POLICE AND C
EVIDENCE ACT

Updated as of March 26, 2018

THE LAW LIBRARY

TABLE OF CONTENTS

Introductory Text

Police and Criminal Evidence Act 1984

1984 CHAPTER 60

An Act to make further provision in relation to the powers and duties of the police, persons in police detention, criminal evidence, police discipline and complaints against the police; to provide for arrangements for obtaining the views of the community on policing and for a rank of deputy chief constable; to amend the law relating to the Police Federations and Police Forces and Police Cadets in Scotland; and for connected purposes.

[31st October 1984]

Be it enacted by the Queen's most Excellent Majesty, by and with the advice and consent of the Lords Spiritual and Temporal, and Commons, in this present Parliament assembled, and by the authority of the same, as follows:—

Modifications etc. (not altering text)

C1. By Criminal Justice Act 1991 (c.53, SIF 39:1), s. 101. (1), Sch. 12 para. 23; S.I. 1991/2208, art. 2. (1), Sch. 1 it is provided (14.10.1991) that in relation to any time before the commencement of s.70 of that 1991 Act (which came into force on 1.10.1992 by S.I. 1992/333, art. 2. (2), Sch. 2) references in any enactment amended by that 1991 Act, to youth courts shall be construed as references to juvenile courts.

C2. Act extended (15.4.1992) by S.I. 1992/975, art. 16. (13).

Act extended (5.6.1992) by S.I. 1992/1302, art. 17. (13).

Act extended (2.8.1993) by S.I. 1993/1813, art. 6, Sch. 3 para. 2. (1)(a); and Act extended by the said S.I. 1993/1813, art. 6, Sch. 3 para. 2 as incorporated (with modifications) (1.12.1997) by S.I. 1994/1405, art. 6, Sch. 3 para. 3

Act amended (17.5.1996) by S.I. 1996/1296, art. 16. (7)(a)

Act amended (16.6.2000) by S.I. 2000/1556, art. 17. (12)

Act extended (temp.) (1.11.1997) by S.I. 1997/2592, arts. 1. (2), 12. (12)

C3. Act: power to apply certain provisions (with modifications) conferred (1.10.2002) by Police Reform Act 2002 (c. 30), ss. 13, 108. (2)-(5), Sch. 3 Pt. 3 para. 19. (6) (with s. 14. (1)); S.I. 2002/2306, art. 4. (e)

Act: power to apply certain provisions (with modifications) conferred (8.11.2006) by Armed Forces Act 2006 (c. 52), ss. 373. (6), 383 (with s. 385)

C4. Act applied (14.2.2000) by 1971 c. 77, s. 28. D(5) (as inserted (14.2.2000) by 1999 c. 33, ss. 131; S.I. 2000/168, art. 2, Sch.)

Act applied (with modifications) (14.10.2002) by The Police and Criminal Evidence Act 1984 (Department of Trade and Industry Investigations) Order 2002 (S.I. 2002/2326), art. 3. (1)(b)

C5. Act modified (11.2.2005) by The Ivory Coast (United Nations Sanctions) Order 2005 (S.I. 2005/253), art. 9. (12)

Act modified (11.3.2005) by Prevention of Terrorism Act 2005 (c. 2), s. 5. (7)(b)(i)

Act applied (with modifications) (1.4.2006) by The Serious Organised Crime and Police Act 2005 (Application and Modification of Certain Enactments to Designated Staff of SOCA) Order 2006 (S.I. 2006/987), art. 3, Sch. 1

C6. Act: certain provisions applied (with modifications) (1.12.2007) by The Police and Criminal

Evidence Act 1984 (Application to Revenue and Customs) Order 2007 (S.I. 2007/3175), arts. 3-19, Schs. 1, 2 (as amended (19.3.2010) by (S.I. 2010/360), {art. 2})
C7. Act: power to apply (with modifications) conferred (21.7.2009) by Borders, Citizenship and Immigration Act 2009 (c. 11), s. 23 (with s. 36. (4))
C8. Act applied (with modifications) (25.6.2013) by The Police and Criminal Evidence Act 1984 (Application to immigration officers and designated customs officials in England and Wales) Order 2013 (S.I. 2013/1542), art. 12. (5)-(8)
C9. Act applied (with modifications) (25.6.2013) by The Police and Criminal Evidence Act 1984 (Application to immigration officers and designated customs officials in England and Wales) Order 2013 (S.I. 2013/1542), art. 3. (5)(6)
C10. Act modified (13.5.2014) by Anti-social Behaviour, Crime and Policing Act 2014 (c. 12), ss. 176. (6), 185. (1) (with ss. 8, 21, 33, 42, 58, 75, 93, 176. (8)); S.I. 2014/949, art. 3, Sch. para. 17
C11. Act applied (with modifications) (4.8.2014) by The Crime and Courts Act 2013 (Application and Modification of Certain Enactments) Order 2014 (S.I. 2014/1704), art. 3, Sch. 1

Part I Powers to Stop and Search

Part I Powers to Stop and Search

Modifications etc. (not altering text)
C1. Pt. I incorporated (E.W.S.) (16.5.2008) by The London Gateway Port Harbour Empowerment Order 2008 (S.I. 2008/1261), art. 52

1 Power of constable to stop and search persons, vehicles etc.

(1) A constable may exercise any power conferred by this section—
    (a) in any place to which at the time when he proposes to exercise the power the public or any section of the public has access, on payment or otherwise, as of right or by virtue of express or implied permission; or
    (b) in any other place to which people have ready access at the time when he proposes to exercise the power but which is not a dwelling.
(2) Subject to subsection (3) to (5) below, a constable—
    (a) may search—
(i) any person or vehicle;
(ii) anything which is in or on a vehicle,
for stolen or prohibited articles [F1, any article to which subsection (8. A) below applies or any firework to which subsection (8. B) below applies] ; and
    (b) may detain a person or vehicle for the purpose of such a search.
(3) This section does not give a constable power to search a person or vehicle or anything in or on a vehicle unless he has reasonable grounds for suspecting that he will find stolen or prohibited articles [F2, any article to which subsection (8. A) below applies or any firework to which subsection (8. B) below applies] .
(4) If a person is in a garden or yard occupied with and used for the purposes of a dwelling or on other land so occupied and used, a constable may not search him in the exercise of the power conferred by this section unless the constable has reasonable grounds for believing—
    (a) that he does not reside in the dwelling; and
    (b) that he is not in the place in question with the express or implied permission of a person who resides in the dwelling.
(5) If a vehicle is in a garden or yard occupied with and used for the purposes of a dwelling or on other land so occupied and used, a constable may not search the vehicle or anything in or on it in

5

the exercise of the power conferred by this section unless he has reasonable grounds for believing—

(a) that the person in charge of the vehicle does not reside in the dwelling; and

(b) that the vehicle is not in the place in question with the express or implied permission of a person who resides in the dwelling.

(6) If in the course of such a search a constable discovers an article which he has reasonable grounds for suspecting to be a stolen or prohibited article [F3, an article to which subsection (8. A) below applies or a firework to which subsection (8. B) below applies] , he may seize it.

(7) An article is prohibited for the purposes of this Part of this Act if it is—

(a) an offensive weapon; or

(b) an article—

(i) made or adapted for use in the course of or in connection with an offence to which this sub-paragraph applies; or

(ii) intended by the person having it with him for such use by him or by some other person.

(8) The offences to which subsection (7)(b)(i) above applies are—

(a) burglary;

(b) theft;

(c) offences under section 12 of the M1. Theft Act 1968 (taking motor vehicle or other conveyance without authority); F4. . .

[F5. (d)fraud (contrary to section 1 of the Fraud Act 2006)][F6; and

(e) offences under section 1 of the Criminal Damage Act 1971 (destroying or damaging property).]

[F7. (8. A)This subsection applies to any article in relation to which a person has committed, or is committing or is going to commit an offence under section 139 [F8or 139. AA] of the Criminal Justice Act 1988.]

[F9. (8. B)This subsection applies to any firework which a person possesses in contravention of a prohibition imposed by fireworks regulations.

(8. C)In this section—

(a) "firework" shall be construed in accordance with the definition of "fireworks" in section 1. (1) of the Fireworks Act 2003; and

(b) "fireworks regulations" has the same meaning as in that Act.]

(9) In this Part of this Act "offensive weapon" means any article—

(a) made or adapted for use for causing injury to persons; or

(b) intended by the person having it with him for such use by him or by some other person.

Amendments (Textual)

F1. Words in s. 1. (2) substituted (1.7.2005) by Serious Organised Crime and Police Act 2005 (c. 15), ss. 115. (2), 178; S.I. 2005/1521, art. 3. (1)(f)

F2. Words in s. 1. (3) substituted (1.7.2005) by Serious Organised Crime and Police Act 2005 (c. 15), ss. 115. (3), 178; S.I. 2005/1521, art. 3. (1)(f)

F3. Words in s. 1. (6) substituted (1.7.2005) by Serious Organised Crime and Police Act 2005 (c. 15), ss. 115. (4), 178; S.I. 2005/1521, art. 3. (1)(f)

F4. Word in s. 1. (8)(c) repealed (20.1.2004) by Criminal Justice Act 2003 (c. 44), ss. 332, 336, Sch. 37 Pt. 1; S.I. 2004/81, art. 2. (1)(2)(g)(i)

F5. S. 1. (8)(d) substituted (15.1.2007) by Fraud Act 2006 (c. 35), ss. 14. (1), 15. (1), Sch. 1 para. 21; S.I. 2006/3200, art. 2

F6. S. 1. (8)(e) and preceding word "and" inserted (20.1.2004) by Criminal Justice Act 2003 (c. 44), ss. 1. (2), 336; S.I. 2004/81, art. 2. (1)(2)(a)

F7. S. 1. (8. A) inserted by Criminal Justice Act 1988 (c. 33, SIF 39:1), s. 140. (1)(c)

F8. Words in s. 1. (8. A) inserted (3.12.2012) by Legal Aid, Sentencing and Punishment of Offenders Act 2012 (c. 10), s. 151. (1), Sch. 26 para. 3; S.I. 2012/2770, art. 2. (f)

F9. S. 1. (8. B)(8. C) inserted (1.7.2005) by Serious Organised Crime and Police Act 2005 (c. 15), ss. 115. (5), 178; S.I. 2005/1521, art. 3. (1)(f)

Modifications etc. (not altering text)

C2. S. 1. (1)-(3) applied (with modifications) (30.4.2017) by The Police and Criminal Evidence Act 1984 (Application to Labour Abuse Prevention Officers) Regulations 2017 (S.I. 2017/520), regs. 1, 2, 3. (a), Sch.
C3. S. 1. (7)(b) modified (15.1.2007) by Fraud Act 2006 (c. 35), ss. 8. (2)(a), 15. (1); S.I. 2006/3200, art. 2
C4. S. 1. (6) applied (with modifications) (30.4.2017) by The Police and Criminal Evidence Act 1984 (Application to Labour Abuse Prevention Officers) Regulations 2017 (S.I. 2017/520), regs. 1, 2, 3. (a), Sch.
Marginal Citations
M11968 c. 60.

2 Provisions relating to search under section 1 and other powers.

(1) A constable who detains a person or vehicle in the exercise—
    (a) of the power conferred by section 1 above; or
    (b) of any other power—
(i) to search a person without first arresting him; or
(ii) to search a vehicle without making an arrest,
need not conduct a search if it appears to him subsequently—
(i) that no search is required; or
(ii) that a search is impracticable.
(2) If a constable contemplates a search, other than a search of an unattended vehicle, in the exercise—
    (a) of the power conferred by section 1 above; or
    (b) of any other power, except the power conferred by section 6 below and the power conferred by section 27. (2) of the M2. Aviation Security Act 1982—
(i) to search a person without first arresting him; or
(ii) to search a vehicle without making an arrest,
it shall be his duty, subject to subsection (4) below, to take reasonable steps before he commences the search to bring to the attention of the appropriate person—
(i) if the constable is not in uniform, documentary evidence that he is a constable; and
(ii) whether he is in uniform or not, the matters specified in subsection (3) below;
and the constable shall not commence the search until he has performed that duty.
(3) The matters referred to in subsection (2)(ii) above are—
    (a) the constable's name and the name of the police station to which he is attached;
    (b) the object of the proposed search;
    (c) the constable's grounds for proposing to make it; and
    (d) the effect of section 3. (7) or (8) below, as may be appropriate.
(4) A constable need not bring the effect of section 3. (7) or (8) below to the attention of the appropriate person if it appears to the constable that it will not be practicable to make the record in section 3. (1) below.
(5) In this section "the appropriate person" means—
    (a) if the constable proposes to search a person, that person; and
    (b) if he proposes to search a vehicle, or anything in or on a vehicle, the person in charge of the vehicle.
(6) On completing a search of an unattended vehicle or anything in or on such a vehicle in the exercise of any such power as is mentioned in subsection (2) above a constable shall leave a notice—
    (a) stating that he has searched it;
    (b) giving the name of the police station to which he is attached;
    (c) stating that an application for compensation for any damage caused by the search may be made to that police station; and

(d) stating the effect of section 3. (8) below.

(7) The constable shall leave the notice inside the vehicle unless it is not reasonably practicable to do so without damaging the vehicle.

(8) The time for which a person or vehicle may be detained for the purposes of such a search is such time as is reasonably required to permit a search to be carried out either at the place where the person or vehicle was first detained or nearby.

(9) Neither the power conferred by section 1 above nor any other power to detain and search a person without first arresting him or to detain and search a vehicle without making an arrest is to be construed—

(a) as authorising a constable to require a person to remove any of his clothing in public other than an outer coat, jacket or gloves; or

(b) as authorising a constable not in uniform to stop a vehicle.

(10) This section and section 1 above apply to vessels, aircraft and hovercraft as they apply to vehicles.

Modifications etc. (not altering text)

C5. S. 2. (1)-(3) applied (with modifications) (30.4.2017) by The Police and Criminal Evidence Act 1984 (Application to Labour Abuse Prevention Officers) Regulations 2017 (S.I. 2017/520), regs. 1, 2, 3. (b), Sch.

C6. S. 2. (8)(9) applied (with modifications) (30.4.2017) by The Police and Criminal Evidence Act 1984 (Application to Labour Abuse Prevention Officers) Regulations 2017 (S.I. 2017/520), regs. 1, 2, 3. (b), Sch.

Marginal Citations

M21982 c. 36.

3 Duty to make records concerning searches.

(1) Where a constable has carried out a search in the exercise of any such power as is mentioned in section 2. (1) above, other than a search—

(a) under section 6 below; or

(b) under section 27. (2) of the M3. Aviation Security Act 1982, [F10a record of the search shall be made] in writing unless it is not practicable to do so.

[F11. (2)If a record of a search is required to be made by subsection (1) above—

(a) in a case where the search results in a person being arrested and taken to a police station, the constable shall secure that the record is made as part of the person's custody record;

(b) in any other case, the constable shall make the record on the spot, or, if that is not practicable, as soon as practicable after the completion of the search.]

F12. (3). . . . .

F12. (4). . . . .

F12. (5). . . . .

(6) The record of a search of a person or a vehicle—

(a) shall state—

(i) the object of the search;

(ii) the grounds for making it;

(iii) the date and time when it was made;

(iv) the place where it was made;

[F13. (v)except in the case of a search of an unattended vehicle, the ethnic origins of the person searched or the person in charge of the vehicle searched (as the case may be); and;]

(b) shall identify the constable [F14who carried out the search].

[F15. (6. A)The requirement in subsection (6)(a)(v) above for a record to state a person's ethnic origins is a requirement to state—

(a) the ethnic origins of the person as described by the person, and

(b) if different, the ethnic origins of the person as perceived by the constable.]

8

(7) [F16. If a record of a search of a person has been made under this section,] the person who was searched shall be entitled to a copy of the record if he asks for one before the end of the period specified in subsection (9) below.

(8) If—

(a) the owner of a vehicle which has been searched or the person who was in charge of the vehicle at the time when it was searched asked for a copy of the record of the search before the end of the period specified in subsection (9) below; and

[F17. (b)a record of the search of the vehicle has been made under this section,] the person who made the request shall be entitled to a copy.

(9) The period mentioned in subsections (7) and (8) above is the period of [F183 months] beginning with the date on which the search was made.

(10) The requirements imposed by this section with regard to records of searches of vehicles shall apply also to records of searches of vessels, aircraft and hovercraft.

Amendments (Textual)

F10. Words in s. 3. (1) substituted (7.3.2011) by Crime and Security Act 2010 (c. 17), ss. 1. (2), 59. (1); S.I. 2011/414, art. 2. (a)

F11. S. 3. (2) substituted (7.3.2011) by Crime and Security Act 2010 (c. 17), ss. 1. (3), 59. (1); S.I. 2011/414, art. 2. (a)

F12. S. 3. (3)-(5) repealed (7.3.2011) by Crime and Security Act 2010 (c. 17), ss. 1. (4), 59. (1); S.I. 2011/414, art. 2. (a)

F13. S. 3. (6)(a)(v) substituted for s. 3. (6)(a)(v)(vi) (7.3.2011) by Crime and Security Act 2010 (c. 17), ss. 1. (5)(a), 59. (1); S.I. 2011/414, art. 2. (a)

F14. Words in s. 3. (6)(b) substituted (7.3.2011) by Crime and Security Act 2010 (c. 17), ss. 1. (5)(b), 59. (1); S.I. 2011/414, art. 2. (a)

F15. S. 3. (6. A) inserted (7.3.2011) by Crime and Security Act 2010 (c. 17), ss. 1. (6), 59. (1); S.I. 2011/414, art. 2. (a)

F16. Words in s. 3. (7) substituted (7.3.2011) by Crime and Security Act 2010 (c. 17), ss. 1. (7), 59. (1); S.I. 2011/414, art. 2. (a)

F17. S. 3. (8)(b) substituted (7.3.2011) by Crime and Security Act 2010 (c. 17), ss. 1. (8), 59. (1); S.I. 2011/414, art. 2. (a)

F18. Words in s. 3. (9) substituted (7.3.2011) by Crime and Security Act 2010 (c. 17), ss. 1. (9), 59. (1); S.I. 2011/414, art. 2. (a)

Modifications etc. (not altering text)

C7. S. 3. (1)(2) applied (with modifications) (30.4.2017) by The Police and Criminal Evidence Act 1984 (Application to Labour Abuse Prevention Officers) Regulations 2017 (S.I. 2017/520), regs. 1, 2, 3. (c), Sch.

C8. S. 3. (6)(6. A) applied (with modifications) (30.4.2017) by The Police and Criminal Evidence Act 1984 (Application to Labour Abuse Prevention Officers) Regulations 2017 (S.I. 2017/520), regs. 1, 2, 3. (c), Sch.

C9. S. 3. (7) applied (with modifications) (30.4.2017) by The Police and Criminal Evidence Act 1984 (Application to Labour Abuse Prevention Officers) Regulations 2017 (S.I. 2017/520), regs. 1, 2, 3. (c), Sch.

C10. S. 3. (9) applied (with modifications) (30.4.2017) by The Police and Criminal Evidence Act 1984 (Application to Labour Abuse Prevention Officers) Regulations 2017 (S.I. 2017/520), regs. 1, 2, 3. (c), Sch.

Marginal Citations

M31982 c. 36.

4 Road checks.

(1) This section shall have effect in relation to the conduct of road checks by police officers for the purpose of ascertaining whether a vehicle is carrying—

(a) a person who has committed an offence other than a road traffic offence or a [F19vehicle] excise offence;

(b) a person who is a witness to such an offence;

(c) a person intending to commit such an offence; or

(d) a person who is unlawfully at large.

(2) For the purposes of this section a road check consists of the exercise in a locality of the power conferred by [F20section 163 of the Road Traffic Act 1988.] in such a way as to stop during the period for which its exercise in that way in that locality continues all vehicles or vehicles selected by any criterion.

(3) Subject to subsection (5) below, there may only be such a road check if a police officer of the rank of superintendent or above authorises it in writing.

(4) An officer may only authorise a road check under subsection (3) above—

(a) for the purpose specified in subsection (1)(a) above, if he has reasonable grounds—

(i) for believing that the offence is [F21an indictable offence] ; and

(ii) for suspecting that the person is, or is about to be, in the locality in which vehicles would be stopped if the road check were authorised;

(b) for the purpose specified in subsection (1)(b) above, if he has reasonable grounds for believing that the offence is [F21an indictable offence] ;

(c) for the purpose specified in subsection (1)(c) above, if he has reasonable grounds—

(i) for believing that the offence would be [F21an indictable offence] ; and

(ii) for suspecting that the person is, or is about to be, in the locality in which vehicles would be stopped if the road check were authorised;

(d) for the purpose specified in subsection (1)(d) above, if he has reasonable grounds for suspecting that the person is, or is about to be, in that locality.

(5) An officer below the rank of superintendent may authorise such a road check if it appears to him that it is required as a matter of urgency for one of the purposes specified in subsection (1) above.

(6) If an authorisation is given under subsection (5) above, it shall be the duty of the officer who gives it—

(a) to make a written record of the time at which he gives it; and

(b) to cause an officer of the rank of superintendent or above to be informed that it has been given.

(7) The duties imposed by subsection (6) above shall be performed as soon as it is practicable to do so.

(8) An officer to whom a report is made under subsection (6) above may, in writing, authorise the road check to continue.

(9) If such an officer considers that the road check should not continue, he shall record in writing—

(a) the fact that it took place; and

(b) the purpose for which it took place.

(10) An officer giving an authorisation under this section shall specify the locality in which vehicles are to be stopped.

(11) An officer giving an authorisation under this section, other than an authorisation under subsection (5) above—

(a) shall specify a period, not exceeding seven days, during which the road check may continue; and

(b) may direct that the road check—

(i) shall be continuous; or

(ii) shall be conducted at specified times,

during that period.

(12) If it appears to an officer of the rank of superintendent or above that a road check ought to continue beyond the period for which it has been authorised he may, from time to time, in writing specify a further period, not exceeding seven days, during which it may continue.

(13) Every written authorisation shall specify—

    (a) the name of the officer giving it;

    (b) the purpose of the road check; and

    (c) the locality in which vehicles are to be stopped.

(14) The duties to specify the purposes of a road check imposed by subsections (9) and (13) above include duties to specify any relevant [F22indictable offence] .

(15) Where a vehicle is stopped in a road check, the person in charge of the vehicle at the time when it is stopped shall be entitled to obtain a written statement of the purpose of the road check if he applies for such a statement not later than the end of the period of twelve months from the day on which the vehicle was stopped.

(16) Nothing in this section affects the exercise by police officers of any power to stop vehicles for purposes other than those specified in subsection (1) above.

Amendments (Textual)

F19. Word in s. 4. (1)(a) substituted (1.9.1994) by 1994 c. 22, ss. 66. (1), 63, Sch. 3 para.19 (with s. 57. (4))

F20. Words substituted by Road Traffic (Consequential Provisions) Act 1988 (c. 54, SIF 107:1), s. 4, Sch. 3 para. 27. (1)

F21. Words in s. 4 substituted (1.1.2006) by Serious Organised Crime and Police Act 2005 (c. 15), ss. 111, 178, Sch. 7 Pt. 3 para. 43. (2)(a); S.I. 2005/3495, art. 2. (1)(m)

F22. Words in s. 4. (14) substituted (1.1.2006) by Serious Organised Crime and Police Act 2005 (c. 15), ss. 111, 178, Sch. 7 Pt. 3 para. 43. (2)(b); S.I. 2005/3495, art. 2. (1)(m)

5 Reports of recorded searches and of road checks.

(1) Every annual report—

    [F23. (a)under section 22 of the M4. Police Act 1996; or]

    (b) made by the Commissioner of Police of the Metropolis,

shall contain information—

(i) about searches recorded under section 3 above which have been carried out in the area to which the report relates during the period to which it relates; and

(ii) about road checks authorised in that area during that period under section 4 above.

(1. A)F24. . . . .

(2) The information about searches shall not include information about specific searches but shall include—

    (a) the total numbers of searches in each month during the period to which the report relates—

(i) for stolen articles;

(ii) for offensive weapons [F25or articles to which section 1. (8. A) above applies]; and

(iii) for other prohibited articles;

    (b) the total number of persons arrested in each such month in consequence of searches of each of the descriptions specified in paragraph (a)(i) to (iii) above.

(3) The information about road checks shall include information—

    (a) about the reason for authorising each road check; and

    (b) about the result of each of them.

Amendments (Textual)

F23. S. 5. (1)(a) substituted (22.8.1996) by 1996 c. 16, ss. 103. (1), 104. (1), Sch. 7 Pt. II para. 34

F24. S. 5. (1. A) repealed (1.4.2006, subject to art. 4. (2)-(7) of the commencing S.I.) by Serious Organised Crime and Police Act 2005 (c. 15), ss. 59, 174, 178, Sch. 4 para. 44, Sch. 17 Pt. 2; S.I. 2006/378, art. 4. (1), Sch. paras. 10, 13. (q)

F25. Words inserted by Criminal Justice Act 1988 (c. 33, SIF 39:1), s. 140. (2)

Marginal Citations

M41996 c. 16.

6 Statutory undertakers etc.

(1) A constable employed by statutory undertakers may stop, detain and search any vehicle before it leaves a goods area included in the premises of the statutory undertakers.

[F26. (1. A)Without prejudice to any powers under subsection (1) above, a constable employed [F27by the [F28. British Transport Police Authority]] may stop, detain and search any vehicle before it leaves a goods area which is included in the premises of any successor of the British Railways Board and is used wholly or mainly for the purposes of a relevant undertaking.]

(2) In this section "goods area" means any area used wholly or mainly for the storage or handling of goods [F29; and "successor of the British Railways Board" and "relevant undertaking" have the same meaning as in the Railways Act 1993 (Consequential Modifications) Order 1999.]

(3) F30. . . . .

(4) F31. . . . .

Amendments (Textual)

F26. S. 6. (1. A) inserted (13.8.1999) by S.I. 1999/1998, art. 5. (1)

F27. Words in s. 6. (1. A) substituted (1.2.2001) by 2000 c. 38, s. 217, Sch. 18 para. 5; S.I. 2001/57, art. 3. (1) (Subject to Sch. 2 Pt II)

F28. Words in s. 6. (1. A) substituted (1.7.2004) by The British Transport Police (Transitional and Consequential Provisions) Order 2004 (S.I. 2004/1573), art. 12. (1)(e)

F29. Words in s. 6. (2) inserted (13.8.1999) by S.I. 1999/1998, art. 5. (2)

F30. S. 6. (3) repealed (1.4.2005) by Energy Act 2004 (c. 20), ss. 197, 198. (2), Sch. 23 Pt. 1; S.I. 2005/877, art. 2. (1), Sch. 1 Table

F31. S. 6. (4) repealed (1.4.2005) by Energy Act 2004 (c. 20), ss. 197, 198. (2), Sch. 23 Pt. 1; S.I. 2005/877, art. 2. (1), Sch. 1 Table

7 Part I—supplementary

(1) The following enactments shall cease to have effect—

    (a) section 8 of the M5. Vagrancy Act 1824;

    (b) section 66 of the M6. Metropolitan Police Act 1839;

    (c) section 11 of the M7. Canals (Offences) Act 1840;

    (d) section 19 of the M8. Pedlars Act 1871;

    (e) section 33 of the M9. County of Merseyside Act 1980; and

    (f) section 42 of the M10. West Midlands County Council Act 1980.

(2) There shall also cease to have effect—

    (a) so much of any enactment contained in an Act passed before 1974, other than—

(i) an enactment contained in public general Act; or

(ii) an enactment relating to statutory undertakers,

as confers power on a constable to search for stolen or unlawfully obtained goods; and

    (b) so much of any enactment relating to statutory undertakers as provides that such a power shall not be exercisable after the end of a specified period.

(3) In this Part of this Act "statutory undertakers" means persons authorised by any enactment to carry on any railway, light railway, road transport, water transport, canal, inland navigation, dock or harbour undertaking.

Marginal Citations

M51824 c. 83.

M61839 c. 47.

M71840 c. 50.

M81871 c. 96.

M91980 c. x.

M101980 c. xi.

Part I—supplementary

7 Part I—supplementary

(1) The following enactments shall cease to have effect—

    (a) section 8 of the M1. Vagrancy Act 1824;

    (b) section 66 of the M2. Metropolitan Police Act 1839;

    (c) section 11 of the M3. Canals (Offences) Act 1840;

    (d) section 19 of the M4. Pedlars Act 1871;

    (e) section 33 of the M5. County of Merseyside Act 1980; and

    (f) section 42 of the M6. West Midlands County Council Act 1980.

(2) There shall also cease to have effect—

    (a) so much of any enactment contained in an Act passed before 1974, other than—

(i) an enactment contained in public general Act; or

(ii) an enactment relating to statutory undertakers,

as confers power on a constable to search for stolen or unlawfully obtained goods; and

    (b) so much of any enactment relating to statutory undertakers as provides that such a power shall not be exercisable after the end of a specified period.

(3) In this Part of this Act "statutory undertakers" means persons authorised by any enactment to carry on any railway, light railway, road transport, water transport, canal, inland navigation, dock or harbour undertaking.

Marginal Citations

M11824 c. 83.

M21839 c. 47.

M31840 c. 50.

M41871 c. 96.

M51980 c. x.

M61980 c. xi.

Part II Powers of Entry, Search and Seizure

Part II Powers of Entry, Search and Seizure

Modifications etc. (not altering text)

C1. Pt. II (ss. 8-23) extended (10.6.1991) by Criminal Justice (International Co-operation) Act 1990 (c. 5, SIF 39:1), s. 7. (1); S.I. 1991/1072, art. 2 Sch. Pt. I

Pt. II (ss. 8-23) applied (with modifications) (17.5.1996) by S.I. 1996/1296, art. 16. (1)

Pt. II (ss. 8-23) amended (17.5.1996) by S.I. 1996/1296, art. 16. (7)(b)

Pt. II (ss. 8-23) applied (with modifications) (15.3.1996) by S.I. 1996/716, art. 16. (1)

Pt. II (ss. 8-23) modified (1.9.2001) by 2001 c. 17, s. 33; S.I. 2001/2161, art. 2 (subject to art. 3)

Pt. II (ss. 8-23): Powers of seizure extended (1.4.2003) by 2001 c. 16, ss. 50, 52-54, 68, Sch. 1 Pt. 1 para 1; S.I. 2003/708, art. 2. (a)(j)

C2. Pt. II (ss. 8-23) amended (26.4.2004) by Crime (International Co-operation) Act 2003 (c. 32), ss. 16. (1), 94; S.I. 2004/786, art. 3. (2)

C3. Pt. II incorporated (16.5.2008) by The London Gateway Port Harbour Empowerment Order 2008 (S.I. 2008/1261), art. 52

8 Power of justice of the peace to authorise entry and search of

premises.

(1) If on an application made by a constable a justice of the peace is satisfied that there are reasonable grounds for believing—

(a) that [F1an indictable offence] has been committed; and

(b) that there is material on premises [F2mentioned in subsection (1. A) below] which is likely to be of substantial value (whether by itself or together with other material) to the investigation of the offence; and

(c) that the material is likely to be relevant evidence; and

(d) that it does not consist of or include items subject to legal privilege, excluded material or special procedure material; and

(e) that any of the conditions specified in subsection (3) below applies,

he may issue a warrant authorising a constable to enter and search the premises [F3in relation to each set of premises specified in the application] .

[F4. (1. A)The premises referred to in subsection (1)(b) above are—

(a) one or more sets of premises specified in the application (in which case the application is for a "specific premises warrant"); or

(b) any premises occupied or controlled by a person specified in the application, including such sets of premises as are so specified (in which case the application is for an "all premises warrant").

(1. B)If the application is for an all premises warrant, the justice of the peace must also be satisfied—

(a) that because of the particulars of the offence referred to in paragraph (a) of subsection (1) above, there are reasonable grounds for believing that it is necessary to search premises occupied or controlled by the person in question which are not specified in the application in order to find the material referred to in paragraph (b) of that subsection; and

(b) that it is not reasonably practicable to specify in the application all the premises which he occupies or controls and which might need to be searched.]

[F5. (1. C)The warrant may authorise entry to and search of premises on more than one occasion if, on the application, the justice of the peace is satisfied that it is necessary to authorise multiple entries in order to achieve the purpose for which he issues the warrant.

(1. D)If it authorises multiple entries, the number of entries authorised may be unlimited, or limited to a maximum.]

(2) A constable may seize and retain anything for which a search has been authorised under subsection (1) above.

(3) The conditions mentioned in subsection (1)(e) above are—

(a) that it is not practicable to communicate with any person entitled to grant entry to the premises;

(b) that it is practicable to communicate with a person entitled to grant entry to the premises but it is not practicable to communicate with any person entitled to grant access to the evidence;

(c) that entry to the premises will not be granted unless a warrant is produced;

(d) that the purpose of a search may be frustrated or seriously prejudiced unless a constable arriving at the premises can secure immediate entry to them.

(4) In this Act "relevant evidence", in relation to an offence, means anything that would be admissible in evidence at a trial for the offence.

(5) The power to issue a warrant conferred by this section is in addition to any such power otherwise conferred.

[F6. (6)This section applies in relation to a relevant offence (as defined in section 28. D(4) of the Immigration Act 1971) as it applies in relation to [F1an indictable offence] .

[F7. (7)Section 4 of the Summary Jurisdiction (Process) Act 1881 (execution of process of English courts in Scotland) shall apply to a warrant issued on the application of an officer of Revenue and Customs under this section by virtue of section 114 below.]]

Amendments (Textual)

F1. Words in s. 8 substituted (1.1.2006) by Serious Organised Crime and Police Act 2005 (c. 15), ss. 111, 178, Sch. 7 Pt. 3 para. 43. (3); S.I. 2005/3495, art. 2. (1)(m)

F2. Words in s. 8. (1)(b) substituted (1.1.2006) by Serious Organised Crime and Police Act 2005 (c. 15), ss. 113. (3)(a), 178; S.I. 2005/3495, art. 2. (1)(n)

F3. Words in s. 8. (1)(e) added (1.1.2006) by Serious Organised Crime and Police Act 2005 (c. 15), ss. 113. (3)(b), 178; S.I. 2005/3495, art. 2. (1)(n)

F4. S. 8. (1. A)(1. B) inserted (1.1.2006) by Serious Organised Crime and Police Act 2005 (c. 15), ss. 113. (4), 178; S.I. 2005/3495, art. 2. (1)(n)

F5. S. 8. (1. C)(1. D) inserted (1.1.2006) by Serious Organised Crime and Police Act 2005 (c. 15), ss. 114. (2), 178; S.I. 2005/3495, art. 2. (1)(n)

F6. S. 8. (6) inserted (14.2.2000) by 1999 c. 33. s. 169. (1), Sch. 14 para. 80. (2); S.I. 2000/168, art. 2, Sch.

F7. S. 8. (7) inserted (19.7.2007) by Finance Act 2007 (c. 11), s. 86

Modifications etc. (not altering text)

C4. Ss. 8, 9, 15, 16, 17. (1)(b(2) (4), 18–20, 21, 22. (1)–(4), 28, 29, 30. (1)–(4)(a)(5)–(11), 31, 32. (1)–(9), 34. (1)–(5), 35, 36, 37, 39, 40–44, 50, 51. (d), 52, 54, 55, 64. (1)–(4)(5)(6), Sch. 1 applied with modifications by S.I. 1985/1800, arts. 3–11, Schs. 1, 2

C5. S. 8 extended (10.6.1991) by Criminal Justice (International Co-operation) Act 1990 (c. 5, SIF 39:1), s. 7. (1); S.I. 1991/1072, art. 2, Sch. Pt. I

S. 8 amended (1.10.1996) by 1996 c. 49, s. 7. (3)(a)(4); S.I. 1996/2053, art. 2, Sch. Pt.III

S. 8 extended (1.10.1997) by 1997 c. 43, ss. 18. (3), 41, Sch. 1 para. 10. (4); S.I. 1997/2200, art. 2. (g) (with art. 5)

S. 8 extended (2.12.2002) by Police Reform Act 2002 (c. 30), s. 38, Sch. 4 Pt. 2 para. 16. (a); S.I. 2002/2750, art. 2. (a)(ii)(d)

C6. S. 8 applied (with modifications) (25.6.2013) by The Police and Criminal Evidence Act 1984 (Application to immigration officers and designated customs officials in England and Wales) Order 2013 (S.I. 2013/1542), arts. 1, 12. (2)-(4), Sch. 2 (with arts. 13-31)

C7. S. 8 applied (2.9.2014) by The Control of Explosives Precursors Regulations 2014 (S.I. 2014/1942), regs. 1. (1), 14

C8. S. 8 applied by 1972 c. 66, s. 9. A (as inserted (20.4.2015 for specified purposes, 26.3.2015 for specified purposes, 26.5.2015 in so far as not already in force) by Deregulation Act 2015 (c. 20), s. 115. (2)(e), Sch. 21 para. 12; S.I. 2015/994, arts. 5, 6. (p))

C9. S. 8 applied (with modifications) (4.11.2015) by The Police and Criminal Evidence Act 1984 (Application to Revenue and Customs) Order 2015 (S.I. 2015/1783), arts. 1, 3. (1), Sch. 1 (with art. 3. (2), (3), 4-19, Sch. 2)

C10. S. 8. (1)-(6) applied (with modifications) (25.6.2013) by The Police and Criminal Evidence Act 1984 (Application to immigration officers and designated customs officials in England and Wales) Order 2013 (S.I. 2013/1542), arts. 1, 3. (2)-(4), Sch. 1 (with arts. 4-11)

C11. S. 8. (1)-(5) applied (with modifications) (30.4.2017) by The Police and Criminal Evidence Act 1984 (Application to Labour Abuse Prevention Officers) Regulations 2017 (S.I. 2017/520), regs. 1, 2, 3. (d), Sch.

C12. S. 8. (2) modified (1.4.2003) by 2001 c. 16, ss. 55, 68, Sch. 1 Pt. 3 para. 84 (with s. 57. (3)); S.I. 2003/708, art. 2. (a)(c)(j)

C13. S. 8. (2) extended (2.12.2002) by Police Reform act 2002 (c. 30), s. 38, {Sch. 4 Pt. 2 para. 16. (c)}; S.I. 2002/2750, art. 2. (a)(ii)(d)

9 Special provisions as to access.

(1) A constable may obtain access to excluded material or special procedure material for the purposes of a criminal investigation by making an application under Schedule 1 below and in accordance with that Schedule.

(2) Any Act (including a local Act) passed before this Act under which a search of premises for

the purposes of a criminal investigation could be authorised by the issue of a warrant to a constable shall cease to have effect so far as it relates to the authorisation of searches—

(a) for items subject to legal privilege; or

(b) for excluded material; or

(c) for special procedure material consisting of documents or records other than documents.

[F8. (2. A)Section 4 of the Summary Jurisdiction (Process) Act 1881 (c. 24) (which includes provision for the execution of process of English courts in Scotland) and section 29 of the Petty Sessions (Ireland) Act 1851 (c. 93) (which makes equivalent provision for execution in Northern Ireland) shall each apply to any process issued by a [F9judge] under Schedule 1 to this Act as it applies to process issued by a magistrates' court under the Magistrates' Courts Act 1980 (c. 43).]

Amendments (Textual)

F8. S. 9. (2. A) inserted (1.8.2001) by 2001 c. 16, s. 86. (1); S.I. 2001/2223, art. 3. (e)

F9. Word in s. 9. (2. A) substituted (1.4.2005) by Courts Act 2003 (c. 39), ss. 65, 110, Sch. 4 para. 5; S.I. 2005/910, art. 3. (u)

Modifications etc. (not altering text)

C14. Ss. 8, 9, 15, 16, 17. (1)(b)(2) (4), 18-20, 21, 22. (1)-(4), 28, 29, 30. (1)-(4)(a)(5)-(11), 31, 32. (1)-(9), 34. (1)-(5), 35, 36, 37, 39, 40-44, 50, 51. (d), 52, 54, 55, 64. (1)-(4)(5)(6), Sch. 1 applied with modifications by S.I. 1985/1800, arts. 3-11, Schs. 1, 2

C15. S. 9 applied (with modifications) (4.11.2015) by The Police and Criminal Evidence Act 1984 (Application to Revenue and Customs) Order 2015 (S.I. 2015/1783), arts. 1, 3. (1), Sch. 1 (with art. 3. (2), (3), 4-19, Sch. 2)

C16. S. 9. (1) extended (2.12.2002) by Police Reform Act 2002 (c. 30), s. 38, Sch. 4 Pt. 2 para. 17. (a); S.I. 2002/2750, art. 2. (a)(ii)(d)

C17. S. 9. (1) applied (with modifications) (25.6.2013) by The Police and Criminal Evidence Act 1984 (Application to immigration officers and designated customs officials in England and Wales) Order 2013 (S.I. 2013/1542), arts. 1, 12. (2)-(4), Sch. 2 (with arts. 13-31)

C18. S. 9. (1) applied (with modifications) (25.6.2013) by The Police and Criminal Evidence Act 1984 (Application to immigration officers and designated customs officials in England and Wales) Order 2013 (S.I. 2013/1542), arts. 1, 3. (2)-(4), Sch. 1 (with arts. 4-11)

C19. S. 9. (1) applied (with modifications) (30.4.2017) by The Police and Criminal Evidence Act 1984 (Application to Labour Abuse Prevention Officers) Regulations 2017 (S.I. 2017/520), regs. 1, 2, 3. (e), Sch.

C20. S. 9. (2) extended by Cinemas Act 1985 (c. 13, SIF 45. A), s. 13. (8)

10 Meaning of "items subject to legal privilege".

(1) Subject to subsection (2) below, in this Act "items subject to legal privilege" means—

(a) communications between a professional legal adviser and his client or any person representing his client made in connection with the giving of legal advice to the client;

(b) communications between a professional legal adviser and his client or any person representing his client or between such an adviser or his client or any such representative and any other person made in connection with or in contemplation of legal proceedings and for the purposes of such proceedings; and

(c) items enclosed with or referred to in such communications and made—

(i) in connection with the giving of legal advice; or

(ii) in connection with or in contemplation of legal proceedings and for the purposes of such proceedings,

when they are in the possession of a person who is entitled to possession of them.

(2) Items held with the intention of furthering a criminal purpose are not items subject to legal privilege.

Modifications etc. (not altering text)

C21. Ss. 10-14 applied (with modifications) (30.4.2017) by The Police and Criminal Evidence Act

1984 (Application to Labour Abuse Prevention Officers) Regulations 2017 (S.I. 2017/520), regs. 1, 2, 3. (w), Sch.

11 Meaning of "excluded material".

(1) Subject to the following provisions of this section, in this Act "excluded material" means—
    (a) personal records which a person has acquired or created in the course of any trade, business, profession or other occupation or for the purposes of any paid or unpaid office and which he holds in confidence;
    (b) human tissue or tissue fluid which has been taken for the purposes of diagnosis or medical treatment and which a person holds in confidence;
    (c) journalistic material which a person holds in confidence and which consists—
(i) of documents; or
(ii) of records other than documents.
(2) A person holds material other than journalistic material in confidence for the purposes of this section if he holds it subject—
    (a) to an express or implied undertaking to hold it in confidence; or
    (b) to a restriction on disclosure or an obligation of secrecy contained in any enactment, including an enactment contained in an Act passed after this Act.
(3) A person holds journalistic material in confidence for the purposes of this section if—
    (a) he holds it subject to such an undertaking, restriction or obligation; and
    (b) it has been continuously held (by one or more persons) subject to such an undertaking, restriction or obligation since it was first acquired or created for the purposes of journalism.
Modifications etc. (not altering text)
C21. Ss. 10-14 applied (with modifications) (30.4.2017) by The Police and Criminal Evidence Act 1984 (Application to Labour Abuse Prevention Officers) Regulations 2017 (S.I. 2017/520), regs. 1, 2, 3. (w), Sch.

12 Meaning of "personal records".

In this Part of this Act "personal records" means documentary and other records concerning an individual (whether living or dead) who can be identified from them and relating—
    (a) to his physical or mental health;
    (b) to spiritual counselling or assistance given or to be given to him; or
    (c) to counselling or assistance given or to be given to him, for the purposes of his personal welfare, by any voluntary organisation or by any individual who—
(i) by reason of his office or occupation has responsibilities for his personal welfare; or
(ii) by reason of an order of a court has responsibilities for his supervision.
Modifications etc. (not altering text)
C21. Ss. 10-14 applied (with modifications) (30.4.2017) by The Police and Criminal Evidence Act 1984 (Application to Labour Abuse Prevention Officers) Regulations 2017 (S.I. 2017/520), regs. 1, 2, 3. (w), Sch.

13 Meaning of "journalistic material".

(1) Subject to subsection (2) below, in this Act "journalistic material" means material acquired or created for the purposes of journalism.
(2) Material is only journalistic material for the purposes of this Act if it is in the possession of a person who acquired or created it for the purposes of journalism.
(3) A person who receives material from someone who intends that the recipient shall use it for the purposes of journalism is to be taken to have acquired it for those purposes.

14 Meaning of "special procedure material".

(1) In this Act "special procedure material" means—
    (a) material to which subsection (2) below applies; and
    (b) journalistic material, other than excluded material.
(2) Subject to the following provisions of this section, this subsection applies to material, other than items subject to legal privilege and excluded material, in the possession of a person who—
    (a) acquired or created it in the course of any trade, business, profession or other occupation or for the purpose of any paid or unpaid office; and
    (b) holds it subject—
(i) to an express or implied undertaking to hold it in confidence; or
(ii) to a restriction or obligation such as is mentioned in section 11. (2)(b) above.
(3) Where material is acquired—
    (a) by an employee from his employer and in the course of his employment; or
    (b) by a company from an associated company,
it is only special procedure material if it was special procedure material immediately before the acquisition.
(4) Where material is created by an employee in the course of his employment, it is only special procedure material if it would have been special procedure material had his employer created it.
(5) Where material is created by a company on behalf of an associated company, it is only special procedure material if it would have been special procedure material had the associated company created it.
(6) A company is to be treated as another's associated company for the purposes of this section if it would be so treated under [F10section 449 of the Corporation Tax Act 2010].
Amendments (Textual)
F10. Words in s. 14. (6) substituted (1.4.2010 with effect as mentioned in s. 1184. (1) of the amending Act) by Corporation Tax Act 2010 (c. 4), ss. 1177, 1184. (1), Sch. 1 para. 193 (with Sch. 2)
Modifications etc. (not altering text)
C21. Ss. 10-14 applied (with modifications) (30.4.2017) by The Police and Criminal Evidence Act 1984 (Application to Labour Abuse Prevention Officers) Regulations 2017 (S.I. 2017/520), regs. 1, 2, 3. (w), Sch.

15 Search warrants—safeguards.

(1) This section and section 16 below have effect in relation to the issue to constables under any enactment, including an enactment contained in an Act passed after this Act, of warrants to enter and search premises; and an entry on or search of premises under a warrant is unlawful unless it complies with this section and section 16 below.
(2) Where a constable applies for any such warrant, it shall be his duty—
    (a) to state—
(i) the ground on which he makes the application; F11. . .
(ii) the enactment under which the warrant would be issued; [F12and]
[F13. (iii)if the application is for a warrant authorising entry and search on more than one occasion, the ground on which he applies for such a warrant, and whether he seeks a warrant authorising an unlimited number of entries, or (if not) the maximum number of entries desired;]
    [F14. (b)to specify the matters set out in subsection (2. A) below; and]

by S.I. 2003/531, arts. 3, 4))

C46. S. 16 modified (2.12.2002) by Police Reform Act 2002 (c. 30), s. 38, Sch. 4 Pt. 2 para. 16. (e); S.I. 2002/2750, art. 2. (a)(ii)(d)

S. 16 modified (20.1.2004) by Police Reform Act 2002 (c. 30), ss. 38, 108, Sch. 4 para. 17. (bc) (as inserted by Criminal Justice Act 2003 (c. 44), ss. 12, 336, Sch. 1 para. 17); S.I. 2004/81, art. 2. (1)(2)(a)

S. 16 modified (27.3.2007 for W. and 6.4.2007 for E.) by Animal Welfare Act 2006 (c. 45), ss. 53, 68, Sch. 2 para. 1. (1) (with ss. 1. (2), 58. (1), 59, 60); S.I. 2007/1030, art. 2. (1)(g); S.I. 2007/499, art. 2. (2)(i)

S. 16 modified (21.8.2007) by The Offshore Marine Conservation (Natural Habitats, &c.) Regulations 2007 (S.I. 2007/1842), reg. 53. (6) (with reg. 3)

C47. S. 16 applied (with modifications) (24.2.2003) by The Proceeds of Crime Act 2002 (Application of Police and Criminal Evidence Act 1984 and Police and Criminal Evidence (Northern Ireland) Order 1989) Order 2003 (S.I. 2003/174), {arts. 3}, 10, Sch. 1

C48. S. 16 applied (31.12.2009) by Banking Act 2009 (c. 1), ss. 194. (7), 263. (1) (with ss. 206, 247); S.I. 2009/3000, art. 4, Sch. para. 2

C49. S. 16 applied (7.6.2010) by The Credit Rating Agencies Regulations 2010 (S.I. 2010/906), reg. 18. (5)

C50. S. 16 applied by S.I. 2010/906, reg. 33. (7) (as inserted (1.7.2011) by The Credit Rating Agencies (Amendment) Regulations 2011 (S.I. 2011/1435), regs. 1, 4. (e) (with reg. 5))

C51. S. 16 applied (with modifications) (25.6.2013) by The Police and Criminal Evidence Act 1984 (Application to immigration officers and designated customs officials in England and Wales) Order 2013 (S.I. 2013/1542), arts. 1, 12. (2)-(4), Sch. 2 (with arts. 13-31)

C52. S. 16 applied (with modifications) (25.6.2013) by The Police and Criminal Evidence Act 1984 (Application to immigration officers and designated customs officials in England and Wales) Order 2013 (S.I. 2013/1542), arts. 1, 3. (2)-(4), Sch. 1 (with arts. 4-11)

C53. S. 16 applied (with modifications) (1.6.2015) by The Proceeds of Crime Act 2002 (Application of Police and Criminal Evidence Act 1984) Order 2015 (S.I. 2015/759), arts. 1. (1), 3 (as amended (31.1.2018 for specified purposes) by The Proceeds of Crime Act 2002 (Application of Police and Criminal Evidence Act 1984) (Amendment) Order 2017 (S.I. 2017/1222), arts. 1. (2)(3), 2. (3))

C54. S. 16 applied (with modifications) (4.11.2015) by The Police and Criminal Evidence Act 1984 (Application to Revenue and Customs) Order 2015 (S.I. 2015/1783), arts. 1, 3. (1), Sch. 1 (with arts. 3. (2)(3), 4-19, Sch. 2)

C55. S. 16 applied (with modifications) (30.4.2017) by The Police and Criminal Evidence Act 1984 (Application to Labour Abuse Prevention Officers) Regulations 2017 (S.I. 2017/520), regs. 1, 2, 3. (g), Sch.

C56. S. 16 applied (30.11.2017) by The Conservation of Offshore Marine Habitats and Species Regulations 2017 (S.I. 2017/1013), regs. 1, 60. (6) (with regs. 3, 4. (2))

C57. S. 16. (3)-(12) applied by 2000 c. 8, s. 131. FB(7) (as inserted (1.11.2012) by The Financial Services and Markets Act 2000 (Short Selling) Regulations 2012 (S.I. 2012/2554), regs. 1. (1), 2. (5))

C58. S. 16. (3)-(12) applied (1.4.2013) by The Financial Services and Markets Act 2000 (Over the Counter Derivatives, Central Counterparties and Trade Repositories) Regulations 2013 (S.I. 2013/504), regs. 1. (2), 17. (10) (with regs. 52-58)

C59. S. 16. (3)-(12) applied (1.3.2014) by Financial Services (Banking Reform) Act 2013 (c. 33), ss. 88. (9), 148. (5); S.I. 2014/377, art. 2. (1)(a), Sch. Pt. 1

C60. S. 16. (3)-(12) applied by 2009 c. 1, s. 83. ZL(9) (as inserted (1.1.2015) by The Bank Recovery and Resolution Order 2014 (S.I. 2014/3329), arts. 1. (2), 97)

C61. S. 16. (3)-(12) applied by 2000 c. 8, s. 122. D(7) (as inserted (3.7.2016) by The Financial Services and Markets Act 2000 (Market Abuse) Regulations 2016 (S.I. 2016/680), regs. 1, 9. (4))

C62. S. 16. (3)-(12) applied (26.6.2017) by The Money Laundering, Terrorist Financing and Transfer of Funds (Information on the Payer) Regulations 2017 (S.I. 2017/692), regs. 1. (2), 70.

(11) (with regs. 8, 15)

Entry and search without search warrant

17 Entry for purpose of arrest etc.

(1) Subject to the following provisions of this section, and without prejudice to any other enactment, a constable may enter and search any premises for the purpose—
    (a) of executing—
(i) a warrant of arrest issued in connection with or arising out of criminal proceedings; or
(ii) a warrant of commitment issued under section 76 of the M1. Magistrates' Courts Act 1980;
    (b) of arresting a person for an [F32indictable] offence;
    (c) of arresting a person for an offence under—
(i) section 1 (prohibition of uniforms in connection with political objects), . . . F33 of the M2. Public Order Act 1936;
(ii) any enactment contained in sections 6 to 8 or 10 of the M3. Criminal Law Act 1977 (offences relating to entering and remaining on property);
[F34. (iii)section 4 of the Public Order Act 1986 (fear or provocation of violence);]
[F35. (iiia)section 4 (driving etc. when under influence of drink or drugs) or 163 (failure to stop when required to do so by constable in uniform) of the Road Traffic Act 1988;
(iiib)section 27 of the Transport and Works Act 1992 (which relates to offences involving drink or drugs);]
[F36. (iv)section 76 of the Criminal Justice and Public Order Act 1994 (failure to comply with interim possession order);]
[F37. (v)any of sections 4, 5, 6. (1) and (2), 7 and 8. (1) and (2) of the Animal Welfare Act 2006 (offences relating to the prevention of harm to animals);]
[F38. (vi)section 144 of the Legal Aid, Sentencing and Punishment of Offenders Act 2012 (squatting in a residential building);]
    [F39. (ca)of arresting, in pursuance of section 32. (1. A) of the Children and Young Persons Act 1969, any child or young person who has been remanded [F40to local authority accommodation or youth detention accommodation under section 91 of the Legal Aid, Sentencing and Punishment of Offenders Act 2012] ;
    [F41. (caa)of arresting a person for an offence to which section 61 of the Animal Health Act 1981 applies;]
    [F42. (cab)of arresting a person under any of the following provisions—
(i) section 30. D(1) or (2. A);
(ii) section 46. A(1) or (1. A);
(iii) section 5. B(7) of the Bail Act 1976 (arrest where a person fails to surrender to custody in accordance with a court order);
(iv) section 7. (3) of the Bail Act 1976 (arrest where a person is not likely to surrender to custody etc);
(v) section 97. (1) of the Legal Aid, Sentencing and Punishment of Offenders Act 2012 (arrest where a child is suspected of breaking conditions of remand);]
    (cb) of recapturing any person who is, or is deemed for any purpose to be, unlawfully at large while liable to be detained—
(i) in a prison, [F43 young offender institution, secure training centre or secure college] , or
(ii) in pursuance of [F44section 92 of the Powers of Criminal Courts (Sentencing) Act 2000] (dealing with children and young persons guilty of grave crimes), in any other place;]
    (d) of recapturing [F45any person whatever] who is unlawfully at large and whom he is pursuing; or
    (e) of saving life or limb or preventing serious damage to property.

(2) Except for the purpose specified in paragraph (e) of subsection (1) above, the powers of entry and search conferred by this section—

(a) are only exercisable if the constable has reasonable grounds for believing that the person whom he is seeking is on the premises; and

(b) are limited, in relation to premises consisting of two or more separate dwellings, to powers to enter and search—

(i) any parts of the premises which the occupiers of any dwelling comprised in the premises use in common with the occupiers of any other such dwelling; and

(ii) any such dwelling in which the constable has reasonable grounds for believing that the person whom he is seeking may be.

(3) The powers of entry and search conferred by this section are only exercisable for the purposes specified in subsection (1)(c)(ii) [F46, (iv) or (vi)] above by a constable in uniform.

(4) The power of search conferred by this section is only a power to search to the extent that is reasonably required for the purpose for which the power of entry is exercised.

(5) Subject to subsection 6 below, all the rules of common law under which a constable has power to enter premises without a warrant are hereby abolished.

(6) Nothing in subsection (5) above affects any power of entry to deal with or prevent a breach of the peace.

Amendments (Textual)

F32. Word in s. 17. (1)(b) substituted (1.1.2006) by Serious Organised Crime and Police Act 2005 (c. 15), ss. 111, 178, Sch. 7 Pt. 3 para. 43. (4); S.I. 2005/3495, art. 2. (1)(m)

F33. Words repealed by Public Order Act 1986 (c. 64, SIF 39:2), s. 40. (2)(3), Sch. 2 para. 7, Sch. 3

F34. S.17. (1)(c)(iii) inserted by Public Order Act 1986 (c. 64, SIF 39:2), s. 40. (2), Sch. 2 para. 7

F35. S. 17. (1)(c)(iiia)(iiib) substituted for s. 17. (1)(c)(iiia) (1.1.2006) by Serious Organised Crime and Police Act 2005 (c. 15), ss. 111, 178, Sch. 7 Pt. 4 para. 58. (a); S.I. 2005/3495, art. 2. (1)(m)

F36. S. 17. (1)(c)(iv) inserted (24.8.1995) by 1994 c. 33, s. 168. (2), Sch. 10 para. 53. (a); S.I. 1995/1957, art. 3

F37. S. 17. (1)(c)(v) inserted (27.3.2007 for W. and 6.4.2007 for E.) by Animal Welfare Act 2006 (c. 45), ss. 24, 68 (with ss. 1. (2), 58. (1), 59, 60); S.I. 2007/1030, art. 2. (2)(g); S.I. 2007/499, art. 2. (2)(g)

F38. S. 17. (1)(c)(vi) inserted (1.9.2012) by Legal Aid, Sentencing and Punishment of Offenders Act 2012 (c. 10), ss. 144. (8)(a), 151. (1); S.I. 2012/1956, art. 2

F39. S. 17. (1)(ca)(cb) inserted (5.9.1995) by 1995 c. 16, s. 2. (1); S.I. 1995/2021, art. 2

F40. Words in s. 17. (1)(ca) substituted (3.12.2012) by Legal Aid, Sentencing and Punishment of Offenders Act 2012 (c. 10), s. 151. (1), Sch. 12 para. 21; S.I. 2012/2906, art. 2. (j) (with art. 7. (2)(3))

F41. S. 17. (1)(caa) inserted (1.1.2006) by Serious Organised Crime and Police Act 2005 (c. 15), ss. 111, 178, Sch. 7 Pt. 4 para. 58. (b); S.I. 2005/3495, art. 2. (1)(m)

F42. S. 17. (1)(cab) inserted (31.1.2017 for specified purposes, 3.4.2017 in so far as not already in force) by Policing and Crime Act 2017 (c. 3), ss. 72, 183. (1), (5)(e); S.I. 2017/399, reg. 2, Sch. para. 21

F43. Words in s. 17. (1)(cb)(i) substituted (20.3.2015) by Criminal Justice and Courts Act 2015 (c. 2), s. 95. (1), Sch. 9 para. 9; S.I. 2015/778, art. 2. (1)(c)

F44. Words in s. 17. (1)(cb) substituted (25.8.2000) by 2000 c. 6, ss. 165, 168. (1), Sch. 9 para. 95

F45. Words in s. 17. (1)(d) substituted (5.9.1995) by 1995 c. 16, s. 2. (1); S.I. 1995/2021, art. 2

F46. Words in s. 17. (3) substituted (1.9.2012) by Legal Aid, Sentencing and Punishment of Offenders Act 2012 (c. 10), ss. 144. (8)(b), 151. (1); S.I. 2012/1956, art. 2

Modifications etc. (not altering text)

C63. S. 17 extended (2.12.2002) Police Reform Act 2002 (c. 30), s. 38, Sch. 4 Pt. 1 para. 8; S.I. 2002/2750, art. 2. (a)(ii)(d)

C64. S. 17 applied (2.9.2014) by The Control of Explosives Precursors Regulations 2014 (S.I.

2014/1942), regs. 1. (1), 14

C65. S. 17 applied by 1972 c. 66, s. 9. A (as inserted (20.4.2015 for specified purposes, 26.3.2015 for specified purposes, 26.5.2015 in so far as not already in force) by Deregulation Act 2015 (c. 20), s. 115. (2)(e), Sch. 21 para. 12; S.I. 2015/994, arts. 5, 6. (p))

C66. S. 17. (1)(a)(i) applied (with modifications) (25.6.2013) by The Police and Criminal Evidence Act 1984 (Application to immigration officers and designated customs officials in England and Wales) Order 2013 (S.I. 2013/1542), arts. 1, 12. (2)-(4), Sch. 2 (with arts. 13-31)

C67. S. 17. (1)(a)(i) applied (with modifications) (4.11.2015) by The Police and Criminal Evidence Act 1984 (Application to Revenue and Customs) Order 2015 (S.I. 2015/1783), arts. 1, 3. (1), Sch. 1 (with art. 3. (2), (3), 4-19, Sch. 2)

C68. S. 17. (1)(a)(i) applied (with modifications) (30.4.2017) by The Police and Criminal Evidence Act 1984 (Application to Labour Abuse Prevention Officers) Regulations 2017 (S.I. 2017/520), regs. 1, 2, 3. (h), Sch.

C69. Ss. 8, 9, 15, 16, 17. (1)(b(2) (4), 18–20, 21, 22. (1)–(4), 28, 29, 30. (1)–(4)(a)(5)–(11), 31, 32. (1)–(9), 34. (1)–(5), 35, 36, 37, 39, 40–44, 50, 51. (d), 52, 54, 55, 64. (1)–(4)(5)(6), Sch. 1 applied with modifications by S.I. 1985/1800, arts. 3–11, Schs. 1, 2

C70. S. 17. (1)(b) applied (with modifications) (25.6.2013) by The Police and Criminal Evidence Act 1984 (Application to immigration officers and designated customs officials in England and Wales) Order 2013 (S.I. 2013/1542), arts. 1, 12. (2)-(4), Sch. 2 (with arts. 13-31)

C71. S. 17. (1)(b) applied (with modifications) (25.6.2013) by The Police and Criminal Evidence Act 1984 (Application to immigration officers and designated customs officials in England and Wales) Order 2013 (S.I. 2013/1542), arts. 1, 3. (2)-(4), Sch. 1 (with arts. 4-11)

C72. S. 17. (1)(b) applied (with modifications) (4.11.2015) by The Police and Criminal Evidence Act 1984 (Application to Revenue and Customs) Order 2015 (S.I. 2015/1783), arts. 1, 3. (1), Sch. 1 (with art. 3. (2), (3), 4-19, Sch. 2)

C73. S. 17. (1)(b) applied (with modifications) (30.4.2017) by The Police and Criminal Evidence Act 1984 (Application to Labour Abuse Prevention Officers) Regulations 2017 (S.I. 2017/520), regs. 1, 2, 3. (h), Sch.

C74. S. 17. (1)(cb) applied (with modifications) (4.11.2015) by The Police and Criminal Evidence Act 1984 (Application to Revenue and Customs) Order 2015 (S.I. 2015/1783), arts. 1, 3. (1), Sch. 1 (with art. 3. (2), (3), 4-19, Sch. 2)

C75. S. 17. (1)(cb)(i) applied (with modifications) (25.6.2013) by The Police and Criminal Evidence Act 1984 (Application to immigration officers and designated customs officials in England and Wales) Order 2013 (S.I. 2013/1542), arts. 1, 3. (2)-(4), Sch. 1 (with arts. 4-11)

C76. S. 17. (1)(cb)(i) applied (with modifications) (25.6.2013) by The Police and Criminal Evidence Act 1984 (Application to immigration officers and designated customs officials in England and Wales) Order 2013 (S.I. 2013/1542), arts. 1, 12. (2)-(4), Sch. 2 (with arts. 13-31)

C77. S. 17. (1)(d) applied (with modifications) (25.6.2013) by The Police and Criminal Evidence Act 1984 (Application to immigration officers and designated customs officials in England and Wales) Order 2013 (S.I. 2013/1542), arts. 1, 3. (2)-(4), Sch. 1 (with arts. 4-11)

C78. S. 17. (1)(d) applied (with modifications) (25.6.2013) by The Police and Criminal Evidence Act 1984 (Application to immigration officers and designated customs officials in England and Wales) Order 2013 (S.I. 2013/1542), arts. 1, 12. (2)-(4), Sch. 2 (with arts. 13-31)

C79. S. 17. (1)(d) applied (with modifications) (4.11.2015) by The Police and Criminal Evidence Act 1984 (Application to Revenue and Customs) Order 2015 (S.I. 2015/1783), arts. 1, 3. (1), Sch. 1 (with art. 3. (2), (3), 4-19, Sch. 2)

C80. S. 17. (2)(4) applied (with modifications) (25.6.2013) by The Police and Criminal Evidence Act 1984 (Application to immigration officers and designated customs officials in England and Wales) Order 2013 (S.I. 2013/1542), arts. 1, 12. (2)-(4), Sch. 2 (with arts. 13-31)

C81. S. 17. (2) applied (with modifications) (25.6.2013) by The Police and Criminal Evidence Act 1984 (Application to immigration officers and designated customs officials in England and Wales) Order 2013 (S.I. 2013/1542), arts. 1, 3. (2)-(4), Sch. 1 (with arts. 4-11)

C82. S. 17. (2) applied (with modifications) (4.11.2015) by The Police and Criminal Evidence Act

1984 (Application to Revenue and Customs) Order 2015 (S.I. 2015/1783), arts. 1, 3. (1), Sch. 1 (with art. 3. (2), (3), 4-19, Sch. 2)
C83. S. 17. (2) applied (with modifications) (30.4.2017) by The Police and Criminal Evidence Act 1984 (Application to Labour Abuse Prevention Officers) Regulations 2017 (S.I. 2017/520), regs. 1, 2, 3. (h), Sch.
C84. S. 17. (4) applied (with modifications) (25.6.2013) by The Police and Criminal Evidence Act 1984 (Application to immigration officers and designated customs officials in England and Wales) Order 2013 (S.I. 2013/1542), arts. 1, 3. (2)-(4), Sch. 1 (with arts. 4-11)
C85. S. 17. (4) applied (with modifications) (4.11.2015) by The Police and Criminal Evidence Act 1984 (Application to Revenue and Customs) Order 2015 (S.I. 2015/1783), arts. 1, 3. (1), Sch. 1 (with art. 3. (2), (3), 4-19, Sch. 2)
C86. S. 17. (4) applied (with modifications) (30.4.2017) by The Police and Criminal Evidence Act 1984 (Application to Labour Abuse Prevention Officers) Regulations 2017 (S.I. 2017/520), regs. 1, 2, 3. (h), Sch.
Marginal Citations
M11980 c. 43.
M21936 c. 6.
M31977 c. 45.

18 Entry and search after arrest.

(1) Subject to the following provisions of this section, a constable may enter and search any premises occupied or controlled by a person who is under arrest for an [F47indictable] offence, if he has reasonable grounds for suspecting that there is on the premises evidence, other than items subject to legal privilege, that relates—
    (a) to that offence; or
    (b) to some other [F47indictable] offence which is connected with or similar to that offence.
(2) A constable may seize and retain anything for which he may search under subsection (1) above.
(3) The power to search conferred by subsection (1) above is only a power to search to the extent that is reasonably required for the purpose of discovering such evidence.
(4) Subject to subsection (5) below, the powers conferred by this section may not be exercised unless an officer of the rank of inspector or above has authorised them in writing.
[F48. (5)A constable may conduct a search under subsection (1)—
    (a) before the person is taken to a police station or released F49... under section 30. A, and
    (b) without obtaining an authorisation under subsection (4),
if the condition in subsection (5. A) is satisfied.
(5. A)The condition is that the presence of the person at a place (other than a police station) is necessary for the effective investigation of the offence.]
(6) If a constable conducts a search by virtue of subsection (5) above, he shall inform an officer of the rank of inspector or above that he has made the search as soon as practicable after he has made it.
(7) An officer who—
    (a) authorises a search; or
    (b) is informed of a search under subsection (6) above, shall make a record in writing—
(i) of the grounds for the search; and
(ii) of the nature of the evidence that was sought.
(8) If the person who was in occupation or control of the premises at the time of the search is in police detention at the time the record is to be made, the officer shall make the record as part of his custody record.
Amendments (Textual)
F47. Words in s. 18. (1) substituted (1.1.2006) by Serious Organised Crime and Police Act 2005

(c. 15), ss. 111, 178, Sch. 7 Pt. 3 para. 43. (5); S.I. 2005/3495, art. 2. (1)(m)

F48. S. 18. (5)(5. A) substituted for s. 18. (5) (20.1.2004) by Criminal Justice Act 2003 (c. 44), ss. 12, 336, Sch. 1 para. 2; S.I. 2004/81, art. 2. (1)(2)(a)

F49. Words in s. 18. (5)(a) omitted (31.1.2017 for specified purposes, 3.4.2017 in so far as not already in force) by virtue of Policing and Crime Act 2017 (c. 3), ss. 53. (2), 183. (1), (5)(e); S.I. 2017/399, reg. 2, Sch. para. 12 (with reg. 5)

Modifications etc. (not altering text)

C87. Ss. 8, 9, 15, 16, 17. (1)(b(2) (4), 18–20, 21, 22. (1)–(4), 28, 29, 30. (1)–(4)(a)(5)–(11), 31, 32. (1)–(9), 34. (1)–(5), 35, 36, 37, 39, 40–44, 50, 51. (d), 52, 54, 55, 64. (1)–(4)(5)(6), Sch. 1 applied with modifications by S.I. 1985/1800, arts. 3–11, Schs. 1, 2

C88. S. 18 extended (2.12.2002) by Police Reform Act 2002 (c. 30), s. 38, Sch. 4 Pt. 2 para. 18. (a); S.I. 2002/2750, art. 2. (a)(ii)(d)

C89. S. 18 applied (with modifications) (25.6.2013) by The Police and Criminal Evidence Act 1984 (Application to immigration officers and designated customs officials in England and Wales) Order 2013 (S.I. 2013/1542), arts. 1, 3. (2)-(4), Sch. 1 (with arts. 4-11)

C90. S. 18 applied (with modifications) (25.6.2013) by The Police and Criminal Evidence Act 1984 (Application to immigration officers and designated customs officials in England and Wales) Order 2013 (S.I. 2013/1542), arts. 1, 12. (2)-(4), Sch. 2 (with arts. 13-31)

C91. S. 18 applied (2.9.2014) by The Control of Explosives Precursors Regulations 2014 (S.I. 2014/1942), regs. 1. (1), 14

C92. S. 18 applied by 1972 c. 66, s. 9. A (as inserted (20.4.2015 for specified purposes, 26.3.2015 for specified purposes, 26.5.2015 in so far as not already in force) by Deregulation Act 2015 (c. 20), s. 115. (2)(e), Sch. 21 para. 12; S.I. 2015/994, arts. 5, 6. (p))

C93. S. 18 applied (with modifications) (4.11.2015) by The Police and Criminal Evidence Act 1984 (Application to Revenue and Customs) Order 2015 (S.I. 2015/1783), arts. 1, 3. (1), Sch. 1 (with art. 3. (2), (3), 4-19, Sch. 2)

C94. S. 18 applied (with modifications) (30.4.2017) by The Police and Criminal Evidence Act 1984 (Application to Labour Abuse Prevention Officers) Regulations 2017 (S.I. 2017/520), regs. 1, 2, 3. (i), Sch.

C95. S. 18. (6) modified (2.12.2002) by Police Reform Act 2002 (c. 30), s. 38, Sch. 4 Pt. 2 para. 18. (b); S.I. 2002/2750, art. 2. (a)(ii)(d)

Seizure etc.

19 General power of seizure etc.

(1) The powers conferred by subsections (2), (3) and (4) below are exercisable by a constable who is lawfully on any premises.

(2) The constable may seize anything which is on the premises if he has reasonable grounds for believing—

(a) that it has been obtained in consequence of the commission of an offence; and

(b) that it is necessary to seize it in order to prevent it being concealed, lost, damaged, altered or destroyed.

(3) The constable may seize anything which is on the premises if he has reasonable grounds for believing—

(a) that it is evidence in relation to an offence which he is investigating or any other offence; and

(b) that it is necessary to seize it in order to prevent the evidence being concealed, lost, altered or destroyed.

(4) The constable may require any information which is [F50stored in any electronic form] and is accessible from the premises to be produced in a form in which it can be taken away and in which

it is visible and legible [F51or from which it can readily be produced in a visible and legible form]if he has reasonable grounds for believing—

(a) that—

(i) it is evidence in relation to an offence which he is investigating or any other offence; or

(ii) it has been obtained in consequence of the commission of an offence; and

(b) that it is necessary to do so in order to prevent it being concealed, lost, tampered with or destroyed.

(5) The powers conferred by this section are in addition to any power otherwise conferred.

(6) No power of seizure conferred on a constable under any enactment (including an enactment contained in an Act passed after this Act) is to be taken to authorise the seizure of an item which the constable exercising the power has reasonable grounds for believing to be subject to legal privilege.

Amendments (Textual)

F50. Words in s. 19. (4) substituted (1.4.2003) by 2001 c. 16, ss. 70, 138. (2) Sch. 2 Pt. II para. 13. (1)(a)(2)(a); S.I. 2003/708, art. 2. (k)

F51. Words in s. 19. (4) inserted (1.4.2003) by 2001 c. 16, ss. 70, 138. (2), Sch. 2 Pt. II para 13. (1)(b)(2)(a); S.I. 2003/708, art. 2. (k)

Modifications etc. (not altering text)

C96. Ss. 8, 9, 15, 16, 17. (1)(b)(2) (4), 18-20, 21, 22. (1)-(4), 28, 29, 30. (1)-(4)(a)(5)-(11), 31, 32. (1)-(9), 34. (1)-(5), 35, 36, 37, 39, 40-44, 50, 51. (d), 52, 54, 55, 64. (1)-(4)(5)(6), Sch. 1 applied with modifications by S.I. 1985/1800, arts. 3-11, Schs. 1, 2

C97. S. 19 extended (2.12.2002) by Police Reform Act 2002 (c. 30), s. 38, Sch. 4 Pt. 2 para. 19. (a); S.I. 2002/2750, art. 2. (a)(ii)(d)

C98. S. 19 applied (with modifications) (25.6.2013) by The Police and Criminal Evidence Act 1984 (Application to immigration officers and designated customs officials in England and Wales) Order 2013 (S.I. 2013/1542), arts. 1, 3. (2)-(4), Sch. 1 (with arts. 4-11)

C99. S. 19 applied (with modifications) (25.6.2013) by The Police and Criminal Evidence Act 1984 (Application to immigration officers and designated customs officials in England and Wales) Order 2013 (S.I. 2013/1542), arts. 1, 12. (2)-(4), Sch. 2 (with arts. 13-31)

C100. S. 19 extended (with modifications) by 2002 c. 30, Sch. 4 para. 2. B(a)-(c) (as inserted (13.5.2014) by Anti-social Behaviour, Crime and Policing Act 2014 (c. 12), s. 185. (1), Sch. 10 para. 4 (with ss. 21, 33, 42, 58, 75, 93); S.I. 2014/949, art. 3, Sch. para. 22)

C101. S. 19 applied (with modifications) (4.11.2015) by The Police and Criminal Evidence Act 1984 (Application to Revenue and Customs) Order 2015 (S.I. 2015/1783), arts. 1, 3. (1), Sch. 1 (with art. 3. (2), (3), 4-19, Sch. 2)

C102. S. 19 applied by 1994 c. 33, s. 139. (10. A)(a) (as inserted (31.1.2017 for specified purposes) by Policing and Crime Act 2017 (c. 3), s. 183. (1)(5)(e), Sch. 17 para. 4. (9))

C103. S. 19 applied (with modifications) (30.4.2017) by The Police and Criminal Evidence Act 1984 (Application to Labour Abuse Prevention Officers) Regulations 2017 (S.I. 2017/520), regs. 1, 2, 3. (j), Sch.

C104. S. 19. (4) modified (1.4.2003) by 2001 c. 16, ss. 63, 138. (2); S.I. 2003/708, art. 2. (a)

C105. S. 19. (6) excluded (1.4.2003) by 2001 c. 16, ss. 50 (2)(4)-(6), 138. (2); S.I. 2003/708, art. 2. (a)

S. 19. (6) excluded (1.4.2003) by 2001 c.16, ss. 51. (2)(4)(5), 138. (2); S.I. 2003/708, art. 2. (a)

C106. S. 19. (6) modified (2.12.2002) by Police Reform Act 2002 (c. 30), s. 38, Sch. 4 Pt. 2 para. 16. (f); S.I. 2002/2750, art. 2. (a)(ii)(d)

S. 19. (6) modified (2.12.2002) by Police Reform Act 2002 (c. 30), s. 38, Sch. 4 Pt. 2 para. 17. (c); S.I. 2002/2750, art. 2. (a)(ii)(d)

S. 19. (6) modified (2.12.2002) by Police Reform Act 2002 (c. 30), s. 38, Sch. 4 Pt. 2 para. 18. (c); S.I. 2002/2750, art. 2. (a)(ii)(d)

S. 19. (6) modified (2.12.2002) by Police Reform Act 2002 (c. 30), s. 38, Sch. 4 Pt. 2 para. 19. (c); S.I. 2002/2750, art. 2. (a)(ii)(d)

20 Extension of powers of seizure to computerised information.

(1) Every power of seizure which is conferred by an enactment to which this section applies on a constable who has entered premises in the exercise of a power conferred by an enactment shall be construed as including a power to require any information [F52stored in any electronic form] contained in a computer and accessible from the premises to be produced in a form in which it can be taken away and in which it is visible and legible [F53or from which it can readily be produced in a visible and legible form].

(2) This section applies—

    (a) to any enactment contained in an Act passed before this Act;

    (b) to sections 8 and 18 above;

    (c) to paragraph 13 of Schedule 1 to this Act; and

    (d) to any enactment contained in an Act passed after this Act.

Amendments (Textual)

F52. Words in s. 20. (1) substituted (1.4.2003) by 2001 c. 16, s. 70, Sch. 2 Pt. II para. 13. (1)(a)(2)(a); S.I. 2003/708, art. 2. (c)(k)

F53. Words in s. 20. (1) inserted (1.4.2003) by 2001 c. 16, s. 70, Sch. 2 Pt. II para. 13. (1)(b)(2)(a); S.I. 2003/708, art. 2. (c)(k)

Modifications etc. (not altering text)

C107. Ss. 8, 9, 15, 16, 17. (1)(b(2) (4), 18–20, 21, 22. (1)–(4), 28, 29, 30. (1)–(4)(a)(5)–(11), 31, 32. (1)–(9), 34. (1)–(5), 35, 36, 37, 39, 40–44, 50, 51. (d), 52, 54, 55, 64. (1)–(4)(5)(6), Sch. 1 applied with modifications by S.I. 1985/1800, arts. 3–11, Schs. 1, 2

C108. S. 20 modified (1.4.2003) by 2001 c. 16, ss. 63, 138. (2); S.I. 2003/708, art. 2. (a)

C109. S. 20 modified (2.12.2002) by Police Reform Act 2002 (c. 30), s. 38, Sch. 4 Pt. 2 para. 16. (g); S.I. 2002/2750, art. 2. (a)(ii)(d)

S. 20 modified (2.12.2002) by Police Reform Act 2002 (c. 30), s. 38, Sch. 4 Pt. 2 para. 17. (d); S.I. 2002/2750, art. 2. (a)(ii)(d)

S. 20 modified (2.12.2002) by Police Reform Act 2002 (c. 30), s. 38, Sch. 4 Pt. 2 para. 18. (d); S.I. 2002/2750, art. 2. (a)(ii)(d)

C110. S. 20 applied (with modifications) (1.4.2003) by The Proceeds of Crime Act 2002 (Investigations in different parts of the United Kingdom) Order 2003 (S.I. 2003/425), art. 5. (9)

S. 20 applied (with modifications) (1.4.2003) by The Proceeds of Crime Act 2002 (Investigations in different parts of the United Kingdom) Order 2003 (S.I. 2003/425), art. 6. (6)

C111. S. 20 excluded (1.4.2003) by The Proceeds of Crime Act 2002 (Investigations in different parts of the United Kingdom) Order 2003 (S.I. 2003/425), art. 15. (8)

S. 20 excluded (1.4.2003) by The Proceeds of Crime Act 2002 (Investigations in different parts of the United Kingdom) Order 2003 (S.I. 2003/425), art. 25. (7)

C112. S. 20 applied (25.7.2003) by The Advanced Television Services Regulations 2003 (S.I. 2003/1901), reg. 8, Sch. para. 12

C113. S. 20 applied (with modifications) (25.6.2013) by The Police and Criminal Evidence Act 1984 (Application to immigration officers and designated customs officials in England and Wales) Order 2013 (S.I. 2013/1542), arts. 1, 3. (2)-(4), Sch. 1 (with arts. 4-11)

C114. S. 20 applied (with modifications) (25.6.2013) by The Police and Criminal Evidence Act 1984 (Application to immigration officers and designated customs officials in England and Wales) Order 2013 (S.I. 2013/1542), arts. 1, 12. (2)-(4), Sch. 2 (with arts. 13-31)

C115. S. 20 applied (with modifications) (4.11.2015) by The Police and Criminal Evidence Act 1984 (Application to Revenue and Customs) Order 2015 (S.I. 2015/1783), arts. 1, 3. (1), Sch. 1 (with art. 3. (2), (3), 4-19, Sch. 2)

C116. S. 20 applied (with modifications) (30.4.2017) by The Police and Criminal Evidence Act 1984 (Application to Labour Abuse Prevention Officers) Regulations 2017 (S.I. 2017/520), regs. 1, 2, 3. (k), Sch.

21 Access and copying.

(1) A constable who seizes anything in the exercise of a power conferred by any enactment, including an enactment contained in an Act passed after this Act, shall, if so requested by a person showing himself—

    (a) to be the occupier of premises on which it was seized; or

    (b) to have had custody or control of it immediately before the seizure,

provide that person with a record of what he seized.

(2) The officer shall provide the record within a reasonable time from the making of the request for it.

(3) Subject to subsection (8) below, if a request for permission to be granted access to anything which—

    (a) has been seized by a constable; and

    (b) is retained by the police for the purpose of investigating an offence,

is made to the officer in charge of the investigation by a person who had custody or control of the thing immediately before it was so seized or by someone acting on behalf of such a person, the officer shall allow the person who made the request access to it under the supervision of a constable.

(4) Subject to subsection (8) below, if a request for a photograph or copy of any such thing is made to the officer in charge of the investigation by a person who had custody or control of the thing immediately before it was so seized, or by someone acting on behalf of such a person, the officer shall—

    (a) allow the person who made the request access to it under the supervision of a constable for the purpose of photographing or copying it; or

    (b) photograph or copy it, or cause it to be photographed or copied.

(5) A constable may also photograph or copy, or have photographed or copied, anything which he has power to seize, without a request being made under subsection (4) above.

(6) Where anything is photographed or copied under subsection (4)(b) above, the photograph or copy shall be supplied to the person who made the request.

(7) The photograph or copy shall be so supplied within a reasonable time from the making of the request.

(8) There is no duty under this section to grant access to, or to supply a photograph or copy of, anything if the officer in charge of the investigation for the purposes of which it was seized has reasonable grounds for believing that to do so would prejudice—

    (a) that investigation;

    (b) the investigation of an offence other than the offence for the purposes of investigating which the thing was seized; or

    (c) any criminal proceedings which may be brought as a result of—

(i) the investigation of which he is in charge; or

(ii) any such investigation as is mentioned in paragraph (b) above.

[F54. (9)The references to a constable in subsections (1), (2), (3)(a) and (5) include a person authorised under section 16. (2) to accompany a constable executing a warrant.]

[F55. (10)The references to a constable in subsections (1) and (2) do not include a constable who has seized a thing under paragraph 19. ZE of Schedule 3 to the Police Reform Act 2002.]

Amendments (Textual)

F54. S. 21. (9) inserted (20.1.2004) by Criminal Justice Act 2003 (c. 44), ss. 12, 336, Sch. 1 para. 3; S.I. 2004/81, art. 2. (1)(2)(a)

F55. S. 21. (10) inserted (31.1.2017 for specified purposes) by Policing and Crime Act 2017 (c. 3), ss. 20. (2), 183. (1)(5)(e)

Modifications etc. (not altering text)

C117. Ss. 8, 9, 15, 16, 17. (1)(b) (2) (4), 18-20, 21, 22. (1)-(4), 28, 29, 30. (1)-(4)(a) (5)-(11), 31, 32. (1)-(9), 34. (1)-(5), 35, 36, 37, 39, 40-44, 50, 51. (d), 52, 54, 55, 64. (1)-(4)(5)(6), Sch. 1

applied with modifications by S.I. 1985/1800, arts. 3-11, Schs. 1, 2

C118. Ss. 21, 22 amended by Drug Trafficking Offences Act 1986 (c. 32, SIF 39:1), s. 29. (1)

S. 21 modified: (3.2.1995) by 1994 c. 37, ss. 57. (1), 69. (2); (1.11.1995) by 1995 c. 11, s. 15. (2) and S.I. 1995/2650, art.2

S. 21 modified (19.2.2001) by 2000 c. 11, s. 37, Sch. 5 para. 17; S.I. 2001/421, art. 2

S. 21 extended (1.11.1995) by 1988 c. 33, s. 93. H (as inserted by 1995 c. 11, s.11; S.I. 1995/2650, art.2)

C119. S. 21 modified (1.9.2001) by S.I. 1996/716, art 17. D (as inserted by S.I. 2001/2563, art. 2)

C120. S. 21 modified (1.9.2001) by 2001 c. 17, s. 37, Sch. 5 Pt. I para. 6. (5); S.I. 2001/2161, art. 2 (subject to art. 3)

S. 21 modified (2.12.2002) by 2002 c. 30, s. 38, Sch. 4 Pt. 2 para. 20; S.I. 2002/2750, art. 2. (a)(ii)(d)

C121. S. 21: power to apply (with modifications) conferred (24.2.2003) by Proceeds of Crime Act 2002 (c. 29), ss. 355. (1)(2)(3)(c), 458. (1)(3); S.I. 2003/120, art. 2, Sch. (subject to transitional provisions and savings in arts. 3-7 (as amended by S.I. 2003/333, art. 14 which in turn is amended by S.I. 2003/531, arts. 3, 4))

C122. S. 21 applied (with modifications) (24.2.2003) by The Proceeds of Crime Act 2002 (Application of Police and Criminal Evidence Act 1984 and Police and Criminal Evidence (Northern Ireland) Order 1989) Order 2003 (S.I. 2003/174), {arts. 4}, 10, Sch. 1

C123. S. 21 applied (25.7.2003) by The Advanced Television Services Regulations 2003 (S.I. 2003/1901), reg. 8, Sch. para. 12 (with reg. 2. (2))

C124. S. 21 applied (31.3.2008) by UK Borders Act 2007 (c. 30), ss. 46. (5), 59; S.I. 2008/309, art. 3 (subject to art. 6)

C125. S. 21 applied (with modifications) (25.6.2013) by The Police and Criminal Evidence Act 1984 (Application to immigration officers and designated customs officials in England and Wales) Order 2013 (S.I. 2013/1542), arts. 1, 12. (2)-(4), Sch. 2 (with arts. 13-31)

C126. S. 21 applied (with modifications) (25.6.2013) by The Police and Criminal Evidence Act 1984 (Application to immigration officers and designated customs officials in England and Wales) Order 2013 (S.I. 2013/1542), arts. 1, 3. (2)-(4), Sch. 1 (with arts. 4-11)

C127. S. 21 applied (with modifications) (1.6.2015) by The Proceeds of Crime Act 2002 (Application of Police and Criminal Evidence Act 1984) Order 2015 (S.I. 2015/759), arts. 1. (1), 4 (as amended (31.1.2018 for specified purposes) by The Proceeds of Crime Act 2002 (Application of Police and Criminal Evidence Act 1984) (Amendment) Order 2017 (S.I. 2017/1222), arts. 1. (2)(3), 2. (4))

C128. S. 21 applied (with modifications) (4.11.2015) by The Police and Criminal Evidence Act 1984 (Application to Revenue and Customs) Order 2015 (S.I. 2015/1783), arts. 1, 3. (1), Sch. 1 (with art. 3. (2), (3), 4-19, Sch. 2)

C129. S. 21 applied by 2007 c. 30, s. 46. B(3) (as inserted (31.1.2017 for specified purposes) by Policing and Crime Act 2017 (c. 3), ss. 160, 183. (1), (5)(e))

C130. Ss. 21, 22 applied by 1994 c. 33, s. 139. (10. A)(b) (as inserted (31.1.2017 for specified purposes) by Policing and Crime Act 2017 (c. 3), s. 183. (1)(5)(e), Sch. 17 para. 4. (9))

C131. S. 21 modified (31.7.2017) by The Criminal Justice (European Investigation Order) Regulations 2017 (S.I. 2017/730), regs. 1. (1), 39. (11) (with reg. 3)

C132. S. 21. (1) modified (2.12.2002) by Police Reform Act 2002 (c. 30), s. 38, Sch. 4 Pt. 2 para. 16. (h); S.I. 2002/2750, art. 2. (a)(ii)(d)

S. 21. (1) modified (2.12.2002) by Police Reform Act 2002 (c. 30), s. 38, Sch. 4 Pt. 2 para. 17. (e); S.I. 2002/2750, art. 2. (a)(ii)(d)

S. 21. (1) modified (2.12.2002) by Police Reform Act 2002 (c. 30), s. 38, Sch. 4 Pt. 2 para. 18. (e); S.I. 2002/2750, art. 2. (a)(ii)(d)

S. 21. (1) modified (2.12.2002) by Police Reform Act 2002 (c. 30), s. 38, Sch. 4 Pt. 2 para. 19. (d); S.I. 2002/2750, art. 2. (a)(ii)(d)

C133. S. 21. (1)(2) modified by 2002 c. 30, Sch. 4 para. 2. B(d) (as inserted (13.5.2014) by Anti-social Behaviour, Crime and Policing Act 2014 (c. 12), s. 185. (1), Sch. 10 para. 4 (with ss. 21, 33,

42, 58, 75, 93); S.I. 2014/949, art. 3, Sch. para. 22)

C134. S. 21. (1)-(9) applied (with modifications) (30.4.2017) by The Police and Criminal Evidence Act 1984 (Application to Labour Abuse Prevention Officers) Regulations 2017 (S.I. 2017/520), regs. 1, 2, 3. (l), Sch. (with reg. 4)

C135. S. 21. (2) modified (2.12.2002) by Police Reform Act 2002 (c. 30), s. 38, Sch. 4 Pt. 2 para. 16. (h); S.I. 2002/2750, art. 2. (a)(ii)(d)

S. 21. (2) modified (2.12.2002) by Police Reform Act 2002 (c. 30), s. 38, Sch. 4 Pt. 2 para. 17. (e); S.I. 2002/2750, art. 2. (a)(ii)(d)

S. 21. (2) modified (2.12.2002) by Police Reform Act 2002 (c. 30), s. 38, Sch. 4 Pt. 2 para. 18. (e); S.I. 2002/2750, art. 2. (a)(ii)(d)

S. 21. (2) modified (2.12.2002) by Police Reform Act 2002 (c. 30), s. 38, Sch. 4 Pt. 2 para. 19. (d); S.I. 2002/2750, art. 2. (a)(ii)(d)

C136. S. 21. (3)-(8) modified (2.12.2002) by Police Reform Act 2002 (c. 30), s. 38, Sch. 4 Pt. 2 para. 16. (i); S.I. 2002/2750, art. 2. (a)(ii)(d)

S. 21. (3)-(8) modified (2.12.2002) by Police Reform Act 2002 (c. 30), s. 38, Sch. 4 Pt. 2 para. 17. (f); S.I. 2002/2750, art. 2. (a)(ii)(d)

S. 21. (3)-(8) modified (2.12.2002) by Police Reform Act 2002 (c. 30), s. 38, Sch. 4 Pt. 2 para. 18. (f); S.I. 2002/2750, art. 2. (a)(ii)(d)

S. 21. (3)-(8) modified (2.12.2002) by Police Reform Act 2002 (c. 30), s. 38, Sch. 4 Pt. 2 para. 19. (e); S.I. 2002/2750, art. 2. (a)(ii)(d)

C137. S. 21. (3)-(8) modified by 2002 c. 30, Sch. 4 para. 2. B(e) (as inserted (13.5.2014) by Anti-social Behaviour, Crime and Policing Act 2014 (c. 12), s. 185. (1), Sch. 10 para. 4 (with ss. 21, 33, 42, 58, 75, 93); S.I. 2014/949, art. 3, Sch. para. 22)

22 Retention.

(1) Subject to subsection (4) below, anything which has been seized by a constable or taken away by a constable following a requirement made by virtue of section 19 or 20 above may be retained so long as is necessary in all the circumstances.

(2) Without prejudice to the generality of subsection (1) above—

(a) anything seized for the purposes of a criminal investigation may be retained, except as provided by subsection (4) below—

(i) for use as evidence at a trial for an offence; or

(ii) for forensic examination or for investigation in connection with an offence; and

(b) anything may be retained in order to establish its lawful owner, where there are reasonable grounds for believing that it has been obtained in consequence of the commission of an offence.

(3) Nothing seized on the ground that it may be used—

(a) to cause physical injury to any person;

(b) to damage property;

(c) to interfere with evidence; or

(d) to assist in escape from police detention or lawful custody,

may be retained when the person from whom it was seized is no longer in police detention or the custody of a court or is in the custody of a court but has been released on bail.

(4) Nothing may be retained for either of the purposes mentioned in subsection (2)(a) above if a photograph or copy would be sufficient for that purpose.

(5) Nothing in this section affects any power of a court to make an order under section 1 of the M4. Police (Property) Act 1897.

[F56. (6)This section also applies to anything retained by the police under section 28. H(5) of the M5. Immigration Act 1971.]

[F57. (7)The reference in subsection (1) to anything seized by a constable includes anything seized by a person authorised under section 16. (2) to accompany a constable executing a warrant.]

Amendments (Textual)

F56. S. 22. (6) inserted (14.2.2000) by 1999 c. 33, s. 169. (1), Sch. 14 para. 80. (3); S.I. 2000/168, art. 2, Sch.

F57. S. 22. (7) inserted (20.1.2004) by Criminal Justice Act 2003 (c. 44), ss. 12, 336, Sch. 1 para. 4; S.I. 2004/81, art. 2. (1)(2)(a)

Modifications etc. (not altering text)

C130. Ss. 21, 22 applied by 1994 c. 33, s. 139. (10. A)(b) (as inserted (31.1.2017 for specified purposes) by Policing and Crime Act 2017 (c. 3), s. 183. (1)(5)(e), Sch. 17 para. 4. (9))

C138. Ss. 21, 22 amended by Drug Trafficking Offences Act 1986 (c. 32, SIF 39:1), s. 29. (1)

S. 22 modified (3.2.1995) by 1994 c. 37, ss. 57. (1), 69. (2); (1.11.1995) by 1995 c. 11, s. 15. (2) and S.I. 1995/2650, art. 2

S. 22 modified (19.2.2001) by 2000 c. 11, s. 37, Sch. 5 para. 17; S.I. 2001/421, art. 2

S. 22 extended (1.11.1995) by 1988 c. 33, s. 93. H (as inserted by 1995 c. 11, s. 11; S.I. 1995/2650, art. 2)

C139. S. 22 modified (1.9.2001) by S.I. 1996/716, art. 17. D (as inserted (1.9.2001) by S.I. 2001/2563, art. 2)

C140. S. 22 applied (1.4.2003) by 2001 c. 16, ss. 57. (1)(a)(4), 138; S.I. 2003/708, art. 2. (a)

C141. S. 22 modified (1.9.2001) by 2001 c. 17, s. 37, Sch. 5 Pt. I para. 6. (5); S.I. 2001/2161, art. 2 (subject to art. 3)

S. 22 modified (2.12.2002) by Police Reform Act 2002 (c. 30), s. 38, Sch. 4 Pt. 2 para. 16. (i); S.I. 2002/2750, art. 2. (a)(ii)(d)

S. 22 modified (2.12.2002) by Police Reform Act 2002 (c. 30), s. 38, Sch. 4 Pt. 2 para. 17. (f); S.I. 2002/2750, art. 2. (a)(ii)(d)

S. 22 modified (2.12.2002) by Police Reform Act 2002 (c. 30), s. 38, Sch. 4 Pt. 2 para. 18. (f); S.I. 2002/2750, art. 2. (a)(ii)(d)

S. 22 modified (2.12.2002) by Police Reform Act 2002 (c. 30), s. 38, Sch. 4 Pt. 2 para. 19. (e); S.I. 2002/2750, art. 2. (a)(ii)(d)

C142. S. 22: power to apply (with modifications) conferred (24.2.2003) by Proceeds of Crime Act 2002 (c. 29), ss. 355. (1)(2)(3)(d), 458; S.I. 2003/120, art. 2, Sch. (subject to transitional provisions and savings in arts. 3-7 (as amended by S.I. 2003/333, art. 14 which in turn is amended by S.I. 2003/531, arts. 3, 4))

C143. S. 22 applied (with modifications) (24.2.2003) by The Proceeds of Crime Act 2002 (Application of Police and Criminal Evidence Act 1984 and Police and Criminal Evidence (Northern Ireland) Order 1989) Order 2003 (S.I. 2003/174), {arts. 5}, 10, Sch. 1

C144. S. 22 modified by 2002 c. 30, Sch. 4 para. 2. B(e) (as inserted (13.5.2014) by Anti-social Behaviour, Crime and Policing Act 2014 (c. 12), s. 185. (1), Sch. 10 para. 4 (with ss. 21, 33, 42, 58, 75, 93); S.I. 2014/949, art. 3, Sch. para. 22)

C145. S. 22 applied (with modifications) (1.6.2015) by The Proceeds of Crime Act 2002 (Application of Police and Criminal Evidence Act 1984) Order 2015 (S.I. 2015/759), arts. 1. (1), 5 (as amended (31.1.2018 for specified purposes) by The Proceeds of Crime Act 2002 (Application of Police and Criminal Evidence Act 1984) (Amendment) Order 2017 (S.I. 2017/1222), art. 1. (2)(3), 2. (5))

C146. Ss. 8, 9, 15, 16, 17. (1)(b)(2) (4), 18-20, 21, 22. (1)-(4), 28, 29, 30. (1)-(4)(a)(5)-(11), 31, 32. (1)-(9), 34. (1)-(5), 35, 36, 37, 39, 40-44, 50, 51. (d), 52, 54, 55, 64. (1)-(4)(5)(6), Sch. 1 applied with modifications by S.I. 1985/1800, arts. 3-11, Schs. 1, 2

C147. S. 22. (1)-(4) applied (with modifications) (25.6.2013) by The Police and Criminal Evidence Act 1984 (Application to immigration officers and designated customs officials in England and Wales) Order 2013 (S.I. 2013/1542), arts. 1, 3. (2)-(4), Sch. 1 (with arts. 4-11)

C148. S. 22. (1)-(4) applied (with modifications) (25.6.2013) by The Police and Criminal Evidence Act 1984 (Application to immigration officers and designated customs officials in England and Wales) Order 2013 (S.I. 2013/1542), arts. 1, 12. (2)-(4), Sch. 2 (with arts. 13-31)

C149. S. 22. (1)-(4) applied (with modifications) (4.11.2015) by The Police and Criminal Evidence Act 1984 (Application to Revenue and Customs) Order 2015 (S.I. 2015/1783), arts. 1, 3. (1), Sch. 1 (with arts. 3. (2)(3), 4-19, Sch. 2)

C150. S. 22. (1) applied (with modifications) (30.4.2017) by The Police and Criminal Evidence Act 1984 (Application to Labour Abuse Prevention Officers) Regulations 2017 (S.I. 2017/520), regs. 1, 2, 3. (m), Sch.
C151. S. 22. (2)(a) applied (with modifications) (30.4.2017) by The Police and Criminal Evidence Act 1984 (Application to Labour Abuse Prevention Officers) Regulations 2017 (S.I. 2017/520), regs. 1, 2, 3. (m), Sch.
C152. S. 22. (3)(4) applied (with modifications) (30.4.2017) by The Police and Criminal Evidence Act 1984 (Application to Labour Abuse Prevention Officers) Regulations 2017 (S.I. 2017/520), regs. 1, 2, 3. (m), Sch.
C153. S. 22. (7) applied (with modifications) (25.6.2013) by The Police and Criminal Evidence Act 1984 (Application to immigration officers and designated customs officials in England and Wales) Order 2013 (S.I. 2013/1542), arts. 1, 3. (2)-(4), Sch. 1 (with arts. 4-11)
C154. S. 22. (7) applied (with modifications) (25.6.2013) by The Police and Criminal Evidence Act 1984 (Application to immigration officers and designated customs officials in England and Wales) Order 2013 (S.I. 2013/1542), arts. 1, 12. (2)-(4), Sch. 2 (with arts. 13-31)
C155. S. 22. (7) applied (with modifications) (4.11.2015) by The Police and Criminal Evidence Act 1984 (Application to Revenue and Customs) Order 2015 (S.I. 2015/1783), arts. 1, 3. (1), Sch. 1 (with arts. 3. (2)(3), 4-19, Sch. 2)
C156. S. 22. (7) applied (with modifications) (30.4.2017) by The Police and Criminal Evidence Act 1984 (Application to Labour Abuse Prevention Officers) Regulations 2017 (S.I. 2017/520), regs. 1, 2, 3. (m), Sch.
Marginal Citations
M41897 c. 30.
M51971 c. 77.

Supplementary

23 Meaning of "premises" etc.

In this Act—
"premises" includes any place and, in particular, includes—
   - any vehicle, vessel, aircraft or hovercraft;
   - any offshore installation;
   - [F58any renewable energy installation;]
   - any tent or movable structure; F59. . .
"offshore installation" has the meaning given to it by section 1 of the M6. Mineral Workings (Offshore Installations) Act 1971.
[F60"renewable energy installation" has the same meaning as in Chapter 2 of Part 2 of the Energy Act 2004.]

Amendments (Textual)
F58. S. 23: in definition of "premises", para. (ba) substituted for word "and" at the end of para. (b) (5.10.2004) by Energy Act 2004 (c. 20), ss. 103. (2)(a), 198. (2); S.I. 2004/2575, art. 2. (1), Sch. 1
F59. S. 23: word at the end of the definition of "premises" repealed (5.10.2004) by Energy Act 2004 (c. 20), ss. 197, 198. (2), Sch. 23 Pt. 1; S.I. 2004/2575, art. 2. (1), Sch. 1 Table
F60. S. 23: definition of "renewable energy installation" inserted (5.10.2004) by Energy Act 2004 (c. 20), ss. 103. (2)(b), 198. (2); S.I. 2004/2575, art. 2. (1), Sch. 1
Modifications etc. (not altering text)
C157. S. 23 applied (with modifications) (30.4.2017) by The Police and Criminal Evidence Act 1984 (Application to Labour Abuse Prevention Officers) Regulations 2017 (S.I. 2017/520), regs. 1, 2, 3. (u), Sch.
Marginal Citations

Part III Arrest

Part III Arrest

Modifications etc. (not altering text)
C1. Pt. III: Powers of seizure extended (1.4.2003) by 2001 c. 16, ss. 50, 52-54, 68, Sch. 1 Pt. 1
para. 1; S.I. 2003/708, art. 2. (j)
Pt. III: Powers of seizure extended (1.4.2003) by 2001 c. 16, ss. 51-54, 68, Sch. 1 Pt. 2 para. 74;
S.I. 2003/708, art. 2. (j)
C2. Pt. III incorporated (16.5.2008) by The London Gateway Port Harbour Empowerment Order
2008 (S.I. 2008/1261), art. 52

[F124 Arrest without warrant: constables

(1) A constable may arrest without a warrant—
   (a) anyone who is about to commit an offence;
   (b) anyone who is in the act of committing an offence;
   (c) anyone whom he has reasonable grounds for suspecting to be about to commit an offence;
   (d) anyone whom he has reasonable grounds for suspecting to be committing an offence.
(2) If a constable has reasonable grounds for suspecting that an offence has been committed, he
may arrest without a warrant anyone whom he has reasonable grounds to suspect of being guilty
of it.
(3) If an offence has been committed, a constable may arrest without a warrant—
   (a) anyone who is guilty of the offence;
   (b) anyone whom he has reasonable grounds for suspecting to be guilty of it.
(4) But the power of summary arrest conferred by subsection (1), (2) or (3) is exercisable only if
the constable has reasonable grounds for believing that for any of the reasons mentioned in
subsection (5) it is necessary to arrest the person in question.
(5) The reasons are—
   (a) to enable the name of the person in question to be ascertained (in the case where the
constable does not know, and cannot readily ascertain, the person's name, or has reasonable
grounds for doubting whether a name given by the person as his name is his real name);
   (b) correspondingly as regards the person's address;
   (c) to prevent the person in question—
(i) causing physical injury to himself or any other person;
(ii) suffering physical injury;
(iii) causing loss of or damage to property;
(iv) committing an offence against public decency (subject to subsection (6)); or
(v) causing an unlawful obstruction of the highway;
   (d) to protect a child or other vulnerable person from the person in question;
   (e) to allow the prompt and effective investigation of the offence or of the conduct of the person
in question;
   (f) to prevent any prosecution for the offence from being hindered by the disappearance of the
person in question.
(6) Subsection (5)(c)(iv) applies only where members of the public going about their normal
business cannot reasonably be expected to avoid the person in question.]
Amendments (Textual)
F1. Ss. 24, 24. A substituted for s. 24 (1.1.2006) by Serious Organised Crime and Police Act 2005

(c. 15), ss. 110. (1), 178; S.I. 2005/3495, art. 2. (1)(m)
Modifications etc. (not altering text)
C3. S. 24 extended (2.8.1993) by S.I. 1993/1813, art. 6, Sch. 3 para. 2. (4).
C4. S. 24 applied (12.5.2005) by The Sudan (United Nations Measures) Order 2005 (S.I. 2005/1259), art. 10. (6)
S. 24 applied (9.6.2005) by The Democratic Republic of the Congo (United Nations Measures) Order 2005 (S.I. 2005/1517), art. 10. (6)
C5. S. 24. (1)-(5)(c)(iii) applied (with modifications) (25.6.2013) by The Police and Criminal Evidence Act 1984 (Application to immigration officers and designated customs officials in England and Wales) Order 2013 (S.I. 2013/1542), arts. 1, 3. (2)-(4), Sch. 1 (with arts. 4-11)
C6. S. 24. (1)-(5)(c)(iii) applied (with modifications) (25.6.2013) by The Police and Criminal Evidence Act 1984 (Application to immigration officers and designated customs officials in England and Wales) Order 2013 (S.I. 2013/1542), arts. 1, 12. (2)-(4), Sch. 2 (with arts. 13-31)
C7. S. 24. (1) applied (6.2.2004) by The Democratic Republic of Congo (Financing and Financial Assistance and Technical Advice, Assistance and Training) (Penalties and Licences) Regulations 2004 (S.I. 2004/221), reg. 4. (2)
S. 24. (1) applied (19.2.2004) by The Sudan (Technical Assistance and Financing and Financial Assistance) (Penalties and Licences) Regulations 2004 (S.I. 2004/373), reg. 4. (2)
S. 24. (1) applied (26.2.2004) by The Liberia (Technical Assistance and Financing and Financial Assistance) (Penalties and Licences) Regulations 2004 (S.I. 2004/432), reg. 4. (2)
C8. S. 24. (1) applied (17.5.2004) by The Burma (Sale, Supply, Export, Technical Assistance, Financing and Financial Assistance and Shipment of Equipment) (Penalties and Licences) Regulations 2004 (S.I. 2004/1315), reg. 4. (2)
C9. S. 24. (1)(b) applied (with modifications) (30.4.2017) by The Police and Criminal Evidence Act 1984 (Application to Labour Abuse Prevention Officers) Regulations 2017 (S.I. 2017/520), regs. 1, 2, 3. (n), Sch.
C10. S. 24. (1)(d) applied (with modifications) (30.4.2017) by The Police and Criminal Evidence Act 1984 (Application to Labour Abuse Prevention Officers) Regulations 2017 (S.I. 2017/520), regs. 1, 2, 3. (n), Sch.
C11. S. 24. (2) applied (with modifications) (4.11.2015) by The Police and Criminal Evidence Act 1984 (Application to Revenue and Customs) Order 2015 (S.I. 2015/1783), arts. 1, 3. (1), Sch. 1 (with art. 3. (2), (3), 4-19, Sch. 2)
C12. S. 24. (2)-(4) applied (with modifications) (30.4.2017) by The Police and Criminal Evidence Act 1984 (Application to Labour Abuse Prevention Officers) Regulations 2017 (S.I. 2017/520), regs. 1, 2, 3. (n), Sch.
C13. S. 24. (2) modified (1.9.2001) by 2001 c. 16, s. 47. (3); S.I. 2001/2223, art. 4. (c)
C14. S. 24. (2) applied by S.I. 1990/1768, art. 8. (10) (as replaced by S.I. 1990/2144, art. 3)
S. 24. (2) extended (15.4.1992) by S.I. 1992/975, art. 16. (13).
S. 24. (2) extended (5.6.1992) by S.I. 1992/1302, art. 17. (13).
s. 24. (2) extended (1.5.1993) by S.I. 1993/1188, art. 16. (11).
S. 24. (2) extended (24.5.1993) by S.I. 1993/1244, art. 22. (13).
S. 24. (2) extended (22.7.1993) by S.I. 1993/1784, art. 13. (12).
S. 24. (2) extended (22.7.1993) by S.I. 1993/1787, art. 10. (12).
S. 24. (2) extended (1.10.1993) by S.I. 1993/2355, art. 12. (12).
S. 24. (2) extended (1.12.1993) by S.I. 1993/2807, art. 19. (12)
S. 24. (2) applied (23.5.1994) by 1994/1323, art. 17. (12)
S. 24. (2) applied (19.10.1994) by S.I. 1994/2673, art. 13. (12)
S. 24. (2) applied (7.2.1995) by S.I. 1995/271, art. 11. (4)
S. 24. (2) applied (15.11.1996) by S.I. 1996/2721, art. 11. (4)
S. 24. (2) extended (1.11.1997) by S.I. 1997/2592, art. 12. (12)
S. 24. (2) applied (with modifications) (15.7.1998) by S.I. 1998/1531, art. 4. (2).
S. 24. (2) extended (3.6.1999) by S.I. 1999/1516, art. 9. (9)
S. 24. (2) extended (14.10.1999) by S.I. 1999/2821, art. 4. (2)

S. 24. (2) extended (14.10.1999) by S.I. 1999/2822, art. 4. (2)

S. 24. (2) extended (26.11.1999) by S.I. 1999/3133, art. 8. (12)

S. 24. (2) applied (16.6.2000) by S.I. 2000/1556, art. 17. (12)

S. 24. (2) applied (28.9.2000) by S.I. 2000/2620, reg. 11. (5)

S. 24. (2) applied (25.5.2000) by S.I. 2000/1408, reg. 3

S. 24. (2) extended (16.2.2001) by S.I. 2001/396, art. 25. (13)

S. 24. (2) applied (10.10.2001) by S.I. 2001/3365, art. 10. (10) (subject to art. 1. (2))

C15. S. 24. (2) applied (with modifications) (25.1.2002) by The Al-Qa'ida and Taliban (United Nations Measures) Order 2002 (S.I. 2002/111), art. 20. (13)

S. 24. (2) applied (with modifications) (31.3.2002) by The Zimbabwe (Sale, Supply, Export and Shipment of Equipment) (Penalties and Licences) Regulations 2002 (S.I. 2002/ 868), {reg. 4. (2)}

S. 24. (2) applied (with modifications) (24.10.2002) by The Somalia (United Nations Sanctions) Order (S.I. 2002/2628), {art. 16. (12)}

C16. S. 24. (2) applied (14.6.2003) by The Iraq (United Nations Sanctions) Order 2003 (S.I. 2003/1519), art. 20. (12)

S. 24. (2) applied (11.2.2005) by The Ivory Coast (United Nations Sanctions) Order 2005 (S.I. 2005/253), art. 9. (12)

C17. S. 24. (2) applied (13.2.2004) by The Liberia (United Nations Sanctions) Order 2004 (S.I. 2004/348), art. 15. (12)

C18. S. 24. (2) applied (10.4.2009) by The Iran (United Nations Sanctions) Order 2009 (S.I. 2009/886), art. 12. (11)

C19. S. 24. (2) applied (10.7.2009) by The North Korea (United Nations Sanctions) Order 2009 (S.I. 2009/1749), art. 14. (11)

C20. S. 24. (4)(5) applied (with modifications) (4.11.2015) by The Police and Criminal Evidence Act 1984 (Application to Revenue and Customs) Order 2015 (S.I. 2015/1783), arts. 1, 3. (1), Sch. 1 (with art. 3. (2), (3), 4-19, Sch. 2)

C21. S. 24. (5)(a)(b) applied (with modifications) (30.4.2017) by The Police and Criminal Evidence Act 1984 (Application to Labour Abuse Prevention Officers) Regulations 2017 (S.I. 2017/520), regs. 1, 2, 3. (n), Sch.

C22. S. 24. (5)(c)(i)-(iii) applied (with modifications) (30.4.2017) by The Police and Criminal Evidence Act 1984 (Application to Labour Abuse Prevention Officers) Regulations 2017 (S.I. 2017/520), regs. 1, 2, 3. (n), Sch.

C23. S. 24. (5)(d)-(f) applied (with modifications) (25.6.2013) by The Police and Criminal Evidence Act 1984 (Application to immigration officers and designated customs officials in England and Wales) Order 2013 (S.I. 2013/1542), arts. 1, 3. (2)-(4), Sch. 1 (with arts. 4-11)

C24. S. 24. (5)(d)-(f) applied (with modifications) (25.6.2013) by The Police and Criminal Evidence Act 1984 (Application to immigration officers and designated customs officials in England and Wales) Order 2013 (S.I. 2013/1542), arts. 1, 12. (2)-(4), Sch. 2 (with arts. 13-31)

C25. S. 24. (5)(d)(e) applied (with modifications) (30.4.2017) by The Police and Criminal Evidence Act 1984 (Application to Labour Abuse Prevention Officers) Regulations 2017 (S.I. 2017/520), regs. 1, 2, 3. (n), Sch.

C26. S. 24. (5)(f) applied (with modifications) (30.4.2017) by The Police and Criminal Evidence Act 1984 (Application to Labour Abuse Prevention Officers) Regulations 2017 (S.I. 2017/520), regs. 1, 2, 3. (n), Sch.

[F224. AArrest without warrant: other persons

(1) A person other than a constable may arrest without a warrant—

  (a) anyone who is in the act of committing an indictable offence;

  (b) anyone whom he has reasonable grounds for suspecting to be committing an indictable offence.

(2) Where an indictable offence has been committed, a person other than a constable may arrest

without a warrant—

    (a) anyone who is guilty of the offence;

    (b) anyone whom he has reasonable grounds for suspecting to be guilty of it.

(3) But the power of summary arrest conferred by subsection (1) or (2) is exercisable only if—

    (a) the person making the arrest has reasonable grounds for believing that for any of the reasons mentioned in subsection (4) it is necessary to arrest the person in question; and

    (b) it appears to the person making the arrest that it is not reasonably practicable for a constable to make it instead.

(4) The reasons are to prevent the person in question—

    (a) causing physical injury to himself or any other person;

    (b) suffering physical injury;

    (c) causing loss of or damage to property; or

    (d) making off before a constable can assume responsibility for him.

[F3. (5)This section does not apply in relation to an offence under Part 3 or 3. A of the Public Order Act 1986.]]

Amendments (Textual)

F2. Ss. 24, 24. A substituted for s. 24 (1.1.2006) by Serious Organised Crime and Police Act 2005 (c. 15), ss. 110, 178; S.I. 2005/3495, art. 2. (m)

F3. S. 24. A(5) added (1.10.2007) by Racial and Religious Hatred Act 2006 (c. 1), ss. 2, 3. (2); S.I. 2007/2490, art. 2. (1)

Modifications etc. (not altering text)

C27. S. 24. A restricted (25.7.2012) by The Police and Crime Commissioner Elections Order 2012 (S.I. 2012/1917), arts. 1. (2), 17. (4)

C28. S. 24. A restricted (16.12.2010) by The National Assembly for Wales Referendum (Assembly Act Provisions) (Referendum Question, Date of Referendum Etc.) Order 2010 (S.I. 2010/2837), art. 26, Sch. 4 para. 2. (4)

C29. S. 24. A restricted (1.1.2007) by Electoral Administration Act 2006 (c. 22), ss. 71, 77; S.I. 2006/3412, art. 3, Sch. 1 para. 9 (with Sch. 2)

S. 24. A restricted (1.2.2007) by The National Assembly for Wales (Representation of The People) Order (S.I. 2007/236), arts. 1. (1), {30. (4)}

25. . . . .

F4. . . . .

Amendments (Textual)

F4. S. 25 repealed (1.1.2006) by Serious Organised Crime and Police Act 2005 (c. 15), ss. 110. (2), 174, 178, Sch. 17 Pt. 2; S.I. 2005/3495, art. 2. (1)(m)(u)(xxiv)

26 Repeal of statutory powers of arrest without warrant or order.

(1) Subject to subsection (2) below, so much of any Act (including a local Act) passed before this Act as enables a constable—

    (a) to arrest a person for an offence without a warrant; or

    (b) to arrest a person otherwise than for an offence without a warrant or an order of a court, shall cease to have effect.

(2) Nothing in subsection (1) above affects the enactments specified in Schedule 2 to this Act.

Modifications etc. (not altering text)

C30. S. 26 excluded by Representation of the People Act 1985 (c. 50, SIF 42), s. 25. (1)

27 Fingerprinting of certain offenders.

F5. (1). . . . .

F5. (1. A). . . . .

F5. (1. B). . . . .

F5. (2). . . . .

F5. (3). . . . .

(4) The Secretary of State may by regulations make provision for recording in national police records convictions for such offences as are specified in the regulations.

[F6. (4. A)In subsection (4) "conviction" includes—

(a) a caution within the meaning of Part 5 of the Police Act 1997; and

(b) a reprimand or warning given under section 65 of the Crime and Disorder Act 1998.]

F7. (4. A). . . . .

(5) Regulations under this section shall be made by statutory instrument and shall be subject to annulment in pursuance of a resolution of either House of Parliament.

Amendments (Textual)

F5. S. 27. (1)-(3) repealed (7.3.2011) by Crime and Security Act 2010 (c. 17), ss. 6. (3), 59. (1); S.I. 2011/414, art. 2. (e)

F6. S. 27. (4. A) inserted (1.7.2012) by Protection of Freedoms Act 2012 (c. 9), ss. 85, 120 (with s. 97); S.I. 2012/1205, art. 3. (w)

F7. S. 27. (4. A) repealed (1.4.2003) by 2001 c. 16, ss. 137, 138. (2), Sch. 7 Pt. 2. (1); S.I. 2003/708, art. 2. (i)(m)

Modifications etc. (not altering text)

C31. S. 27. (1) extended (2.12.2002) by Police Reform Act 2002 (c. 30), s. 38, Sch. 4 Pt. 3 para. 25; S.I. 2002/2750, art. 2. (a)(ii)(d)

28 Information to be given on arrest.

(1) Subject to subsection (5) below, where a person is arrested, otherwise than by being informed that he is under arrest, the arrest is not lawful unless the person arrested is informed that he is under arrest as soon as is practicable after his arrest.

(2) Where a person is arrested by a constable, subsection (1) above applies regardless of whether the fact of the arrest is obvious.

(3) Subject to subsection (5) below, no arrest is lawful unless the person arrested is informed of the ground for the arrest at the time of, or as soon as is practicable after, the arrest.

(4) Where a person is arrested by a constable, subsection (3) above applies regardless of whether the ground for the arrest is obvious.

(5) Nothing in this section is to be taken to require a person to be informed—

(a) that he is under arrest; or

(b) of the ground for the arrest,

if it was not reasonably practicable for him to be so informed by reason of his having escaped from arrest before the information could be given.

Modifications etc. (not altering text)

C32. Ss. 8, 9, 15, 16, 17. (1)(b(2) (4), 18–20, 21, 22. (1)–(4), 28, 29, 30. (1)–(4)(a)(5)–(11), 31, 32. (1)–(9), 34. (1)–(5), 35, 36, 37, 39, 40–44, 50, 51. (d), 52, 54, 55, 64. (1)–(4)(5)(6), Sch. 1 applied with modifications by S.I. 1985/1800, arts. 3–11, Schs. 1, 2

C33. S. 28 applied (with modifications) (25.6.2013) by The Police and Criminal Evidence Act 1984 (Application to immigration officers and designated customs officials in England and Wales) Order 2013 (S.I. 2013/1542), arts. 1, 12. (2)-(4), Sch. 2 (with arts. 13-31)

C34. S. 28 applied (with modifications) (25.6.2013) by The Police and Criminal Evidence Act 1984 (Application to immigration officers and designated customs officials in England and Wales) Order 2013 (S.I. 2013/1542), arts. 1, 3. (2)-(4), Sch. 1 (with arts. 4-11)

C35. S. 28 applied (with modifications) (4.11.2015) by The Police and Criminal Evidence Act 1984 (Application to Revenue and Customs) Order 2015 (S.I. 2015/1783), arts. 1, 3. (1), Sch. 1

(with art. 3. (2), (3), 4-19, Sch. 2)
C36. S. 28 applied (with modifications) by 1994 c. 33, s. 137. D(2)(a) Sch. 7. B Pt. 1 (as inserted (31.1.2017 for specified purposes) by Policing and Crime Act 2017 (c. 3), s. 116. (1)(3)183. (1)(5)(e), Sch. 16)
C37. S. 28 applied (with modifications) (30.4.2017) by The Police and Criminal Evidence Act 1984 (Application to Labour Abuse Prevention Officers) Regulations 2017 (S.I. 2017/520), regs. 1, 2, 3. (o), Sch.

29 Voluntary attendance at police station etc.

Where for the purpose of assisting with an investigation a person attends voluntarily at a police station or at any other place where a constable is present or accompanies a constable to a police station or any such other place without having been arrested—
    (a) he shall be entitled to leave at will unless he is placed under arrest;
    (b) he shall be informed at once that he is under arrest if a decision is taken by a constable to prevent him from leaving at will.
Modifications etc. (not altering text)
C38. Ss. 8, 9, 15, 16, 17. (1)(b(2) (4), 18–20, 21, 22. (1)–(4), 28, 29, 30. (1)–(4)(a)(5)–(11), 31, 32. (1)–(9), 34. (1)–(5), 35, 36, 37, 39, 40–44, 50, 51. (d), 52, 54, 55, 64. (1)–(4)(5)(6), Sch. 1 applied with modifications by S.I. 1985/1800, arts. 3–11, Schs. 1, 2
C39. S. 29 applied (with modifications) (25.6.2013) by The Police and Criminal Evidence Act 1984 (Application to immigration officers and designated customs officials in England and Wales) Order 2013 (S.I. 2013/1542), arts. 1, 12. (2)-(4), Sch. 2 (with arts. 13-31)
C40. S. 29 applied (with modifications) (25.6.2013) by The Police and Criminal Evidence Act 1984 (Application to immigration officers and designated customs officials in England and Wales) Order 2013 (S.I. 2013/1542), arts. 1, 3. (2)-(4), Sch. 1 (with arts. 4-11)
C41. S. 29 applied (with modifications) (4.11.2015) by The Police and Criminal Evidence Act 1984 (Application to Revenue and Customs) Order 2015 (S.I. 2015/1783), arts. 1, 3. (1), Sch. 1 (with art. 3. (2), (3), 4-19, Sch. 2)
C42. S. 29 applied (with modifications) (30.4.2017) by The Police and Criminal Evidence Act 1984 (Application to Labour Abuse Prevention Officers) Regulations 2017 (S.I. 2017/520), regs. 1, 2, 3. (p), Sch.

30 Arrest elsewhere than at police station.

[F8. (1)Subsection (1. A) applies where a person is, at any place other than a police station—
    (a) arrested by a constable for an offence, or
    (b) taken into custody by a constable after being arrested for an offence by a person other than a constable.
(1. A)The person must be taken by a constable to a police station as soon as practicable after the arrest.
(1. B)Subsection (1. A) has effect subject to section 30. A (release [F9of a person arrested elsewhere than at police station]) and subsection (7)(release without bail).]
(2) Subject to subsections (3) and (5) below, the police station to which an arrested person is taken under [F10subsection (1. A)] above shall be a designated police station.
(3) A constable to whom this subsection applies may take an arrested person to any police station unless it appears to the constable that it may be necessary to keep the arrested person in police detention for more than six hours.
(4) Subsection (3) above applies—
    (a) to a constable who is working in a locality covered by a police station which is not a designated police station; and
    (b) to a constable belonging to a body of constables maintained by an authority other than a

[F11local policing body].

(5) Any constable may take an arrested person to any police station if—

(a) either of the following conditions is satisfied—

(i) the constable has arrested him without the assistance of any other constable and no other constable is available to assist him;

(ii) the constable has taken him into custody from a person other than a constable without the assistance of any other constable and no other constable is available to assist him; and

(b) it appears to the constable that he will be unable to take the arrested person to a designated police station without the arrested person injuring himself, the constable or some other person.

(6) If the first police station to which an arrested person is taken after his arrest is not a designated police station, he shall be taken to a designated police station not more than six hours after his arrival at the first police station unless he is released previously.

[F12. (7)A person arrested by a constable at any place other than a police station must be released without bail if the condition in subsection (7. A) is satisfied.

(7. A)The condition is that, at any time before the person arrested reaches a police station, a constable is satisfied that there are no grounds for keeping him under arrest F13....]

(8) A constable who releases a person under subsection (7) above shall record the fact that he has done so.

(9) The constable shall made the record as soon as is practicable after the release.

[F14. (10)Nothing in subsection (1. A) or in section 30. A prevents a constable delaying taking a person to a police station or releasing him [F15under section 30. A] if the condition in subsection (10. A) is satisfied.

(10. A)The condition is that the presence of the person at a place (other than a police station) is necessary in order to carry out such investigations as it is reasonable to carry out immediately.

(11) Where there is any such delay the reasons for the delay must be recorded when the person first arrives at the police station or (as the case may be) is released [F15under section 30. A].]

(12) Nothing in [F16subsection (1. A) or section 30. A] above shall be taken to affect—

(a) paragraphs 16. (3) or 18. (1) of Schedule 2 to the M1. Immigration Act 1971;

(b) section 34. (1) of the M2. Criminal Justice Act 1972; or

[F17. (c)any provision of the Terrorism Act 2000.]

(13) Nothing in subsection (1) above shall be taken to affect paragraph 18. (3) of Schedule 2 to the Immigration Act 1971.

Amendments (Textual)

F8. S. 30. (1)-(1. B) substituted (20.1.2004) for s. 30. (1) by Criminal Justice Act 2003 (c. 44), ss. 4. (2), 336; S.I. 2004/81, art. 2. (1)(2)(a)

F9. Words in s. 30. (1)(b) substituted (31.1.2017 for specified purposes, 3.4.2017 in so far as not already in force) by Policing and Crime Act 2017 (c. 3), ss. 53. (3)(a), 183. (1), (5)(e); S.I. 2017/399, reg. 2, Sch. para. 12 (with reg. 5)

F10. Words in s. 30. (2) substituted (20.1.2004) by Criminal Justice Act 2003 (c. 44), ss. 4. (3), 336; S.I. 2004/81, art. 2. (1)(2)(a)

F11. Words in s. 30. (4)(b) substituted (16.1.2012) by Police Reform and Social Responsibility Act 2011 (c. 13), s. 157. (1), Sch. 16 para. 161; S.I. 2011/3019, art. 3, Sch. 1

F12. S. 30. (7)(7. A) substituted for s. 30. (7) (20.1.2004) by Criminal Justice Act 2003 (c. 44), ss. 4. (4), 336; S.I. 2004/81, art. 2. (1)(2)(a)

F13. Words in s. 30. (7. A) omitted (31.1.2017 for specified purposes, 3.4.2017 in so far as not already in force) by virtue of Policing and Crime Act 2017 (c. 3), ss. 53. (3)(b), 183. (1), (5)(e); S.I. 2017/399, reg. 2, Sch. para. 12 (with reg. 5)

F14. S. 30. (10)(10. A)(11) substituted (20.1.2004) for s. 30. (10)(11) by Criminal Justice Act 2003 (c. 44), ss. 4. (5), 336; S.I. 2004/81, art. 2. (1)(2)(a)

F15. Words in s. 30. (10)(11) substituted (31.1.2017 for specified purposes, 3.4.2017 in so far as not already in force) by Policing and Crime Act 2017 (c. 3), ss. 53. (3)(c), 183. (1), (5)(e); S.I. 2017/399, reg. 2, Sch. para. 12 (with reg. 5)

F16. Words in s. 30. (12) substituted (20.1.2004) by Criminal Justice Act 2003 (c. 44), ss. 4. (6),

336; S.I. 2004/81, art. 2. (1)(2)(a)

F17. S. 30. (12)(c) substituted (19.2.2001) by 2000 c. 11, ss. 125, Sch. 15 para. 5. (2) (with s. 129. (1)(b)); 2001/421, art. 2

Modifications etc. (not altering text)

C43. S. 30 extended (2.8.1993) by S.I. 1993/1813, art. 6, Sch. 3 para. 2. (6); s. 30 extended by the said S.I. 1993/1813, art. 6, Sch. 3 para. 2 as in corporated (with modifications) (1.12.1997) by S.I. 1994/1405, art. 6, Sch. 3 para. 3

C44. S. 30 modified (2.12.2002) by Police Reform Act 2002 (c. 30), s. 38, Sch. 4 Pt. 4 para. 34. (1)(b); S.I. 2002/2750, art. 2. (a)(ii)(d)

C45. S. 30 applied (with modifications) by Criminal Justice Act 2003 (c. 44), s. 24. B(1)-(3) (as inserted (29.6.2007) by Police and Justice Act 2006 (c. 48), ss. 18. (1), 53 (with s. 18. (2)); S.I. 2007/1614, art. 2. (e))

C46. S. 30. (1)-(4)(a) applied (with modifications) (25.6.2013) by The Police and Criminal Evidence Act 1984 (Application to immigration officers and designated customs officials in England and Wales) Order 2013 (S.I. 2013/1542), arts. 1, 12. (2)-(4), Sch. 2 (with arts. 13-31)

C47. S. 30. (1)-(4)(a) applied (with modifications) (25.6.2013) by The Police and Criminal Evidence Act 1984 (Application to immigration officers and designated customs officials in England and Wales) Order 2013 (S.I. 2013/1542), arts. 1, 3. (2)-(4), Sch. 1 (with arts. 4-11)

C48. S. 30. (1)-(4)(a) applied (with modifications) (4.11.2015) by The Police and Criminal Evidence Act 1984 (Application to Revenue and Customs) Order 2015 (S.I. 2015/1783), arts. 1, 3. (1), Sch. 1 (with art. 3. (2), (3), 4-19, Sch. 2)

C49. S. 30. (1)(a) applied (with modifications) (30.4.2017) by The Police and Criminal Evidence Act 1984 (Application to Labour Abuse Prevention Officers) Regulations 2017 (S.I. 2017/520), regs. 1, 2, 3. (q), Sch.

C50. S. 30. (1. A)(1. B) applied (with modifications) (30.4.2017) by The Police and Criminal Evidence Act 1984 (Application to Labour Abuse Prevention Officers) Regulations 2017 (S.I. 2017/520), regs. 1, 2, 3. (q), Sch.

C51. Ss. 8, 9, 15, 16, 17. (1)(b(2) (4), 18–20, 21, 22. (1)–(4), 28, 29, 30. (1)–(4)(a)(5)–(11), 31, 32. (1)–(9), 34. (1)–(5), 35, 36, 37, 39, 40–44, 50, 51. (d), 52, 54, 55, 64. (1)–(4)(5)(6), Sch. 1 applied with modifications by S.I. 1985/1800, arts. 3–11, Schs. 1, 2

C52. S. 30. (5)-(13) applied (with modifications) (25.6.2013) by The Police and Criminal Evidence Act 1984 (Application to immigration officers and designated customs officials in England and Wales) Order 2013 (S.I. 2013/1542), arts. 1, 3. (2)-(4), Sch. 1 (with arts. 4-11)

C53. S. 30. (5)-(13) applied (with modifications) (25.6.2013) by The Police and Criminal Evidence Act 1984 (Application to immigration officers and designated customs officials in England and Wales) Order 2013 (S.I. 2013/1542), arts. 1, 12. (2)-(4), Sch. 2 (with arts. 13-31)

C54. S. 30. (5)-(11) applied (with modifications) (4.11.2015) by The Police and Criminal Evidence Act 1984 (Application to Revenue and Customs) Order 2015 (S.I. 2015/1783), arts. 1, 3. (1), Sch. 1 (with art. 3. (2), (3), 4-19, Sch. 2)

C55. S. 30. (7)-(11) applied (with modifications) (30.4.2017) by The Police and Criminal Evidence Act 1984 (Application to Labour Abuse Prevention Officers) Regulations 2017 (S.I. 2017/520), regs. 1, 2, 3. (q), Sch.

Marginal Citations

M11971 c. 77.

M21972 c. 71.

[F1830. A [F19. Release of a person arrested] elsewhere than at police station

(1) A constable may release F20... a person who is arrested or taken into custody in the circumstances mentioned in section 30. (1)[F21—

    (a) without bail unless subsection (1. A) applies, or

(b) on bail if subsection (1. A) applies.]

[F22. (1. A)This subsection applies if—

(a) the constable is satisfied that releasing the person on bail is necessary and proportionate in all the circumstances (having regard, in particular, to any conditions of bail which would be imposed), and

(b) a police officer of the rank of inspector or above authorises the release on bail (having considered any representations made by the person).]

(2) A person may be released F23... under subsection (1) at any time before he arrives at a police station.

(3) A person released on bail under subsection (1) must be required to attend a police station.

[F24. (3. A)Where a constable releases a person on bail under subsection (1)—

(a) no recognizance for the person's surrender to custody shall be taken from the person,

(b) no security for the person's surrender to custody shall be taken from the person or from anyone else on the person's behalf,

(c) the person shall not be required to provide a surety or sureties for his surrender to custody, and

(d) no requirement to reside in a bail hostel may be imposed as a condition of bail.

(3. B)Subject to subsection (3. A), where a constable releases a person on bail under subsection (1) the constable may impose, as conditions of the bail, such requirements as appear to the constable to be necessary—

(a) to secure that the person surrenders to custody,

(b) to secure that the person does not commit an offence while on bail,

(c) to secure that the person does not interfere with witnesses or otherwise obstruct the course of justice, whether in relation to himself or any other person, or

(d) for the person's own protection or, if the person is [F25under the age of 18], for the person's own welfare or in the person's own interests.

(4) Where a person is released on bail under subsection (1), a requirement may be imposed on the person as a condition of bail only under the preceding provisions of this section.]

(5) The police station which the person is required to attend may be any police station.

Amendments (Textual)

F18. Ss. 30. A-30. D inserted (20.1.2004) by Criminal Justice Act 2003 (c. 44), ss. 4. (7), 336; S.I. 2004/81, art. 2. (1)(2)(a)

F19. Words in s. 30. A substituted (31.1.2017 for specified purposes, 3.4.2017 in so far as not already in force) by Policing and Crime Act 2017 (c. 3), ss. 52. (2), 183. (1), (5)(e); S.I. 2017/399, reg. 2, Sch. para. 12 (with reg. 5)

F20. Words in s. 30. A(1) omitted (31.1.2017 for specified purposes, 3.4.2017 in so far as not already in force) by virtue of Policing and Crime Act 2017 (c. 3), ss. 52. (3)(a), 183. (1), (5)(e); S.I. 2017/399, reg. 2, Sch. para. 12 (with reg. 5)

F21. Words in s. 30. A(1) inserted (31.1.2017 for specified purposes, 3.4.2017 in so far as not already in force) by Policing and Crime Act 2017 (c. 3), ss. 52. (3)(b), 183. (1), (5)(e); S.I. 2017/399, reg. 2, Sch. para. 12 (with reg. 5)

F22. S. 30. A(1. A) inserted (31.1.2017 for specified purposes, 3.4.2017 in so far as not already in force) by Policing and Crime Act 2017 (c. 3), ss. 52. (4), 183. (1), (5)(e); S.I. 2017/399, reg. 2, Sch. para. 12 (with reg. 5)

F23. Words in s. 30. A(2) omitted (31.1.2017 for specified purposes, 3.4.2017 in so far as not already in force) by virtue of Policing and Crime Act 2017 (c. 3), ss. 52. (5), 183. (1), (5)(e); S.I. 2017/399, reg. 2, Sch. para. 12 (with reg. 5)

F24. S. 30. A(3. A)-(4) substituted (1.4.2007) for s. 30. A(4) by Police and Justice Act 2006 (c. 48), ss. 10, 53, Sch. 6 para. 2; S.I. 2007/709, art. 3. (i) (subject to arts. 6, 7)

F25. Words in s. 30. A(3. B)(d) substituted (31.1.2017 for specified purposes, 3.4.2017 in so far as not already in force) by Policing and Crime Act 2017 (c. 3), ss. 73. (2), 183. (1), (5)(e); S.I. 2017/399, reg. 2, Sch. para. 22

Modifications etc. (not altering text)

C56. Ss. 30. A-30. D applied (with modifications) by Criminal Justice Act 2003 (c. 44), s. 24.
B(1)-(3) (as inserted (29.6.2007) by Police and Justice Act 2006 (c. 48), ss. 18. (1), 53 (with s. 18.
(2)); S.I. 2007/1614, art. 2. (e))

30. BF26... section 30. A: notices

(1) Where a constable [F27releases] a person under section 30. A, he must give that person a
notice in writing before he is released.
(2) The notice must state—
    (a) the offence for which he was arrested, F28...
    (b) the ground on which he was arrested [F29and
    (c) whether the person is being released without bail or on bail].
(3) [F30. A notice given to a person who is released on bail] must inform him that he is required to
attend a police station.
[F31. (4)The notice must also specify—
    (a) the police station which the person is required to attend, and
    (b) the time on the bail end date when the person is required to attend the police station.]
[F32. (4. A)If the person is granted bail subject to conditions under section 30. A(3. B), the notice
also—
    (a) must specify the requirements imposed by those conditions,
    (b) must explain the opportunities under sections 30. CA(1) and 30. CB(1) for variation of those
conditions, F33...
    F33. (c). . . . .]
F34. (5). . . . .
(6) The person may be required to attend a different police station from that specified in the notice
under subsection (1) or [F35to attend at a different time or an additional time].
[F36. (6. A)A person may not be required under subsection (6) to attend a police station at a time
which is after the bail end date in relation to the person.]
(7) He must be given notice in writing of any such change as is mentioned in subsection (6) but
more than one such notice may be given to him.
[F37. (8)In this section "bail end date", in relation to a person, means the last day of the period of
28 days beginning with the day after the day on which the person was arrested for the offence in
relation to which bail is granted under section 30. A.]
Amendments (Textual)
F18. Ss. 30. A-30. D inserted (20.1.2004) by Criminal Justice Act 2003 (c. 44), ss. 4. (7), 336; S.I.
2004/81, art. 2. (1)(2)(a)
F26. Words in s. 30. B omitted (31.1.2017 for specified purposes, 3.4.2017 in so far as not already
in force) by virtue of Policing and Crime Act 2017 (c. 3), ss. 53. (5), 183. (1), (5)(e); S.I.
2017/399, reg. 2, Sch. para. 12 (with reg. 5)
F27. Word in s. 30. B(1) substituted (31.1.2017 for specified purposes, 3.4.2017 in so far as not
already in force) by Policing and Crime Act 2017 (c. 3), ss. 53. (6), 183. (1), (5)(e); S.I. 2017/399,
reg. 2, Sch. para. 12 (with reg. 5)
F28. Word in s. 30. B(2) omitted (31.1.2017 for specified purposes, 3.4.2017 in so far as not
already in force) by virtue of Policing and Crime Act 2017 (c. 3), ss. 53. (7)(a), 183. (1), (5)(e);
S.I. 2017/399, reg. 2, Sch. para. 12 (with reg. 5)
F29. S. 30. B(2)(c) and word inserted (31.1.2017 for specified purposes, 3.4.2017 in so far as not
already in force) by Policing and Crime Act 2017 (c. 3), ss. 53. (7)(b), 183. (1), (5)(e); S.I.
2017/399, reg. 2, Sch. para. 12 (with reg. 5)
F30. Words in s. 30. B(3) substituted (31.1.2017 for specified purposes, 3.4.2017 in so far as not
already in force) by Policing and Crime Act 2017 (c. 3), ss. 53. (8), 183. (1), (5)(e); S.I. 2017/399,
reg. 2, Sch. para. 12 (with reg. 5)
F31. S. 30. B(4) substituted (31.1.2017 for specified purposes, 3.4.2017 in so far as not already in

force) by Policing and Crime Act 2017 (c. 3), ss. 62. (3), 183. (1), (5)(e); S.I. 2017/399, reg. 2, Sch. para. 14 (with reg. 5)

F32. S. 30. B(4. A) inserted (1.4.2007) by Police and Justice Act 2006 (c. 48), ss. 10, 53, Sch. 6 para. 3; S.I. 2007/709, art. 3. (i) (subject to arts. 6, 7)

F33. S. 30. B(4. A)(c) and word omitted (31.1.2017 for specified purposes, 3.4.2017 in so far as not already in force) by virtue of Policing and Crime Act 2017 (c. 3), ss. 62. (4), 183. (1), (5)(e); S.I. 2017/399, reg. 2, Sch. para. 14 (with reg. 5)

F34. S. 30. B(5) omitted (31.1.2017 for specified purposes, 3.4.2017 in so far as not already in force) by virtue of Policing and Crime Act 2017 (c. 3), ss. 62. (5), 183. (1), (5)(e); S.I. 2017/399, reg. 2, Sch. para. 14 (with reg. 5)

F35. Word in s. 30. B(6) substituted (31.1.2017 for specified purposes, 3.4.2017 in so far as not already in force) by Policing and Crime Act 2017 (c. 3), ss. 62. (6), 183. (1), (5)(e); S.I. 2017/399, reg. 2, Sch. para. 14 (with reg. 5)

F36. S. 30. B(6. A) inserted (31.1.2017 for specified purposes, 3.4.2017 in so far as not already in force) by Policing and Crime Act 2017 (c. 3), ss. 62. (7), 183. (1), (5)(e); S.I. 2017/399, reg. 2, Sch. para. 14 (with reg. 5)

F37. S. 30. B(8) inserted (31.1.2017 for specified purposes, 3.4.2017 in so far as not already in force) by Policing and Crime Act 2017 (c. 3), ss. 62. (8), 183. (1), (5)(e); S.I. 2017/399, reg. 2, Sch. para. 14 (with reg. 5)

Modifications etc. (not altering text)

C57. Ss. 30. A-30. D applied (with modifications) by Criminal Justice Act 2003 (c. 44), s. 24. B(1)-(3) (as inserted (29.6.2007) by Police and Justice Act 2006 (c. 48), ss. 18. (1), 53 (with s. 18. (2)); S.I. 2007/1614, art. 2. (e))

30. CF38... section 30. A: supplemental

(1) A person who has been required to attend a police station is not required to do so if he is given notice in writing that his attendance is no longer required.

(2) If a person is required to attend a police station which is not a designated police station he must be—

    (a) released, or

    (b) taken to a designated police station,

not more than six hours after his arrival.

(3) Nothing in the Bail Act 1976 applies in relation to bail under section 30. A.

(4) Nothing in section 30. A or 30. B or in this section prevents the re-arrest without a warrant of a person released F39... under section 30. A if[F40, since the person's release, new evidence has come to light or an examination or analysis of existing evidence has been made which could not reasonably have been made before the person's release].

Amendments (Textual)

F18. Ss. 30. A-30. D inserted (20.1.2004) by Criminal Justice Act 2003 (c. 44), ss. 4. (7), 336; S.I. 2004/81, art. 2. (1)(2)(a)

F38. Words in s. 30. C omitted (31.1.2017 for specified purposes, 3.4.2017 in so far as not already in force) by virtue of Policing and Crime Act 2017 (c. 3), ss. 53. (9)(a), 183. (1), (5)(e); S.I. 2017/399, reg. 2, Sch. para. 12 (with reg. 5)

F39. Words in s. 30. C(4) omitted (31.1.2017 for specified purposes, 3.4.2017 in so far as not already in force) by virtue of Policing and Crime Act 2017 (c. 3), ss. 53. (9)(b), 183. (1), (5)(e); S.I. 2017/399, reg. 2, Sch. para. 12 (with reg. 5)

F40. Words in s. 30. C(4) substituted (31.1.2017 for specified purposes, 3.4.2017 in so far as not already in force) by Policing and Crime Act 2017 (c. 3), ss. 65. (2), 183. (1), (5)(e); S.I. 2017/399, reg. 2, Sch. para. 17 (with reg. 5)

Modifications etc. (not altering text)

C58. Ss. 30. A-30. D applied (with modifications) by Criminal Justice Act 2003 (c. 44), s. 24.

B(1)-(3) (as inserted (29.6.2007) by Police and Justice Act 2006 (c. 48), ss. 18. (1), 53 (with s. 18. (2)); S.I. 2007/1614, art. 2. (e))

[F4130. CABail under section 30. A: variation of conditions by police

(1) Where a person released on bail under section 30. A(1) is on bail subject to conditions—
    (a) a relevant officer at the police station at which the person is required to attend, F42...
    F42. (b). . . . .
may, at the request of the person but subject to subsection (2), vary the conditions.

(2) On any subsequent request made in respect of the same grant of bail, subsection (1) confers power to vary the conditions of the bail only if the request is based on information that, in the case of the previous request or each previous request, was not available to the relevant officer considering that previous request when he was considering it.

(3) Where conditions of bail granted to a person under section 30. A(1) are varied under subsection (1)—
    (a) paragraphs (a) to (d) of section 30. A(3. A) apply,
    (b) requirements imposed by the conditions as so varied must be requirements that appear to the relevant officer varying the conditions to be necessary for any of the purposes mentioned in paragraphs (a) to (d) of section 30. A(3. B), and
    (c) the relevant officer who varies the conditions must give the person notice in writing of the variation.

(4) Power under subsection (1) to vary conditions is, subject to subsection (3)(a) and (b), power—
    (a) to vary or rescind any of the conditions, and
    (b) to impose further conditions.

(5) In this section "relevant officer", in relation to a designated police station, means a custody officer but, in relation to any other police station—
    (a) means a constable F43. . . who is not involved in the investigation of the offence for which the person making the request under subsection (1) was under arrest when granted bail under section 30. A(1), if such a constable F44. . . is readily available, and
    (b) if no such constable F45. . . is readily available—
(i) means a constable other than the one who granted bail to the person, if such a constable is readily available, and
(ii) if no such constable is readily available, means the constable who granted bail.
Amendments (Textual)
F18. Ss. 30. A-30. D inserted (20.1.2004) by Criminal Justice Act 2003 (c. 44), ss. 4. (7), 336; S.I. 2004/81, art. 2. (1)(2)(a)
F41. Ss. 30. CA, 30. CB inserted (1.4.2007) by Police and Justice Act 2006 (c. 48), ss. 10, 53, Sch. 6 para. 4; S.I. 2007/709, art. 3. (i) (subject to arts. 6, 7)
F42. S. 30. CA(1)(b) and word omitted (31.1.2017 for specified purposes, 3.4.2017 in so far as not already in force) by virtue of Policing and Crime Act 2017 (c. 3), ss. 62. (9), 183. (1), (5)(e); S.I. 2017/399, reg. 2, Sch. para. 14 (with reg. 5)
F43. Words in s. 30. CA(5)(a) repealed (12.1.2010) by Policing and Crime Act 2009 (c. 26), ss. 112. (1)(2), 116. (6), Sch. 7 para. 123. (2)(a)(i), Sch. 8 Pt. 13
F44. Words in s. 30. CA(5)(a) repealed (12.1.2010) by Policing and Crime Act 2009 (c. 26), ss. 112. (1)(2), 116. (6), Sch. 7 para. 123. (2)(a)(ii), Sch. 8 Pt. 13
F45. Words in s. 30. CA(5)(b) repealed (12.1.2010) by Policing and Crime Act 2009 (c. 26), ss. 112. (1)(2), 116. (6), Sch. 7 para. 123. (2)(b), Sch. 8 Pt. 13
Modifications etc. (not altering text)
C59. Ss. 30. A-30. D applied (with modifications) by Criminal Justice Act 2003 (c. 44), s. 24.
B(1)-(3) (as inserted (29.6.2007) by Police and Justice Act 2006 (c. 48), ss. 18. (1), 53 (with s. 18. (2)); S.I. 2007/1614, art. 2. (e))

30. CBBail under section 30. A: variation of conditions by court

(1) Where a person released on bail under section 30. A(1) is on bail subject to conditions, a magistrates' court may, on an application by or on behalf of the person, vary the conditions if—

(a) the conditions have been varied under section 30. CA(1) since being imposed under section 30. A(3. B),

(b) a request for variation under section 30. CA(1) of the conditions has been made and refused, or

(c) a request for variation under section 30. CA(1) of the conditions has been made and the period of 48 hours beginning with the day when the request was made has expired without the request having been withdrawn or the conditions having been varied in response to the request.

(2) In proceedings on an application for a variation under subsection (1), a ground may not be relied upon unless—

(a) in a case falling within subsection (1)(a), the ground was relied upon in the request in response to which the conditions were varied under section 30. CA(1), or

(b) in a case falling within paragraph (b) or (c) of subsection (1), the ground was relied upon in the request mentioned in that paragraph,

but this does not prevent the court, when deciding the application, from considering different grounds arising out of a change in circumstances that has occurred since the making of the application.

(3) Where conditions of bail granted to a person under section 30. A(1) are varied under subsection (1)—

(a) paragraphs (a) to (d) of section 30. A(3. A) apply,

(b) requirements imposed by the conditions as so varied must be requirements that appear to the court varying the conditions to be necessary for any of the purposes mentioned in paragraphs (a) to (d) of section 30. A(3. B), and

(c) that bail shall not lapse but shall continue subject to the conditions as so varied.

(4) Power under subsection (1) to vary conditions is, subject to subsection (3)(a) and (b), power—

(a) to vary or rescind any of the conditions, and

(b) to impose further conditions.]

Amendments (Textual)

F18. Ss. 30. A-30. D inserted (20.1.2004) by Criminal Justice Act 2003 (c. 44), ss. 4. (7), 336; S.I. 2004/81, art. 2. (1)(2)(a)

F41. Ss. 30. CA, 30. CB inserted (1.4.2007) by Police and Justice Act 2006 (c. 48), ss. 10, 53, Sch. 6 para. 4; S.I. 2007/709, art. 3. (i) (subject to arts. 6, 7)

Modifications etc. (not altering text)

C60. Ss. 30. A-30. D applied (with modifications) by Criminal Justice Act 2003 (c. 44), s. 24. B(1)-(3) (as inserted (29.6.2007) by Police and Justice Act 2006 (c. 48), ss. 18. (1), 53 (with s. 18. (2)); S.I. 2007/1614, art. 2. (e))

30. DFailure to answer to bail under section 30. A

(1) A constable may arrest without a warrant a person who—

(a) has been released on bail under section 30. A subject to a requirement to attend a specified police station, but

(b) fails to attend the police station at the specified time.

(2) A person arrested under subsection (1) must be taken to a police station (which may be the specified police station or any other police station) as soon as practicable after the arrest.

[F46. (2. A)A person who has been released on bail under section 30. A may be arrested without a warrant by a constable if the constable has reasonable grounds for suspecting that the person has broken any of the conditions of bail.

(2. B)A person arrested under subsection (2. A) must be taken to a police station (which may be the specified police station mentioned in subsection (1) or any other police station) as soon as practicable after the arrest.]

(3) In subsection (1), "specified" means specified in a notice under subsection (1) F47... of section 30. B or, if notice of change has been given under subsection (7) of that section, in that notice.

(4) For the purposes of—

(a) section 30 (subject to the [F48obligations in subsections (2) and (2. B)]), and

(b) section 31,

an arrest under this section is to be treated as an arrest for an offence.]

Amendments (Textual)

F18. Ss. 30. A-30. D inserted (20.1.2004) by Criminal Justice Act 2003 (c. 44), ss. 4. (7), 336; S.I. 2004/81, art. 2. (1)(2)(a)

F46. S. 30. D(2. A)(2. B) inserted (1.4.2007) by Police and Justice Act 2006 (c. 48), ss. 10, 53, Sch. 6 para. 5. (2); S.I. 2007/709, art. 3. (i) (subject to arts. 6, 7)

F47. Words in s. 30. D(3) omitted (31.1.2017 for specified purposes, 3.4.2017 in so far as not already in force) by virtue of Policing and Crime Act 2017 (c. 3), ss. 62. (10), 183. (1), (5)(e); S.I. 2017/399, reg. 2, Sch. para. 14 (with reg. 5)

F48. Words in s. 30. D(4)(a) substituted (1.4.2007) by Police and Justice Act 2006 (c. 48), ss. 10, 53, Sch. 6 para. 5. (3); S.I. 2007/709, art. 3. (i) (subject to arts. 6, 7)

Modifications etc. (not altering text)

C61. Ss. 30. A-30. D applied (with modifications) by Criminal Justice Act 2003 (c. 44), s. 24. B(1)-(3) (as inserted (29.6.2007) by Police and Justice Act 2006 (c. 48), ss. 18. (1), 53 (with s. 18. (2)); S.I. 2007/1614, art. 2. (e))

31 Arrest for further offence.

Where—

(a) a person—

(i) has been arrested for an offence; and

(ii) is at a police station in consequence of that arrest; and

(b) it appears to a constable that, if he were released from that arrest, he would be liable to arrest for some other offence,

he shall be arrested for that other offence.

Modifications etc. (not altering text)

C62. Ss. 8, 9, 15, 16, 17. (1)(b) (2) (4), 18-20, 21, 22. (1)-(4), 28, 29, 30. (1)-(4)(a)(5)-(11), 31, 32. (1)-(9), 34. (1)-(5), 35, 36, 37, 39, 40-44, 50, 51. (d), 52, 54, 55, 64. (1)-(4)(5)(6), Sch. 1 applied with modifications by S.I. 1985/1800, arts. 3-11, Schs. 1, 2

C63. S. 31 applied (with modifications) by Criminal Justice Act 2003 (c. 44), s. 24. B(1)-(3) (as inserted (29.6.2007) by Police and Justice Act 2006 (c. 48), ss. 18. (1), 53 (with s. 18. (2)); S.I. 2007/1614, art. 2. (e))

C64. S. 31 applied (with modifications) (25.6.2013) by The Police and Criminal Evidence Act 1984 (Application to immigration officers and designated customs officials in England and Wales) Order 2013 (S.I. 2013/1542), arts. 1, 12. (2)-(4), Sch. 2 (with arts. 13-31)

C65. S. 31 applied (with modifications) (25.6.2013) by The Police and Criminal Evidence Act 1984 (Application to immigration officers and designated customs officials in England and Wales) Order 2013 (S.I. 2013/1542), arts. 1, 3. (2)-(4), Sch. 1 (with arts. 4-11)

C66. S. 31 applied (with modifications) (4.11.2015) by The Police and Criminal Evidence Act 1984 (Application to Revenue and Customs) Order 2015 (S.I. 2015/1783), arts. 1, 3. (1), Sch. 1 (with art. 3. (2), (3), 4-19, Sch. 2)

32 Search upon arrest.

(1) A constable may search an arrested person, in any case where the person to be searched has been arrested at a place other than a police station, if the constable has reasonable grounds for believing that the arrested person may present a danger to himself or others.

(2) Subject to subsections (3) to (5) below, a constable shall also have power in any such case—

(a) to search the arrested person for anything—

(i) which he might use to assist him to escape from lawful custody; or

(ii) which might be evidence relating to an offence; and

[F49. (b)if the offence for which he has been arrested is an indictable offence, to enter and search any premises in which he was when arrested or immediately before he was arrested for evidence relating to the offence.]

(3) The power to search conferred by subsection (2) above is only a power to search to the extent that is reasonably required for the purpose of discovering any such thing or any such evidence.

(4) The powers conferred by this section to search a person are not to be construed as authorising a constable to require a person to remove any of his clothing in public other than an outer coat, jacket or gloves [F50but they do authorise a search of a person's mouth].

(5) A constable may not search a person in the exercise of the power conferred by subsection (2)(a) above unless he has reasonable grounds for believing that the person to be searched may have concealed on him anything for which a search is permitted under that paragraph.

(6) A constable may not search premises in the exercise of the power conferred by subsection (2)(b) above unless he has reasonable grounds for believing that there is evidence for which a search is permitted under that paragraph on the premises.

(7) In so far as the power of search conferred by subsection (2)(b) above relates to premises consisting of two or more separate dwellings, it is limited to a power to search—

(a) any dwelling in which the arrest took place or in which the person arrested was immediately before his arrest; and

(b) any parts of the premises which the occupier of any such dwelling uses in common with the occupiers of any other dwellings comprised in the premises.

(8) A constable searching a person in the exercise of the power conferred by subsection (1) above may seize and retain anything he finds, if he has reasonable grounds for believing that the person searched might use it to cause physical injury to himself or to any other person.

(9) A constable searching a person in the exercise of the power conferred by subsection (2)(a) above may seize and retain anything he finds, other than an item subject to legal privilege, if he has reasonable grounds for believing—

(a) that he might use it to assist him to escape from lawful custody; or

(b) that it is evidence of an offence or has been obtained in consequence of the commission of an offence.

(10) Nothing in this section shall be taken to affect the power conferred by [F51section 43 of the Terrorism Act 2000].

Amendments (Textual)

F49. S. 32. (2)(b) substituted (1.1.2006) by Serious Organised Crime and Police Act 2005 (c. 15), ss. 111, 178, Sch. 7 Pt. 3 para. 43. (6); S.I. 2005/3495, art. 2. (1)(m)

F50. Words in s. 32. (4) inserted (10.4.1995) by 1994 c. 33, s. 59. (2); S.I. 1995/721, art. 2, Sch.

F51. Words in s. 32. (10) substituted (19.2.2001) by 2000 c. 11, ss. 125. (1), Sch. 15 para. 5. (3) (with s. 29. (1)); S.I. 2001/421

Modifications etc. (not altering text)

C67. S. 32 modified (3.11.1994) by 1994 c. 33, ss. 166. (5), 172. (2)(4)

C68. S. 32 extended (1.1.2006) by Police Refom Act 2002 (c. 30), Sch. 4 para. 2. A (as inserted by Serious Organised Crime and Police Act 2005 (c. 15), ss. 122, 178, Sch. 8 Pt. 1 para. 4; S.I. 2005/3495, art. 2. (1)(q)(r))

C69. Ss. 8, 9, 15, 16, 17. (1)(b)(2) (4), 18-20, 21, 22. (1)-(4), 28, 29, 30. (1)-(4)(a)(5)-(11), 31, 32. (1)-(9), 34. (1)-(5), 35, 36, 37, 39, 40-44, 50, 51. (d), 52, 54, 55, 64. (1)-(4)(5)(6), Sch. 1 applied with modifications by S.I. 1985/1800, arts. 3-11, Schs. 1, 2

C70. S. 32. (1)-(9) applied (with modifications) (25.6.2013) by The Police and Criminal Evidence

Act 1984 (Application to immigration officers and designated customs officials in England and Wales) Order 2013 (S.I. 2013/1542), arts. 1, 12. (2)-(4), Sch. 2 (with arts. 13-31)
C71. S. 32. (1)-(9) applied (with modifications) (25.6.2013) by The Police and Criminal Evidence Act 1984 (Application to immigration officers and designated customs officials in England and Wales) Order 2013 (S.I. 2013/1542), arts. 1, 3. (2)-(4), Sch. 1 (with arts. 4-11)
C72. S. 32. (1)-(9) applied (with modifications) (4.11.2015) by The Police and Criminal Evidence Act 1984 (Application to Revenue and Customs) Order 2015 (S.I. 2015/1783), arts. 1, 3. (1), Sch. 1 (with art. 3. (2), (3), 4-19, Sch. 2)
C73. S. 32. (1)-(9) applied (with modifications) (30.4.2017) by The Police and Criminal Evidence Act 1984 (Application to Labour Abuse Prevention Officers) Regulations 2017 (S.I. 2017/520), regs. 1, 2, 3. (r), Sch.
C74. S. 32. (2)(b) modified (30.5.2006) by London Olympic Games and Paralympic Games Act 2006 (c. 12), ss. 31. (7), 40. (1)-(3); S.I. 2006/1118, art. 3. (1)

[F5233 Execution of warrant not in possession of constable.

In section 125 of the M3. Magistrates' Courts Act 1980—
   (a) in subsection (3), for the words "arrest a person charged with an offence" there shall be substituted the words "which this subsection applies";
   (b) the following subsection shall be added after that subsection—
"(4)The warrants to which subsection (3) above applies are—
   (a) a warrant to arrest a person in connection with an offence;
   (b) without prejudice to paragraph (a) above, a warrant under section 186. (3) of the M4. Army Act 1955, section 186. (3) of the M5. Air Force Act 1955, section 105. (3) of the M6. Naval Discipline Act 1957 or Schedule 5 to the M7. Reserve Forces Act 1980 (desertion etc.);
   (c) a warrant under—
(i) section 102 or 104 of the M8. General Rate Act 1967 (insufficiency of distress);
(ii) section 18. (4) of the M9. Domestic Proceedings and Magistrates' Courts Act 1978 (protection of parties to marriage and children of family); and
(iii) section 55, 76, 93 or 97 above."]
Amendments (Textual)
F52. S. 33 repealed (19.2.2001) by 1999 c. 22, s. 106, Sch. 15 Pt. V(8) (with Sch. 14 paras. 7. (2), 36. (9)); S.I. 2001/168, art 2. (b)
Marginal Citations
M31980 c. 43.
M41955 c. 18
M51955 c. 19
M61957 c. 53
M71980 c. 9
M81967 c. 9
M91978 c. 22

Part IV Detention

Part IV Detention

Modifications etc. (not altering text)
C1. Pt. IV (ss. 34-52) modified (2.8.1993) by S.I. 1993/1813, art. 6, Sch. 3 paras. 4. (6)(b)(c)(7), 5. (9)(b)(c), 6. (9)(b)(c); Pt. IV (ss. 34-52) modified by the said S.I. 1993/1813, art. 6, Sch. 3 para. 4 as incorporated (with modifications) (1.12.1997) by S.I. 1994/1405, art. 6, Sch. 3 para. 5

Pt. IV (ss. 34-52) modified by The Nationality, Immigration and Asylum Act 2002 (Juxtaposed Controls) Order 2003 (S.I. 2003/2818), art. 7. (6)(c) (the modification coming into force in accordance with art. 1. (2) of the modifying S.I.)

Pt. IV (ss. 34-52) modified by The Nationality, Immigration and Asylum Act 2002 (Juxtaposed Controls) Order 2003 (S.I. 2003/2818), art. 15. (2) (the modification coming into force in accordance with art. 1. (2) of the modifying S.I.)

Pt. IV (ss. 34-52) modified by The Nationality, Immigration and Asylum Act 2002 (Juxtaposed Controls) Order 2003 (S.I. 2003/2818), art. 16. (4) (the modification coming into force in accordance with art. 1. (2) of the modifying S.I.)

Pt. IV (ss. 34-52) modified (30.3.2004) by Railways and Transport Safety Act 2003 (c. 20), ss. 85. (4)(a), 120 (with s. 90); S.I. 2004/827, art. 3. (h)

Pt. IV (ss. 34-52) modified (30.3.2004) by Railways and Transport Safety Act 2003 (c. 20), ss. 97. (4)(a), 120 (with s. 100); S.I. 2004/827, art. 3. (t)

C2. Pt. IV (ss. 34-52) applied (with modifications) (4.4.2005) Criminal Justice Act 2003 (c. 44), ss. 87. (3), 336; S.I. 2005/950, art. 2. (1), Sch. 1 para. 5 (subject to art. 2. (2), Sch. 2) (as amended by S.I. 2005/2122, art. 2)

C3. Pt. IV incorporated (16.5.2008) by The London Gateway Port Harbour Empowerment Order 2008 (S.I. 2008/1261), art. 52

34 Limitations on police detention.

(1) A person arrested for an offence shall not be kept in police detention except in accordance with the provisions of this Part of this Act.

(2) Subject to subsection (3) below, if at any time a custody officer—

(a) becomes aware, in relation to any person in police detention, that the grounds for the detention of that person have ceased to apply; and

(b) is not aware of any other grounds on which the continued detention of that person could be justified under the provision of this part of this Act,

it shall be the duty of the custody officer, subject to subsection (4) below, to order his immediate release from custody.

(3) No person in police detention shall be released except on the authority of a custody officer at the police station where his detention was authorised or, if it was authorised at more than one station, a custody officer at the station where it was last authorised.

(4) A person who appears to the custody officer to have been unlawfully at large when he was arrested is not to be released under subsection (2) above.

(5) A person whose release is ordered under subsection (2) above shall be released [F1—

(a) without bail unless subsection (5. A) applies, or

(b) on bail if subsection (5. A) applies.]

[F2. (5. A)This subsection applies if—

(a) it appears to the custody officer—

(i) that there is need for further investigation of any matter in connection with which the person was detained at any time during the period of the person's detention, or

(ii) that, in respect of any such matter, proceedings may be taken against the person or the person may be given a youth caution under section 66. ZA of the Crime and Disorder Act 1998, and

(b) the pre-conditions for bail are satisfied.]

[F3. (5. B)Subsection (5. C) applies where—

(a) a person is released under subsection (5), and

(b) the custody officer determines that—

(i) there is not sufficient evidence to charge the person with an offence, or

(ii) there is sufficient evidence to charge the person with an offence but the person should not be charged with an offence or given a caution in respect of an offence.

(5. C)The custody officer must give the person notice in writing that the person is not to be

prosecuted.

(5. D)Subsection (5. C) does not prevent the prosecution of the person for an offence if new evidence comes to light after the notice was given.

(5. E)In this Part "caution" includes—

(a) a conditional caution within the meaning of Part 3 of the Criminal Justice Act 2003;

(b) a youth conditional caution within the meaning of Chapter 1 of Part 4 of the Crime and Disorder Act 1998;

(c) a youth caution under section 66. ZA of that Act.]

(6) For the purposes of this Part of this Act a person arrested under [F4section 6. D of the Road Traffic Act 1988][F5or section 30. (2) of the Transport and Works Act 1992 (c. 42)] is arrested for an offence.

[F6. (7)For the purposes of this Part a person who—

(a) attends a police station to answer to bail granted under section 30. A,

(b) returns to a police station to answer to bail granted under this Part, or

(c) is arrested under section 30. D or 46. A,

is to be treated as arrested for an offence and that offence is the offence in connection with which he was granted bail.

[F7. But this subsection is subject to section 47. (6) (which provides for the calculation of certain periods, where a person has been granted bail under this Part, by reference to time when the person is in police detention only).]]

F8[(8)Subsection (7) does not apply in relation to a person who is granted bail subject to the duty mentioned in section 47. (3)(b) and who either—

(a) attends a police station to answer to such bail, or

(b) is arrested under section 46. A for failing to do so,

(provision as to the treatment of such persons for the purposes of this Part being made by section 46. ZA).]

Amendments (Textual)

F1. Words in s. 34. (5) substituted (31.1.2017 for specified purposes, 3.4.2017 in so far as not already in force) by Policing and Crime Act 2017 (c. 3), ss. 54. (2), 183. (1), (5)(e); S.I. 2017/399, reg. 2, Sch. para. 12 (with reg. 5)

F2. S. 34. (5. A) inserted (31.1.2017 for specified purposes, 3.4.2017 in so far as not already in force) by Policing and Crime Act 2017 (c. 3), ss. 54. (3), 183. (1), (5)(e); S.I. 2017/399, reg. 2, Sch. para. 12 (with reg. 5)

F3. S. 34. (5. B)-(5. E) inserted (31.1.2017 for specified purposes, 3.4.2017 in so far as not already in force) by Policing and Crime Act 2017 (c. 3), ss. 66. (2), 183. (1), (5)(e); S.I. 2017/399, reg. 2, Sch. para. 18

F4. Words in s. 34. (6) substituted (30.3.2004) by Railways and Transport Safety Act 2003 (c. 20), ss. 107, 120, Sch. 7 para. 12; S.I. 2004/827, art. 3. (bb)(ii)

F5. Words in s. 34. (6) inserted (1.4.2003) by Police Reform Act 2002 (c. 30), ss. 53. (1), 108. (2)-(5); S.I. 2003/808, art. 2. (d)

F6. S. 34. (7) substituted (20.1.2004) by Criminal Justice Act 2003 (c. 44), ss. 12, 336, Sch. 1 para. 5; S.I. 2004/81, art. 2. (1)(2)(a)

F7. Words in s. 34. (7) inserted (retrospectively) by Police (Detention and Bail) Act 2011 (c. 9), s. 1. (2)(3)

F8. S. 34. (8) inserted (1.4.2007 for specified purposes, 14.11.2008 for specified purposes, 3.10.2011 for specified purposes, 8.10.2012 in so far as not already in force) by Police and Justice Act 2006 (c. 48), ss. 46. (2), 53. (1); S.I. 2007/709, art. 3. (n) (with art. 6); S.I. 2008/2785, art. 2; S.I. 2011/2144, art. 2. (1)(b); S.I. 2012/2373, art. 2. (b)

Modifications etc. (not altering text)

C4. Ss. 8, 9, 15, 16, 17. (1)(b)(2) (4), 18-20, 21, 22. (1)-(4), 28, 29, 30. (1)-(4)(a)(5)-(11), 31, 32. (1)-(9), 34. (1)-(5), 35, 36, 37, 39, 40-44, 50, 51. (d), 52, 54, 55, 64. (1)-(4)(5)(6), Sch. 1 applied with modifications by S.I. 1985/1800, arts. 3-11, Schs. 1, 2

C5. S. 34. (1)-(5) modified (2.8.1993) by S.I. 1993/1813, art. 6, Sch. 3 para. 3. (3).

C6. S. 34. (1)-(5) applied (with modifications) by Criminal Justice Act 2003 (c. 44), s. 24. B(1)-(3) (as inserted (29.6.2007) by Police and Justice Act 2006 (c. 48), ss. 18. (1), 53 (with s. 18. (2)); S.I. 2006/1614, art. 2. (e))

C7. S. 34. (1)-(5) applied (with modifications) (25.6.2013) by The Police and Criminal Evidence Act 1984 (Application to immigration officers and designated customs officials in England and Wales) Order 2013 (S.I. 2013/1542), arts. 1, 12. (2)-(4), Sch. 2 (with arts. 13-31)

C8. S. 34. (1)-(5) applied (with modifications) (4.11.2015) by The Police and Criminal Evidence Act 1984 (Application to Revenue and Customs) Order 2015 (S.I. 2015/1783), arts. 1, 3. (1), Sch. 1 (with art. 3. (2), (3), 4-19, Sch. 2)

35 Designated police stations.

(1) The chief officer of police for each police area shall designate the police stations in his area which, subject to [F9sections 30. (3) and (5), 30. A(5) and 30. D(2)] , are to be the stations in that area to be used for the purpose of detaining arrested persons.

(2) A chief officer's duty under subsection (1) above is to designate police stations appearing to him to provide enough accommodation for that purpose.

[F10. (2. A)The Chief Constable of the British Transport Police Force may designate police stations which (in addition to those designated under subsection (1) above) may be used for the purpose of detaining arrested persons.]

(3) Without prejudice to section 12 of the M1. Interpretation Act 1978 (continuity of duties) a chief officer—

    (a) may designate a station which was not previously designated; and

    (b) may direct that a designation of a station previously made shall cease to operate.

(4) In this Act "designated police station" means a police station for the time being designated under this section.

Amendments (Textual)

F9. Words in s. 35. (1) substituted (20.1.2004) by Criminal Justice Act 2003 (c. 44), ss. 12, 336, Sch. 1 para. 6; S.I. 2004/81, art. 2. (1)(2)(a)

F10. S. 35. (2. A) inserted (14.12.2001) by 2001 c. 24, ss. 101, Sch. 7 para. 12

Modifications etc. (not altering text)

C9. Ss. 8, 9, 15, 16, 17. (1)(b)(2) (4), 18-20, 21, 22. (1)-(4), 28, 29, 30. (1)-(4)(a)(5)-(11), 31, 32. (1)-(9), 34. (1)-(5), 35, 36, 37, 39, 40-44, 50, 51. (d), 52, 54, 55, 64. (1)-(4)(5)(6), Sch. 1 applied with modifications by S.I. 1985/1800, arts. 3-11, Schs. 1, 2

C10. S. 35 amended (1.7.2004) by Railways and Transport Safety Act 2003 (c. 20), ss. 73, 120, Sch. 5 para. 4 (with s. 72); S.I. 2004/1572, art. 3. (ddd)(jjj)

C11. S. 35 applied (with modifications) (25.6.2013) by The Police and Criminal Evidence Act 1984 (Application to immigration officers and designated customs officials in England and Wales) Order 2013 (S.I. 2013/1542), arts. 1, 12. (2)-(4), Sch. 2 (with arts. 13-31)

C12. S. 35. (1)(2) applied (with modifications) (4.11.2015) by The Police and Criminal Evidence Act 1984 (Application to Revenue and Customs) Order 2015 (S.I. 2015/1783), arts. 1, 3. (1), Sch. 1 (with art. 3. (2), (3), 4-19, Sch. 2)

C13. S. 35. (3)(4) applied (with modifications) (4.11.2015) by The Police and Criminal Evidence Act 1984 (Application to Revenue and Customs) Order 2015 (S.I. 2015/1783), arts. 1, 3. (1), Sch. 1 (with art. 3. (2), (3), 4-19, Sch. 2)

Marginal Citations

M11978 c. 30.

36 Custody officers at police stations.

(1) One or more custody officers shall be appointed for each designated police station.

(2) A custody officer for [F11a police station designated under section 35. (1) above] shall be

appointed—

(a) by the chief officer of police for the area in which the designated police station is situated; or

(b) by such other police officer as the chief officer of police for that area may direct.

F12 [(2. A)A custody officer for a police station designated under section 35. (2. A) above shall be appointed—

(a) by the Chief Constable of the British Police Transport Force; or

(b) by such other member of that Force as that Chief Constable may direct.]

[F13. (3)No officer may be appointed a custody officer unless the officer is of at least the rank of sergeant.]

(4) An officer of any rank may perform the functions of a custody officer at a designated police station if a custody officer is not readily available to perform them.

(5) Subject to the following provisions of this section and to section 39. (2) below, none of the functions of a custody officer in relation to a person shall be performed by [F14an officer] who at the time when the function falls to be performed is involved in the investigation of an offence for which that person is in police detention at that time.

(6) Nothing in subsection (5) above is to be taken to prevent a custody officer—

(a) performing any function assigned to custody officers—

(i) by this Act; or

(ii) by a code of practice issued under this Act;

(b) carrying out the duty imposed on custody officers by section 39 below;

(c) doing anything in connection with the identification of a suspect; or

(d) doing anything under [F15sections 7 and 8 of the Road Traffic Act 1988].

(7) Where an arrested person is taken to a police station which is not a designated police station, the functions in relation to him which at a designated police station would be the functions of a custody officer shall be performed—

(a) by an officer F16. . . who is not involved in the investigation of an offence for which he is in police detention, if [F17such an officer] is readily available; and

(b) if no [F18such officer] is readily available, by the officer who took him to the station or any other officer.

[F19. (7. A)Subject to subsection (7. B), subsection (7) applies where a person attends a police station which is not a designated station to answer to bail granted under section 30. A as it applies where a person is taken to such a station.

(7. B)Where subsection (7) applies because of subsection (7. A), the reference in subsection (7)(b) to the officer who took him to the station is to be read as a reference to the officer who granted him bail.]

(8) References to a custody officer in [F20section 34 above or in] the following provisions of this Act include references to [F21an officer] other than a custody officer who is performing the functions of a custody officer by virtue of subsection (4) or (7) above.

(9) Where by virtue of subsection (7) above an officer of a force maintained by a [F22local policing body] who took an arrested person to a police station is to perform the functions of a custody officer in relation to him, the officer shall inform an officer who—

(a) is attached to a designated police station; and

(b) is of at least the rank of inspector,

that he is to do so.

(10) The duty imposed by subsection (9) above shall be performed as soon as it is practicable to perform it.

(11) F23. . . . .

Amendments (Textual)

F11. Words in s. 36. (2) substituted (14.12.2001) by 2001 c. 24, s. 107, Sch. 7 para. 13. (2)

F12. S. 36. (2. A) inserted (14.12.2001) by 2001 c. 24, s. 107, Sch. 7 para. 13. (3)

F13. S. 36. (3) substituted (12.1.2010) by Policing and Crime Act 2009 (c. 26), ss. 112. (1), 116. (6), Sch. 7 para. 123. (3)(a)

F14. Words in s. 36. (5) substituted (12.1.2010) by Policing and Crime Act 2009 (c. 26), ss. 112.

(1), 116. (6), Sch. 7 para. 123. (3)(b)

F15. Words substituted by Road Traffic (Consequential Provisions) Act 1988 (c.54, SIF 107:1), s. 4, Sch. 3 para. 27. (3)

F16. Words in s. 36. (7)(a) repealed (12.1.2010) by Policing and Crime Act 2009 (c. 26), ss. 112. (1)(2), 116. (6), Sch. 7 para. 123. (3)(c)(i), Sch. 8 Pt. 13

F17. Words in s. 36. (7)(a) substituted (12.1.2010) by Policing and Crime Act 2009 (c. 26), ss. 112. (1), 116. (6), Sch. 7 para. 123. (3)(c)(i)

F18. Words in s. 36. (7)(b) substituted (12.1.2010) by Policing and Crime Act 2009 (c. 26), ss. 112. (1), 116. (6), Sch. 7 para. 123. (3)(c)(ii)

F19. S. 36. (7. A)(7. B) inserted (20.1.2004) by Criminal Justice Act 2003 (c. 44), ss. 12, 336, Sch. 1 para. 7; S.I. 2004/81, art. 2. (1)(2)(a)

F20. Words in s. 36. (8) inserted (7.3.2011) by Serious Organised Crime and Police Act 2005 (c. 15), ss. 121. (5)(a), 178. (8); S.I. 2011/410, art. 2. (f)

F21. Words in s. 36. (8) substituted (12.1.2010) by Policing and Crime Act 2009 (c. 26), ss. 112. (1), 116. (6), Sch. 7 para. 123. (3)(d)

F22. Words in s. 36. (9) substituted (16.1.2012) by Police Reform and Social Responsibility Act 2011 (c. 13), s. 157. (1), Sch. 16 para. 162; S.I. 2011/3019, art. 3, Sch. 1

F23. S. 36. (11) repealed (12.1.2010) by Policing and Crime Act 2009 (c. 26), ss. 112. (1)(2), 116. (6), Sch. 7 para. 123. (3)(e), Sch. 8 Pt. 13

Modifications etc. (not altering text)

C14. Ss. 8, 9, 15, 16, 17. (1)(b)(2) (4), 18-20, 21, 22. (1)-(4), 28, 29, 30. (1)-(4)(a)(5)-(11), 31, 32. (1)-(9), 34. (1)-(5), 35, 36, 37, 39, 40-44, 50, 51. (d), 52, 54, 55, 64. (1)-(4)(5)(6), Sch. 1 applied with modifications by S.I. 1985/1800, arts. 3-11, Schs. 1, 2

C15. S. 36 modified (2.8.1993) by S.I. 1993/1813, art. 6, Sch. 3 para. 3. (3); s. 36 modified by the said S.I.1993/1813, art. 6, Sch. 3 para. 3. (3) as incorporated (with modifications) (1.12.1997) by S.I. 1994/1405, art. 6, Sch. 3 para. 4. (b)

C16. S. 36 amended (1.7.2004) by Railways and Transport Safety Act 2003 (c. 20), ss. 73, 120, Sch. 5 para. 4 (with s. 72); S.I. 2004/1572, art. 3. (ddd)(jjj)

C17. S. 36 applied (with modifications) by Criminal Justice Act 2003 (c. 44), s. 24. B(1)-(3) (as inserted (29.6.2007) by Police and Justice Act 2006 (c. 48), ss. 18. (1), 53 (with s. 18. (2)); S.I. 2007/1614, art. 2. (e))

C18. S. 36. (1)(2) applied (with modifications) (25.6.2013) by The Police and Criminal Evidence Act 1984 (Application to immigration officers and designated customs officials in England and Wales) Order 2013 (S.I. 2013/1542), arts. 1, 12. (2)-(4), Sch. 2 (with arts. 13-31)

C19. S. 36. (1)(2) applied (with modifications) (4.11.2015) by The Police and Criminal Evidence Act 1984 (Application to Revenue and Customs) Order 2015 (S.I. 2015/1783), arts. 1, 3. (1), Sch. 1 (with art. 3. (2), (3), 4-19, Sch. 2)

C20. S. 36. (3)-(6)(c) applied (with modifications) (25.6.2013) by The Police and Criminal Evidence Act 1984 (Application to immigration officers and designated customs officials in England and Wales) Order 2013 (S.I. 2013/1542), arts. 1, 12. (2)-(4), Sch. 2 (with arts. 13-31)

C21. S. 36. (3)(4) applied (with modifications) (4.11.2015) by The Police and Criminal Evidence Act 1984 (Application to Revenue and Customs) Order 2015 (S.I. 2015/1783), arts. 1, 3. (1), Sch. 1 (with art. 3. (2), (3), 4-19, Sch. 2)

C22. S. 36. (5)(6) applied (with modifications) (4.11.2015) by The Police and Criminal Evidence Act 1984 (Application to Revenue and Customs) Order 2015 (S.I. 2015/1783), arts. 1, 3. (1), Sch. 1 (with art. 3. (2), (3), 4-19, Sch. 2)

C23. S. 36. (7)(8) extended (2.8.1993) by S.I. 1993/1813, art. 6, Sch. 3 paras. 1. (2)(b), 3. (2); s. 36. (7)(8) extended by the said S.I. 1993/1813, art. 6, Sch. 3 paras. 3. (2), 4 as incorporated (with modifications) (1.12.1997) by S.I. 1994/1405, art. 6, Sch. 3 paras. 4. (b), 5

C24. S. 36. (7) applied (with modifications) (25.6.2013) by The Police and Criminal Evidence Act 1984 (Application to immigration officers and designated customs officials in England and Wales) Order 2013 (S.I. 2013/1542), arts. 1, 12. (2)-(4), Sch. 2 (with arts. 13-31)

C25. S. 36. (7)(8) applied (with modifications) (4.11.2015) by The Police and Criminal Evidence

Act 1984 (Application to Revenue and Customs) Order 2015 (S.I. 2015/1783), arts. 1, 3. (1), Sch. 1 (with art. 3. (2), (3), 4-19, Sch. 2)

C26. S. 36. (8)-(10) applied (with modifications) (25.6.2013) by The Police and Criminal Evidence Act 1984 (Application to immigration officers and designated customs officials in England and Wales) Order 2013 (S.I. 2013/1542), arts. 1, 12. (2)-(4), Sch. 2 (with arts. 13-31)

C27. S. 36. (9)(10) applied (with modifications) (4.11.2015) by The Police and Criminal Evidence Act 1984 (Application to Revenue and Customs) Order 2015 (S.I. 2015/1783), arts. 1, 3. (1), Sch. 1 (with art. 3. (2), (3), 4-19, Sch. 2)

37 Duties of custody officer before charge.

(1) Where—

(a) a person is arrested for an offence—

(i) without a warrant; or

(ii) under a warrant not endorsed for bail, F24. . .

(b) . . . .

the custody officer at each police station where he is detained after his arrest shall determine whether he has before him sufficient evidence to charge that person with the offence for which he was arrested and may detain him at the police station for such period as is necessary to enable him to do so.

(2) If the custody officer determines that he does not have such evidence before him, the person arrested shall be released[F25—

(a) without bail unless the pre-conditions for bail are satisfied, or

(b) on bail if those pre-conditions are satisfied,

(subject to subsection (3))].

(3) If the custody officer has reasonable grounds for [F26believing that the person's detention without being charged is necessary to secure or preserve evidence relating to an offence for which the person is under arrest or to obtain such evidence by questioning the person], he may authorise the person arrested to be kept in police detention.

(4) Where a custody officer authorises a person who has not been charged to be kept in police detention, he shall, as soon as is practicable, make a written record of the grounds for the detention.

(5) Subject to subsection (6) below, the written record shall be made in the presence of the person arrested who shall at that time be informed by the custody officer of the grounds for his detention.

(6) Subsection (5) above shall not apply where the person arrested is, at the time when the written record is made—

(a) incapable of understanding what is said to him;

(b) violent or likely to become violent; or

(c) in urgent need of medical attention.

[F27. (6. A)Subsection (6. B) applies where—

(a) a person is released under subsection (2), and

(b) the custody officer determines that—

(i) there is not sufficient evidence to charge the person with an offence, or

(ii) there is sufficient evidence to charge the person with an offence but the person should not be charged with an offence or given a caution in respect of an offence.

(6. B)The custody officer must give the person notice in writing that the person is not to be prosecuted.

(6. C)Subsection (6. B) does not prevent the prosecution of the person for an offence if new evidence comes to light after the notice was given.]

(7) Subject to section 41. (7) below, if the custody officer determines that he has before him sufficient evidence to charge the person arrested with the offence for which he was arrested, the person arrested—

[F28. (a)[F29 shall be—

(i) released without charge and on bail, or

(ii) kept in police detention,

for the purpose] of enabling the Director of Public Prosecutions to make a decision under section 37. B below,

[F30. (b)shall be released without charge and without bail unless the pre-conditions for bail are satisfied,

(c) shall be released without charge and on bail if those pre-conditions are satisfied but not for the purpose mentioned in paragraph (a), or]

(d) shall be charged.]

[F31. (7. A)The decision as to how a person is to be dealt with under subsection (7) above shall be that of the custody officer.

(7. B)Where a person is [F32dealt with under subsection (7)(a)] above, it shall be the duty of the custody officer to inform him that he is being released [F33, or (as the case may be) detained,] to enable the Director of Public Prosecutions to make a decision under section 37. B below.]

(8) Where—

(a) a person is released under subsection (7)(b) [F34or (c)] above; and

(b) at the time of his release a decision whether he should be prosecuted for the offence for which he was arrested has not been taken,

it shall be the duty of the custody officer so to inform him.

[F35. (8. ZA)Where—

(a) a person is released under subsection (7)(b) or (c), and

(b) the custody officer makes a determination as mentioned in subsection (6. A)(b),

subsections (6. B) and (6. C) apply.]

[F36. (8. A)Subsection (8. B) applies if the offence for which the person is arrested is one in relation to which a sample could be taken under section 63. B below and the custody officer—

(a) is required in pursuance of subsection (2) above to release the person arrested and decides to release him on bail, or

(b) decides in pursuance of subsection (7)(a) or [F37. (c)] above to release the person without charge and on bail.

(8. B)The detention of the person may be continued to enable a sample to be taken under section 63. B, but this subsection does not permit a person to be detained for a period of more than 24 hours after the relevant time.]

(9) If the person arrested is not in a fit state to be dealt with under subsection (7) above, he may be kept in police detention until he is.

(10) The duty imposed on the custody officer under subsection (1) above shall be carried out by him as soon as practicable after the person arrested arrives at the police station or, in the case of a person arrested at the police station, as soon as practicable after the arrest.

F38. (11). . . . .

F38. (12). . . . .

F38. (13). . . . .

F38. (14). . . . .

(15) In this Part of this Act—

"arrested juvenile" means a person arrested with or without a warrant who appears to be [F39 under the age of 18] F40 . . .;

"endorsed for bail" means endorsed with a direction for bail in accordance with section 117. (2) of the M2. Magistrates' Courts Act 1980.

Amendments (Textual)

F24. S. 37. (1)(b) and the word "or" preceeding it repealed (10.4.1995) by 1994 c. 33, ss. 29. (4)(a)(5), 168. (3), Sch.11; S.I. 1995/721, art. 2, Sch. AppendixB

F25. Words in s. 37. (2) substituted (31.1.2017 for specified purposes, 3.4.2017 in so far as not already in force) by Policing and Crime Act 2017 (c. 3), ss. 54. (5), 183. (1), (5)(e); S.I. 2017/399, reg. 2, Sch. para. 12 (with reg. 5)

F26. Words in s. 37. (3) substituted (31.1.2017 for specified purposes, 3.4.2017 in so far as not already in force) by Policing and Crime Act 2017 (c. 3), ss. 54. (6), 183. (1), (5)(e); S.I. 2017/399, reg. 2, Sch. para. 12 (with reg. 5)

F27. S. 37. (6. A)-(6. C) inserted (31.1.2017 for specified purposes, 3.4.2017 in so far as not already in force) by Policing and Crime Act 2017 (c. 3), ss. 66. (4), 183. (1), (5)(e); S.I. 2017/399, reg. 2, Sch. para. 18

F28. S. 37. (7)(a)-(d) substituted for s. 37. (7)(a)(b) (29.1.2004) by Criminal Justice Act 2003 (c. 44), ss. 28, 336, Sch. 2 para. 2. (2); S.I. 2004/81, art. 4. (1)(2)(c)

F29. Words in s. 37. (7)(a) substituted (15.1.2007) by Police and Justice Act 2006 (c. 48), ss. 11, 53; S.I. 2006/3364, art. 2. (c)

F30. S. 37. (7)(b)(c) substituted (31.1.2017 for specified purposes, 3.4.2017 in so far as not already in force) by Policing and Crime Act 2017 (c. 3), ss. 54. (7), 183. (1), (5)(e); S.I. 2017/399, reg. 2, Sch. para. 12 (with reg. 5)

F31. S. 37. (7. A)(7. B) inserted (29.1.2004) by Criminal Justice Act 2003 (c. 44), ss. 28, 336, Sch. 2 para. 2. (3); S.I. 2004/81, art. 4. (1)(2)(c)

F32. Words in s. 37. (7. B) substituted (15.1.2007) by Police and Justice Act 2006 (c. 48), ss. 52, 53, Sch. 14 para. 9. (a); S.I. 2006/3364, art. 2. (j)(k) (as amended by S.I. 2007/29, art. 2)

F33. Words in s. 37. (7. B) inserted (15.1.2007) by Police and Justice Act 2006 (c. 48), ss. 52, 53, Sch. 14 para. 9. (b); S.I. 2006/3364, art. 2. (j)(k) (as amended by S.I. 2007/29, art. 2)

F34. Words in s. 37. (8)(a) inserted (29.1.2004) by Criminal Justice Act 2003 (c. 44), ss. 28, 336, Sch. 2 para. 2. (4); S.I. 2004/81, art. 4. (1)(2)(c)

F35. S. 37. (8. ZA) inserted (31.1.2017 for specified purposes, 3.4.2017 in so far as not already in force) by Policing and Crime Act 2017 (c. 3), ss. 66. (5), 183. (1), (5)(e); S.I. 2017/399, reg. 2, Sch. para. 18

F36. S. 37. (8. A)(8. B) inserted (1.12.2005) by Drugs Act 2005 (c. 17), ss. 23, 24, Sch. 1 para. 2; S.I. 2005/3053, art. 2. (1)(f)

F37. Word in s. 37. (8. A)(b) substituted (31.1.2017 for specified purposes, 3.4.2017 in so far as not already in force) by Policing and Crime Act 2017 (c. 3), ss. 54. (8), 183. (1), (5)(e); S.I. 2017/399, reg. 2, Sch. para. 12 (with reg. 5)

F38. S. 37. (11)-(14) repealed (1.10.1992) by Criminal Justice Act 1991 (c. 53), s. 72, 101. (2), Sch. 13; S.I. 1992/333, art. 2. (2), Sch. 2.

F39. Words in s. 37. (15) substituted (26.10.2015) by Criminal Justice and Courts Act 2015 (c. 2), ss. 42, 95. (1); S.I. 2015/1778, art. 3. (a)

F40. Words in s. 37. (15) repealed (14.10.1991) by Children Act 1989 (c. 41, SIF 20), s. 108. (7), Sch. 15 (with Sch. 14 paras. 1. (1), 27. (4)); S.I. 1991/828, art. 3. (2)

Modifications etc. (not altering text)

C28. Ss. 8, 9, 15, 16, 17. (1)(b(2) (4), 18–20, 21, 22. (1)–(4), 28, 29, 30. (1)–(4)(a)(5)–(11), 31, 32. (1)–(9), 34. (1)–(5), 35, 36, 37, 39, 40–44, 50, 51. (d), 52, 54, 55, 64. (1)–(4)(5)(6), Sch. 1 applied with modifications by S.I. 1985/1800, arts. 3–11, Schs. 1, 2

C29. S. 37 modified (2.8.1993) by S.I. 1993/1813, art. 6, Sch. 3 paras. 3. (3), 4. (4)(a), 5. (7)(a), 6. (7)(a); s. 37 modified by the said S.I. 1993/1813, art. 6, Sch. 3 paras. 4, 5, 6 as incorporated (with modifications) (1.12.1997) by S.I. 1994/1405, art. 6, Sch. 3 paras. 5, 6, 7

C30. Ss. 37-37. B modified (18.4.2005) by Commissioners for Revenue and Customs Act 2005 (c. 11), ss. 50, 53. (1) {Sch. 4 para. 30}; S.I. 2005/1126, art. 2. (2)(h)

Ss. 37-37. B modified (1.4.2006) by Serious Organised Crime and Police Act 2005 (c. 15), ss. 40, 178; S.I. 2006/378, art. 4. (1), Sch. para. 6 (subject to art. 4. (2)-(7))

C31. Ss. 37-37. B modified (21.7.2009) by Borders, Citizenship and Immigration Act 2009 (c. 11), s. 31. (4) (with s. 36. (4))

C32. S. 37 applied (with modifications) (4.11.2015) by The Police and Criminal Evidence Act 1984 (Application to Revenue and Customs) Order 2015 (S.I. 2015/1783), arts. 1, 3. (1), Sch. 1 (with art. 3. (2), (3), 4-19, Sch. 2)

C33. S. 37. (1)-(8) applied (with modifications) (25.6.2013) by The Police and Criminal Evidence Act 1984 (Application to immigration officers and designated customs officials in England and

Wales) Order 2013 (S.I. 2013/1542), arts. 1, 12. (2)-(4), Sch. 2 (with arts. 13-31)

C34. S. 37. (4)-(6) applied (with modifications) by Criminal Justice Act 2003 (c. 44), s. 24. B(1)-(3) (as inserted by Police and Justice Act 2006 (c. 48), ss. 18. (1), 53 (with s. 18. (2)); S.I. 2007/1614, art. 2. (e))

C35. S. 37. (9)(10) applied (with modifications) (25.6.2013) by The Police and Criminal Evidence Act 1984 (Application to immigration officers and designated customs officials in England and Wales) Order 2013 (S.I. 2013/1542), arts. 1, 12. (2)-(4), Sch. 2 (with arts. 13-31)

Marginal Citations

M21980 c. 43.

[F4137. AGuidance

(1) The Director of Public Prosecutions may issue guidance—

    (a) for the purpose of enabling custody officers to decide how persons should be dealt with under section 37. (7) above or 37. C(2) [F42or 37. CA(2)] below, and

    (b) as to the information to be sent to the Director of Public Prosecutions under section 37. B(1) below.

(2) The Director of Public Prosecutions may from time to time revise guidance issued under this section.

(3) Custody officers are to have regard to guidance under this section in deciding how persons should be dealt with under section 37. (7) above or 37. C(2) [F43or 37. CA(2)] below.

(4) A report under section 9 of the Prosecution of Offences Act 1985 (report by DPP to Attorney General) must set out the provisions of any guidance issued, and any revisions to guidance made, in the year to which the report relates.

(5) The Director of Public Prosecutions must publish in such manner as he thinks fit—

    (a) any guidance issued under this section, and

    (b) any revisions made to such guidance.

(6) Guidance under this section may make different provision for different cases, circumstances or areas.]

Amendments (Textual)

F41. S. 37. A inserted (29.1.2004) by Criminal Justice Act 2003 (c. 44), ss. 28, 336, Sch. 2 para. 3; S.I. 2004/81, art. 4. (1)(2)(c)

F42. Words in s. 37. A(1)(a) inserted (1.4.2007) by Police and Justice Act 2006 (c. 48), ss. 10, 53, Sch. 6 para. 8. (2); S.I. 2007/709, art. 3. (i) (subject to arts. 6, 7)

F43. Words in s. 37. A(3) inserted (1.4.2007) by Police and Justice Act 2006 (c. 48), ss. 10, 53, Sch. 6 para. 8. (2); S.I. 2007/709, art. 3. (i) (subject to arts. 6, 7)

Modifications etc. (not altering text)

C36. S. 37. A applied (with modifications) (25.6.2013) by The Police and Criminal Evidence Act 1984 (Application to immigration officers and designated customs officials in England and Wales) Order 2013 (S.I. 2013/1542), arts. 1, 12. (2)-(4), Sch. 2 (with arts. 13-31)

C37. Ss. 37-37. B modified (18.4.2005) by Commissioners for Revenue and Customs Act 2005 (c. 11), ss. 50, 53. (1) {Sch. 4 para. 30}; S.I. 2005/1126, art. 2. (2)(h)

Ss. 37-37. B modified (1.4.2006) by Serious Organised Crime and Police Act 2005 (c. 15), ss. 40, 178; S.I. 2006/378, art. 4. (1), Sch. para. 6 (subject to art. 4. (2)-(7))

C38. Ss. 37-37. B modified (21.7.2009) by Borders, Citizenship and Immigration Act 2009 (c. 11), s. 31. (4) (with s. 36. (4))

[F4437. BConsultation with the Director of Public Prosecutions

(1) Where a person is [F45dealt with under section 37. (7)(a)] above, an officer involved in the investigation of the offence shall, as soon as is practicable, send to the Director of Public Prosecutions such information as may be specified in guidance under section 37. A above.

(2) The Director of Public Prosecutions shall decide whether there is sufficient evidence to charge the person with an offence.

(3) If he decides that there is sufficient evidence to charge the person with an offence, he shall decide—

(a) whether or not the person should be charged and, if so, the offence with which he should be charged, and

(b) whether or not the person should be given a caution and, if so, the offence in respect of which he should be given a caution.

(4) The Director of Public Prosecutions [F46shall give notice] of his decision to an officer involved in the investigation of the offence.

[F47. (4. A)Notice under subsection (4) above shall be in writing, but in the case of a person kept in police detention under section 37. (7)(a) above it may be given orally in the first instance and confirmed in writing subsequently.]

(5) If his decision is—

(a) that there is not sufficient evidence to charge the person with an offence, or

(b) that there is sufficient evidence to charge the person with an offence but that the person should not be charged with an offence or given a caution in respect of an offence,

a custody officer shall give the person notice in writing that he is not to be prosecuted.

[F48. (5. A)Subsection (5) does not prevent the prosecution of the person for an offence if new evidence comes to light after the notice was given.]

(6) If the decision of the Director of Public Prosecutions is that the person should be charged with an offence, or given a caution in respect of an offence, the person shall be charged or cautioned accordingly.

(7) But if his decision is that the person should be given a caution in respect of the offence and it proves not to be possible to give the person such a caution [F49 (whether because of section 17 of the Criminal Justice and Courts Act 2015 or for any other reason)] , he shall instead be charged with the offence.

(8) For the purposes of this section, a person is to be charged with an offence either—

[F50. (a)when he is in police detention at a police station (whether because he has returned to answer bail, because he is detained under section 37. (7)(a) above or for some other reason), or]

(b) in accordance with section 29 of the Criminal Justice Act 2003.

F51. (9). . . . .]

Amendments (Textual)

F44. S. 37. B inserted (29.1.2004 for certain purposes, 3.7.2004 for certain further purposes and 1.10.2007 otherwise) by Criminal Justice Act 2003 (c. 44), ss. 28, 336, Sch. 2 para. 3; S.I. 2004/81, art. 4. (1)(2)(c); S.I. 2004/1629, art. 2. (1)(2)(b)(c): S.I. 2007/2874, art. 2

F45. Words in s. 37. B(1) substituted (15.1.2007) by Police and Justice Act 2006 (c. 48), ss. 52, 53, Sch. 14 para. 10. (2); S.I. 2006/3364, art. 2. (j)(k) (as amended by S.I. 2007/29, art. 2)

F46. Words in s. 37. B(4) substituted (15.1.2007) by Police and Justice Act 2006 (c. 48), ss. 52, 53, Sch. 14 para. 10. (3); S.I. 2006/3364, art. 2. (j)(k) (as amended by S.I. 2007/29, art. 2)

F47. S. 37. B(4. A) inserted (15.1.2007) by Police and Justice Act 2006 (c. 48), ss. 52, 53, Sch. 14 para. 10. (4); S.I. 2006/3364, art. 2. (j)(k) (as amended by S.I. 2007/29, art. 2)

F48. S. 37. B(5. A) inserted (31.1.2017 for specified purposes, 3.4.2017 in so far as not already in force) by Policing and Crime Act 2017 (c. 3), ss. 66. (7), 183. (1), (5)(e); S.I. 2017/399, reg. 2, Sch. para. 18

F49. Words in s. 37. B(7) inserted (13.4.2015) by Criminal Justice and Courts Act 2015 (c. 2), ss. 18. (5), 95. (1); S.I. 2015/778, art. 3, Sch. 1 para. 14

F50. S. 37. B(8)(a) substituted (15.1.2007) by Police and Justice Act 2006 (c. 48), ss. 52, 53, Sch. 14 para. 10. (5); S.I. 2006/3364, art. 2. (j)(k) (as amended by S.I. 2007/29, art. 2)

F51. S. 37. B(9) omitted (31.1.2017 for specified purposes, 3.4.2017 in so far as not already in force) by virtue of Policing and Crime Act 2017 (c. 3), ss. 66. (8), 183. (1), (5)(e); S.I. 2017/399, reg. 2, Sch. para. 18

Modifications etc. (not altering text)

C39. Ss. 37-37. B modified (21.7.2009) by Borders, Citizenship and Immigration Act 2009 (c. 11), s. 31. (4) (with s. 36. (4))
C40. Ss. 37-37. B modified (18.4.2005) by Commissioners for Revenue and Customs Act 2005 (c. 11), ss. 50, 53. (1) {Sch. 4 para. 30}; S.I. 2005/1126, art. 2. (2)(h)
Ss. 37-37. B modified (1.4.2006) by Serious Organised Crime and Police Act 2005 (c. 15), ss. 40, 178; S.I. 2006/378, art. 4. (1), Sch. para. 6 (subject to art. 4. (2)-(7))
C41. S. 37. B applied (with modifications) (25.6.2013) by The Police and Criminal Evidence Act 1984 (Application to immigration officers and designated customs officials in England and Wales) Order 2013 (S.I. 2013/1542), arts. 1, 12. (2)-(4), Sch. 2 (with arts. 13-31)

[F5237. CBreach of bail following release under section 37(7)(a)

(1) This section applies where—
   (a) a person released on bail under section 37. (7)(a) above or subsection (2)(b) below is arrested under section 46. A below in respect of that bail, and
   (b) at the time of his detention following that arrest at the police station mentioned in section 46. A(2) below, notice under section 37. B(4) above has not been given.
(2) The person arrested—
   (a) shall be charged, or
   (b) shall be released without charge, either on bail or without bail.
(3) The decision as to how a person is to be dealt with under subsection (2) above shall be that of a custody officer.
(4) A person released on bail under subsection (2)(b) above shall be released on bail subject to the same conditions (if any) which applied immediately before his arrest.]
Amendments (Textual)
F52. S. 37. C inserted (29.1.2004) by Criminal Justice Act 2003 (c. 44), ss. 28, 336, Sch. 2 para. 3; S.I. 2004/81, art. 4. (1)(2)(c)

[F5337. CABreach of bail following release under [F54section 37(7)(c)]

(1) This section applies where a person released on bail under [F55section 37. (7)(c)] above or subsection (2)(b) below—
   (a) is arrested under section 46. A below in respect of that bail, and
   (b) is being detained following that arrest at the police station mentioned in section 46. A(2) below.
(2) The person arrested—
   (a) shall be charged, or
   (b) shall be released without charge [F56—
(i) without bail unless the pre-conditions for bail are satisfied, or
(ii) on bail if those pre-conditions are satisfied.]
(3) The decision as to how a person is to be dealt with under subsection (2) above shall be that of a custody officer.
(4) A person released on bail under subsection (2)(b) above shall be released on bail subject to the same conditions (if any) which applied immediately before his arrest [F57. (and the reference in section 50. A to any conditions of bail which would be imposed is to be read accordingly)].
[F58. (5)Subsection (6) applies where—
   (a) a person is released under subsection (2), and
   (b) a custody officer determines that—
(i) there is not sufficient evidence to charge the person with an offence, or
(ii) there is sufficient evidence to charge the person with an offence but the person should not be

charged with an offence or given a caution in respect of an offence.

(6) The custody officer must give the person notice in writing that the person is not to be prosecuted.

(7) Subsection (6) does not prevent the prosecution of the person for an offence if new evidence comes to light after the notice was given.]]

Amendments (Textual)

F53. S. 37. CA inserted (1.4.2007) by Police and Justice Act 2006 (c. 48), ss. 10, 53, Sch. 6 para. 8. (1); S.I. 2007/709, art. 3. (i) (subject to arts. 6, 7)

F54. Words in s. 37. CA heading substituted (31.1.2017 for specified purposes, 3.4.2017 in so far as not already in force) by Policing and Crime Act 2017 (c. 3), ss. 55. (2), 183. (1), (5)(e); S.I. 2017/399, reg. 2, Sch. para. 12 (with reg. 5)

F55. Words in s. 37. CA(1) substituted (31.1.2017 for specified purposes, 3.4.2017 in so far as not already in force) by Policing and Crime Act 2017 (c. 3), ss. 55. (2), 183. (1), (5)(e); S.I. 2017/399, reg. 2, Sch. para. 12 (with reg. 5)

F56. Words in s. 37. CA(2)(b) substituted (31.1.2017 for specified purposes, 3.4.2017 in so far as not already in force) by Policing and Crime Act 2017 (c. 3), ss. 55. (3), 183. (1), (5)(e); S.I. 2017/399, reg. 2, Sch. para. 12 (with reg. 5)

F57. Words in s. 37. CA(4) inserted (31.1.2017 for specified purposes, 3.4.2017 in so far as not already in force) by Policing and Crime Act 2017 (c. 3), ss. 55. (4), 183. (1), (5)(e); S.I. 2017/399, reg. 2, Sch. para. 12 (with reg. 5)

F58. Ss. 37. CA(5)-(7) inserted (31.1.2017 for specified purposes, 3.4.2017 in so far as not already in force) by Policing and Crime Act 2017 (c. 3), ss. 66. (9), 183. (1), (5)(e); S.I. 2017/399, reg. 2, Sch. para. 18

[F5937. DRelease [F60on bail under section 37]: further provision

F61. (1). . . . .

F61. (2). . . . .

F61. (3). . . . .

(4) Where a person released on bail under section 37. (7)(a) or 37. C(2)(b) above returns to a police station to answer bail or is otherwise in police detention at a police station, he may be kept in police detention to enable him to be dealt with in accordance with section 37. B or 37. C above or to enable the power under [F62section 47. (4. A)] to be exercised.

[F63. (4. A)Where a person released on bail under [F64section 37. (7)(c)] or 37. CA(2)(b) above returns to a police station to answer bail or is otherwise in police detention at a police station, he may be kept in police detention to enable him to be dealt with in accordance with section 37. CA above or to enable the power under [F62section 47. (4. A)] to be exercised.

(5) If the person mentioned in subsection (4) or (4. A) above is not in a fit state to enable him to be dealt with as mentioned in that subsection or to enable the power under [F62section 47. (4. A)] to be exercised, he may be kept in police detention until he is.]

(6) Where a person is kept in police detention by virtue of subsection (4) [F65, (4. A)] or (5) above, section 37. (1) to (3) and (7) above (and section 40. (8) below so far as it relates to section 37. (1) to (3)) shall not apply to the offence in connection with which he was released on bail under section [F6637. (7), 37. C(2)(b) or 37. CA(2)(b)] above.]

Amendments (Textual)

F59. S. 37. D inserted (29.1.2004) by Criminal Justice Act 2003 (c. 44), ss. 28, 336, Sch. 2 para. 3; S.I. 2004/81, art. 4. (1)(2)(c)

F60. Words in s. 37. D heading substituted (1.4.2007) by Police and Justice Act 2006 (c. 48), ss. 10, 53, Sch. 6 para. 9. (2); S.I. 2007/709, art. 3. (i) (subject to arts. 6, 7)

F61. Ss. 37. D(1)-(3) omitted (31.1.2017 for specified purposes, 3.4.2017 in so far as not already in force) by virtue of Policing and Crime Act 2017 (c. 3), ss. 64. (3), 183. (1), (5)(e); S.I. 2017/399, reg. 2, Sch. para. 16 (with reg. 5)Text here

F62. Words in ss. 37. D(4)-(5) substituted (31.1.2017 for specified purposes, 3.4.2017 in so far as not already in force) by Policing and Crime Act 2017 (c. 3), ss. 64. (4), 183. (1), (5)(e); S.I. 2017/399, reg. 2, Sch. para. 16 (with reg. 5)

F63. S. 37. D(4. A)(5) substituted (1.4.2007) for s. 37. D(5) by Police and Justice Act 2006 (c. 48), ss. 10, 53, Sch. 6 para. 10. (2); S.I. 2007/709, art. 3. (i) (subject to arts. 6, 7)

F64. Words in s. 37. D(4. A) substituted (31.1.2017 for specified purposes, 3.4.2017 in so far as not already in force) by Policing and Crime Act 2017 (c. 3), ss. 55. (5), 183. (1), (5)(e); S.I. 2017/399, reg. 2, Sch. para. 12 (with reg. 5)

F65. Word in s. 37. D(6) inserted (1.4.2007) by Police and Justice Act 2006 (c. 48), ss. 10, 53, Sch. 6 para. 10. (3)(a); S.I. 2007/709, art. 3. (i) (subject to arts. 6, 7)

F66. Words in s. 37. D(6) substituted (1.4.2007) by Police and Justice Act 2006 (c. 48), ss. 10, 53, Sch. 6 para. 10. (3)(b); S.I. 2007/709, art. 3. (i) (subject to arts. 6, 7)

38 Duties of custody officer after charge.

(1) Where a person arrested for an offence otherwise than under a warrant endorsed for bail is charged with an offence, the custody officer shall [F67, subject to section 25 of the Criminal Justice and Public Order Act 1994,] order his release from police detention, either on bail or without bail, unless—

(a) If the person arrested is not an arrested juvenile—

(i) his name or address cannot be ascertained or the custody officer has reasonable grounds for doubting whether a name or address furnished by him as his name or address is his real name or address;

F68[F69. (ii)the custody officer has reasonable grounds for believing that the person arrested will fail to appear in court to answer to bail;

(iii) in the case of a person arrested for an imprisonable offence, the custody officer has reasonable grounds for believing that the detention of the person arrested is necessary to prevent him from committing an offence;

[F69. (iiia)in a case where a sample may be taken from the person under section 63. B below, the custody officer has reasonable grounds for believing that the detention of the person is necessary to enable the sample to be taken from him;]

(iv) in the case of a person arrested for an offence which is not an imprisonable offence, the custody officer has reasonable grounds for believing that the detention of the person arrested is necessary to prevent him from causing physical injury to any other person or from causing loss of or damage to property;

(v) the custody officer has reasonable grounds for believing that the detention of the person arrested is necessary to prevent him from interfering with the administration of justice or with the investigation of offences or of a particular offence; or

(vi) the custody officer has reasonable grounds for believing that the detention of the person arrested is necessary for his own protection;]

(b) if he is an arrested juvenile—

(i) any of the requirements of paragraph (a) above is satisfied [F70. (but, in the case of paragraph (a)(iiia) above, only if the arrested juvenile has attained the minimum age)] ; or

(ii) the custody officer has reasonable grounds for believing that he ought to be detained in his own interests.

[F71. (c)the offence with which the person is charged is murder.]

(2) If the release of a person arrested is not required by subsection (1) above, the custody officer may authorise him to be kept in police detention [F72but may not authorise a person to be kept in police detension by virtue of subsection (1)(a)(iiia) after the end of the period of six hours beginning when he was charged with the offence].

F73[(2. A)The custody officer, in taking the decisions required by subsection (1)(a) and (b) above (except (a)(i) and (vi) and (b)(ii)), shall have regard to the same considerations as those which a court is required to have regard to in taking the corresponding decisions under paragraph [F742. (1)] of Part I of Schedule 1 to the M3. Bail Act 1976 [F75. (disregarding [F76paragraphs 1. A and 2. (2)] of that Part)] .]

(3) Where a custody officer authorises a person who has been charged to be kept in police detention, he shall, as soon as practicable, make a written record of the grounds for the detention.

(4) Subject to subsection (5) below, the written record shall be made in the presence of the person charged who shall at that time be informed by the custody officer of the grounds for his detention.

(5) Subsection (4) above shall not apply where the person charged is, at the time when the written record is made—

(a) incapable of understanding what is said to him;

(b) violent or likely to become violent; or

(c) in urgent need of medical attention.

[F77. (6)Where a custody officer authorises an arrested juvenile to be kept in police detention under subsection (1) above, the custody officer shall, unless he certifies—

(a) that, by reason of such circumstances as are specified in the certificate, it is impracticable for him to do so; or

(b) in the case of an arrested juvenile who has attained the [F78age of 12 years], that no secure accommodation is available and that keeping him in other local authority accommodation would not be adequate to protect the public from serious harm from him,

secure that the arrested juvenile is moved to local authority accommodation.]

F77[F79. (6. A)In this section—

"local authority accommodation" means accommodation provided by or on behalf of a local authority (within the meaning of the Children Act 1989);

[F80"minimum age" means the age specified in [F81section 63. B(3)(b) below];]

"secure accommodation" means accommodation provided for the purpose of restricting liberty;

[F82"sexual offence" means an offence specified in Part 2 of Schedule 15 to the Criminal Justice Act 2003;

"violent offence" means murder or an offence specified in Part 1 of that Schedule;]

and any reference, in relation to an arrested juvenile charged with a violent or sexual offence, to protecting the public from serious harm from him shall be construed as a reference to protecting members of the public from death or serious personal injury, whether physical or psychological, occasioned by further such offences committed by him.]

[F79. (6. B)Where an arrested juvenile is moved to local authority accommodation under subsection (6) above, it shall be lawful for any person acting on behalf of the authority to detain him.]

(7) A certificate made under subsection (6) above in respect of an arrested juvenile shall be produced to the court before which he is first brought thereafter.

F83[(7. A)In this section "imprisonable offence" has the same meaning as in Schedule 1 to the Bail Act 1976.]

(8) In this Part of this Act "local authority" has the same meaning as in the [F84. Children Act 1989].

Amendments (Textual)

F67. Words in s. 38. (1) inserted (10.4.1995) by 1994 c. 33, s. 168. (2), Sch. 10 para. 54; S.I. 1995/721, art. 2, Sch.

F68. S. 38. (1)(a)(ii)-(vi) substituted (10.4.1995) for sub-paras (ii)(iii) by 1994 c. 33, s. 28. (2); S.I. 1995/721, art. 2, Sch.

F69. S. 38. (1)(a)(iiia) substituted (1.12.2005) by Drugs Act 2005 (c. 17), ss. 23. (1), 24, Sch. 1 para. 3. (a); S.I. 2005/3053, art. 2. (1)(f)

F70. Words in s. 38. (1)(b)(i) inserted (1.8.2004 for certain purposes and 1.12.2005 for further purposes) by Criminal Justice Act 2003 (c. 44), ss. 5. (2)(a)(ii), 336; S.I. 2004/1867, art. 2; S.I. 2005/3055, art. 2

F71. S. 38. (1)(c) added (1.2.2010) by Coroners and Justice Act 2009 (c. 25), ss. 177. (1), 182, Sch. 21 para. 77 (with s. 180, Sch. 22); S.I. 2010/145, art. 2. (2), Sch. para. 25. (b)

F72. Words in s. 38. (2) inserted (for certain purposes on 20.6.2001, 2.7.2001, 20.5.2002, 2.9.2002, 1.4.2003, 1.4.2004, 1.4.2005 and 1.12.2005) by 2000 c. 43, ss. 57. (3)(b), 80. (1); S.I. 2001/2232, art. 2. (f); S.I. 2002/1149, art. 2; S.I. 2002/1862, art. 2; S.I. 2003/709, art. 2; S.I. 2004/780, art. 2; S.I. 2005/596, art. 2; S.I. 2005/3054, art. 2

F73. S. 38. (2. A) inserted (10.4.1995) by 1994 c. 33, s. 28. (3); S.I. 1995/721, art. 2, Sch.

F74. Words in s. 38. (2. A) substituted (5.4.2004) by Criminal Justice Act 2003 (c. 44), ss. 331, 336, Sch. 36 para. 5. (a); S.I. 2004/829, art. 2. (1)(2)(k)

F75. Words in s. 38. (2. A) inserted (5.4.2004) by Criminal Justice Act 2003 (c. 44), ss. 331, 336, Sch. 36 para. 5. (b); S.I. 2004/829, art. 2. (1)(2)(k)

F76. Words in s. 38. (2. A) substituted (3.12.2012) by Legal Aid, Sentencing and Punishment of Offenders Act 2012 (c. 10), s. 151. (1), Sch. 11 para. 34; S.I. 2012/2906, art. 2. (i)

F77. S. 38. (6)(6. A) substituted (1.10.1992) by Criminal Justice Act 1991 (c. 53), s. 59; S.I. 1992/333, art. 2. (2), Sch. 2.

F78. Words in s. 38. (6)(b) substituted (3.2.1995) by 1994 c. 33, s. 24; S.I. 1995/127, art. 2. (1), Sch. 1

F79. S. 38. (6. A)(6. B) inserted (14.10.1991) by Children Act 1989 (c. 41, SIF 20), s. 108. (5), Sch. 13 para. 53. (2) (with Sch. 14 para. 1. (1)); S.I. 1991/828, art. 3. (2)

F80. S. 38. (6. A): definition of "minimum age" inserted (1.8.2004 for certain purposes and 1.12.2005 for further purposes) by Criminal Justice Act 2003 (c. 44), ss. 5. (2)(b), 336; S.I. 2004/1867, art. 2; S.I. 2005/3055, art. 2

F81. S. 38. (6. A): words in the definition of "minimum age" substituted (1.12.2005) by Drugs Act 2005 (c. 17), ss. 23. (1), 24, Sch. 1 para. 3. (b); S.I. 2005/3053, art. 2. (1)(f)

F82. S. 38. (6. A): definitions of "sexual offence" and "violent offence" substituted (4.4.2005) by Criminal Justice Act 2003 (c. 44), ss. 304, 336, Sch. 32 para. 44; S.I. 2005/950, art. 2. (1), Sch. 1 paras. 23, 42. (20) (subject to art. 2. (2), Sch. 2) (as amended by S.I. 2005/2122, art. 2)

F83. S. 38. (7. A) inserted (10.4.1995) by 1994 c. 33, s. 28. (4); S.I. 1995/721, art. 2, Sch.

F84. Words in s. 38. (8) substituted (14.10.1991) by Children Act 1989 (c. 41, SIF 20), s. 108. (5), Sch. 13 para. 53. (3) (with Sch. 14 para. 1. (1)); S.I. 1991/828, art. 3. (2)

Modifications etc. (not altering text)

C42. S. 38 modified (4.4.2005) by Criminal Justice Act 2003 (c. 44), ss. 88. (1)(a), 336; S.I. 2005/950, art. 2. (1), Sch. 1 para. 5 (subject to art. 2. (2), Sch. 2) (as amended by S.I. 2005/2122, art. 2)

S. 38 modified (4.4.2005) by Criminal Justice Act 2003 (c. 44), ss. 88. (1)(b), 336; S.I. 2005/950, art. 2. (1), Sch. 1 para. 5 (subject to art. 2. (2), Sch. 2) (as amended by S.I. 2005/2122, art. 2)

C43. S. 38 applied (with modifications) by Criminal Justice Act 2003 (c. 44), s. 24. B(1)-(3) (as inserted (29.6.2007) by Police and Justice Act 2006 (c. 48), ss. 18. (1), 53 (with s. 18. (2)); S.I. 2007/1614, art. 2. (e))

Marginal Citations

M31976 c. 63.

39 Responsibilities in relation to persons detained.

(1) Subject to subsections (2) and (4) below, it shall be the duty of the custody officer at a police station to ensure—

(a) that all persons in police detention at that station are treated in accordance with this Act and any code of practice issued under it and relating to the treatment of persons in police detention; and

(b) that all matters relating to such persons which are required by this Act or by such codes of practice to be recorded are recorded in the custody records relating to such persons.

(2) If the custody officer, in accordance with any code of practice issued under this Act, transfers or permits the transfer of a person in police detention—

(a) to the custody of [F85another police officer at the police station where the person is in police detention, for the purpose of an interview that is part of the investigation of an offence for which the person is in police detention or otherwise in connection with the investigation of such an offence]; or

(b) to the custody of an officer who has charge of that person outside the police station, the custody officer shall cease in relation to that person to be subject to the duty imposed on him by subsection (1)(a) above; and it shall be the duty of the officer to whom the transfer is made to ensure that he is treated in accordance with the provisions of this Act and of any such codes of practice as are mentioned in subsection (1) above.

(3) If the person detained is subsequently returned to the custody officer, it shall be the duty of the officer investigating the offence to report to the custody officer as to the manner in which this section and the codes of practice have been complied with while that person was in his custody.

[F86. (3. A)Subsections (3. B) and (3. C) apply if the custody officer, in accordance with any code of practice issued under this Act, transfers or permits the transfer of a person in police detention to an officer mentioned in subsection (2)(a) for the purpose of an interview that is to be conducted to any extent by means of a live link by another police officer who is investigating the offence but is not at the police station where the person in police detention is held at the time of the interview.

(3. B)The officer who is not at the police station has the same duty as the officer mentioned in subsection (2)(a) to ensure that the person is treated in accordance with the provisions of this Act and of any such codes of practice as are mentioned in subsection (1).

(3. C)If the person detained is subsequently returned to the custody of the custody officer, the officer who is not at the police station also has the same duty under subsection (3) as the officer mentioned in subsection (2)(a).

(3. D)For the purpose of subsection (3. C), subsection (3) applies as if the reference to "in his custody" were a reference to "being interviewed".

(3. E)In subsection (3. A), "live link" means an arrangement by which the officer who is not at the police station is able to see and hear, and to be seen and heard by, the person in police detention, any legal representative of that person and the officer who has custody of that person at the police station (and for this purpose any impairment of eyesight or hearing is to be disregarded).]

(4) If an arrested juvenile is [F87moved to local authority accommodation] under section 38. (6) above, the custody officer shall cease in relation to that person to be subject to the duty imposed on him by subsection (1) above.

F88. (5). . . . .

(6) Where—

(a) an officer of higher rank than the custody officer F89. . . gives directions relating to a person in police detention; and

(b) the directions are at variance—

(i) with any decision made or action taken by the custody officer in the performance of a duty imposed on him under this Part of this Act; or

(ii) with any decision or action which would but for the directions have been made or taken by him in the performance of such a duty,

the custody officer shall refer the matter at once to an officer of the rank of superintendent or above who is responsible for the police station for which the custody officer is acting as custody officer.

(7) F90. . . . .

Amendments (Textual)

F85. Words in s. 39. (2)(a) substituted (31.1.2017 for specified purposes, 3.4.2017 in so far as not already in force) by Policing and Crime Act 2017 (c. 3), ss. 75. (2), 183. (1), (5)(e); S.I. 2017/399, reg. 2, Sch. para. 24

F86. S. 39. (3. A)-(3. E) inserted (31.1.2017 for specified purposes, 3.4.2017 in so far as not already in force) by Policing and Crime Act 2017 (c. 3), ss. 75. (3), 183. (1), (5)(e); S.I. 2017/399, reg. 2, Sch. para. 24

F87. Words in s. 39. (4) substituted (14.10.1991) by Children Act 1989 (c. 41, SIF 20), s. 108. (5), Sch. 13, para. 54; S.I. 1991/828, art. 3. (2)

F88. S. 39. (5) repealed (14.10.1991) by Children Act 1989 (c. 41, SIF 20), s. 108. (7), Sch.15; S.I. 1991/828, art. 3. (2)

F89. Words in s. 39. (6)(a) repealed (12.1.2010) by Policing and Crime Act 2009 (c. 26), ss. 112. (1)(2), 116. (6), Sch. 7 para. 123. (4)(a), Sch. 8 Pt. 13

F90. S. 39. (7) repealed (12.1.2010) by Policing and Crime Act 2009 (c. 26), ss. 112. (1)(2), 116. (6), Sch. 7 para. 123. (4)(b), Sch. 8 Pt. 13

Modifications etc. (not altering text)

C44. Ss. 8, 9, 15, 16, 17. (1)(b(2) (4), 18–20, 21, 22. (1)–(4), 28, 29, 30. (1)–(4)(a)(5)–(11), 31, 32. (1)–(9), 34. (1)–(5), 35, 36, 37, 39, 40–44, 50, 51. (d), 52, 54, 55, 64. (1)–(4)(5)(6), Sch. 1 applied with modifications by S.I. 1985/1800, arts. 3–11, Schs. 1, 2

C45. S. 39 modified (2.8.1993) by S.I. 1993/1813, art. 6, Sch. 3 para. 3. (3).

S. 39 extended (27.7.1999) by 1999 c. 23, ss. 61. (3), 68. (4)(e) (with s. 63. (2), Sch. 7 paras. 3. (3), 5. (2))

C46. S. 39 applied (with modifications) by Criminal Justice Act 2003 (c. 44), s. 24. B(1)-(3) (as inserted (29.6.2007) by Police and Justice Act 2006 (c. 48), ss. 18. (1), 53 (with s. 18. (2)); S.I. 2007/1614, art. 2. (e))

C47. S. 39 applied (with modifications) (25.6.2013) by The Police and Criminal Evidence Act 1984 (Application to immigration officers and designated customs officials in England and Wales) Order 2013 (S.I. 2013/1542), arts. 1, 12. (2)-(4), Sch. 2 (with arts. 13-31)

C48. S. 39 applied (with modifications) (4.11.2015) by The Police and Criminal Evidence Act 1984 (Application to Revenue and Customs) Order 2015 (S.I. 2015/1783), arts. 1, 3. (1), Sch. 1 (with art. 3. (2), (3), 4-19, Sch. 2)

C49. S. 39. (2) modified (2.12.2002) by Police Reform Act 2002 (c. 30), s. 38, Sch. 4 Pt. 4 para. 35. (5); S.I. 2002/2750, art. 2. (a)(ii)(d)

S. 39. (2)(3) modified (2.12.2002) by Police Reform Act 2002 (c. 30), s. 38, Sch. 4 Pt. 2 para. 22. (3); S.I. 2002/2750, art. 2. (a)(ii)(d)

40 Review of police detention.

(1) Reviews of the detention of each person in police detention in connection with the investigation of an offence shall be carried out periodically in accordance with the following provisions of this section—

(a) in the case of a person who has been arrested and charged, by the custody officer; and

(b) in the case of a person who has been arrested but not charged, by an officer of at least the rank of inspector who has not been directly involved in the investigation.

(2) The officer to whom it falls to carry out a review is referred to in this section as a "review officer".

(3) Subject to subsection (4) below—

(a) the first review shall be not later than six hours after the detention was first authorised;

(b) the second review shall be not later than nine hours after the first;

(c) subsequent reviews shall be at intervals of not more than nine hours.

(4) A review may be postponed—

(a) if, having regard to all the circumstances prevailing at the latest time for it specified in subsection (3) above, it is not practicable to carry out the review at that time;

(b) without prejudice to the generality of paragraph (a) above—

(i) if at that time the person in detention is being questioned by a police officer and the review officer is satisfied that an interruption of the questioning for the purpose of carrying out the review would prejudice the investigation in connection with which he is being questioned; or

(ii) if at that time no review officer is readily available.

(5) If a review is postponed under subsection (4) above it shall be carried out as soon as practicable after the latest time specified for it in subsection (3) above.

(6) If a review is carried out after postponement under subsection (4) above, the fact that it was so

carried out shall not affect any requirement of this section as to the time at which any subsequent review is to be carried out.

(7) The review officer shall record the reasons for any postponement of a review in the custody record.

(8) Subject to subsection (9) below, where the person whose detention is under review has not been charged before the time of the review, section 37. (1) to (6) above shall have effect in relation to him, but with [F91the modifications specified in subsection (8. A)]

[F92. (8. A)The modifications are—

(a) the substitution of references to the person whose detention is under review for references to the person arrested;

(b) the substitution of references to the review officer for references to the custody officer; and

(c) in subsection (6), the insertion of the following paragraph after paragraph (a)—
"(aa)asleep;"]

(9) Where a person has been kept in police detention by virtue of section 37. (9) [F93or 37. D(5)] above, section 37. (1) to (6) shall not have effect in relation to him but it shall be the duty of the review officer to determine whether he is yet in a fit state.

(10) Where the person whose detention is under review has been charged before the time of the review, section 38. (1) to [F94. (6. B)] above shall have effect in relation to him, but with [F95the modifications specified in subsection (10. A)] .

[F96. (10. A)The modifications are—

(a) the substitution of a reference to the person whose detention is under review for any reference to the person arrested or to the person charged; and

(b) in subsection (5), the insertion of the following paragraph after paragraph (a)—
"(aa)asleep;"]

(11) Where—

(a) an officer of higher rank than the review officer gives directions relating to a person in police detention; and

(b) the directions are at variance—

(i) with any decision made or action taken by the review officer in the performance of a duty imposed on him under this Part of this Act; or

(ii) with any decision or action which would but for the directions have been made or taken by him in the performance of such a duty,

the review officer shall refer the matter at once to an officer of the rank of superintendent or above who is responsible for the police station for which the review officer is acting as review officer in connection with the detention.

(12) Before determining whether to authorise a person's continued detention the review officer shall give—

(a) that person (unless he is asleep); or

(b) any solicitor representing him who is available at the time of the review,

an opportunity to make representations to him about the detention.

(13) Subject to subsection (14) below, the person whose detention is under review or his solicitor may make representations under subsection (12) above either orally or in writing.

(14) The review officer may refuse to hear oral representations from the person whose detention is under review if he considers that he is unfit to make such representations by reason of his condition or behaviour.

Amendments (Textual)

F91. Words in s. 40. (8) substituted (1.4.2003) by Police Reform Act 2002 (c. 30), ss. {52. (1)}, 108. (2)-(5); S.I. 2003/808, art. 2. (d)

F92. S. 40. (8. A) inserted (1.4.2003) by Police Reform Act 2002 (c. 30), ss. {52. (2)}, 108. (2)-(5); S.I. 2003/808, art. 2. (d)

F93. Words in s. 40. (9) inserted (29.1.2004) by Criminal Justice Act 2003 (c. 44), ss. 28, 336, Sch. 2 para. 4; S.I. 2004/81, art. 4. (1)(2)(c)

F94. Word in s. 40. (10) substituted (1.4.2003) by Police Reform Act 2002 (c. 30), ss. {52. (3)(a)},

108. (2)-(5); S.I. 2003/808, art. 2. (d)

F95. Words in s. 40. (10) substituted (1.4.2003) by Police Reform Act 2002 (c. 30), ss. {52. (3)(b)}, 108. (2)-(5); S.I. 2003/808, art. 2. (d)

F96. S. 40. (10. A) inserted (1.4.2003) by Police Reform Act 2002 (c. 30), ss. {52. (4)}, 108. (2)-(5); S.I. 2003/808, art. 2. (d)

Modifications etc. (not altering text)

C50. Ss. 8, 9, 15, 16, 17. (1)(b(2) (4), 18–20, 21, 22. (1)–(4), 28, 29, 30. (1)–(4)(a)(5)–(11), 31, 32. (1)–(9), 34. (1)–(5), 35, 36, 37, 39, 40–44, 50, 51. (d), 52, 54, 55, 64. (1)–(4)(5)(6), Sch. 1 applied with modifications by S.I. 1985/1800, arts. 3–11, Schs. 1, 2

C51. S. 40 modified (2.8.1993) by S.I. 1993/1813, art. 6, Sch. 3 paras. 3. (3), 4. (4)(b), 5. (7)(b), 6. (7)(b); s. 40 modified by the said S.I. 1993/1813, art. 6, Sch. 3 paras. 4, 5, 6 as incorporated (with modifications) (1.12.1997) by S.I. 1994/1405, art. 6, Sch. 3 paras. 5, 6, 7

C52. S. 40 applied (with modifications) by Criminal Justice Act 2003 (c. 44), s. 24. B(4) (as inserted (29.6.2007) by Police and Justice Act 2006 (c. 48), ss. 18. (1), 53 (with s. 18. (2)); S.I. 2007/1614, art. 2. (e))

C53. S. 40 applied (with modifications) (4.11.2015) by The Police and Criminal Evidence Act 1984 (Application to Revenue and Customs) Order 2015 (S.I. 2015/1783), arts. 1, 3. (1), Sch. 1 (with art. 3. (2), (3), 4-19, Sch. 2)

C54. S. 40. (1)-(9) applied (with modifications) (25.6.2013) by The Police and Criminal Evidence Act 1984 (Application to immigration officers and designated customs officials in England and Wales) Order 2013 (S.I. 2013/1542), arts. 1, 12. (2)-(4), Sch. 2 (with arts. 13-31)

C55. S. 40. (11)-(14) applied (with modifications) (25.6.2013) by The Police and Criminal Evidence Act 1984 (Application to immigration officers and designated customs officials in England and Wales) Order 2013 (S.I. 2013/1542), arts. 1, 12. (2)-(4), Sch. 2 (with arts. 13-31)

C56. S. 40. (13) amended by S.I. 1991/2684, arts. 1, 2, 4 and Sch.1

C57. S. 40. (13) applied (with modifications) (23.12.2011) by The Legal Services Act 2007 (Designation as a Licensing Authority) (No. 2) Order 2011 (S.I. 2011/2866), art. 1. (2), Sch. 2

[F9740. A Use of telephone for review under s. 40.

[F98. (1)A review under section 40. (1)(b) may be carried out by means of a discussion, conducted by telephone, with one or more persons at the police station where the arrested person is held.

(2) But subsection (1) does not apply if—

(a) the review is of a kind authorised by regulations under section 45. A to be carried out using[F99a live link]; and

(b) it is reasonably practicable to carry it out in accordance with those regulations.]

(3) Where any review is carried out under this section by an officer who is not present at the station where the arrested person is held—

(a) any obligation of that officer to make a record in connection with the carrying out of the review shall have effect as an obligation to cause another officer to make the record;

(b) any requirement for the record to be made in the presence of the arrested person shall apply to the making of that record by that other officer; and

(c) the requirements under section 40. (12) and (13) above for—

(i) the arrested person, or

(ii) a solicitor representing him,

to be given any opportunity to make representations (whether in writing or orally) to that officer shall have effect as a requirement for that person, or such a solicitor, to be given an opportunity to make representations in a manner authorised by subsection (4) below.

(4) Representations are made in a manner authorised by this subsection—

(a) in a case where facilities exist for the immediate transmission of written representations to the officer carrying out the review, if they are made either—

(i) orally by telephone to that officer; or

(ii) in writing to that officer by means of those facilities;
and
    (b) in any other case, if they are made orally by telephone to that officer.
(5) In this section "[F100live link]" has the same meaning as in section 45. A below.]
Amendments (Textual)
F97. S. 40. A inserted (1.10.2001) by 2001 c. 16, s. 72. (3); S.I. 2001/3150, art. 2. (a)
F98. S. 40. A(1)(2) substituted (20.1.2004) by Criminal Justice Act 2003 (c. 44), ss. 6, 336; S.I. 2004/81, art. 2. (1)(2)(a)
F99. Words in s. 40. A(2)(a) substituted (31.1.2017 for specified purposes, 3.4.2017 in so far as not already in force) by Policing and Crime Act 2017 (c. 3), ss., 74. (5)(a), 183. (5)(e); S.I. 2017/399, reg. 2, Sch. para. 23
F100. Words in s. 40. A(5) substituted (31.1.2017 for specified purposes, 3.4.2017 in so far as not already in force) by Policing and Crime Act 2017 (c. 3), ss., 75. (5)(b), 183. (5)(e); S.I. 2017/399, reg. 2, Sch. para. 24
Modifications etc. (not altering text)
C58. S. 40. A(1) applied (with modifications) (25.6.2013) by The Police and Criminal Evidence Act 1984 (Application to immigration officers and designated customs officials in England and Wales) Order 2013 (S.I. 2013/1542), arts. 1, 12. (2)-(4), Sch. 2 (with arts. 13-31)
C59. S. 40. A(3)(4) applied (with modifications) (25.6.2013) by The Police and Criminal Evidence Act 1984 (Application to immigration officers and designated customs officials in England and Wales) Order 2013 (S.I. 2013/1542), arts. 1, 12. (2)-(4), Sch. 2 (with arts. 13-31)

41 Limits on period of detention without charge.

(1) Subject to the following provisions of this section and to sections 42 and 43 below, a person shall not be kept in police detention for more than 24 hours without being charged.
(2) The time from which the period of detention of a person is to be calculated (in this Act referred to as "the relevant time")—
    (a) in the case of a person to whom this paragraph applies, shall be—
(i) the time at which that person arrives at the relevant police station; or
(ii) the time 24 hours after the time of that person's arrest,
whichever is the earlier;
    (b) in the case of a person arrested outside England and Wales, shall be—
(i) the time at which that person arrives at the first police station to which he is taken in the police area in England or Wales in which the offence for which he was arrested is being investigated; or
(ii) the time 24 hours after the time of that person's entry into England and Wales,
whichever is the earlier;
    (c) in the case of a person who—
(i) attends voluntarily at a police station; or
(ii) accompanies a constable to a police station without having been arrested,
and is arrested at the police station, the time of his arrest;
    [F101. (ca)in the case of a person who attends a police station to answer to bail granted under section 30. A, the time when he arrives at the police station;]
    (d) in any other case, except where subsection (5) below applies, shall be the time at which the person arrested arrives at the first police station to which he is taken after his arrest.
(3) Subsection (2)(a) above applies to a person if—
    (a) his arrest is sought in one police area in England and Wales;
    (b) he is arrested in another police area; and
    (c) he is not questioned in the area in which he is arrested in order to obtain evidence in relation to an offence for which he is arrested;
and in sub-paragraph (i) of that paragraph "the relevant police station" means the first police station to which he is taken in the police area in which his arrest was sought.

(4) Subsection (2) above shall have effect in relation to a person arrested under section 31 above as if every reference in it to his arrest or his being arrested were a reference to his arrest or his being arrested for the offence for which he was originally arrested.

(5) If—

(a) a person is in police detention in a police area in England and Wales ("the first area"); and

(b) his arrest for an offence is sought in some other police area in England and Wales ("the second area"); and

(c) he is taken to the second area for the purposes of investigating that offence, without being questioned in the first area in order to obtain evidence in relation to it,

the relevant time shall be—

(i) the time 24 hours after he leaves the place where he is detained in the first area; or

(ii) the time at which he arrives at the first police station to which he is taken in the second area, whichever is the earlier.

(6) When a person who is in police detention is removed to hospital because he is in need of medical treatment, any time during which he is being questioned in hospital or on the way there or back by a police officer for the purpose of obtaining evidence relating to an offence shall be included in any period which falls to be calculated for the purposes of this Part of this Act, but any other time while he is in hospital or on his way there or back shall not be so included.

(7) Subject to subsection (8) below, a person who at the expiry of 24 hours after the relevant time is in police detention and has not been charged shall be released at that time [F102—

(a) without bail unless the pre-conditions for bail are satisfied, or

(b) on bail if those pre-conditions are satisfied.]

(8) Subsection (7) above does not apply to a person whose detention for more than 24 hours after the relevant time has been authorised or is otherwise permitted in accordance with section 42 or 43 below.

(9) A person released under subsection (7) above shall not be re-arrested without a warrant for the offence for which he was previously arrested unless [F103, since the person's release, new evidence has come to light or an examination or analysis of existing evidence has been made which could not reasonably have been made before] his release[F104; but this subsection does not prevent an arrest under section 46. A below.]

[F105. (10)Subsection (11) applies where—

(a) a person is released under subsection (7), and

(b) a custody officer determines that—

(i) there is not sufficient evidence to charge the person with an offence, or

(ii) there is sufficient evidence to charge the person with an offence but the person should not be charged with an offence or given a caution in respect of an offence.

(11) The custody officer must give the person notice in writing that the person is not to be prosecuted.

(12) Subsection (11) does not prevent the prosecution of the person for an offence if new evidence comes to light after the notice was given.]

Amendments (Textual)

F101. S. 41. (2)(ca) inserted (20.1.2004) by Criminal Justice Act 2003 (c. 44), ss. 12, 336, Sch. 1 para. 8; S.I. 2004/81, art. 2. (1)(2)(a)

F102. Words in s. 41. (7) substituted (31.1.2017 for specified purposes, 3.4.2017 in so far as not already in force) by Policing and Crime Act 2017 (c. 3), ss. 56. (1), 183. (1), (5)(e); S.I. 2017/399, reg. 2, Sch. para. 12 (with reg. 5)

F103. Words in s. 41. (9) substituted (31.1.2017 for specified purposes, 3.4.2017 in so far as not already in force) by Policing and Crime Act 2017 (c. 3), ss. 65. (3), 183. (1), (5)(e); S.I. 2017/399, reg. 2, Sch. para. 17 (with reg. 5)

F104. Words in s. 41. (9) inserted (10.4.1995) by 1994 c. 33, s. 29. (4)(b)(5); S.I. 1995/721, art. 2,Sch.

F105. S. 41. (10)-(12) inserted (31.1.2017 for specified purposes, 3.4.2017 in so far as not already in force) by Policing and Crime Act 2017 (c. 3), ss. 67. (2), 183. (1), (5)(e); S.I. 2017/399, reg. 2,

Sch. para. 18

Modifications etc. (not altering text)

C60. Ss. 8, 9, 15, 16, 17. (1)(b)(2) (4), 18–20, 21, 22. (1)–(4), 28, 29, 30. (1)–(4)(a)(5)–(11), 31, 32. (1)–(9), 34. (1)–(5), 35, 36, 37, 39, 40–44, 50, 51. (d), 52, 54, 55, 64. (1)–(4)(5)(6), Sch. 1 applied with modifications by S.I. 1985/1800, arts. 3–11, Schs. 1, 2

C61. S. 41 extended (2.8.1993) by S.I. 1993/1813, art. 6, Sch. 3 para. 2. (6); s. 41 extended by the said S.I. 1993/1813, art. 6, Sch. 3 paras. 2, 5, 6 as incorporated (with modifications) (1.12.1997) by S.I. 1994/1405, art. 6, Sch. 3 paras. 3, 6, 7

S. 41 modified (2.8.1993) by S.I. 1993/1813, art. 6, Sch. 3 paras. 3. (3), 4. (4)(b), 5. (7)(b), 6. (7)(b); s. 41 modified by the said S.I. 1993/1813, art. 6, Sch. 3 paras. 4, 5, 6 as incorporated (with modifications) (1.12.1997) by S.I. 1994/1405, art. 6, Sch. 3 paras. 5, 6, 7

C62. S. 41. (1)(2)(b)(c)(d)(4)-(9) applied (with modifications) (25.6.2013) by The Police and Criminal Evidence Act 1984 (Application to immigration officers and designated customs officials in England and Wales) Order 2013 (S.I. 2013/1542), arts. 1, 12. (2)-(4), Sch. 2 (with arts. 13-31)

C63. S. 41. (1)(2)(4)(6)-(9) applied (with modifications) (4.11.2015) by The Police and Criminal Evidence Act 1984 (Application to Revenue and Customs) Order 2015 (S.I. 2015/1783), arts. 1, 3. (1), Sch. 1 (with art. 3. (2), (3), 4-19, Sch. 2)

42 Authorisation of continued detention.

(1) Where a police officer of the rank of superintendent or above who is responsible for the police station at which a person is detained has reasonable grounds for believing that—

(a) the detention of that person without charge is necessary to secure or preserve evidence relating to an offence for which he is under arrest or to obtain such evidence by questioning him;

[F106. (b)an offence for which he is under arrest is an [F107indictable] offence; and]

(c) the investigation is being conducted diligently and expeditiously,

he may authorise the keeping of that person in police detention for a period expiring at or before 36 hours after the relevant time.

(2) Where an officer such as is mentioned in subsection (1) above has authorised the keeping of a person in police detention for a period expiring less than 36 hours after the relevant time, such an officer may authorise the keeping of that person in police detention for a further period expiring not more than 36 hours after that time if the conditions specified in subsection (1) above are still satisfied when he gives the authorisation.

(3) If it is proposed to transfer a person in police detention to another police area, the officer determining whether or not to authorise keeping him in detention under subsection (1) above shall have regard to the distance and the time the journey would take.

(4) No authorisation under subsection (1) above shall be given in respect of any person—

(a) more than 24 hours after the relevant time; or

(b) before the second review of his detention under section 40 above has been carried out.

(5) Where an officer authorises the keeping of a person in police detention under subsection (1) above, it shall be his duty—

(a) to inform that person of the grounds for his continued detention; and

(b) to record the grounds in that person's custody record.

(6) Before determining whether to authorise the keeping of a person in detention under subsection (1) or (2) above, an officer shall give—

(a) that person; or

(b) any solicitor representing him who is available at the time when it falls to the officer to determine whether to give the authorisation,

an opportunity to make representations to him about the detention.

(7) Subject to subsection (8) below, the person in detention or his solicitor may make representations under subsection (6) above either orally or in writing.

(8) The officer to whom it falls to determine whether to give the authorisation may refuse to hear

oral representations from the person in detention if he considers that he is unfit to make such representations by reason of his condition or behaviour.

(9) Where—

(a) an officer authorises the keeping of a person in detention under subsection (1) above; and

(b) at the time of the authorisation he has not yet exercised a right conferred on him by section 56 or 58 below,

the officer—

(i) shall inform him of that right;

(ii) shall decide whether he should be permitted to exercise it;

(iii) shall record the decision in his custody record; and

(iv) if the decision is to refuse to permit the exercise of the right, shall also record the grounds for the decision in that record.

(10) Where an officer has authorised the keeping of a person who has not been charged in detention under subsection (1) or (2) above, he shall be released from detentionF108..., not later than 36 hours after the relevant time [F109—

(a) without bail unless the pre-conditions for bail are satisfied, or

(b) on bail if those pre-conditions are satisfied,

(subject to subsection (10. A))].

[F110. (10. A)Subsection (10) does not apply if—

(a) the person has been charged with an offence, or

(b) the person's continued detention is authorised or otherwise permitted in accordance with section 43.]

(11) A person released under subsection (10) above shall not be re-arrested without a warrant for the offence for which he was previously arrested unless [F111, since the person's release, new evidence has come to light or an examination or analysis of existing evidence has been made which could not reasonably have been made before] his release[F112; but this subsection does not prevent an arrest under section 46. A below.]

[F113. (12)Subsection (13) applies where—

(a) a person is released under subsection (10), and

(b) a custody officer determines that—

(i) there is not sufficient evidence to charge the person with an offence, or

(ii) there is sufficient evidence to charge the person with an offence but the person should not be charged with an offence or given a caution in respect of an offence.

(13) The custody officer must give the person notice in writing that the person is not to be prosecuted.

(14) Subsection (13) does not prevent the prosecution of the person for an offence if new evidence comes to light after the notice was given.]

Amendments (Textual)

F106. S. 42. (1)(b) substituted (20.1.2004) by Criminal Justice Act 2003 (c. 44), ss. 7, 336; S.I. 2004/81, art. 2. (1)(2)(a)

F107. Word in s. 42. (1)(b) substituted (1.1.2006) by Serious Organised Crime and Police Act 2005 (c. 15), ss. 111, 178, Sch. 7 Pt. 3 para. 43. (7); S.I. 2005/3495, art. 2. (1)(m)

F108. Words in s. 42. (10) omitted (31.1.2017 for specified purposes, 3.4.2017 in so far as not already in force) by virtue of Policing and Crime Act 2017 (c. 3), ss. 56. (3)(a), 183. (1), (5)(e); S.I. 2017/399, reg. 2, Sch. para. 12 (with reg. 5)

F109. Words in s. 42. (10) substituted (31.1.2017 for specified purposes, 3.4.2017 in so far as not already in force) by Policing and Crime Act 2017 (c. 3), ss. 56. (3)(b), 183. (1), (5)(e); S.I. 2017/399, reg. 2, Sch. para. 12 (with reg. 5)

F110. S. 42. (10. A) inserted (31.1.2017 for specified purposes, 3.4.2017 in so far as not already in force) by Policing and Crime Act 2017 (c. 3), ss. 56. (4), 183. (1), (5)(e); S.I. 2017/399, reg. 2, Sch. para. 12 (with reg. 5)

F111. Words in s. 42. (11) substituted (31.1.2017 for specified purposes, 3.4.2017 in so far as not already in force) by Policing and Crime Act 2017 (c. 3), ss. 65. (4), 183. (1), (5)(e); S.I. 2017/399, reg. 2, Sch. para. 17 (with reg. 5)

F112. Words in s. 42. (11) inserted (10.4.1995) by 1994 c. 33, s. 29. (4)(b)(5); S.I. 1995/721, art. 2, Sch.

F113. S. 42. (12)-(14) inserted (31.1.2017 for specified purposes, 3.4.2017 in so far as not already in force) by Policing and Crime Act 2017 (c. 3), ss. 67. (3), 183. (1), (5)(e); S.I. 2017/399, reg. 2, Sch. para. 18

Modifications etc. (not altering text)

C64. Ss. 8, 9, 15, 16, 17. (1)(b(2) (4), 18–20, 21, 22. (1)–(4), 28, 29, 30. (1)–(4)(a)(5)–(11), 31, 32. (1)–(9), 34. (1)–(5), 35, 36, 37, 39, 40–44, 50, 51. (d), 52, 54, 55, 64. (1)–(4)(5)(6), Sch. 1 applied with modifications by S.I. 1985/1800, arts. 3–11, Schs. 1, 2

C65s. 42 modified (2.8.1993) by S.I. 1993/1813, art. 6, Sch. 3 paras. 3. (3), 4. (4)(b), 5. (7)(b), 6. (7)(b); s. 42 modified by the said S.I. 1993/1813, art. 6, Sch. 3 paras. 4, 5, 6 as incorporated (with modifications) (1.12.1997) by S.I. 1994/1405, art. 6, Sch. 3 paras. 5, 6, 7

C66. S. 42 applied (with modifications) (25.6.2013) by The Police and Criminal Evidence Act 1984 (Application to immigration officers and designated customs officials in England and Wales) Order 2013 (S.I. 2013/1542), arts. 1, 12. (2)-(4), Sch. 2 (with arts. 13-31)

C67. S. 42. (1)(2) applied (with modifications) (4.11.2015) by The Police and Criminal Evidence Act 1984 (Application to Revenue and Customs) Order 2015 (S.I. 2015/1783), arts. 1, 3. (1), Sch. 1 (with art. 3. (2), (3), 4-19, Sch. 2)

C68. S. 42. (4)-(11) applied (with modifications) (4.11.2015) by The Police and Criminal Evidence Act 1984 (Application to Revenue and Customs) Order 2015 (S.I. 2015/1783), arts. 1, 3. (1), Sch. 1 (with art. 3. (2), (3), 4-19, Sch. 2)

C69. S. 42. (7) amended by S.I. 1991/2684, arts. 1, 2, 4 and Sch. 1

C70. S. 42. (7) applied (with modifications) (23.12.2011) by The Legal Services Act 2007 (Designation as a Licensing Authority) (No. 2) Order 2011 (S.I. 2011/2866), art. 1. (2), Sch. 2

43 Warrants of further detention.

(1) Where, on an application on oath made by a constable and supported by an information, a magistrates' court is satisfied that there are reasonable grounds for believing that the further detention of the person to whom the application relates is justified, it may issue a warrant of further detention authorising the keeping of that person in police detention.

(2) A court may not hear an application for a warrant of further detention unless the person to whom the application relates—

  (a) has been furnished with a copy of the information; and

  (b) has been brought before the court for the hearing.

(3) The person to whom the application relates shall be entitled to be legally represented at the hearing and, if he is not so represented but wishes to be so represented—

  (a) the court shall adjourn the hearing to enable him to obtain representation; and

  (b) he may be kept in police detention during the adjournment.

(4) A person's further detention is only justified for the purposes of this section or section 44 below if—

  (a) his detention without charge is necessary to secure or preserve evidence relating to an offence for which he is under arrest or to obtain such evidence by questioning him;

  (b) an offence for which he is under arrest is [F114an indictable offence] ; and

  (c) the investigation is being conducted diligently and expeditiously.

(5) Subject to subsection (7) below, an application for a warrant of further detention may be made—

  (a) at any time before the expiry of 36 hours after the relevant time; or

  (b) in a case where—

(i) it is not practicable for the magistrates' court to which the application will be made to sit at the expiry of 36 hours after the relevant time; but

(ii) the court will sit during the 6 hours following the end of that period,
at any time before the expiry of the said 6 hours.
(6) In a case to which subsection (5)(b) above applies—
    (a) the person to whom the application relates may be kept in police detention until the application is heard; and
    (b) the custody officer shall make a note in that person's custody record—
(i) of the fact that he was kept in police detention for more than 36 hours after the relevant time; and
(ii) of the reason why he was so kept.
(7) If—
    (a) an application for a warrant of further detention is made after the expiry of 36 hours after the relevant time; and
    (b) it appears to the magistrates' court that it would have been reasonable for the police to make it before the expiry of that period,
the court shall dismiss the application.
(8) Where on an application such as is mentioned in subsection (1) above a magistrates' court is not satisfied that there are reasonable grounds for believing that the further detention of the person to whom the application relates is justified, it shall be its duty—
    (a) to refuse the application; or
    (b) to adjourn the hearing of it until a time not later than 36 hours after the relevant time.
(9) The person to whom the application relates may be kept in police detention during the adjournment.
(10) A warrant of further detention shall—
    (a) state the time at which it is issued;
    (b) authorise the keeping in police detention of the person to whom it relates for the period stated in it.
(11) Subject to subsection (12) below, the period stated in a warrant of further detention shall be such period as the magistrates' court thinks fit, having regard to the evidence before it.
(12) The period shall not be longer than 36 hours.
(13) If it is proposed to transfer a person in police detention to a police area other than that in which he is detained when the application for a warrant of further detention is made, the court hearing the application shall have regard to the distance and the time the journey would take.
(14) Any information submitted in support of an application under this section shall state—
    (a) the nature of the offence for which the person to whom the application relates has been arrested;
    (b) the general nature of the evidence on which that person was arrested;
    (c) what inquiries relating to the offence have been made by the police and what further inquiries are proposed by them;
    (d) the reasons for believing the continued detention of that person to be necessary for the purposes of such further inquiries.
(15) Where an application under this section is refused, the person to whom the application relates shall forthwith be charged or, subject to subsection (16) below, released [F115—
    (a) without bail unless the pre-conditions for bail are satisfied, or
    (b) on bail if those pre-conditions are satisfied.]
(16) A person need not be released under subsection (15) above—
    (a) before the expiry of 24 hours after the relevant time; or
    (b) before the expiry of any longer period for which his continued detention is or has been authorised under section 42 above.
(17) Where an application under this section is refused, no further application shall be made under this section in respect of the person to whom the refusal relates, unless supported by evidence which has come to light since the refusal.
(18) Where a warrant of further detention is issued, the person to whom it relates shall [F116, unless the person is charged, be released from police detention upon or before the expiry of the

warrant—
(a) without bail unless the pre-conditions for bail are satisfied, or
(b) on bail if those pre-conditions are satisfied.]
(19) A person released under subsection (18) above shall not be re-arrested without a warrant for the offence for which he was previously arrested unless [F117, since the person's release, new evidence has come to light or an examination or analysis of existing evidence has been made which could not reasonably have been made before] his release[F118; but this subsection does not prevent an arrest under section 46. A below.]
[F119. (20)Subsection (21) applies where—
(a) a person is released under subsection (15) or (18), and
(b) a custody officer determines that—
(i) there is not sufficient evidence to charge the person with an offence, or
(ii) there is sufficient evidence to charge the person with an offence but the person should not be charged with an offence or given a caution in respect of an offence.
(21) The custody officer must give the person notice in writing that the person is not to be prosecuted.
(22) Subsection (21) does not prevent the prosecution of the person for an offence if new evidence comes to light after the notice was given.]
Amendments (Textual)
F114. Words in s. 43. (4)(b) substituted (1.1.2006) by Serious Organised Crime and Police Act 2005 (c. 15), ss. 111, 178, Sch. 7 Pt. 3 para. 43. (8); S.I. 2005/3495, art. 2. (1)(m)
F115. Words in s. 43. (15) substituted (31.1.2017 for specified purposes, 3.4.2017 in so far as not already in force) by Policing and Crime Act 2017 (c. 3), ss. 57. (2), 183. (1), (5)(e); S.I. 2017/399, reg. 2, Sch. para. 12 (with reg. 5)
F116. Words in s. 43. (18) substituted (31.1.2017 for specified purposes, 3.4.2017 in so far as not already in force) by Policing and Crime Act 2017 (c. 3), ss. 57. (3), 183. (1), (5)(e); S.I. 2017/399, reg. 2, Sch. para. 12 (with reg. 5)
F117. Words in s. 43. (19) substituted (31.1.2017 for specified purposes, 3.4.2017 in so far as not already in force) by Policing and Crime Act 2017 (c. 3), ss. 65. (5), 183. (1), (5)(e); S.I. 2017/399, reg. 2, Sch. para. 17 (with reg. 5)
F118. Words in s. 43. (19) inserted (10.4.1995) by 1994 c. 33, s. 29. (4)(b)(5); S.I. 1995/721, art. 2, Sch.
F119. S. 43. (20)-(22) inserted (31.1.2017 for specified purposes, 3.4.2017 in so far as not already in force) by Policing and Crime Act 2017 (c. 3), ss. 67. (4), 183. (1), (5)(e); S.I. 2017/399, reg. 2, Sch. para. 18
Modifications etc. (not altering text)
C71. Ss. 8, 9, 15, 16, 17. (1)(b(2) (4), 18–20, 21, 22. (1)–(4), 28, 29, 30. (1)–(4)(a)(5)–(11), 31, 32. (1)–(9), 34. (1)–(5), 35, 36, 37, 39, 40–44, 50, 51. (d), 52, 54, 55, 64. (1)–(4)(5)(6), Sch. 1 applied with modifications by S.I. 1985/1800, arts. 3–11, Schs. 1, 2
C72. S. 43 modified (2.8.1993) by S.I. 1993/1813, art. 6, Sch. 3 paras. 4. (4)(b), 5. (7)(b), 6. (7)(b); s. 43 modified by the said S.I. 1993/1813, art. 6, Sch. 3 paras. 4, 5, 6 as incorporated (with modifications) (1.12.1997) by S.I. 1994/1405, art. 6, Sch. 3 paras. 5, 6, 7
C73. S. 43 applied (with modifications) (25.6.2013) by The Police and Criminal Evidence Act 1984 (Application to immigration officers and designated customs officials in England and Wales) Order 2013 (S.I. 2013/1542), arts. 1, 12. (2)-(4), Sch. 2 (with arts. 13-31)
C74. S. 43 applied (with modifications) (30.4.2017) by The Police and Criminal Evidence Act 1984 (Application to Labour Abuse Prevention Officers) Regulations 2017 (S.I. 2017/520), regs. 1, 2, 3. (s), Sch.
C75. S. 43. (1)-(12)(14)-(19) applied (with modifications) (4.11.2015) by The Police and Criminal Evidence Act 1984 (Application to Revenue and Customs) Order 2015 (S.I. 2015/1783), arts. 1, 3. (1), Sch. 1 (with art. 3. (2), (3), 4-19, Sch. 2)

44 Extension of warrants of further detention.

(1) On an application on oath made by a constable and supported by an information a magistrates' court may extend a warrant of further detention issued under section 43 above if it is satisfied that there are reasonable grounds for believing that the further detention of the person to whom the application relates is justified.

(2) Subject to subsection (3) below, the period for which a warrant of further detention may be extended shall be such period as the court thinks fit, having regard to the evidence before it.

(3) The period shall not—

    (a) be longer than 36 hours; or

    (b) end later than 96 hours after the relevant time.

(4) Where a warrant of further detention has been extended under subsection (1) above, or further extended under this subsection, for a period ending before 96 hours after the relevant time, on an application such as is mentioned in that subsection a magistrates' court may further extend the warrant if it is satisfied as there mentioned; and subsections (2) and (3) above apply to such further extensions as they apply to extensions under subsection (1) above.

(5) A warrant of further detention shall, if extended or further extended under this section, be endorsed with a note of the period of the extension.

(6) Subsections (2), (3) and (14) of section 43 above shall apply to an application made under this section as they apply to an application made under that section.

(7) Where an application under this section is refused, the person to whom the application relates shall forthwith be charged or, subject to subsection (8) below, released [F120—

    (a) without bail unless the pre-conditions for bail are satisfied, or

    (b) on bail if those pre-conditions are satisfied.]

(8) A person need not be released under subsection (7) above before the expiry of any period for which a warrant of further detention issued in relation to him has been extended or further extended on an earlier application made under this section.

[F121. (9)Subsection (10) applies where—

    (a) a person is released under subsection (7), and

    (b) a custody officer determines that—

(i) there is not sufficient evidence to charge the person with an offence, or

(ii) there is sufficient evidence to charge the person with an offence but the person should not be charged with an offence or given a caution in respect of an offence.

(10) The custody officer must give the person notice in writing that the person is not to be prosecuted.

(11) Subsection (10) does not prevent the prosecution of the person for an offence if new evidence comes to light after the notice was given.]

Amendments (Textual)

F120. Words in s. 44. (7) substituted (31.1.2017 for specified purposes, 3.4.2017 in so far as not already in force) by Policing and Crime Act 2017 (c. 3), ss. 57. (4), 183. (1), (5)(e); S.I. 2017/399, reg. 2, Sch. para. 12 (with reg. 5)

F121. S. 44. (9)-(11) inserted (31.1.2017 for specified purposes, 3.4.2017 in so far as not already in force) by Policing and Crime Act 2017 (c. 3), ss. 67. (5), 183. (1), (5)(e); S.I. 2017/399, reg. 2, Sch. para. 18

Modifications etc. (not altering text)

C76. Ss. 8, 9, 15, 16, 17. (1)(b(2) (4), 18–20, 21, 22. (1)–(4), 28, 29, 30. (1)–(4)(a)(5)–(11), 31, 32. (1)–(9), 34. (1)–(5), 35, 36, 37, 39, 40–44, 50, 51. (d), 52, 54, 55, 64. (1)–(4)(5)(6), Sch. 1 applied with modifications by S.I. 1985/1800, arts. 3–11, Schs. 1, 2

C77. S. 44 applied (with modifications) (25.6.2013) by The Police and Criminal Evidence Act 1984 (Application to immigration officers and designated customs officials in England and Wales) Order 2013 (S.I. 2013/1542), arts. 1, 12. (2)-(4), Sch. 2 (with arts. 13-31)

C78. S. 44 applied (with modifications) (4.11.2015) by The Police and Criminal Evidence Act

1984 (Application to Revenue and Customs) Order 2015 (S.I. 2015/1783), arts. 1, 3. (1), Sch. 1 (with art. 3. (2), (3), 4-19, Sch. 2)
C79. S. 44 applied (with modifications) (30.4.2017) by The Police and Criminal Evidence Act 1984 (Application to Labour Abuse Prevention Officers) Regulations 2017 (S.I. 2017/520), regs. 1, 2, 3. (t), Sch.

45 Detention before charge—supplementary.

(1) In [F122sections 43, 44 and 45. ZB] of this Act "magistrates' court" means a court consisting of two or more justices of the peace sitting otherwise than in open court.
(2) Any reference in this Part of this Act to a period of time or a time of day is to be treated as approximate only.
Amendments (Textual)
F122. Words in s. 45. (1) substituted (31.1.2017 for specified purposes, 3.4.2017 in so far as not already in force) by Policing and Crime Act 2017 (c. 3), ss. 74. (3), 183. (1), (5)(e); S.I. 2017/399, reg. 2, Sch. para. 23

[F123. Use of live links

Amendments (Textual)
F123. S. 45. ZA 45. ZB and crossheading inserted (31.1.2017 for specified purposes, 3.4.2017 in so far as not already in force) by Policing and Crime Act 2017 (c. 3), ss. 74. (2), 183. (1), (5)(e); S.I. 2017/399, reg. 2, Sch. para. 23

45. ZAFunctions of extending detention: use of live links

(1) The functions of a police officer under section 42. (1) or (2) may be performed, in relation to an arrested person who is held at a police station, by an officer who is not present at the police station but has access to the use of a live link if—
    (a) a custody officer considers that the use of the live link is appropriate,
    (b) the arrested person has had advice from a solicitor on the use of the live link, and
    (c) the appropriate consent to the use of the live link has been given.
(2) In subsection (1)(c), "the appropriate consent" means—
    (a) in relation to a person who has attained the age of 18, the consent of that person;
    (b) in relation to a person who has not attained that age but has attained the age of 14, the consent of that person and of his or her parent or guardian;
    (c) in relation to a person who has not attained the age of 14, the consent of his or her parent or guardian.
(3) The consent of a person who has not attained the age of 18 (but has attained the age of 14), or who is a vulnerable adult, may only be given in the presence of an appropriate adult.
(4) Section 42 applies with the modifications set out in subsections (5) to (7) below in any case where the functions of a police officer under that section are, by virtue of subsection (1), performed by an officer who is not at the police station where the arrested person is held.
(5) Subsections (5)(b) and (9)(iii) and (iv) of that section are each to be read as if, instead of requiring the officer to make a record, they required the officer to cause another police officer to make a record.
(6) Subsection (6) of that section is to be read as if it required the officer to give the persons mentioned in that subsection an opportunity to make representations—
    (a) if facilities exist for the immediate transmission of written representations to the officer, either in writing by means of those facilities or orally by means of the live link, or
    (b) in any other case, orally by means of the live link.

(7) Subsection (9) of that section is to be read as if the reference in paragraph (b) to the right conferred by section 58 were omitted.

(8) In this section—

"live link" means an arrangement by which an officer who is not present at the police station where an arrested person is held is able to see and hear, and to be seen and heard by, the arrested person and the arrested person's solicitor (and for this purpose any impairment of eyesight or hearing is to be disregarded);

"vulnerable adult" means a person aged 18 or over who may have difficulty understanding the purpose of an authorisation under section 42. (1) or (2) or anything that occurs in connection with a decision whether to give such an authorisation (whether because of a mental disorder or for any other reason);

"appropriate adult", in relation to a person who has not attained the age of 18, means—

- the persons's parent or guardian or, if the person is in the care of a local authority or voluntary organisation, a person representing that authority or organisation,

- a social worker of a local authority, or

- if no person falling within paragraph (a) or (b) is available, any responsible person aged 18 or over who is not a police officer or a person employed for, or engaged on, police purposes;

"appropriate adult", in relation to a vulnerable adult, means—

- a relative, guardian or other person responsible for the vulnerable adult's care,

- a person who is experienced in dealing with vulnerable adults but who is not a police officer or a person employed for, or engaged on, police purposes, or

- if no person falling within paragraph (a) or (b) is available, any responsible person aged 18 or over who is not a police officer or a person employed for, or engaged on, police purposes.

(9) In subsection (8), in both definitions of "appropriate adult", "police purposes" has the meaning given by section 101. (2) of the Police Act 1996.

45. ZBWarrants for further detention: use of live links

(1) A magistrates' court may give a live link direction for the purpose of the hearing of an application under section 43 for a warrant authorising further detention of a person, or the hearing of an application under section 44 for an extension of such a warrant, if—

(a) a custody officer considers that the use of a live link for that purpose is appropriate,

(b) the person to whom the application relates has had legal advice on the use of the live link,

(c) the appropriate consent to the use of the live link has been given, and

(d) it is not contrary to the interests of justice to give the direction.

(2) In subsection (1)(c), "the appropriate consent" means—

(a) in relation to a person who has attained the age of 18, the consent of that person;

(b) in relation to a person who has not attained that age but has attained the age of 14, the consent of that person and of his or her parent or guardian;

(c) in relation to a person who has not attained the age of 14, the consent of his or her parent or guardian.

(3) Where a live link direction is given, the requirement under section 43. (2)(b) for the person to whom the application relates to be brought before the court for the hearing does not apply.

(4) In this section—

"live link direction" means a direction that a live link be used for the purposes of the hearing;

"live link" means an arrangement by which a person (when not in the place where the hearing is being held) is able to see and hear, and to be seen and heard by, the court during a hearing (and for this purpose any impairment of eyesight or hearing is to be disregarded);

"vulnerable adult" means a person aged 18 or over who may have difficulty understanding the purpose of the hearing or what occurs at it (whether because of a mental disorder or for any other reason);

"appropriate adult", in relation to a person aged under 18, means—

- the person's parent or guardian or, if the person is in the care of a local authority or voluntary organisation, a person representing that authority or organisation,

- a social worker of a local authority, or

- if no person falling within paragraph (a) or (b) is available, any responsible person aged 18 or over who is not a police officer or a person employed for, or engaged on, police purposes; "appropriate adult", in relation to a vulnerable adult, means—

- a relative, guardian or other person responsible for the appropriate adult's care,

- a person who is experienced in dealing with vulnerable adults but who is not a police officer or a person employed for, or engaged on, police purposes, or

- if no person falling within paragraph (a) or (b) is available, any responsible person aged 18 or over who is not a police officer or a person employed for, or engaged on, police purposes.

(5) In subsection (4), in both definitions of "appropriate adult", "police purposes" has the meaning given by section 101. (2) of the Police Act 1996.]

[F12445. A [F125. Use of live links for other decisions about detention]

(1) Subject to the following provisions of this section, the Secretary of State may by regulations provide that, in the case of an arrested person who is held in a police station, some or all of the functions mentioned in subsection (2) may be performed (notwithstanding anything in the preceding provisions of this Part) by an officer who—

(a) is not present in that police station; but

(b) has access to the use of[F126a live link].

(2) Those functions are—

(a) the functions in relation to an arrested person taken to [F127, or answering to bail at,] a police station that is not a designated police station which, in the case of an arrested person taken to a station that is a designated police station, are functions of a custody officer under section 37, 38 or 40 above; and

(b) the function of carrying out a review under section 40. (1)(b) above (review, by an officer of at least the rank of inspector, of the detention of person arrested but not charged).

(3) Regulations under this section shall specify the use to be made in the performance of the functions mentioned in subsection (2) above of [F128a live link].

(4) Regulations under this section shall not authorise the performance of any of the functions mentioned in subsection (2)(a) above by such an officer as is mentioned in subsection (1) above unless he is a custody officer for a designated police station.

(5) Where any functions mentioned in subsection (2) above are performed in a manner authorised by regulations under this section—

(a) any obligation of the officer performing those functions to make a record in connection with the performance of those functions shall have effect as an obligation to cause another officer to make the record; and

(b) any requirement for the record to be made in the presence of the arrested person shall apply to the making of that record by that other officer.

(6) Where the functions mentioned in subsection (2)(b) are performed in a manner authorised by regulations under this section, the requirements under section 40. (12) and (13) above for—

(a) the arrested person, or

(b) a solicitor representing him,

to be given any opportunity to make representations (whether in writing or orally) to the person performing those functions shall have effect as a requirement for that person, or such a solicitor, to be given an opportunity to make representations in a manner authorised by subsection (7) below.

(7) Representations are made in a manner authorised by this subsection—

(a) in a case where facilities exist for the immediate transmission of written representations to the officer performing the functions, if they are made either—

(i) orally to that officer by means of [F129the live link] used by him for performing those functions; or

(ii) in writing to that officer by means of the facilities available for the immediate transmission of the representations;

and

(b) in any other case if they are made orally to that officer by means of [F130the live link] used by him for performing the functions.

(8) Regulations under this section may make different provision for different cases and may be made so as to have effect in relation only to the police stations specified or described in the regulations.

(9) Regulations under this section shall be made by statutory instrument and shall be subject to annulment in pursuance of a resolution of either House of Parliament.

[F131. (10)In this section, "live link", in relation to any functions, means an arrangement by which the functions may be performed by an officer who is not present at the police station where an arrested person is held but who is able (for the purpose of the functions) to see and hear, and to be seen and heard by, the arrested person and any legal representative of that person (and for this purpose any impairment of eyesight or hearing is to be disregarded).]]

Amendments (Textual)

F124. S. 45. A inserted (1.4.2003) by 2001 c. 16, ss. 73. (3), 138. (2); S.I. 2003/708, art. 2. (d)

F125. S. 45. A heading substituted (31.1.2017 for specified purposes, 3.4.2017 in so far as not already in force) by Policing and Crime Act 2017 (c. 3), ss. 74. (4)(a), 183. (1), (5)(e); S.I. 2017/399, reg. 2, Sch. para. 23

F126. Words in s. 45. A(1)(b) substituted (31.1.2017 for specified purposes, 3.4.2017 in so far as not already in force) by Policing and Crime Act 2017 (c. 3), ss. 74. (4)(b), 183. (1), (5)(e); S.I. 2017/399, reg. 2, Sch. para. 23

F127. Words in s. 45. A(2)(a) inserted (20.1.2004) by Criminal Justice Act 2003 (c. 44), ss. 12, 336, Sch. 1 Pt. 1 para. 9; S.I. 2004/81, art. 2. (1)(2)(a)

F128. Words in s. 45. A(3) substituted (31.1.2017 for specified purposes, 3.4.2017 in so far as not already in force) by Policing and Crime Act 2017 (c. 3), ss. 74. (4)(c), 183. (1), (5)(e); S.I. 2017/399, reg. 2, Sch. para. 23

F129. Words in s. 45. A(7)(a)(i) substituted (31.1.2017 for specified purposes, 3.4.2017 in so far as not already in force) by Policing and Crime Act 2017 (c. 3), ss. 74. (4)(d), 183. (1), (5)(e); S.I. 2017/399, reg. 2, Sch. para. 23

F130. Words in s. 45. A(7)(b) substituted (31.1.2017 for specified purposes, 3.4.2017 in so far as not already in force) by Policing and Crime Act 2017 (c. 3), ss. 74. (4)(d), 183. (1), (5)(e); S.I. 2017/399, reg. 2, Sch. para. 23

F131. S. 45. A(10) substituted (31.1.2017 for specified purposes, 3.4.2017 in so far as not already in force) by Policing and Crime Act 2017 (c. 3), ss. 74. (4)(e), 183. (1), (5)(e); S.I. 2017/399, reg. 2, Sch. para. 23

Detention—miscellaneous

46 Detention after charge.

(1) Where a person—

(a) is charged with an offence; and

(b) after being charged—

(i) is kept in police detention; or

(ii) is detained by a local authority in pursuance of arrangements made under section 38. (6) above,

he shall be brought before a magistrates' court in accordance with the provisions of this section.

(2) If he is to be brought before a magistrates' court [F132in the local justice] area in which the police station at which he was charged is situated, he shall be brought before such a court as soon as is practicable and in any event not later than the first sitting after he is charged with the offence.

(3) If no magistrates' court [F133in that area] is due to sit either on the day on which he is charged or on the next day, the custody officer for the police station at which he was charged shall inform the [F134designated officer]for the area that there is a person in the area to whom subsection (2) above applies.

(4) If the person charged is to be brought before a magistrates' court [F135in a local justice] area other than that in which the police station at which he was charged is situated, he shall be removed to that area as soon as is practicable and brought before such a court as soon as is practicable after his arrival in the area and in any event not later than the first sitting of a magistrates' court [F136in that area] after his arrival in the area.

(5) If no magistrates' court [F137in that area] is due to sit either on the day on which he arrives in the area or on the next day—

(a) he shall be taken to a police station in the area; and

(b) the custody officer at that station shall inform the [F138designated officer] for the area that there is a person in the area to whom subsection (4) applies.

(6) Subject to subsection (8) below, where [F139the designated officer for a local justice] area has been informed—

(a) under subsection (3) above that there is a person in the area to whom subsection (2) above applies; or

(b) under subsection (5) above that there is a person in the area to whom subsection (4) above applies,

[F140the designated officer] shall arrange for a magistrates' court to sit not later than the day next following the relevant day.

(7) In this section "the relevant day"—

(a) in relation to a person who is to be brought before a magistrates' court [F141in the local justice] area in which the police station at which he was charged is situated, means the day on which he was charged; and

(b) in relation to a person who is to be brought before a magistrates' court [F142in any other local justice] area, means the day on which he arrives in the area.

(8) Where the day next following the relevant day is Christmas Day, Good Friday or a Sunday, the duty of the [F143designated officer] under subsection (6) above is a duty to arrange for a magistrates' court to sit not later than the first day after the relevant day which is not one of those days.

(9) Nothing in this section requires a person who is in hospital to be brought before a court if he is not well enough.

Amendments (Textual)

F132. Words in s. 46. (2) substituted (1.4.2005) by Courts Act 2003 (c. 39), ss. 109. (1), 110, Sch. 8 para. 282. (2); S.I. 2005/910, art. 3. (y)

F133. Words in s. 46. (3) substituted (1.4.2005) by Courts Act 2003 (c. 39), ss. 109. (1), 110, Sch. 8 para. 282. (3)(a); S.I. 2005/910, art. 3. (y)

F134. Words in s. 46. (3) substituted (1.4.2005) by Courts Act 2003 (c. 39), ss. 109. (1), 110, Sch. 8 para. 282. (3)(b); S.I. 2005/910, art. 3. (y)

F135. Words in s. 46. (4) substituted (1.4.2005) by Courts Act 2003 (c. 39), ss. 109. (1), 110, Sch. 8 para. 282. (4)(a); S.I. 2005/910, art. 3. (y)

F136. Words in s. 46. (4) substituted (1.4.2005) by Courts Act 2003 (c. 39), ss. 109. (1), 110, Sch. 8 para. 282. (4)(b); S.I. 2005/910, art. 3. (y)

F137. Words in s. 46. (5) substituted (1.4.2005) by Courts Act 2003 (c. 39), ss. 109. (1), 110, Sch. 8 para. 282. (5)(a); S.I. 2005/910, art. 3. (y)

F138. Words in s. 46. (5) substituted (1.4.2005) by Courts Act 2003 (c. 39), ss. 109. (1), 110, Sch. 8 para. 282. (5)(b); S.I. 2005/910, art. 3. (y)

F139. Words in s. 46. (6) substituted (1.4.2005) by Courts Act 2003 (c. 39), ss. 109. (1), 110, Sch.

8 para. 282. (6)(a); S.I. 2005/910, art. 3. (y)

F140. Words in s. 46. (6) substituted (1.4.2005) by Courts Act 2003 (c. 39), ss. 109. (1), 110, Sch. 8 para. 282. (6)(b); S.I. 2005/910, art. 3. (y)

F141. Words in s. 46. (7) substituted (1.4.2005) by Courts Act 2003 (c. 39), ss. 109. (1), 110, Sch. 8 para. 282. (7)(a); S.I. 2005/910, art. 3. (y)

F142. Words in s. 46. (7) substituted (1.4.2005) by Courts Act 2003 (c. 39), ss. 109. (1), 110, Sch. 8 para. 282. (7)(b); S.I. 2005/910, art. 3. (y)

F143. Words in s. 46. (8) substituted (1.4.2005) by Courts Act 2003 (c. 39), ss. 109. (1), 110, Sch. 8 para. 282. (8); S.I. 2005/910, art. 3. (y)

Modifications etc. (not altering text)

C80. S. 46 excluded (4.4.2005) by Criminal Justice Act 2003 (c. 44), ss. 88. (2), 336; S.I. 2005/950, art. 2. (1), Sch. 1 para. 5 (subject to art. 2. (2), Sch. 2) (as amended by S.I. 2005/2122, art. 2)

C81. S. 46 applied (with modifications) (25.6.2013) by The Police and Criminal Evidence Act 1984 (Application to immigration officers and designated customs officials in England and Wales) Order 2013 (S.I. 2013/1542), arts. 1, 12. (2)-(4), Sch. 2 (with arts. 13-31)

F144[46. ZAPersons granted live link bail

(1) This section applies in relation to bail granted under this Part subject to the duty mentioned in section 47. (3)(b)("live link bail").

(2) An accused person who attends a police station to answer to live link bail is not to be treated as in police detention for the purposes of this Act.

(3) Subsection (2) does not apply in relation to an accused person if—

F145[(a)at any time before the beginning of proceedings in relation to a live link direction under section 57. C of the Crime and Disorder Act 1998 in relation to him, he informs a constable that he does not intend to give his consent to the direction;]

F146. (b)[at any time before the beginning of proceedings in relation to a live link direction under section 57. C of the Crime and Disorder Act 1998 in relation to the accused person,]a constable informs him that a live link will not be available for his use for the purposes of that section;

F147[(c)proceedings in relation to a live link direction under that section have begun but he does not give his consent to the direction; or]

(d) the court determines for F148[any reason] not to give such a direction.

(4) If F149[paragraph (b) or (d) of subsection (3) applies] in relation to a person, he is to be treated for the purposes of this Part—

(a) as if he had been arrested for and charged with the offence in connection with which he was granted bail, and

(b) as if he had been so charged at the time when that paragraph first applied in relation to him.

(5) An accused person who is arrested under section 46. A for failing to attend at a police station to answer to live link bail, and who is brought to a police station in accordance with that section, is to be treated for the purposes of this Part—

(a) as if he had been arrested for and charged with the offence in connection with which he was granted bail, and

(b) as if he had been so charged at the time when he is brought to the station.

(6) Nothing in subsection (4) or (5) affects the operation of section 47. (6).]

Amendments (Textual)

F144. S. 46. ZA inserted (1.4.2007 for specified purposes, 14.11.2008 for specified purposes, 3.10.2011 for specified purposes, 8.10.2012 in so far as not already in force) by Police and Justice Act 2006 (c. 48), ss. 46. (3), 53. (1); S.I. 2007/709, art. 3. (n) (with art. 6); S.I. 2008/2785, art. 2; S.I. 2011/2144, art. 2. (1)(b); S.I. 2012/2373, art. 2. (b)

F145. S. 46. ZA(3)(a) repealed (14.12.2009 for specified purposes, 6.4.2010 for specified purposes, 3.10.2011 for specified purposes, 8.10.2012 in so far as not already in force) by Coroners and Justice Act 2009 (c. 25), ss. 107. (2)(a)(i), 182. (5), Sch. 23 Pt. 3 (with s. 180); S.I. 2009/3253, art. 3. (1)(b) (with art. 4); S.I. 2010/816, art. 4; S.I. 2011/2148, art. 2; S.I. 2012/2374, art. 3. (b)(e)

F146. Words in s. 46. ZA(3)(b) substituted (14.12.2009 for specified purposes, 3.10.2011 for specified purposes, 8.10.2012 in so far as not already in force) by Coroners and Justice Act 2009 (c. 25), ss. 107. (2)(a)(ii), 182. (5) (with s. 180); S.I. 2009/3253, art. 3. (1)(b) (with art. 4); S.I. 2011/2148, art. 2; S.I. 2012/2374, art. 3. (b)

F147. S. 46. ZA(3)(c) repealed (14.12.2009 for specified purposes, 6.4.2010 for specified purposes, 3.10.2011 for specified purposes, 8.10.2012 in so far as not already in force) by Coroners and Justice Act 2009 (c. 25), ss. 107. (2)(a)(iii), 182. (5), Sch. 23 Pt. 3 (with s. 180); S.I. 2009/3253, art. 3. (1)(b) (with art. 4); S.I. 2010/816, art. 4; S.I. 2011/2148, art. 2; S.I. 2012/2374, art. 3. (b)(e)

F148. Words in s. 46. ZA(3)(d) substituted (14.12.2009 for specified purposes, 3.10.2011 for specified purposes, 8.10.2012 in so far as not already in force) by Coroners and Justice Act 2009 (c. 25), ss. 107. (2)(a)(iv), 182. (5) (with s. 180); S.I. 2009/3253, art. 3. (1)(b) (with art. 4); S.I. 2011/2148, art. 2; S.I. 2012/2374, art. 3. (b)

F149. Words in s. 46. ZA(4) substituted (14.12.2009 for specified purposes, 3.10.2011 for specified purposes, 8.10.2012 in so far as not already in force) by Coroners and Justice Act 2009 (c. 25), ss. 107. (2)(b), 182. (5) (with s. 180); S.I. 2009/3253, art. 3. (1)(b) (with art. 4); S.I. 2011/2148, art. 2; S.I. 2012/2374, art. 3. (b)

[F15046. A Power of arrest for failure to answer to police bail.

(1) A constable may arrest without a warrant any person who, having been released on bail under this Part of this Act subject to a duty to attend at a police station, fails to attend at that police station at the time appointed for him to do so.

F151[(1. ZA)The reference in subsection (1) to a person who fails to attend at a police station at the time appointed for him to do so includes a reference to a person who—

(a) attends at a police station to answer to bail granted subject to the duty mentioned in section 47. (3)(b), but

(b) leaves the police station at any time before the beginning of proceedings in relation to a live link direction under section 57. C of the Crime and Disorder Act 1998 in relation to him [F152, without informing a constable that he does not intend to give his consent to the direction.]]

F153[(1. ZB)The reference in subsection (1) to a person who fails to attend at a police station at the time appointed for the person to do so includes a reference to a person who—

(a) attends at a police station to answer to bail granted subject to the duty mentioned in section 47. (3)(b), but

(b) refuses to be searched under section 54. B.]

[F154. (1. A)A person who has been released on bail under [F155this Part] may be arrested without warrant by a constable if the constable has reasonable grounds for suspecting that the person has broken any of the conditions of bail.]

(2) A person who is arrested under this section shall be taken to the police station appointed as the place at which he is to surrender to custody as soon as practicable after the arrest.

(3) For the purposes of—

(a) section 30 above (subject to the obligation in subsection (2) above), and

(b) section 31 above,

an arrest under this section shall be treated as an arrest for an offence.]

Amendments (Textual)

F150. S. 46. A inserted (10.4.1995) by 1994 c. 33, s. 29. (2)(5); S.I. 1995/721, art. 2,Sch.

F151. S. 46. A(1. ZA) inserted (1.4.2007 for specified purposes, 14.11.2008 for specified purposes, 3.10.2011 for specified purposes, 8.10.2012 in so far as not already in force) by Police and Justice Act 2006 (c. 48), ss. 46. (4), 53. (1); S.I. 2007/709, art. 3. (n) (with art. 6); S.I. 2008/2785, art. 2; S.I. 2011/2144, art. 2. (1)(b); S.I. 2012/2373, art. 2. (b)

F152. Words in s. 46. A(1. ZA) omitted (14.12.2009 in relation to the relevant local justice areas specified in art. 3. (2) of the first commencing S.I.) by virtue of and repealed (prosp.) by Coroners and Justice Act 2009 (c. 25), ss. 107. (3), 178, 182, Sch. 23 Pt. 3 (with s. 180, Sch. 22); S.I. 2009/3253, art. 3. (1)(b)(2) (with art. 4)

F153. S. 46. A(1. ZB) inserted (14.12.2009 for specified purposes, 3.10.2011 for specified purposes, 8.10.2012 in so far as not already in force) by Coroners and Justice Act 2009 (c. 25), ss. 108. (2), 182. (5) (with s. 180); S.I. 2009/3253, art. 3. (1)(c); S.I. 2011/2148, art. 2; S.I. 2012/2374, art. 3. (c)

F154. S. 46. A(1. A) inserted (29.1.2004) by Criminal Justice Act 2003 (c. 44), ss. 28, 336, Sch. 2 para. 5; S.I. 2004/81, art. 4. (1)(2)(c)

F155. Words in s. 46. A(1. A) substituted (31.1.2017 for specified purposes, 3.4.2017 in so far as not already in force) by Policing and Crime Act 2017 (c. 3), ss. 61. (2), 183. (1), (5)(e); S.I. 2017/399, reg. 2, Sch. para. 13

Modifications etc. (not altering text)

C82. S. 46. A applied (with modifications) by Criminal Justice Act 2003 (c. 44), s. 24. B(5)(b) (as inserted (29.6.2007) by Police and Justice Act 2006 (c. 48), ss. 18. (1), 53 (with s. 18. (2)); S.I. 2007/1614, art. 2. (e))

C83. S. 46. A(1) applied (with modifications) (25.6.2013) by The Police and Criminal Evidence Act 1984 (Application to immigration officers and designated customs officials in England and Wales) Order 2013 (S.I. 2013/1542), arts. 1, 12. (2)-(4), Sch. 2 (with arts. 13-31)

C84. S. 46. A(1) applied (with modifications) (25.6.2013) by The Police and Criminal Evidence Act 1984 (Application to immigration officers and designated customs officials in England and Wales) Order 2013 (S.I. 2013/1542), arts. 1, 3. (2)-(4), Sch. 1 (with arts. 4-11)

C85. S. 46. A(1)(1. A) applied (with modifications) (4.11.2015) by The Police and Criminal Evidence Act 1984 (Application to Revenue and Customs) Order 2015 (S.I. 2015/1783), arts. 1, 3. (1), Sch. 1 (with art. 3. (2), (3), 4-19, Sch. 2)

C86. Ss. 46. A(1. A)-(3) applied (with modifications) (25.6.2013) by The Police and Criminal Evidence Act 1984 (Application to immigration officers and designated customs officials in England and Wales) Order 2013 (S.I. 2013/1542), arts. 1, 12. (2)-(4), Sch. 2 (with arts. 13-31)

C87. Ss. 46. A(1. A)-(3) applied (with modifications) (25.6.2013) by The Police and Criminal Evidence Act 1984 (Application to immigration officers and designated customs officials in England and Wales) Order 2013 (S.I. 2013/1542), arts. 1, 3. (2)-(4), Sch. 1 (with arts. 4-11)

47 Bail after arrest.

(1) [F156. Subject to the following provisions of this section], a release on bail of a person under this Part of this Act shall be a release on bail granted in accordance with [F157sections 3, 3. A, 5 and 5. A of the Bail Act 1976 as they apply to bail granted by a constable].

F158[(1. A)The normal powers to impose conditions of bail shall be available to him where a custody officer releases a person on bail under [F159this Part (except sections 37. C(2)(b) and 37. CA(2)(b))]. In this subsection, "the normal powers to impose conditions of bail" has the meaning given in section 3. (6) of the Bail Act 1976.]

[F160. (1. B)No application may be made under section 5. B of the Bail Act 1976 if a person is released on bail under section F161[F162... 37. C(2)(b) or 37. CA(2)(b)] above.

(1. C)Subsections (1. D) to (1. F) below apply where a person released on bail under section F163[F164... 37. C(2)(b) or 37. CA(2)(b)] above is on bail subject to conditions.

(1. D)The person shall not be entitled to make an application under section 43. B of the Magistrates' Courts Act 1980.

(1. E) A magistrates' court may, on an application by or on behalf of the person, vary the conditions of bail; and in this subsection "vary" has the same meaning as in the Bail Act 1976.

(1. F)Where a magistrates' court varies the conditions of bail under subsection (1. E) above, that bail shall not lapse but shall continue subject to the conditions as so varied.]

(2) Nothing in the Bail Act 1976 shall prevent the re-arrest without warrant of a person released on bail subject to a duty to attend at a police station if[F165, since the person's release, new evidence has come to light or an examination or analysis of existing evidence has been made which could not reasonably have been made before the person's release].

(3) Subject to [F166subsections (3. A) and (4)] below, in this Part of this Act references to "bail" are references to bail subject to a duty—

[F167. (a)to appear before a magistrates' court at such time and such place as the custody officer may appoint;

(b) to attend at such police station as the custody officer may appoint at such time as he may appoint for the purposes of—

(i) proceedings in relation to a live link direction under section 57. C of the Crime and Disorder Act 1998 (use of live link direction at preliminary hearings where accused is at police station); and

(ii) any preliminary hearing in relation to which such a direction is given; or

(c) to attend at such police station as the custody officer may appoint at such time as he may appoint for purposes other than those mentioned in paragraph (b) [F168. (subject to section 47. ZA)].]

[F169. (3. A)Where a custody officer grants bail to a person subject to a duty to appear before a magistrates' court, he shall appoint for the appearance—

(a) a date which is not later than the first sitting of the court after the person is charged with the offence; or

(b) where he is informed by the [F170designated officer for the relevant local justice] area that the appearance cannot be accommodated until a later date, that later date.]

(4) Where a custody officer has granted bail to a person subject to a duty to appear at a police station, the custody officer may give notice in writing to that person that his attendance at the police station is not required.

[F171. (4. A)Where a person has been granted bail under this Part subject to a duty to attend at a police station, a custody officer may subsequently appoint a different time, or an additional time, at which the person is to attend at the police station to answer bail.

(4. B)The custody officer must give the person notice in writing of the exercise of the power under subsection (4. A).

(4. C)The exercise of the power under subsection (4. A) does not affect the conditions of bail (if any).

(4. D)A custody officer may not appoint a time for a person's attendance under subsection (4. A) which is after the end of the applicable bail period in relation to the person.

(4. E)Subsection (4. D) is subject to section 47. ZL.]

F172. (5). . . . .

(6) Where a person [F173who has been granted bail [F174under this Part] and either has attended at the police station in accordance with the grant of bail or has been arrested under section 46. A above is detained at a police station], any time during which he was in police detention prior to being granted bail shall be included as part of any period which falls to be calculated under this Part of this Act [F175and any time during which he was on bail shall not be so included].

(7) Where a person who was released on bail [F176under this Part] subject to a duty to attend at a police station is re-arrested, the provisions of this Part of this Act shall apply to him as they apply to a person arrested for the first time [F177; but this subsection does not apply to a person who is arrested under section 46. A above or has attended a police station in accordance with the grant of bail (and who accordingly is deemed by section 34. (7) above to have been arrested for an offence) F178[or to a person to whom section 46. ZA(4) or (5) applies.]]

(8) In the M4. Magistrates' Court Act 1980—

(a) the following section shall be substituted for section 43—

"43 Bail on arrest

(1) Where a person has been granted bail under the Police and Criminal Evidence Act 1984

87

subject to a duty to appear before a magistrates' court, the court before which he is to appear may appoint a later time as the time at which he is to appear and may enlarge the recognizances of any sureties for him at that time.

(2) The recognizance of any surety for any person granted bail subject to a duty to attend at a police station may be enforced as if it were conditioned for his appearance before a magistrates' court for the petty sessions area in which the police station named in the recognizance is situated."; and

(b) the following subsection shall be substituted for section 117. (3)—

"(3)Where a warrant has been endorsed for bail under subsection (1) above—

(a) where the person arrested is to be released on bail on his entering into a recognizance without sureties, it shall not be necessary to take him to a police station, but if he is so taken, he shall be released from custody on his entering into the recognizance; and

(b) where he is to be released on his entering into a recognizance with sureties, he shall be taken to a police station on his arrest, and the custody officer there shall (subject to his approving any surety tendered in compliance with the endorsement) release him from custody as directed in the endorsement.".

Amendments (Textual)

F156. Words in s. 47. (1) substituted (29.1.2004) by Criminal Justice Act 2003 (c. 44), ss. 28, 336, Sch. 2 para. 6. (2); S.I. 2004/81, art. 4. (1)(2)(c)

F157. Words in s. 47. (1) substituted (10.4.1995) by 1994 c. 33, s. 27. (1)(a); S.I. 1995/721, art. 2, Sch.

F158. S. 47. (1. A) inserted (10.4.1995) by 1994 c. 33, s. 27. (1)(b); S.I. 1995/721, art. 2, Sch.

F159. Words in s. 47. (1. A) substituted (31.1.2017 for specified purposes, 3.4.2017 in so far as not already in force) by Policing and Crime Act 2017 (c. 3), ss. 61. (4), 183. (1), (5)(e); S.I. 2017/399, reg. 2, Sch. para. 13

F160. S. 47. (1. B)-(1. F) inserted (29.1.2004) by Criminal Justice Act 2003 (c. 44), ss. 28, 336, Sch. 2 para. 6. (4); S.I. 2004/81, art. 4. (1)(2)(c)

F161. Word in s. 47. (1. B) omitted (31.1.2017 for specified purposes, 3.4.2017 in so far as not already in force) by virtue of Policing and Crime Act 2017 (c. 3), ss. 61. (5), 183. (1), (5)(e); S.I. 2017/399, reg. 2, Sch. para. 13

F162. Words in s. 47. (1. B) substituted (1.4.2007) by Police and Justice Act 2006 (c. 48), ss. 10, 53, Sch. 6 para. 11; S.I. 2007/709, art. 3. (i) (subject to arts. 6, 7)

F163. Word in s. 47. (1. C) omitted (31.1.2017 for specified purposes, 3.4.2017 in so far as not already in force) by virtue of Policing and Crime Act 2017 (c. 3), ss. 61. (5), 183. (1), (5)(e); S.I. 2017/399, reg. 2, Sch. para. 13

F164. Words in s. 47. (1. C) substituted (1.4.2007) by Police and Justice Act 2006 (c. 48), ss. 10, 53, Sch. 6 para. 11; S.I. 2007/709, art. 3. (i) (subject to arts. 6, 7)

F165. Words in s. 47. (2) substituted (31.1.2017 for specified purposes, 3.4.2017 in so far as not already in force) by Policing and Crime Act 2017 (c. 3), ss. 65. (6), 183. (1), (5)(e); S.I. 2017/399, reg. 2, Sch. para. 17 (with reg. 5)

F166. Words in s. 47. (3) substituted (30.9.1998 for the purposes specified in S.I. 1998/2327, art. 3. (2), Sch. 2 and otherwise 1.11.1999) by 1998 c. 37, s. 46. (1); S.I. 1998/2327, art. 3. (2), Sch. 2 and S.I. 1999/2976, art. 2

F167. S. 47. (3)(a)-(c) substituted for s. 47. (3)(a) (1.4.2007 for specified purposes, 14.11.2008 for specified purposes, 3.10.2011 for specified purposes, 8.10.2012 in so far as not already in force) by Police and Justice Act 2006 (c. 48), ss. 46. (5)(a), 53. (1); S.I. 2007/709, art. 3. (n) (with art. 6); S.I. 2008/2785, art. 2; S.I. 2011/2144, art. 2. (1)(b); S.I. 2012/2373, art. 2. (b)Text here

F168. Words in s. 47. (3)(c) inserted (31.1.2017 for specified purposes, 3.4.2017 in so far as not already in force) by Policing and Crime Act 2017 (c. 3), ss. 64. (6), 183. (1), (5)(e); S.I. 2017/399, reg. 2, Sch. para. 16 (with reg. 5)

F169. S. 47. (3. A) inserted (30.9.1998 for the purposes specified in S.I. 1998/2327, art. 3. (2), Sch. 2 and otherwise 1.11.1999) by 1998 c. 37, s. 46. (2); S.I. 1998/2327, art. 3. (2), Sch. 2; S.I. 1999/2976, art. 2.

F170. Words in s. 47. (3. A)(b) substituted (1.4.2005) by Courts Act 2003 (c. 39), ss. 109. (1), 110, Sch. 8 para. 283; S.I. 2005/910, art. 3. (y)

F171. S. 47. (4. A)-(4. E) inserted (31.1.2017 for specified purposes, 3.4.2017 in so far as not already in force) by Policing and Crime Act 2017 (c. 3), ss. 64. (7), 183. (1), (5)(e); S.I. 2017/399, reg. 2, Sch. para. 16 (with reg. 5)

F172. S. 47. (5) repealed (10.4.1995) by 1994 c. 33, ss. 29. (4)(c)(5), 168. (3), Sch. 11; S.I. 1995/721, art. 2, Sch. Appendix B

F173. Words in s. 47. (6) substituted (10.4.1995) by 1994 c. 33, s. 29. (4)(d)(5); S.I. 1995/721, art. 2, Sch.

F174. Words in s. 47. (6) inserted (20.1.2004) by Criminal Justice Act 2003 (c. 44), ss. 12, 336, Sch. 1 Pt. 1 para. 10. (a); S.I. 2004/81, art. 2. (1)(2)(a)

F175. Words in s. 47. (6) inserted (retrospectively) by Police (Detention and Bail) Act 2011 (c. 9), s. 1. (1)(3)

F176. Words in s. 47. (7) inserted (20.1.2004) by Criminal Justice Act 2003 (c. 44), ss. 12, 336, Sch. 1 Pt. 1 para. 10. (b); S.I. 2004/81, art. 2. (1)(2)(a)

F177. Words in s. 47. (7) inserted (10.4.1995) by 1994 c. 33, s. 29. (4)(e)(5); S.I. 1995/721, art. 2, Sch.

F178. Words in s. 47. (7) inserted (1.4.2007 for specified purposes, 14.11.2008 for specified purposes, 3.10.2011 for specified purposes, 8.10.2012 in so far as not already in force) by Police and Justice Act 2006 (c. 48), ss. 46. (5)(b), 53. (1); S.I. 2007/709, art. 3. (n) (with art. 6); S.I. 2008/2785, art. 2; S.I. 2011/2144, art. 2. (1)(b); S.I. 2012/2373, art. 2. (b)

Modifications etc. (not altering text)

C88. S. 47 applied (with modifications) by Criminal Justice Act 2003 (c. 44), s. 24. B(5)(c) (as inserted (29.6.2007) by Police and Justice Act 2006 (c. 48), ss. 18. (1), 53 (with s. 18. (2)); S.I. 2007/1614, art. 2. (e))

C89. S. 47. (3) excluded (4.4.2005) by Criminal Justice Act 2003 (c. 44), ss. 88. (1)(b), 336; S.I. 2005/950, art. 2. (1), Sch. 1 para. 5 (subject to art. 2. (2), Sch. 2) (as amended by S.I. 2005/2122, art. 2)

Marginal Citations

M41980 c. 43.

[F17947. ZALimits on period of bail without charge

(1) This section applies in relation to the power conferred on a custody officer, when releasing a person on bail under this Part, to appoint a time for the person to attend at a police station in accordance with section 47. (3)(c).

(2) The power must be exercised so as to appoint a time on the day on which the applicable bail period in relation to the person ends, unless subsection (3) or (4) applies.

(3) This subsection applies where—

   (a) at the time of the exercise of the power the person is on bail under this Part in relation to one or more offences other than the relevant offence, and

   (b) the custody officer believes that it is appropriate to align the person's attendance in relation to the relevant offence with the person's attendance in relation to the one or more other offences.

(4) This subsection applies where the custody officer believes that a decision as to whether to charge the person with the relevant offence would be made before the end of the applicable bail period in relation to the person.

(5) Where subsection (3) or (4) applies, the power may be exercised so as to appoint a time on a day falling before the end of the applicable bail period in relation to the person.

(6) This section is subject to section 47. ZL.

(7) In this section references to attendance are to attendance at a police station in accordance with section 47. (3)(c).

(8) In this Part the "relevant offence", in relation to a person, means the offence in respect of

which the power mentioned in subsection (1) is exercised in relation to the person.

Amendments (Textual)

F179. Ss. 47. ZA-47. ZM inserted (31.1.2017 for specified purposes, 3.4.2017 in so far as not already in force) by Policing and Crime Act 2017 (c. 3), ss. 63, 183. (1), (5)(e); S.I. 2017/399, reg. 2, Sch. para. 15 (with reg. 5)

47. ZBApplicable bail period: initial limit

(1) In this Part the "applicable bail period", in relation to a person, means—

    (a) in an SFO case, the period of 3 months beginning with the person's bail start date, or

    (b) in an FCA case or any other case, the period of 28 days beginning with the person's bail start date.

(2) The applicable bail period in relation to a person may be extended under sections 47. ZD to 47. ZG or treated as extended under section 47. ZJ(3).

(3) Subsection (1) and sections 47. ZD to 47. ZG are subject to sections 47. ZL and 47. ZM.

(4) For the purposes of this Part—

    (a) a person's bail start date is the day after the day on which the person was arrested for the relevant offence,

    (b) an "FCA case" is a case in which—

(i) the relevant offence in relation to the person is being investigated by the Financial Conduct Authority, and

(ii) a senior officer confirms that sub-paragraph (i) applies,

    (c) an "SFO case" is a case in which—

(i) the relevant offence in relation to the person is being investigated by the Director of the Serious Fraud Office, and

(ii) a senior officer confirms that sub-paragraph (i) applies, and

    (d) "senior officer" means a police officer of the rank of superintendent or above.

Amendments (Textual)

F179. Ss. 47. ZA-47. ZM inserted (31.1.2017 for specified purposes, 3.4.2017 in so far as not already in force) by Policing and Crime Act 2017 (c. 3), ss. 63, 183. (1), (5)(e); S.I. 2017/399, reg. 2, Sch. para. 15 (with reg. 5)

47. ZCApplicable bail period: conditions A to D in sections 47. ZD to 47. ZG

(1) This section applies for the purposes of sections 47. ZD to 47. ZG.

(2) Condition A is that the decision-maker has reasonable grounds for suspecting the person in question to be guilty of the relevant offence.

(3) Condition B is that the decision-maker has reasonable grounds for believing—

    (a) in a case where the person in question is or is to be released on bail under section 37. (7)(c) or 37. CA(2)(b), that further time is needed for making a decision as to whether to charge the person with the relevant offence, or

    (b) otherwise, that further investigation is needed of any matter in connection with the relevant offence.

(4) Condition C is that the decision-maker has reasonable grounds for believing—

    (a) in a case where the person in question is or is to be released on bail under section 37. (7)(c) or 37. CA(2)(b), that the decision as to whether to charge the person with the relevant offence is being made diligently and expeditiously, or

    (b) otherwise, that the investigation is being conducted diligently and expeditiously.

(5) Condition D is that the decision-maker has reasonable grounds for believing that the release on bail of the person in question is necessary and proportionate in all the circumstances (having

regard, in particular, to any conditions of bail which are, or are to be, imposed).

(6) In this section "decision-maker" means—

(a) in relation to a condition which falls to be considered by virtue of section 47. ZD, the senior officer in question;

(b) in relation to a condition which falls to be considered by virtue of section 47. ZE, the appropriate decision-maker in question;

(c) in relation to a condition which falls to be considered by virtue of section 47. ZF or 47. ZG, the court in question.

Amendments (Textual)

F179. Ss. 47. ZA-47. ZM inserted (31.1.2017 for specified purposes, 3.4.2017 in so far as not already in force) by Policing and Crime Act 2017 (c. 3), ss. 63, 183. (1), (5)(e); S.I. 2017/399, reg. 2, Sch. para. 15 (with reg. 5)

47. ZDApplicable bail period: extension of initial limit in standard cases

(1) This section applies in relation to a person if—

(a) the applicable bail period in relation to the person is the period mentioned in section 47. ZB(1)(b),

(b) that period has not ended, and

(c) a senior officer is satisfied that conditions A to D are met in relation to the person.

(2) The senior officer may authorise the applicable bail period in relation to the person to be extended so that it ends at the end of the period of 3 months beginning with the person's bail start date.

(3) Before determining whether to give an authorisation under subsection (2) in relation to a person, the senior officer must arrange for the person or the person's legal representative to be informed that a determination is to be made.

(4) In determining whether to give an authorisation under subsection (2) in relation to a person, the senior officer must consider any representations made by the person or the person's legal representative.

(5) The senior officer must arrange for the person or the person's legal representative to be informed whether an authorisation under subsection (2) has been given in relation to the person.

Amendments (Textual)

F179. Ss. 47. ZA-47. ZM inserted (31.1.2017 for specified purposes, 3.4.2017 in so far as not already in force) by Policing and Crime Act 2017 (c. 3), ss. 63, 183. (1), (5)(e); S.I. 2017/399, reg. 2, Sch. para. 15 (with reg. 5)

47. ZEApplicable bail period: extension of limit in designated cases

(1) This section applies in relation to a person if—

(a) the person's case is an SFO case, or

(b) a senior officer has authorised an extension of the applicable bail period in relation to the person under section 47. ZD.

(2) A qualifying prosecutor may designate the person's case as being an exceptionally complex case (a "designated case").

(3) If an appropriate decision-maker is satisfied that conditions A to D are met in relation to the person in a designated case, the decision-maker may authorise the applicable bail period in relation to the person to be extended so that it ends at the end of the period of 6 months beginning with the person's bail start date.

(4) An appropriate decision-maker is—

(a) a member of staff of the Financial Conduct Authority who is of the description designated for the purposes of this paragraph by the Chief Executive of the Authority (in an FCA case),

(b) a member of the Serious Fraud Office who is of the Senior Civil Service (in an SFO case), or

(c) a qualifying police officer (in any other case).

(5) Before determining whether to give an authorisation under subsection (3) in relation to a person—

(a) the appropriate decision-maker must arrange for the person or the person's legal representative to be informed that a determination is to be made, and

(b) if the appropriate decision-maker is a qualifying police officer, the officer must consult a qualifying prosecutor.

(6) In determining whether to give an authorisation under subsection (3) in relation to a person, the appropriate decision-maker must consider any representations made by the person or the person's legal representative.

(7) The appropriate decision-maker must arrange for the person or the person's legal representative to be informed whether an authorisation under subsection (3) has been given in relation to the person.

(8) Any designation under subsection (2) must be made, and any authorisation under subsection (3) must be given, before the applicable bail period in relation to the person has ended.

(9) In this section—

"qualifying police officer" means a police officer of the rank of commander or assistant chief constable or above, and

"qualifying prosecutor" means a prosecutor of the description designated for the purposes of this section by the Chief Executive of the Financial Conduct Authority, the Director of the Serious Fraud Office or the Director of Public Prosecutions.

Amendments (Textual)

F179. Ss. 47. ZA-47. ZM inserted (31.1.2017 for specified purposes, 3.4.2017 in so far as not already in force) by Policing and Crime Act 2017 (c. 3), ss. 63, 183. (1), (5)(e); S.I. 2017/399, reg. 2, Sch. para. 15 (with reg. 5)

47. ZFApplicable bail period: first extension of limit by court

(1) This section applies in relation to a person if—

(a) the person's case is an SFO case,

(b) a senior officer has authorised an extension of the applicable bail period in relation to the person under section 47. ZD, or

(c) an appropriate decision-maker has authorised an extension of the applicable bail period in relation to the person under section 47. ZE.

(2) Before the applicable bail period in relation to the person ends a qualifying applicant may apply to a magistrates' court for it to authorise an extension of the applicable bail period in relation to the person under this section.

(3) If the court is satisfied that—

(a) conditions B to D are met in relation to the person, and

(b) the case does not fall within subsection (7),

it may authorise the applicable bail period to be extended as specified in subsection (4).

(4) The applicable bail period is to end—

(a) in a case falling within subsection (1)(a) or (b), at the end of the period of 6 months beginning with the person's bail start date;

(b) in a case falling within subsection (1)(c), at the end of the period of 9 months beginning with the person's bail start date.

(5) If the court is satisfied that—

(a) conditions B to D are met in relation to the person, and

(b) the case falls within subsection (7),

it may authorise the applicable bail period to be extended as specified in subsection (6).

(6) The applicable bail period is to end—

(a) in a case falling within subsection (1)(a) or (b), at the end of the period of 9 months beginning with the person's bail start date;

(b) in a case falling within subsection (1)(c), at the end of the period of 12 months beginning with the person's bail start date.

(7) A case falls within this subsection if the nature of the decision or further investigations mentioned in condition B means that that decision is unlikely to be made or those investigations completed if the applicable bail period in relation to the person is not extended as specified in subsection (6).

(8) In this section "qualifying applicant" means—

(a) a constable,

(b) a member of staff of the Financial Conduct Authority who is of the description designated for the purposes of this subsection by the Chief Executive of the Authority,

(c) a member of the Serious Fraud Office, or

(d) a Crown Prosecutor.

Amendments (Textual)

F179. Ss. 47. ZA-47. ZM inserted (31.1.2017 for specified purposes, 3.4.2017 in so far as not already in force) by Policing and Crime Act 2017 (c. 3), ss. 63, 183. (1), (5)(e); S.I. 2017/399, reg. 2, Sch. para. 15 (with reg. 5)

47. ZGApplicable bail period: subsequent extensions of limit by court

(1) Subsections (2) to (6) apply where a court has authorised an extension of the applicable bail period in relation to a person under section 47. ZF.

(2) Before the applicable bail period in relation to the person ends a qualifying applicant may apply to a magistrates' court for it to authorise an extension of the applicable bail period in relation to the person under this section.

(3) If the court is satisfied that—

(a) conditions B to D are met in relation to the person, and

(b) the case does not fall within subsection (8),

it may authorise the applicable bail period to be extended as specified in subsection (4).

(4) The applicable bail period is to end at the end of the period of 3 months beginning with the end of the current applicable bail period in relation to the person.

(5) If the court is satisfied that—

(a) conditions B to D are met in relation to the person, and

(b) the case falls within subsection (8),

it may authorise the applicable bail period to be extended as specified in subsection (6).

(6) The applicable bail period is to end at the end of the period of 6 months beginning with the end of the current applicable bail period in relation to the person.

(7) Where a court has authorised an extension of the applicable bail period in relation to a person under subsection (3) or (5), a qualifying applicant may make further applications under subsection (2) (and subsections (3) to (6) apply accordingly).

(8) A case falls within this subsection if the nature of the decision or further investigations mentioned in condition B means that that decision is unlikely to be made or those investigations completed if the current applicable bail period in relation to the person is not extended as specified in subsection (6).

(9) For the purposes of this section—

(a) references to the current applicable bail period in relation to a person are to the applicable bail period applying to the person when the application under this section is made (subject to section 47. ZJ(3)), and

(b) "qualifying applicant" has the same meaning as in section 47. ZF.

Amendments (Textual)

F179. Ss. 47. ZA-47. ZM inserted (31.1.2017 for specified purposes, 3.4.2017 in so far as not already in force) by Policing and Crime Act 2017 (c. 3), ss. 63, 183. (1), (5)(e); S.I. 2017/399, reg. 2, Sch. para. 15 (with reg. 5)

47. ZHSections 47. ZF and 47. ZG: withholding sensitive information

(1) This section applies where a qualifying applicant makes an application to a magistrates' court under section 47. ZF or 47. ZG in relation to a person.

(2) The qualifying applicant may apply to the court for it to authorise the specified information to be withheld from the person and any legal representative of the person.

(3) The court may grant an application under subsection (2) only if satisfied that there are reasonable grounds for believing that the specified information is sensitive information.

(4) For the purposes of this section information is sensitive information if its disclosure would have one or more of the following results—

(a) evidence connected with an indictable offence would be interfered with or harmed;

(b) a person would be interfered with or physically injured;

(c) a person suspected of having committed an indictable offence but not yet arrested for the offence would be alerted;

(d) the recovery of property obtained as a result of an indictable offence would be hindered.

(5) In this section "specified information" means the information specified in the application under subsection (2).

Amendments (Textual)

F179. Ss. 47. ZA-47. ZM inserted (31.1.2017 for specified purposes, 3.4.2017 in so far as not already in force) by Policing and Crime Act 2017 (c. 3), ss. 63, 183. (1), (5)(e); S.I. 2017/399, reg. 2, Sch. para. 15 (with reg. 5)

47. ZISections 47. ZF to 47. ZH: proceedings in magistrates' court

(1) An application made to a magistrates' court under section 47. ZF or 47. ZG in relation to a person is to be determined by a single justice of the peace on written evidence unless subsection (2) or (3) applies.

(2) This subsection applies if—

(a) the effect of the application would be to extend the applicable bail period in relation to the person so that it ends at or before the end of the period of 12 months beginning with the person's bail start date, and

(b) a single justice of the peace considers that the interests of justice require an oral hearing.

(3) This subsection applies if—

(a) the effect of the application would be to extend the applicable bail period in relation to the person so that it ends after the end of the period of 12 months beginning with the person's bail start date, and

(b) the person, or the person who made the application, requests an oral hearing.

(4) If subsection (2) or (3) applies, the application is to be determined by two or more justices of the peace sitting otherwise than in open court.

(5) Where an application under section 47. ZF or 47. ZG in relation to a person is to be determined as mentioned in subsection (4), the justices may direct that the person and any legal representative of the person be excluded from any part of the hearing.

(6) The justices may give a direction under subsection (5) only if satisfied that there are reasonable

grounds for believing that sensitive information would be disclosed at the part of the hearing in question.

(7) An application under section 47. ZH is to be determined by a single justice of the peace on written evidence unless the justice determines that the interests of justice require an oral hearing.

(8) If the justice makes a determination under subsection (7)—

(a) the application is to be determined by two or more justices of the peace sitting otherwise than in open court, and

(b) the justices hearing the application must direct that the person to whom the application relates and any legal representative of the person be excluded from the hearing.

(9) In this section "sensitive information" has the meaning given in section 47. ZH(4).

Amendments (Textual)

F179. Ss. 47. ZA-47. ZM inserted (31.1.2017 for specified purposes, 3.4.2017 in so far as not already in force) by Policing and Crime Act 2017 (c. 3), ss. 63, 183. (1), (5)(e); S.I. 2017/399, reg. 2, Sch. para. 15 (with reg. 5)

47. ZJSections 47. ZF and 47. ZG: late applications to magistrates' court

(1) This section applies where—

(a) an application under section 47. ZF or 47. ZG is made to a magistrates' court before the end of the applicable bail period in relation to a person, but

(b) it is not practicable for the court to determine the application before the end of that period.

(2) The court must determine the application as soon as is practicable.

(3) The applicable bail period in relation to the person is to be treated as extended until the application is determined.

(4) If it appears to the court that it would have been reasonable for the application to have been made in time for it to have been determined by the court before the end of the applicable bail period in relation to the person, it may refuse the application.

Amendments (Textual)

F179. Ss. 47. ZA-47. ZM inserted (31.1.2017 for specified purposes, 3.4.2017 in so far as not already in force) by Policing and Crime Act 2017 (c. 3), ss. 63, 183. (1), (5)(e); S.I. 2017/399, reg. 2, Sch. para. 15 (with reg. 5)

47. ZKRules

Criminal Procedure Rules may make provision in connection with applications under sections 47. ZF, 47. ZG and 47. ZH and the proceedings for determining such applications.

Amendments (Textual)

F179. Ss. 47. ZA-47. ZM inserted (31.1.2017 for specified purposes, 3.4.2017 in so far as not already in force) by Policing and Crime Act 2017 (c. 3), ss. 63, 183. (1), (5)(e); S.I. 2017/399, reg. 2, Sch. para. 15 (with reg. 5)

47. ZLApplicable bail period and bail return date: special case of release on bail under section 37(7)(a) or 37. C(2)(b)

(1) This section applies where a person is released on bail under section 37. (7)(a) or 37. C(2)(b).

(2) The running of the applicable bail period in relation to the person—

(a) does not begin (in the case of a first release on bail), or

(b) is suspended (in any other case),

(subject to subsection (6)).

(3) Accordingly section 47. ZA does not apply to the exercise of the power mentioned in section

47. ZA(1) when releasing the person on bail.

(4) Subsections (5) and (6) apply if a DPP request is made in relation to the person.

(5) A custody officer must exercise the power mentioned in section 47. (4. A) to appoint a different time for the person to attend at the police station (and section 47. (4. B) to (4. D) applies accordingly).

(6) The applicable bail period in relation to the person—

(a) begins to run on the day on which the DPP request is made (in the case of a first release on bail), or

(b) resumes running on that day (in any other case).

(7) Subsection (8) applies where—

(a) a DPP request has been made in relation to the person, and

(b) the applicable bail period in relation to the person would end before the end of the period of 7 days beginning with the day on which the DPP request was made.

(8) The running of the applicable bail period in relation to the person is suspended for the number of days necessary to secure that the applicable bail period ends at the end of the period of 7 days beginning with the day on which the DPP request was made.

(9) Subsections (10) and (11) apply if the DPP request made in relation to the person is met.

(10) The running of the applicable bail period in relation to the person is suspended.

(11) Accordingly section 47. (4. D) does not apply to any exercise of the power under section 47. (4. A).

(12) For the purposes of this section—

(a) a "DPP request", in relation to a person, means a request by the Director of Public Prosecutions for the further information specified in the request to be provided before the Director decides under section 37. B(2) whether there is sufficient evidence to charge the person with the relevant offence,

(b) a DPP request is met when the further information specified in the request is provided, and

(c) references to the case of a first release on bail are to a case where the person has not been released on bail in relation to the relevant offence under any other provision of this Part or under section 30. A.

Amendments (Textual)

F179. Ss. 47. ZA-47. ZM inserted (31.1.2017 for specified purposes, 3.4.2017 in so far as not already in force) by Policing and Crime Act 2017 (c. 3), ss. 63, 183. (1), (5)(e); S.I. 2017/399, reg. 2, Sch. para. 15 (with reg. 5)

47. ZMApplicable bail period: special cases of release on bail under section 30. A and periods in hospital

(1) Subsections (2) and (3) apply where a person was released on bail under section 30. A.

(2) The period of 28 days mentioned in section 30. B(8) in relation to the person is to be treated as being the period of 28 days mentioned in section 47. ZB(1)(b) in relation to the person.

(3) Any reference to the relevant offence, in relation to the person, is to be read as a reference to the offence in respect of which the power in section 30. A(1) was exercised.

(4) Subsection (5) applies if, at any time on the day on which the applicable bail period in relation to a person would end, the person is in hospital as an in-patient.

(5) The running of the applicable bail period in relation to the person is to be treated as having been suspended for any day on which the patient was in hospital as an in-patient.]

Amendments (Textual)

F179. Ss. 47. ZA-47. ZM inserted (31.1.2017 for specified purposes, 3.4.2017 in so far as not already in force) by Policing and Crime Act 2017 (c. 3), ss. 63, 183. (1), (5)(e); S.I. 2017/399, reg. 2, Sch. para. 15 (with reg. 5)

[F18047. A Early administrative hearings conducted by justices' clerks.

Where a person has been charged with an offence at a police station, any requirement imposed under this Part for the person to appear or be brought before a magistrates' court shall be taken to be satisfied if the person appears or is brought before [F181a justices' clerk] in order for the clerk to conduct a hearing under section 50 of the Crime and Disorder Act 1998 (early administrative hearings).]

Amendments (Textual)

F180. S. 47. A inserted (30.9.1998) by 1998 c. 37, s. 119, Sch. 8 para.62; S.I. 1998/2327, art. 2. (2)(t).

F181. Words in s. 47. A substituted (1.4.2005) by Courts Act 2003 (c. 39), ss. 109. (1), 110, Sch. 8 para. 284; S.I. 2005/910, art. 3. (y)

48 Remands to police detention.

In section 128 of the Magistrates' Courts Act 1980—

(a) in subsection (7) for the words "the custody of a constable" there shall be substituted the words "detention at a police station";

(b) after subsection (7) there shall be inserted the following subsection—

"(8)Where a person is committed to detention at a police station under subsection (7) above—

(a) he shall not be kept in such detention unless there is a need for him to be so detained for the purposes of inquiries into other offences;

(b) if kept in such detention, he shall be brought back before the magistrates' court which committed him as soon as that need ceases;

(c) he shall be treated as a person in police detention to whom the duties under section 39 of the Police and Criminal Evidence Act 1984 (responsibilities in relation to persons detained) relate;

(d) his detention shall be subject to periodic review at the times set out in section 40 of that Act (review of police detention).".

49 Police detention to count towards custodial sentence.

(1) In subsection (1) of section 67 of the M5. Criminal Justice Act 1967 (computation of custodial sentences) for the words from "period", in the first place where it occurs, to "the offender" there shall be substituted the words "relevant period, but where he".

(2) The following subsection shall be inserted after that subsection—

"(1. A)In subsection (1) above "relevant period" means—

(a) any period during which the offender was in police detention in connection with the offence for which the sentence was passed; or

(b) any period during which he was in custody—

(i) by reason only of having been committed to custody by an order of a court made in connection with any proceedings relating to that sentence or the offence for which it was passed or any proceedings from which those proceedings arose; or

(ii) by reason of his having been so committed and having been concurrently detained otherwise than by order of a court.".

(3) The following subsections shall be added after subsection (6) of that section—

"(7)A person is in police detention for the purposes of this section—

(a) at any time when he is in police detention for the purposes of the Police and Criminal Evidence Act 1984; and

(b) at any time when he is detained under section 12 of the Prevention of Terrorism (Temporary Provisions) Act 1984.

(8) No period of police detention shall be taken into account under this section unless it falls after the coming into force of section 49 of the Police and Criminal Evidence Act 1984.".
Marginal Citations
M51967 c. 80.

50 Records of detention.

(1) Each police force shall keep written records showing on an annual basis—

(a) the number of persons kept in police detention for more than 24 hours and subsequently released without charge;

(b) the number of applications for warrants of further detention and the results of the applications; and

(c) in relation to each warrant of further detention—

(i) the period of further detention authorised by it;

(ii) the period which the person named in it spent in police detention on its authority; and

(iii) whether he was charged or released without charge.

(2) Every annual report—

F182[(a)under section 22 of the Police Act 1996; or]

(b) made by the Commissioner of Police of the Metropolis,

shall contain information about the matters mentioned in subsection (1) above in respect of the period to which the report relates.

Amendments (Textual)
F182. S. 50. (2)(a) substituted (22.8.1996) by 1996 c. 16, ss. 103, 104. (1) Sch. 7 Pt. II para.35
Modifications etc. (not altering text)
C90. Ss. 8, 9, 15, 16, 17. (1)(b(2) (4), 18–20, 21, 22. (1)–(4), 28, 29, 30. (1)–(4)(a)(5)–(11), 31, 32. (1)–(9), 34. (1)–(5), 35, 36, 37, 39, 40–44, 50, 51. (d), 52, 54, 55, 64. (1)–(4)(5)(6), Sch. 1 applied with modifications by S.I. 1985/1800, arts. 3–11, Schs. 1, 2
C91. S. 50 modified (2.8.1993) by S.I. 1993/1813, art. 6, Sch. 3 para. 3. (3).
C92. S. 50 applied (with modifications) (25.6.2013) by The Police and Criminal Evidence Act 1984 (Application to immigration officers and designated customs officials in England and Wales) Order 2013 (S.I. 2013/1542), arts. 1, 12. (2)-(4), Sch. 2 (with arts. 13-31)
C93. S. 50 applied (with modifications) (4.11.2015) by The Police and Criminal Evidence Act 1984 (Application to Revenue and Customs) Order 2015 (S.I. 2015/1783), arts. 1, 3. (1), Sch. 1 (with art. 3. (2), (3), 4-19, Sch. 2)

[F18350. AInterpretation of references to pre-conditions for bail

For the purposes of this Part the following are the pre-conditions for bail in relation to the release of a person by a custody officer—

(a) that the custody officer is satisfied that releasing the person on bail is necessary and proportionate in all the circumstances (having regard, in particular, to any conditions of bail which would be imposed), and

(b) that an officer of the rank of inspector or above authorises the release on bail (having considered any representations made by the person or the person's legal representative).]

Amendments (Textual)
F183. S. 50. A inserted (31.1.2017 for specified purposes, 3.4.2017 in so far as not already in force) by Policing and Crime Act 2017 (c. 3), ss. 58, 183. (1), (5)(e); S.I. 2017/399, reg. 2, Sch. para. 12 (with reg. 5)

51 Savings.

Nothing in this Part of this Act shall affect—

(a) the powers conferred on immigration officers by section 4 of and Schedule 2 to the M6. Immigration Act 1971 (administrative provisions as to control on entry etc.);

[F184. (b)the powers conferred by virtue of section 41 of, or Schedule 7 to, the Terrorism Act 2000 (powers of arrest and detention);]

(c) F185. . . . .

(d) any right of a person in police detention to apply for a writ of habeas corpus or other prerogative remedy.

Amendments (Textual)

F184. S. 51. (b) substituted (19.2.2001) by 2000 c. 11, s. 125. (1), Sch. 15 para. 5. (4); S.I.2001/421, art. 2

F185. S. 51. (c) repealed (28.3.2009 for certain purposes and otherwise prosp.) by Armed Forces Act 2006 (c. 52), ss. 378, 383, Sch. 17; S.I. 2009/812, art. 3 (with transitional provisions in S.I. 2009/1059)

Modifications etc. (not altering text)

C94. S. 51. (b) applied (with modifications) (25.6.2013) by The Police and Criminal Evidence Act 1984 (Application to immigration officers and designated customs officials in England and Wales) Order 2013 (S.I. 2013/1542), arts. 1, 3. (2)-(4), Sch. 1 (with arts. 4-11)

C95. Ss. 8, 9, 15, 16, 17. (1)(b(2) (4), 18–20, 21, 22. (1)–(4), 28, 29, 30. (1)–(4)(a)(5)–(11), 31, 32. (1)–(9), 34. (1)–(5), 35, 36, 37, 39, 40–44, 50, 51. (d), 52, 54, 55, 64. (1)–(4)(5)(6), Sch. 1 applied with modifications by S.I. 1985/1800, arts. 3–11, Schs. 1, 2

C96. S. 51. (d) applied (with modifications) (4.11.2015) by The Police and Criminal Evidence Act 1984 (Application to Revenue and Customs) Order 2015 (S.I. 2015/1783), arts. 1, 3. (1), Sch. 1 (with art. 3. (2), (3), 4-19, Sch. 2)

Marginal Citations

M61971 c. 77.

F18652. . . . .

Amendments (Textual)

F186. S. 52 repealed (14.10.1991) by Children Act 1989 (c. 41, SIF 20), s. 108. (7), Sch.15; S.I. 1991/828, art. 3. (2)

Part V Questioning and Treatment of Persons by Police

Part V Questioning and Treatment of Persons by Police

Modifications etc. (not altering text)

C1. Pt. V incorporated (16.5.2008) by The London Gateway Port Harbour Empowerment Order 2008 (S.I. 2008/1261), art. 52

53 Abolition of certain powers of constables to search persons.

(1) Subject to subsection (2) below, there shall cease to have effect any Act (including a local Act) passed before this Act in so far as it authorises—

(a) any search by a constable of a person in police detention at a police station; or

(b) an intimate search of a person by a constable;

and any rule of common law which authorises a search such as is mentioned in paragraph (a) or

(b) above is abolished.

F1. (2). . . . .

Amendments (Textual)

F1. S. 53. (2) repealed by Prevention of Terrorism (Temporary Provisions) Act 1989 (c. 4, SIF 39:2), s. 25. (2), Sch. 9 Pt. I

54 Searches of detained persons.

(1) F2. The custody officer at a police station shall ascertain . . . everything which a person has with him when he is—

  (a) brought to the station after being arrested elsewhere or after being committed to custody by an order of sentence of a court; or

  F3[F4. (b)arrested at the station or detained there [F5, as a person falling within section 34. (7), under section 37 above [F6or as a person to whom section 46. ZA(4) or (5) applies]].]

[F7. (2)The custody officer may record or cause to be recorded all or any of the things which he ascertains under subsection (1).

(2. A)In the case of an arrested person, any such record may be made as part of his custody record.]

(3) Subject to subsection (4) below, a custody officer may seize and retain any such thing or cause any such thing to be seized and retained.

(4) Clothes and personal effects may only be seized if the custody officer—

  (a) believes that the person from whom they are seized may use them—

(i) to cause physical injury to himself or any other person;

(ii) to damage property;

(iii) to interfere with evidence; or

(iv) to assist him to escape; or

  (b) has reasonable grounds for believing that they may be evidence relating to an offence.

(5) Where anything is seized, the person from whom it is seized shall be told the reason for the seizure unless he is—

  (a) violent or likely to become violent; or

  (b) incapable of understanding what is said to him.

(6) Subject to subsection (7) below, a person may be searched if the custody officer considers it necessary to enable him to carry out his duty under subsection (1) above and to the extent that the custody officer considers necessary for that purpose.

[F8. (6. A)A person who is in custody at a police station or is in police detention otherwise than at a police station may at any time be searched in order to ascertain whether he has with him anything which he could use for any of the purposes specified in subsection (4)(a) above.

(6. B)Subject to subsection (6. C) below, a constable may seize and retain, or cause to be seized and retained, anything found on such a search.

(6. C)A constable may only seize clothes and personal effects in the circumstances specified in subsection (4) above.]

(7) An intimate search may not be conducted under this section.

(8) A search under this section shall be carried out by a constable.

(9) The constable carrying out a search shall be of the same sex as the person searched.

Amendments (Textual)

F2. Words in s. 54. (1) repealed (20.1.2004) by Criminal Justice Act 2003 (c. 44), ss. 8. (1), 332, 336, Sch. 37 Pt. 1; S.I. 2004/81, art. 2. (1)(2)(a)(f)(g)(i)

F3. Words in s. 54. (1)(b) inserted (1.4.2007 for specified purposes, 14.11.2008 for specified purposes, 3.10.2011 for specified purposes, 8.10.2012 in so far as not already in force) by Police and Justice Act 2006 (c. 48), ss. 46. (6), 53. (1); S.I. 2007/709, art. 3. (n) (with art. 6); S.I. 2008/2785, art. 2; S.I. 2011/2144, art. 2. (1)(b); S.I. 2012/2373, art. 2. (b)

F4. S. 54. (1)(b) substituted by Criminal Justice Act 1988 (c. 33, SIF 39:1), s. 147. (a)

F5. Words in s. 54. (1)(b) substituted (10.4.1995) by 1994 c. 33, s. 168. (2), Sch. 10 para.55; S.I. 1995/721, art. 2, Sch. Appendix A

F6. Words in s. 54. (1)(b) inserted (1.4.2007 for certain purposes, otherwise prosp.) by Police and Justice Act 2006 (c. 48), ss. 46. (6), 53; S.I. 2007/709, art. 3. (n) (subject to arts. 6, 7)

F7. S. 54. (2)(2. A) substituted (20.1.2004) for s. 54. (2) by Criminal Justice Act 2003 (c. 44), ss. 8. (2), 336; S.I. 2004/81, art. 2. (1)(2)(a)

F8. S. 54. (6. A)–(6. C) inserted by Criminal Justice Act 1988 (c. 33, SIF 39:1), s. 147. (b) Modifications etc. (not altering text)

C2. Ss. 8, 9, 15, 16, 17. (1)(b(2) (4), 18–20, 21, 22. (1)–(4), 28, 29, 30. (1)–(4)(a)(5)–(11), 31, 32. (1)–(9), 34. (1)–(5), 35, 36, 37, 39, 40–44, 50, 51. (d), 52, 54, 55, 64. (1)–(4)(5)(6), Sch. 1 applied with modifications by S.I. 1985/1800, arts. 3–11, Schs. 1, 2

S. 54. (1)(3)(4)(6)(6. A)(8)(9) applied (with modifications) (1.2.1997) by S.I. 1997/15, art. 2. (1),Sch.

S. 54. (5)(7) applied (1.2.1997) by S.I. 1997/15, art. 2. (1),Sch.

C3. S. 54 extended (2.8.1993) by S.I. 1993/1813, art. 6, Sch. 3 paras. 1. (2)(b), 3. (2)(3); s. 54 extended by the said S.I. 1993/1813, art. 6, Sch. 3 paras. 3, 4 as incorporated (with modifications) (1.12.1997) by S.I. 1994/1405, art. 6, Sch. 3 paras. 4. (b), 5

S. 54 extended (2.12.2002) by 2002 c. 30, s. 38, Sch. 4 Pt. 3 para. 26. (1); S.I. 2002/2750, (art. 2. (a)(ii)(d))

C4. S. 54 applied (with modifications) (1.1.2004) by The Extradition Act 2003 (Police Powers) Order 2003 (S.I. 2003/3106), art. 2

S. 54 applied (with modifications) by Criminal Justice Act 2003 (c. 44), s. 24. B(6) (as inserted (29.6.2007) by Police and Justice Act 2006 (c. 48), ss. 18. (1), 53 (with s. 18. (2)); S.I. 2007/1614, art. 2. (e))

C5. S. 54: power to apply (with modifications) conferred (1.1.2004) by Extradition Act 2003 (c. 41), ss. 171. (3)(a), 221; S.I. 2003/3103, art. 2 (subject to savings in Order (as amended by S.I. 2003/3312, art. 2. (2) and S.I. 2003/3258, art. 2. (2)))

C6. S. 54 applied (with modifications) (31.12.2006) by The Police and Criminal Evidence Act 1984 (Application to the Armed Forces) Order 2006 (S.I. 2006/2015), arts. 2, 3, Schs. 1-3

C7. S. 54 applied (with modifications) (25.6.2013) by The Police and Criminal Evidence Act 1984 (Application to immigration officers and designated customs officials in England and Wales) Order 2013 (S.I. 2013/1542), arts. 1, 12. (2)-(4), Sch. 2 (with arts. 13-31)

C8. S. 54 applied (with modifications) (4.11.2015) by The Police and Criminal Evidence Act 1984 (Application to Revenue and Customs) Order 2015 (S.I. 2015/1783), arts. 1, 3. (1), Sch. 1 (with art. 3. (2), (3), 4-19, Sch. 2)

C9. S. 54. (6. A)(6. B) extended (2.12.2002) by Police Reform Act 2002 (c. 30), s. 38, Sch. 4 Pt. 4 para. 34. (2)(a); S.I. 2002/2750, art. 2. (a)(ii)(d)

S. 54. (6. A)(6. B) extended (2.12.2002) by Police Reform Act 2002 (c. 30), s. 38, Sch. 4 Pt. 4 para. 35. (4)(a); S.I. 2002/2750, art. 2. (a)(ii)(d)

C10. S. 54. (6. C) applied (2.12.2002) by Police Reform Act 2002 (c. 30), s. 38, Sch. 4 Pt. 3 para. 26. (2); S.I. 2002/2750, art. 2. (a)(ii)(d)

S. 54. (6. C) applied (2.12.2002) by Police Reform Act 2002 (c. 30), s. 38, Sch. 4 Pt. 4 para. 34. (2)(b); S.I. 2002/2750, art. 2. (a)(ii)(d)

S. 54. (6. C) applied (2.12.2002) by Police Reform Act 2002 (c. 30), s. 38, Sch. 4 Pt. 4 para. 35. (4)(b); S.I. 2002/2750, art. 2. (a)(ii)(d)

C11. S. 54. (9) applied (2.12.2002) by Police Reform Act 2002 (c. 30), s. 38, Sch. 4 Pt. 3 para. 26. (2); S.I. 2002/2750, art. 2. (a)(ii)(d)

S. 54. (9) applied (2.12.2002) by Police Reform Act 2002 (c. 30), s. 38, Sch. 4 Pt. 4 para. 34. (2)(b); S.I. 2002/2750, art. 2. (a)(ii)(d)

S. 54. (9) applied (2.12.2002) by Police Reform Act 2002 (c. 30), s. 38, Sch. 4 Pt. 4 para. 35. (4)(b); S.I. 2002/2750, art. 2. (a)(ii)(d)

[F954. A Searches and examination to ascertain identity

(1) If an officer of at least the rank of inspector authorises it, a person who is detained in a police station may be searched or examined, or both—

  (a) for the purpose of ascertaining whether he has any mark that would tend to identify him as a person involved in the commission of an offence; or

  (b) for the purpose of facilitating the ascertainment of his identity.

(2) An officer may only give an authorisation under subsection (1) for the purpose mentioned in paragraph (a) of that subsection if—

  (a) the appropriate consent to a search or examination that would reveal whether the mark in question exists has been withheld; or

  (b) it is not practicable to obtain such consent.

(3) An officer may only give an authorisation under subsection (1) in a case in which subsection (2) does not apply if—

  (a) the person in question has refused to identify himself; or

  (b) the officer has reasonable grounds for suspecting that that person is not who he claims to be.

(4) An officer may give an authorisation under subsection (1) orally or in writing but, if he gives it orally, he shall confirm it in writing as soon as is practicable.

(5) Any identifying mark found on a search or examination under this section may be photographed—

  (a) with the appropriate consent; or

  (b) if the appropriate consent is withheld or it is not practicable to obtain it, without it.

(6) Where a search or examination may be carried out under this section, or a photograph may be taken under this section, the only persons entitled to carry out the search or examination, or to take the photograph, are[F10 constables]

(7) A person may not under this section carry out a search or examination of a person of the opposite sex or take a photograph of any part of the body of a person of the opposite sex.

(8) An intimate search may not be carried out under this section.

(9) A photograph taken under this section—

  (a) may be used by, or disclosed to, any person for any purpose related to the prevention or detection of crime, the investigation of an offence or the conduct of a prosecution; and

  (b) after being so used or disclosed, may be retained but may not be used or disclosed except for a purpose so related.

(10) In subsection —

  (a) the reference to crime includes a reference to any conduct which—

(i) constitutes one or more criminal offences (whether under the law of a part of the United Kingdom or of a country or territory outside the United Kingdom); or

(ii) is, or corresponds to, any conduct which, if it all took place in any one part of the United Kingdom, would constitute one or more criminal offences;

and

  (b) the references to an investigation and to a prosecution include references, respectively, to any investigation outside the United Kingdom of any crime or suspected crime and to a prosecution brought in respect of any crime in a country or territory outside the United Kingdom.

(11) In this section—

  (a) references to ascertaining a person's identity include references to showing that he is not a particular person; and

  (b) references to taking a photograph include references to using any process by means of which a visual image may be produced, and references to photographing a person shall be construed accordingly.

(12) In this section "mark" includes features and injuries; and a mark is an identifying mark for the purposes of this section if its existence in any person's case facilitates the ascertainment of his identity or his identification as a person involved in the commission of an offence.

[F11. (13)Nothing in this section applies to a person arrested under an extradition arrest power.]]

Amendments (Textual)

F9. S. 54. A inserted (14.12.2001) by 2001 c. 24, s. 90. (1)

F10. Words in s. 54. A(6) substituted (2.12.2002) by Police Reform Act 2002 (c.30), s. 107, Sch. 7 {para. 9. (2)}; S.I. 2002/2750, art. 2. (b)(ii)

F11. S. 54. A(13) inserted (1.1.2004) by Extradition Act 2003 (c. 41), ss. 169. (2), 221; S.I. 2003/3103, art. 2 (subject to savings in Order (as amended by S.I. 2003/3312, art. 2. (2) and S.I. 2003/3258, art. 2. (2)))

Modifications etc. (not altering text)

C12. S. 54. A applied (with modifications) (25.6.2013) by The Police and Criminal Evidence Act 1984 (Application to immigration officers and designated customs officials in England and Wales) Order 2013 (S.I. 2013/1542), arts. 1, 12. (2)-(4), Sch. 2 (with arts. 13-31)

C13. S. 54. A applied (with modifications) (31.12.2006) by The Police and Criminal Evidence Act 1984 (Application to the Armed Forces) Order 2006 (S.I. 2006/2015), arts. 2, 3, Schs. 1-3

S. 54. A applied (with modifications) by Criminal Justice Act 2003 (c. 44), s. 24. B(7) (as inserted (29.6.2007) by Police and Justice Act 2006 (c. 48), ss. 18. (1), 53 (with s. 18. (2)); S.I. 2007/1614, art. 2. (e))

F12[54. BSearches of persons answering to live link bail

(1) A constable may search at any time—

    (a) any person who is at a police station to answer to live link bail; and

    (b) any article in the possession of such a person.

(2) If the constable reasonably believes a thing in the possession of the person ought to be seized on any of the grounds mentioned in subsection (3), the constable may seize and retain it or cause it to be seized and retained.

(3) The grounds are that the thing—

    (a) may jeopardise the maintenance of order in the police station;

    (b) may put the safety of any person in the police station at risk; or

    (c) may be evidence of, or in relation to, an offence.

(4) The constable may record or cause to be recorded all or any of the things seized and retained pursuant to subsection (2).

(5) An intimate search may not be carried out under this section.

(6) The constable carrying out a search under subsection (1) must be of the same sex as the person being searched.

(7) In this section "live link bail" means bail granted under Part 4 of this Act subject to the duty mentioned in section 47. (3)(b).]

Amendments (Textual)

F12. Ss. 54. B, 54. C inserted (14.12.2009 for specified purposes, 3.10.2011 for specified purposes, 8.10.2012 in so far as not already in force) by Coroners and Justice Act 2009 (c. 25), ss. 108. (1), 182. (5) (with s. 180); S.I. 2009/3253, art. 3. (1)(c); S.I. 2011/2148, art. 2; S.I. 2012/2374, art. 3. (c)

F12[54. CPower to retain articles seized

(1) Except as provided by subsections (2) and (3), a constable may retain a thing seized under section 54. B until the time when the person from whom it was seized leaves the police station.

(2) A constable may retain a thing seized under section 54. B in order to establish its lawful owner, where there are reasonable grounds for believing that it has been obtained in consequence of the commission of an offence.

(3) If a thing seized under section 54. B may be evidence of, or in relation to, an offence, a constable may retain it—

(a) for use as evidence at a trial for an offence; or

(b) for forensic examination or for investigation in connection with an offence.

(4) Nothing may be retained for either of the purposes mentioned in subsection (3) if a photograph or copy would be sufficient for that purpose.

(5) Nothing in this section affects any power of a court to make an order under section 1 of the Police (Property) Act 1897.

(6) The references in this section to anything seized under section 54. B include anything seized by a person to whom paragraph 27. A of Schedule 4 to the Police Reform Act 2002 applies.]

Amendments (Textual)

F12. Ss. 54. B, 54. C inserted (14.12.2009 for specified purposes, 3.10.2011 for specified purposes, 8.10.2012 in so far as not already in force) by Coroners and Justice Act 2009 (c. 25), ss. 108. (1), 182. (5) (with s. 180); S.I. 2009/3253, art. 3. (1)(c); S.I. 2011/2148, art. 2; S.I. 2012/2374, art. 3. (c)

55. Intimate searches

(1) Subject to the following provisions of this section, if an officer of at least the rank of [F13inspector] has reasonable grounds for believing—

(a) that a person who has been arrested and is in police detention may have concealed on him anything which—

(i) he could use to cause physical injury to himself or others; and

(ii) he might so use while he is in police detention or in the custody of a court; or

(b) that such a person—

(i) may have a Class A drug concealed on him; and

(ii) was in possession of it with the appropriate criminal intent before his arrest,

he may authorise [F14an intimate search] of that person.

(2) An officer may not authorise an intimate search of a person for anything unless he has reasonable grounds for believing that it cannot be found without his being intimately searched.

(3) An officer may give an authorisation under subsection (1) above orally or in writing but, if he gives it orally, he shall confirm it in writing as soon as is practicable.

[F15. (3. A)A drug offence search shall not be carried out unless the appropriate consent has been given in writing.

(3. B)Where it is proposed that a drug offence search be carried out, an appropriate officer shall inform the person who is to be subject to it—

(a) of the giving of the authorisation for it; and

(b) of the grounds for giving the authorisation.]

(4) An intimate search which is only a drug offence search shall be by way of examination by a suitably qualified person.

(5) Except as provided by subsection (4) above, an intimate search shall be by way of examination by a suitably qualified person unless an officer of at least the rank of [F13inspector] considers that this is not practicable.

(6) An intimate search which is not carried out as mentioned in subsection (5) above shall be carried out by a constable.

(7) A constable may not carry out an intimate search of a person of the opposite sex.

(8) No intimate search may be carried out except—

(a) at a police station;

(b) at a hospital;

(c) at a registered medical practitioner's surgery; or

(d) at some other place used for medical purposes.

(9) An intimate search which is only a drug offence search may not be carried out at a police station.

(10) If an intimate search of a person is carried out, the custody record relating to him shall state—

(a) which parts of his body were searched; and

(b) why they were searched.

[F16. (10. A)If the intimate search is a drug offence search, the custody record relating to that person shall also state—

(a) the authorisation by virtue of which the search was carried out;

(b) the grounds for giving the authorisation; and

(c) the fact that the appropriate consent was given.]

(11) The information required to be recorded by [F17subsections (10) and (10. A)] above shall be recorded as soon as practicable after the completion of the search.

(12) The custody officer at a police station may seize and retain anything which is found on an intimate search of a person, or cause any such thing to be seized and retained—

(a) if he believes that the person from whom it is seized may use it—

(i) to cause physical injury to himself or any other person;

(ii) to damage property;

(iii) to interfere with evidence; or

(iv) to assist him to escape; or

(b) if he has reasonable grounds for believing that it may be evidence relating to an offence.

(13) Where anything is seized under this section, the person from whom it is seized shall be told the reason for the seizure unless he is—

(a) violent or likely to become violent; or

(b) incapable of understanding what is said to him.

[F18. (13. A)Where the appropriate consent to a drug offence search of any person was refused without good cause, in any proceedings against that person for an offence—

(a) the court, in determining whether there is a case to answer;

(b) a judge, in deciding whether to grant an application made by the accused under paragraph 2 of Schedule 3 to the Crime and Disorder Act 1998 (applications for dismissal); and

(c) the court or jury, in determining whether that person is guilty of the offence charged, may draw such inferences from the refusal as appear proper.]

(14) Every annual report—

[F19. (a)under section 22 of the M1. Police Act 1996; or]

(b) made by the Commissioner of Police of the Metropolis, shall contain information about searches under this section which have been carried out in the area to which the report relates during the period to which it relates.

(14. A)F20. . . . .

(15) The information about such searches shall include—

(a) the total number of searches;

(b) the number of searches conducted by way of examination by a suitably qualified person;

(c) the number of searches not so conducted but conducted in the presence of such a person; and

(d) the result of the searches carried out.

(16) The information shall also include, as separate items—

(a) the total number of drug offence searches; and

(b) the result of those searches.

(17) In this section—

"the appropriate criminal intent" means an intent to commit an offence under—

(a) section 5. (3) of the M2. Misuse of Drugs Act 1971 (possession of controlled drug with intent to supply to another); or

(b) section 68. (2) of the M3. Customs and Excise Management Act 1979 (exportation etc. with intent to evade a prohibition or restriction);

[F21"appropriate officer" means—

- a constable,

- F22...F23. . .

- F23. . . . .]

"Class A drug" has the meaning assigned to it by section 2. (1)(b) of the Misuse of Drugs Act

1971;

"drug offence search" means an intimate search for a Class A drug which an officer has authorised by virtue of subsection (1)(b) above; and

"suitably qualified person" means—

  (a) a registered medical practitioner; or

  (b) a registered nurse.

Amendments (Textual)

F13. Words in s. 55. (1)(5) inserted (1.4.2003) by 2001 c. 16, ss. 79, 138. (2); S.I. 2003/708, art. 2. (g)

F14. Words substituted by Criminal Justice Act 1988 (c. 33, SIF 39:1), s. 170. (1), Sch. 15 para. 99

F15. S. 55. (3. A)(3. B) inserted (1.1.2006) by Drugs Act 2005 (c. 17), ss. 3. (2), 24; S.I. 2005/3053, art. 3. (b)

F16. S. 55. (10. A) inserted (1.1.2006) by Drugs Act 2005 (c. 17), ss. 3. (3), 24; S.I. 2005/3053, art. 3. (b)

F17. Words in s. 55. (11) substituted (1.1.2006) by Drugs Act 2005 (c. 17), ss. 3. (4), 24; S.I. 2005/3053, art. 3. (b)

F18. S. 55. (13. A) inserted (1.1.2006) by Drugs Act 2005 (c. 17), ss. 3. (5), 24; S.I. 2005/3053, art. 3. (b)

F19. S. 55. (14)(a) substituted (22.8.1996) by 1996 c. 16, ss. 103. (1), 104. (1), Sch. 7 Pt. II para. 36

F20. S. 55. (14. A) repealed (1.4.2006) by Serious Organised Crime and Police Act 2005 (c. 15), ss. 59, 174, 178, Sch. 4 para. 45, Sch. 17 Pt. 2; S.I. 2006/378, art. 4. (1), Sch. paras. 10, 12, 13. (q) (subject to art. 4. (2)-(7))

F21. S. 55. (17): definition of "appropriate officer" inserted (1.1.2006) by Drugs Act 2005 (c. 17), ss. 3. (6), 24; S.I. 2005/3053, art. 3. (b)

F22. Words in s. 55. (17) omitted (31.1.2017 for specified purposes, 15.12.2017 in so far as not already in force) by virtue of Policing and Crime Act 2017 (c. 3), s. 183. (1)(5)(e), Sch. 12 para. 7. (2); S.I. 2017/1139, reg. 2. (k) (as amended by S.I. 2017/1162, reg. 2)

F23. Words in s. 55. (17) definition of "appropriate officer" repealed (12.1.2010) by Policing and Crime Act 2009 (c. 26), ss. 112. (1)(2), 116. (6), Sch. 7 para. 123. (5), Sch. 8 Pt. 13

Modifications etc. (not altering text)

C14. Ss. 8, 9, 15, 16, 17. (1)(b(2) (4), 18–20, 21, 22. (1)–(4), 28, 29, 30. (1)–(4)(a)(5)–(11), 31, 32. (1)–(9), 34. (1)–(5), 35, 36, 37, 39, 40–44, 50, 51. (d), 52, 54, 55, 64. (1)–(4)(5)(6), Sch. 1 applied with modifications by S.I. 1985/1800, arts. 3–11, Schs. 1, 2

S. 55. (1)-(3)(5)(6)-(10)(12)(17) applied (with modifications) (1.2.1997) by S.I. 1997/15, art. 2. (1), Sch.

S. 55. (4)(11)(13) applied (1.2.1997) by S.I. 1997/15, art. 2. (1), Sch.

C15. S. 55 extended (2.8.1993) by S.I. 1993/1813, art. 6, Sch. 3 paras. 1. (2)(b), 3. (2)(3); s. 55 extended by the said S.I. 1993/1813, art. 6, Sch. 3 paras. 3, 4 as incorporated (with modifications) (1.12.1997) by S.I. 1994/1405, art. 6, Sch. 3 paras. 4. (b), 5

C16. S. 55: power to apply (with modifications) conferred (1.1.2004) by Extradition Act 2003 (c. 41), ss. 171. (3)(b), 221; S.I. 2003/3103, art. 2 (subject to savings in Order (as amended by S.I. 2003/3312, art. 2. (2) and S.I. 2003/3258, art. 2. (2)))

C17. S. 55 applied (with modifications) (1.1.2004) by The Extradition Act 2003 (Police Powers) Order 2003 (S.I. 2003/3106), art. 2

C18. S. 55 applied (with modifications) (31.12.2006) by The Police and Criminal Evidence Act 1984 (Application to the Armed Forces) Order 2006 (S.I. 2006/2015), arts. 2, 3, Schs. 1-3

C19. S. 55 applied (with modifications) (4.11.2015) by The Police and Criminal Evidence Act 1984 (Application to Revenue and Customs) Order 2015 (S.I. 2015/1783), arts. 1, 3. (1), Sch. 1 (with art. 3. (2), (3), 4-19, Sch. 2)

C20. S. 55. (1)(a)(2)(3)(5)-(8)(10)(11)-(13)(14)(15)(17) applied (with modifications) (25.6.2013) by The Police and Criminal Evidence Act 1984 (Application to immigration officers and designated customs officials in England and Wales) Order 2013 (S.I. 2013/1542), arts. 1, 12. (2)-(4), Sch. 2 (with arts. 13-31)

C21. S. 55. (6) extended (2.12.2002) by Police Reform Act 2002 (c. 30), s. 38, Sch. 4 Pt. 3 para. 28. (1); S.I. 2002/2750, art. 2. (a)(ii)(d)

C22. S. 55. (7) applied (2.12.2002) by Police Reform Act 2002 (c. 30), s. 38, Sch. 4 Pt. 3 para. 28. (2); S.I. 2002/2750, art. 2. (a)(ii)(d)

Marginal Citations

M11996 C. 16.

M21971 c. 38.

M31979 c. 2.

[F2455. AX-rays and ultrasound scans

(1) If an officer of at least the rank of inspector has reasonable grounds for believing that a person who has been arrested for an offence and is in police detention—

    (a) may have swallowed a Class A drug, and

    (b) was in possession of it with the appropriate criminal intent before his arrest,

the officer may authorise that an x-ray is taken of the person or an ultrasound scan is carried out on the person (or both).

(2) An x-ray must not be taken of a person and an ultrasound scan must not be carried out on him unless the appropriate consent has been given in writing.

(3) If it is proposed that an x-ray is taken or an ultrasound scan is carried out, an appropriate officer must inform the person who is to be subject to it—

    (a) of the giving of the authorisation for it, and

    (b) of the grounds for giving the authorisation.

(4) An x-ray may be taken or an ultrasound scan carried out only by a suitably qualified person and only at—

    (a) a hospital,

    (b) a registered medical practitioner's surgery, or

    (c) some other place used for medical purposes.

(5) The custody record of the person must also state—

    (a) the authorisation by virtue of which the x-ray was taken or the ultrasound scan was carried out,

    (b) the grounds for giving the authorisation, and

    (c) the fact that the appropriate consent was given.

(6) The information required to be recorded by subsection (5) must be recorded as soon as practicable after the x-ray has been taken or ultrasound scan carried out (as the case may be).

(7) Every annual report—

    (a) under section 22 of the Police Act 1996, or

    (b) made by the Commissioner of Police of the Metropolis,

must contain information about x-rays which have been taken and ultrasound scans which have been carried out under this section in the area to which the report relates during the period to which it relates.

(8) The information about such x-rays and ultrasound scans must be presented separately and must include—

    (a) the total number of x-rays;

    (b) the total number of ultrasound scans;

    (c) the results of the x-rays;

    (d) the results of the ultrasound scans.

(9) If the appropriate consent to an x-ray or ultrasound scan of any person is refused without good cause, in any proceedings against that person for an offence—

    (a) the court, in determining whether there is a case to answer,

(b) a judge, in deciding whether to grant an application made by the accused under paragraph 2 of Schedule 3 to the Crime and Disorder Act 1998 (applications for dismissal), and

(c) the court or jury, in determining whether that person is guilty of the offence charged, may draw such inferences from the refusal as appear proper.

(10) In this section "the appropriate criminal intent", "appropriate officer", "Class A drug" and "suitably qualified person" have the same meanings as in section 55 above.]

Amendments (Textual)

F24. S. 55. A inserted (1.1.2006) by Drugs Act 2005 (c. 17), ss. 5. (1), 24; S.I. 2005/3053, art. 3. (c)

Modifications etc. (not altering text)

C23. S. 55. A applied (with modifications) (31.12.2006) by The Police and Criminal Evidence Act 1984 (Application to the Armed Forces) Order 2006 (S.I. 2006/2015), arts. 2, 3, Schs. 1-3

S. 55. A applied (with modifications) by Criminal Justice Act 2003 (c. 44), s. 24. B(1)-(3) (as inserted (29.6.2007) by Police and Justice Act 2006 (c. 48), ss. 18. (1), 53 (with s. 18. (2)); S.I. 2007/1614, art. 2. (e))

56 Right to have someone informed when arrested.

(1) Where a person has been arrested and is being held in custody in a police station or other premises, he shall be entitled, if he so requests, to have one friend or relative or other person who is known to him or who is likely to take an interest in his welfare told, as soon as is practicable except to the extent that delay is permitted by this section, that he has been arrested and is being detained there.

(2) Delay is only permitted—

(a) in the case of a person who is in police detention for [F25an indictable offence] ; and

(b) if an officer of at least the rank of [F26inspector] authorises it.

(3) In any case the person in custody must be permitted to exercise the right conferred by subsection (1) above within 36 hours from the relevant time, as defined in section 41. (2) above.

(4) An officer may give an authorisation under subsection (2) above orally or in writing but, if he gives it orally, he shall confirm it in writing as soon as is practicable.

(5) [F27. Subject to sub-section (5. A) below] An officer may only authorise delay where he has reasonable grounds for believing that telling the named person of the arrest—

(a) will lead to interference with or harm to evidence connected with [F28an indictable offence] or interference with or physical injury to other persons; or

(b) will lead to the alerting of other persons suspected of having committed such an offence but not yet arrested for it; or

(c) will hinder the recovery of any property obtained as a result of such an offence.

[F29. (5. A)An officer may also authorise delay where he has reasonable grounds for believing that—

(a) the person detained for [F30the indictable offence] has benefited from his criminal conduct, and

(b) the recovery of the value of the property constituting the benefit will be hindered by telling the named person of the arrest.

(5. B)For the purposes of subsection (5. A) above the question whether a person has benefited from his criminal conduct is to be decided in accordance with Part 2 of the Proceeds of Crime Act 2002.]

(6) If a delay is authorised—

(a) the detained person shall be told the reason for it; and

(b) the reason shall be noted on his custody record.

(7) The duties imposed by subsection (6) above shall be performed as soon as is practicable.

(8) The rights conferred by this section on a person detained at a police station or other premises are exercisable whenever he is transferred from one place to another; and this section applies to

each subsequent occasion on which they are exercisable as it applies to the first such occasion.
(9) There may be no further delay in permitting the exercise of the right conferred by subsection
(1) above once the reason for authorising delay ceases to subsist.
[F31. (10)Nothing in this section applies to a person arrested or detained under the terrorism
provisions.]
Amendments (Textual)
F25. Words in s. 56. (2)(a) substituted (1.1.2006) by Serious Organised Crime and Police Act
2005 (c. 15), ss. 111, 178, Sch. 7 Pt. 3 para. 43. (9)(a); S.I. 2005/3495, art. 2. (1)(m)
F26. Word in s. 56. (2)(b) substituted (1.4.2003) by Criminal Justice and Police Act 2001 (c. 16),
ss. 74, 138. (2)-(4); S.I. 2003/708, art. 2. (e)
F27. Words inserted by Drug Trafficking Offences Act 1986 (c. 32, SIF 39:1), s. 32. (1)
F28. Words in s. 56. (5)(a) substituted (1.1.2006) by Serious Organised Crime and Police Act
2005 (c. 15), ss. 111, 178, Sch. 7 Pt. 3 para. 43. (9)(a); S.I. 2005/3495, art. 2. (1)(m)
F29. S. 56. (5. A)(5. B) substituted (24.3.2003) for s. 56. (5. A) by Proceeds of Crime Act 2002 (c.
29), ss. 456, 458. (1)(3), Sch. 11 para. 14. (2); S.I. 2003/333, art. 2, Sch. (subject to transitional
provisions and savings in arts. 3-14) (as amended by S.I. 2003/531, arts. 3, 4)
F30. Words in s. 56. (5. A)(a) substituted (1.1.2006) by Serious Organised Crime and Police Act
2005 (c. 15), ss. 111, 178, Sch. 7 Pt. 3 para. 43. (9)(b); S.I. 2005/3495, art. 2. (1)(m)
F31. S. 56. (10) substituted (19.2.2001) for s. 56. (10)(11) by 2000 c. 11, s. 125, Sch. 15 para. 5.
(5) (with s. 129. (1)); S.I. 2001/421, art. 2
Modifications etc. (not altering text)
C24. S. 56 applied with modifications by S.I. 1985/1800, arts. 3–11, Schs. 1, 2 and Criminal
Justice Act 1988 (c. 33, SIF 39:1), s. 99. (4)
S. 56. (1)-(6)(8) applied (with modifications) (1.2.1997) by S.I. 1997/15, art. 2. (1), Sch.
S. 56. (7)(9) applied (1.2.1997) by S.I. 1997/15, art. 2. (1), Sch.
C25. S. 56 extended (2.8.1993) by S.I. 1993/1813, art. 6, Sch. 3 paras. 1. (2)(b), 3. (2)(3); s. 56
extended by the said S.I. 1993/1813, art. 6, Sch. 3 paras. 3. (3), 4 as incorporated (with
modifications) (1.12.1997) by S.I. 1994/1405, art. 6, Sch. 3 paras. 4. (b)(d), 5
C26. S. 56 applied by The Nationality, Immigration and Asylum Act 2002 (Juxtaposed Controls)
Order 2003 (S.I. 2003/2818), art. 5. (3) (the amendment coming into force in accordance with art.
1. (2) of the amending S.I.)
C27. S. 56: power to apply (with modifications) conferred (1.1.2004) by Extradition Act 2003 (c.
41), ss. 171. (3)(c), 221; S.I. 2003/3103, art. 2 (subject to savings in Order (as amended by S.I.
2003/3312, art. 2. (2) and S.I. 2003/3258, art. 2. (2)))
C28. S. 56 applied (with modifications) (1.1.2004) The Extradition Act 2003 (Police Powers)
Order 2003 (S.I. 2003/3106), art. 2
C29. S. 56 applied (with modifications) (31.12.2006) by The Police and Criminal Evidence Act
1984 (Application to the Armed Forces) Order 2006 (S.I. 2006/2015), arts. 2, 3, Schs. 1-3
C30. S. 56 applied (with modifications) (25.6.2013) by The Police and Criminal Evidence Act
1984 (Application to immigration officers and designated customs officials in England and Wales)
Order 2013 (S.I. 2013/1542), arts. 1, 12. (2)-(4), Sch. 2 (with arts. 13-31)
C31. S. 56 applied (with modifications) by 1994 c. 33, s. 137. D(2)(b) Sch. 7. B Pt. 1 (as inserted
(31.1.2017 for specified purposes) by Policing and Crime Act 2017 (c. 3), s. 116. (1)(3)183.
(1)(5)(e), Sch. 16)
C32. S. 56. (1)-(9) modified (2.8.1993) by S.I. 1993/1813, art. 6, Sch. 3 para. 3. (3).
C33. S. 56. (1)-(9) applied (with modifications) (4.11.2015) by The Police and Criminal Evidence
Act 1984 (Application to Revenue and Customs) Order 2015 (S.I. 2015/1783), arts. 1, 3. (1), Sch.
1 (with art. 3. (2), (3), 4-19, Sch. 2)

57 Additional rights of children and young persons.

The following subsections shall be substituted for section 34. (2) of the M4. Children and Young

Persons Act 1933—

"(2)Where a child or young person is in police detention, such steps as are practicable shall be taken to ascertain the identity of a person responsible for his welfare.

(3) If it is practicable to ascertain the identity of a person responsible for the welfare of the child or young person, that person shall be informed, unless it is not practicable to do so—

(a) that the child or young person has been arrested;

(b) why he has been arrested; and

(c) where he is being detained.

(4) Where information falls to be given under subsection (3) above, it shall be given as soon as it is practicable to do so.

(5) For the purposes of this section the persons who may be responsible for the welfare of a child or young person are—

(a) his parent or guardian; or

(b) any other person who has for the time being assumed responsibility for his welfare.

(6) If it is practicable to give a person responsible for the welfare of the child or young person the information required by subsection (3) above, that person shall be given it as soon as it is practicable to do so.

(7) If it appears that at the time of his arrest a supervision order, as defined in section 11 of the Children and Young Persons Act 1969, is in force in respect of him, the person responsible for his supervision shall also be informed as described in subsection (3) above as soon it is reasonably practicable to do so.

(8) The reference to a parent or guardian in subsection (5) above is—

(a) in the case of a child or young person in the care of a local authority, a reference to that authority; and

(b) in the case of a child or young person in the care of a voluntary organisation in which parental rights and duties with respect to him are vested by virtue of a resolution under section 64. (1) of the Child Care Act 1980, a reference to that organisation.

(9) The rights conferred on a child or young person by subsections (2) to (8) above are in addition to his rights under section 56 of the Police and Criminal Evidence Act 1984.

(10) The reference in subsection (2) above to a child or young person who is in police detention includes a reference to a child or young person who has been detained under the terrorism provisions; and in subsection (3) above "arrest" includes such detention.

(11) In subsection (10) above "the terrorism provisions" has the meaning assigned to it by section 65 of the Police and Criminal Evidence Act 1984".

Modifications etc. (not altering text)

C34. S. 57. (1)–(9) expressed to be applied with modifications by S.I. 1985/1800, arts. 3–11, Schs. 1, 2

C35. S. 57 applied (with modifications) (25.6.2013) by The Police and Criminal Evidence Act 1984 (Application to immigration officers and designated customs officials in England and Wales) Order 2013 (S.I. 2013/1542), arts. 1, 12. (2)-(4), Sch. 2 (with arts. 13-31)

C36. S. 57 applied (with modifications) (4.11.2015) by The Police and Criminal Evidence Act 1984 (Application to Revenue and Customs) Order 2015 (S.I. 2015/1783), arts. 1, 3. (1), Sch. 1 (with art. 3. (2), (3), 4-19, Sch. 2)

Marginal Citations

M41933 c. 12.

58 Access to legal advice.

(1) A person arrested and held in custody in a police station or other premises shall be entitled, if he so requests, to consult a solicitor privately at any time.

(2) Subject to subsection (3) below, a request under subsection (1) above and the time at which it was made shall be recorded in the custody record.

(3) Such a request need not be recorded in the custody record of a person who makes it at a time while he is at a court after being charged with an offence.

(4) If a person makes such a request, he must be permitted to consult a solicitor as soon as is practicable except to the extent that delay is permitted by this section.

(5) In any case he must be permitted to consult a solicitor within 36 hours from the relevant time, as defined in section 41. (2) above.

(6) Delay in compliance with a request is only permitted—

    (a) in the case of a person who is in police detention for [F32an indictable offence] ; and

    (b) if an officer of at least the rank of superintendent authorises it.

(7) An officer may give an authorisation under subsection (6) above orally or in writing but, if he gives it orally, he shall confirm it in writing as soon as is practicable.

(8) [F33. Subject to sub-section (8. A) below] An officer may only authorise delay where he has reasonable grounds for believing that the exercise of the right conferred by subsection (1) above at the time when the person detained desires to exercise it—

    (a) will lead to interference with or harm to evidence connected with [F34an indictable offence] or interference with or physical injury to other persons; or

    (b) will lead to the alerting of other persons suspected of having committed such an offence but not yet arrested for it; or

    (c) will hinder the recovery of any property obtained as a result of such an offence.

[F35. (8. A)An officer may also authorise delay where he has reasonable grounds for believing that—

    (a) the person detained for [F36the indictable offence] has benefited from his criminal conduct, and

    (b) the recovery of the value of the property constituting the benefit will be hindered by the exercise of the right conferred by subsection (1) above.

(8. B)For the purposes of subsection (8. A) above the question whether a person has benefited from his criminal conduct is to be decided in accordance with Part 2 of the Proceeds of Crime Act 2002.]

(9) If delay is authorised—

    (a) the detained person shall be told the reasons for it; and

    (b) the reason shall be noted on his custody record.

(10) The duties imposed by subsection (9) above shall be performed as soon as is practicable.

(11) There may be no further delay in permitting the exercise of the right conferred by subsection (1) above once the reason for authorising delay ceases to subsist.

[F37. (12)Nothing in this section applies to a person arrested or detained under the terrorism provisions.]

Amendments (Textual)

F32. Words in s. 58. (6)(a) substituted (1.1.2006) by Serious Organised Crime and Police Act 2005 (c. 15), ss. 111, 178, Sch. 7 Pt. 3 para. 43. (10)(a); S.I. 2005/3495, art. 2. (1)(m)

F33. Words inserted by Drug Trafficking Offences Act 1986 (c. 32, SIF 39:1), s. 32. (2)

F34. Words in s. 58. (8)(a) substituted (1.1.2006) by Serious Organised Crime and Police Act 2005 (c. 15), ss. 111, 178, Sch. 7 Pt. 3 para. 43. (10)(a); S.I. 2005/3495, art. 2. (1)(m)

F35. S. 58. (8. A)(8. B) substituted (24.3.2003) for s. 58. (8. A) by Proceeds of Crime Act 2002 (c. 29), ss. 456, 458. (1)(3), Sch. 11 para. 14. (3); S.I. 2003/333, art. 2, Sch. (subject to transitional provisions and savings in arts. 3-14) (as amended by S.I. 2003/531, arts. 3, 4)

F36. Words in s. 58. (8. A)(a) substituted (1.1.2006) by Serious Organised Crime and Police Act 2005 (c. 15), ss. 111, 178, Sch. 7 Pt. 3 para. 43. (10)(b); S.I. 2005/3495, art. 2. (1)(m)

F37. S. 58. (12) substituted (19.2.2001) for s. 58. (12)-(18) by 2000 c. 11, s. 125, Sch. 15 para. 5. (6) (with s. 129. (1)); S.I. 2000/421, art. 2

Modifications etc. (not altering text)

C37. S. 58 applied with modifications by S.I. 1985/1882, art. 4, 1985/1800, arts. 3-11, Schs. 1, 2 and Criminal Justice Act 1988 (c. 33, SIF 39:1), s. 99. (4)

S. 58. (1)(2)(4)(6)-(9) applied (with modifications) (1.2.1997) by S.I. 1997/15, art. 2. (1), Sch.

S. 58. (10)(11) applied (1.2.1997) by S.I. 1997/15, art. 2. (1), Sch.

C38. S. 58 extended (2.8.1993) by S.I. 1993/1813, art. 6, Sch. 3 paras. 1. (2)(b), 3. (2)(3); s. 58 extended by the said S.I. 1993/1813, art. 6, Sch. 3 paras. 3. (3), 4 as incorporated (with modifications) (1.12.1997) by S.I. 1994/1405, art. 6, Sch. 3 paras. 4. (b)(d), 5

C39. S. 58: power to apply (with modifications) conferred (1.1.2004) by Extradition Act 2003 (c. 41), ss. 171. (3)(d), 221; S.I. 2003/3103, art. 2 (subject to savings in Order (as amended by S.I. 2003/3312, art. 2. (2) and S.I. 2003/3258, art. 2. (2)))

C40. S. 58 applied (with modifications) (1.1.2004) The Extradition Act 2003 (Police Powers) Order 2003 (S.I. 2003/3106), art. 2

C41. S. 58 applied (with modifications) (31.12.2006) by The Police and Criminal Evidence Act 1984 (Application to the Armed Forces) Order 2006 (S.I. 2006/2015), arts. 2, 3, Schs. 1-3

C42. S. 58 applied (with modifications) (25.6.2013) by The Police and Criminal Evidence Act 1984 (Application to immigration officers and designated customs officials in England and Wales) Order 2013 (S.I. 2013/1542), arts. 1, 12. (2)-(4), Sch. 2 (with arts. 13-31)

C43. S. 58 applied (with modifications) by 1994 c. 33, s. 137. D(2)(c) Sch. 7. B Pt. 1 (as inserted (31.1.2017 for specified purposes) by Policing and Crime Act 2017 (c. 3), s. 116. (1)(3)183. (1)(5)(e), Sch. 16)

C44. S. 58. (1)-(11) modified (2.8.1993) by S.I. 1993/1813, art. 6, Sch. 3 para. 3. (3).

C45. S. 58. (1)-(11) applied (with modifications) (4.11.2015) by The Police and Criminal Evidence Act 1984 (Application to Revenue and Customs) Order 2015 (S.I. 2015/1783), arts. 1, 3. (1), Sch. 1 (with art. 3. (2), (3), 4-19, Sch. 2)

F3859. . . . .

Amendments (Textual)

F38. S. 59 repealed by Legal Aid Act 1988 (c. 34, SIF 77:1), s. 45, Sch. 6

F3960[F39. Audio recording] of interviews.

(1) It shall be the duty of the Secretary of State—

(a) to issue a code of practice in connection with the[F40audio recording] of interviews of persons suspected of the commission of criminal offences which are held by police officers at police stations; and

(b) to make an order requiring the [F40audio recording] of interviews of persons suspected of the commission of criminal offences, or of such descriptions of criminal offences as may be specified in the order, which are so held, in accordance with the code as it has effect for the time being.

(2) An order under subsection (1) above shall be made by statutory instrument and shall be subject to annulment in pursuance of a resolution of either House of Parliament.

Amendments (Textual)

F39. Words in s. 60 heading substituted (31.1.2017 for specified purposes, 31.3.2017 in so far as not already in force) by Policing and Crime Act 2017 (c. 3), ss. 76. (2)(b), 183. (5)(e)(6)(a)

F40. Words in s. 60. (1)(a)(b) substituted (31.1.2017 for specified purposes, 31.3.2017 in so far as not already in force) by Policing and Crime Act 2017 (c. 3), ss. 76. (2)(a), 183. (5)(e)(6)(a)

Commencement Information

I1. S. 60 wholly in force; s. 60 not in force at Royal Assent see s. 121; s. 60. (1)(a) in force at 1.1.1986 by S.I. 1985/1934; s. 60. (1)(b) in force in specified areas and s. 60. (2) wholly in force at 29.11.1991 by S.I. 1991/2686, art. 2, Sch.; s. 60. (1)(b) in force in the Thames Valley police area at 9.11.1992 by S.I. 1992/2802, art. 2.

[F4160. A Visual recording of interviews

(1) The Secretary of State shall have power—

(a) to issue a code of practice for the visual recording of interviews held by police officers at police stations; and

(b) to make an order requiring the visual recording of interviews so held, and requiring the visual recording to be in accordance with the code for the time being in force under this section.

(2) A requirement imposed by an order under this section may be imposed in relation to such cases or police stations in such areas, or both, as may be specified or described in the order.

(3) An order under subsection (1) above shall be made by statutory instrument and shall be subject to annulment in pursuance of a resolution of either House of Parliament.

(4) In this section—

(a) references to any interview are references to an interview of a person suspected of a criminal offence; and

(b) references to a visual recording include references to a visual recording in which an audio recording is comprised.]

Amendments (Textual)

F41. S. 60. A inserted (19.6.2001) by 2001 c. 16, s. 76. (1); S.I. 2001/2223, art. 2. (a)

[F4260. BNotification of decision not to prosecute person interviewed

(1) This section applies where—

(a) a person suspected of the commission of a criminal offence is interviewed by a police officer but is not arrested for the offence, and

(b) the police officer in charge of investigating the offence determines that—

(i) there is not sufficient evidence to charge the person with an offence, or

(ii) there is sufficient evidence to charge the person with an offence but the person should not be charged with an offence or given a caution in respect of an offence.

(2) A police officer must give the person notice in writing that the person is not to be prosecuted.

(3) Subsection (2) does not prevent the prosecution of the person for an offence if new evidence comes to light after the notice was given.

(4) In this section "caution" includes—

(a) a conditional caution within the meaning of Part 3 of the Criminal Justice Act 2003;

(b) a youth conditional caution within the meaning of Chapter 1 of Part 4 of the Crime and Disorder Act 1998;

(c) a youth caution under section 66. ZA of that Act.]

Amendments (Textual)

F42. S. 60. B inserted (31.1.2017 for specified purposes, 3.4.2017 in so far as not already in force) by Policing and Crime Act 2017 (c. 3), ss. 77, 183. (1), (5)(e); S.I. 2017/399, reg. 2, Sch. para. 25

61. Finger-printing.

(1) Except as provided by this section no person's fingerprints may be taken without the appropriate consent.

(2) Consent to the taking of a person's fingerprints must be in writing if it is given at a time when he is at a police station.

[F43. (3)The fingerprints of a person detained at a police station may be taken without the appropriate consent if—

(a) he is detained in consequence of his arrest for a recordable offence; and

(b) he has not had his fingerprints taken in the course of the investigation of the offence by the police.]

F44 [(3. A)[F45. Where a person mentioned in paragraph (a) of subsection (3) or (4) has already had his fingerprints taken in the course of the investigation of the offence by the police], that fact shall be disregarded for the purposes of that subsection if—

(a) the fingerprints taken on the previous occasion do not constitute a complete set of his fingerprints; or

(b) some or all of the fingerprints taken on the previous occasion are not of sufficient quality to allow satisfactory analysis, comparison or matching (whether in the case in question or generally).]

[F46. (4)The fingerprints of a person detained at a police station may be taken without the appropriate consent if—

(a) he has been charged with a recordable offence or informed that he will be reported for such an offence; and

(b) he has not had his fingerprints taken in the course of the investigation of the offence by the police.]

[F47. (4. A)The fingerprints of a person who has answered to bail at a court or police station may be taken without the appropriate consent at the court or station if—

(a) the court, or

(b) an officer of at least the rank of inspector,

authorises them to be taken.

(4. B)A court or officer may only give an authorisation under subsection (4. A) if—

(a) the person who has answered to bail has answered to it for a person whose fingerprints were taken on a previous occasion and there are reasonable grounds for believing that he is not the same person; or

(b) the person who has answered to bail claims to be a different person from a person whose fingerprints were taken on a previous occasion.]

(5) An officer may give an authorisation under [F48subsection (4. A)] above orally or in writing but, if he gives it orally, he shall confirm it in writing as soon as is practicable.

[F49. (5. A)The fingerprints of a person may be taken without the appropriate consent if (before or after the coming into force of this subsection) he has been arrested for a recordable offence and released and—

(a) F50... he has not had his fingerprints taken in the course of the investigation of the offence by the police; or

(b) F51... he has had his fingerprints taken in the course of that investigation][F52but

(i) subsection (3. A)(a) or (b) above applies, or

(ii) subsection (5. C) below applies.]

[F53. (5. B)The fingerprints of a person not detained at a police station may be taken without the appropriate consent if (before or after the coming into force of this subsection) he has been charged with a recordable offence or informed that he will be reported for such an offence and—

(a) he has not had his fingerprints taken in the course of the investigation of the offence by the police; or

(b) he has had his fingerprints taken in the course of that investigation] [F54but

(i) subsection (3. A)(a) or (b) above applies, or

(ii) subsection (5. C) below applies.]

[F55. (5. C)This subsection applies where—

(a) the investigation was discontinued but subsequently resumed, and

(b) before the resumption of the investigation the fingerprints were destroyed pursuant to section 63. D(3) below.]

[F56. (6)Subject to this section, the fingerprints of a person may be taken without the appropriate consent if (before or after the coming into force of this subsection)—

(a) he has been convicted of a recordable offence, [F57 or]

(b) he has been given a caution in respect of a recordable offence which, at the time of the caution, he has admitted, [F58 and]

F59. (c). . . . .

either of the conditions mentioned in subsection (6. ZA) below is met.

(6. ZA)The conditions referred to in subsection (6) above are—

(a) the person has not had his fingerprints taken since he was convicted, [F60or cautioned] ;

(b) he has had his fingerprints taken since then but subsection (3. A)(a) or (b) above applies.

(6. ZB)Fingerprints may only be taken as specified in subsection (6) above with the authorisation of an officer of at least the rank of inspector.

(6. ZC)An officer may only give an authorisation under subsection (6. ZB) above if the officer is satisfied that taking the fingerprints is necessary to assist in the prevention or detection of crime.]

[F61. (6. A)A constable may take a person's fingerprints without the appropriate consent if—

(a) the constable reasonably suspects that the person is committing or attempting to commit an offence, or has committed or attempted to commit an offence; and

(b) either of the two conditions mentioned in subsection (6. B) is met.

(6. B)The conditions are that—

(a) the name of the person is unknown to, and cannot be readily ascertained by, the constable;

(b) the constable has reasonable grounds for doubting whether a name furnished by the person as his name is his real name.

(6. C)The taking of fingerprints by virtue of subsection (6. A) does not count for any of the purposes of this Act as taking them in the course of the investigation of an offence by the police.]

[F62. (6. D)Subject to this section, the fingerprints of a person may be taken without the appropriate consent if—

(a) under the law in force in a country or territory outside England and Wales the person has been convicted of an offence under that law (whether before or after the coming into force of this subsection and whether or not he has been punished for it);

(b) the act constituting the offence would constitute a qualifying offence if done in England and Wales (whether or not it constituted such an offence when the person was convicted); and

(c) either of the conditions mentioned in subsection (6. E) below is met.

(6. E)The conditions referred to in subsection (6. D)(c) above are—

(a) the person has not had his fingerprints taken on a previous occasion under subsection (6. D) above;

(b) he has had his fingerprints taken on a previous occasion under that subsection but subsection (3. A)(a) or (b) above applies.

(6. F)Fingerprints may only be taken as specified in subsection (6. D) above with the authorisation of an officer of at least the rank of inspector.

(6. G)An officer may only give an authorisation under subsection (6. F) above if the officer is satisfied that taking the fingerprints is necessary to assist in the prevention or detection of crime.]

[F63. (7)Where a person's fingerprints are taken without the appropriate consent by virtue of any power conferred by this section—

(a) before the fingerprints are taken, the person shall be informed of—

(i) the reason for taking the fingerprints;

(ii) the power by virtue of which they are taken; and

(iii) in a case where the authorisation of the court or an officer is required for the exercise of the power, the fact that the authorisation has been given; and

(b) those matters shall be recorded as soon as practicable after the fingerprints are taken.]

[F64. (7. A)If a person's fingerprints are taken at a police station, [F65or by virtue of [F66subsection (4. A), (6. A)] at a place other than a police station,] whether with or without the appropriate consent—

(a) before the fingerprints are taken, an officer [F67. (or, where by virtue of subsection (4. A), (6. A) or (6. BA) the fingerprints are taken at a place other than a police station, the constable taking the fingerprints)] shall inform him that they may be the subject of a speculative search; and

(b) the fact that the person has been informed of this possibility shall be recorded as soon as is practicable after the fingerprints have been taken.]

(8) If he is detained at a police station when the fingerprints are taken, [F68the matters referred to in subsection (7)(a)(i) to (iii) above] [F69and, in the case falling within subsection (7. A) above,

the fact referred to in paragraph (b) of that subsection] shall be recorded on his custody record.

F70. (8. A). . . . .

[F71. (8. B)Any power under this section to take the fingerprints of a person without the appropriate consent, if not otherwise specified to be exercisable by a constable, shall be exercisable by a constable.]

(9) Nothing in this section—

(a) affects any power conferred by paragraph 18. (2) of Schedule 2 to the M5. Immigration Act 1971; or

[F72. (b)applies to a person arrested or detained under the terrorism provisions.]

[F73. (10)Nothing in this section applies to a person arrested under an extradition arrest power.]

Amendments (Textual)

F43. S. 61. (3) substituted (5.4.2004) by Criminal Justice Act 2003 (c. 44), ss. 9. (2), 336; S.I. 2004/829, art. 2. (1)(2)(a) (subject to art. 2. (3)-(6))

F44. S. 61. (3. A) inserted (1.1.2003) by 2001 c. 16, s. 78. (3); S.I. 2002/3032, art. 2. (a)

F45. Words in s. 61. (3. A) substituted (5.4.2004) by Criminal Justice Act 2003 (c. 44), ss. 9. (3), 336; S.I. 2004/829, art. 2. (1)(2)(a) (subject to art. 2. (3)-(6))

F46. S. 61. (4) substituted (5.4.2004) by Criminal Justice Act 2003 (c. 44), ss. 9. (2), 336; S.I. 2004/829, art. 2. (1)(2)(a) (subject to art. 2. (3)-(6))

F47. S. 61. (4. A)(4. B) inserted (1.1.2003) by 2001 c. 16, s. 78. (4); S.I. 2002/3032, art. 2. (a)

F48. Words in s. 61. (5) substituted (5.4.2004) by Criminal Justice Act 2003 (c. 44), ss. 9. (4), 336; S.I. 2004/829, art. 2. (1)(2)(a) (subject to art. 2. (3)-(6))

F49. S. 61. (5. A) inserted (7.3.2011) by Crime and Security Act 2010 (c. 17), ss. 2. (1), 59. (1); S.I. 2011/414, art. 2. (b)

F50. Words in s. 61. (5. A)(a) omitted (31.1.2017 for specified purposes, 3.4.2017 in so far as not already in force) by virtue of Policing and Crime Act 2017 (c. 3), ss. 59. (2)(a), 183. (1), (5)(e); S.I. 2017/399, reg. 2, Sch. para. 12

F51. Words in s. 61. (5. A)(b) omitted (31.1.2017 for specified purposes, 3.4.2017 in so far as not already in force) by virtue of Policing and Crime Act 2017 (c. 3), ss. 59. (2)(b), 183. (1), (5)(e); S.I. 2017/399, reg. 2, Sch. para. 12

F52. Words in s. 61. (5. A)(b) substituted (13.5.2014) by Anti-social Behaviour, Crime and Policing Act 2014 (c. 12), ss. 144. (1)(a), 185. (1) (with ss. 21, 33, 42, 58, 75, 93); S.I. 2014/949, art. 3, Sch. para. 13

F53. S. 61. (5. B) inserted (7.3.2011) by Crime and Security Act 2010 (c. 17), ss. 2. (2), 59. (1); S.I. 2011/414, art. 2. (b)

F54. Words in s. 61. (5. B)(b) substituted (13.5.2014) by Anti-social Behaviour, Crime and Policing Act 2014 (c. 12), ss. 144. (1)(a), 185. (1) (with ss. 21, 33, 42, 58, 75, 93); S.I. 2014/949, art. 3, Sch. para. 13

F55. S. 61. (5. C) inserted (13.5.2014) by Anti-social Behaviour, Crime and Policing Act 2014 (c. 12), ss. 144. (1)(b), 185. (1) (with ss. 21, 33, 42, 58, 75, 93); S.I. 2014/949, art. 3, Sch. para. 13

F56. S. 61. (6)-(6. ZC) substituted for s. 61. (6) (7.3.2011) by Crime and Security Act 2010 (c. 17), ss. 2. (3), 59. (1); S.I. 2011/414, art. 2. (b)

F57. Word in s. 61. (6)(a) inserted (8.4.2013) by Legal Aid, Sentencing and Punishment of Offenders Act 2012 (c. 10), s. 151. (1), Sch. 24 para. 7. (2)(a) (with s. 135. (4)); S.I. 2013/453, art. 4. (f)

F58. Word in s. 61. (6)(b) substituted (8.4.2013) by Legal Aid, Sentencing and Punishment of Offenders Act 2012 (c. 10), s. 151. (1), Sch. 24 para. 7. (2)(b) (with s. 135. (4)); S.I. 2013/453, art. 4. (f)

F59. S. 61. (6)(c) omitted (8.4.2013) by virtue of Legal Aid, Sentencing and Punishment of Offenders Act 2012 (c. 10), s. 151. (1), Sch. 24 para. 7. (2)(c) (with s. 135. (4)); S.I. 2013/453, art. 4. (f)

F60. Words in s. 61. (6. ZA)(a) substituted (8.4.2013) by Legal Aid, Sentencing and Punishment of Offenders Act 2012 (c. 10), s. 151. (1), Sch. 24 para. 7. (3) (with s. 135. (4)); S.I. 2013/453, art. 4. (f)

F61. S. 61. (6. A)-(6. C) inserted (7.3.2011) by Serious Organised Crime and Police Act 2005 (c. 15), ss. 117. (2), 178. (8); S.I. 2011/410, art. 2. (a)

F62. S. 61. (6. D)-(6. G) inserted (7.3.2011) by Crime and Security Act 2010 (c. 17), ss. 3. (1), 59. (1); S.I. 2011/414, art. 2. (b)

F63. S. 61. (7) substituted (7.3.2011) by Crime and Security Act 2010 (c. 17), ss. 4. (1), 59. (1); S.I. 2011/414, art. 2. (b)

F64. S. 61. (7. A) inserted (10.4.1995) by 1994 c. 33, s. 168. (2), Sch. 10 para. 56. (a); S.I. 1995/721, art. 2, Sch. Appendix A

F65. Words in s. 61. (7. A) inserted (7.3.2011) by Serious Organised Crime and Police Act 2005 (c. 15), ss. 117. (4)(a), 178. (8); S.I. 2011/410, art. 2. (b)

F66. Words in s. 61. (7. A) substituted (7.3.2011) by Crime and Security Act 2010 (c. 17), ss. 4. (2)(a), 59. (1); S.I. 2011/414, art. 2. (b)

F67. S. 61. (7. A)(a): By Crime and Security Act 2010 (c. 17), ss. 4. (2)(b), 59. (1); S.I. 2011/414, art. 2. (b), it is provided that the words "(or, in a subsection (6. A) case, the constable)" (which were inserted (prosp.) by 2005 c. 15, s. 117. (4)(b)) be substituted (7.3.2011)

F68. Words in s. 61. (8) substituted (7.3.2011) by Crime and Security Act 2010 (c. 17), ss. 4. (3), 59. (1); S.I. 2011/414, art. 2. (b)

F69. Words in s. 61. (8) inserted (10.4.1995) by 1994 c. 33, s. 168. (2), Sch. 10 para. 56. (b); S.I. 1995/721, art. 2, Sch. Appendix A

F70. S. 61. (8. A) repealed (12.1.2010) by Policing and Crime Act 2009 (c. 26), ss. 112. (1)(2), 116. (6), Sch. 7 para. 127. (2), Sch. 8 Pt. 13

F71. S. 61. (8. B) substituted (7.3.2011) by Crime and Security Act 2010 (c. 17), ss. 2. (4), 59. (1); S.I. 2011/414, art. 2. (b)

F72. S. 61. (9)(b) substituted (19.2.2001) by 2000 c. 11, s. 125, Sch. 15 para. 5. (7) (with s. 129. (1)); S.I. 2001/421 art. 2

F73. S. 61. (10) inserted (1.1.2004) by Extradition Act 2003 (c. 41), ss. 169. (3), 221; S.I. 2003/3103, art. 2 (subject to savings in Order (as amended by S.I. 2003/3312, art. 2. (2) and S.I. 2003/3258, art. 2. (2)))

Modifications etc. (not altering text)

C46. S. 61 applied (with modifications) by S.I. 1985/1882, art. 6

C47. S. 61 modified (2.8.1993) by S.I. 1993/1813, art. 6, Sch. 3 para. 3. (2); and s. 61 modified by the said S.I. 1993/1813, art. 6, Sch. 3 para. 3 as incorporated (with modifications) (1.12.1997) by S.I. 1994/1405, art. 6, Sch. 3 para. 4

S. 61. (1) applied (1.2.1997) by S.I. 1997/15, art. 2. (1), Sch.

S. 61. (2)-(7. A) applied (with modifications) (1.2.1997) by S.I. 1997/15, art. 2. (1), Sch.

C48. S. 61 extended (2.12.2002) by Police Reform Act 2002 (c. 30), s. 38, Sch. 4 Pt. 3 para. 29. (a); S.I. 2002/2750, art. 2. (a)(ii)(d)

C49. S. 61 applied (with modifications) (31.12.2006) by The Police and Criminal Evidence Act 1984 (Application to the Armed Forces) Order 2006 (S.I. 2006/2015), arts. 2, 3, Schs. 1-3

C50. S. 61. (1)-(8) modified (E.W.) (temp.) by Prevention of Terrorism (Temporary Provisions) Act 1989 (c. 4, SIF 39:2), ss. 15. (10), 16. (1)(3)(4), 27. (5), Sch. 5 para. 7. (6)

C51. S. 61. (7. A)(a) modified (2.12.2002) by Police Reform Act 2002 (c. 30), s. 38, Sch. 4 Pt. 3 para. 29. (b); S.I. 2002/2750, art. 2. (a)(ii)(d)

Marginal Citations

M51971 c. 77.

[F7461. AImpressions of footwear

(1) Except as provided by this section, no impression of a person's footwear may be taken without the appropriate consent.

(2) Consent to the taking of an impression of a person's footwear must be in writing if it is given at a time when he is at a police station.

(3) Where a person is detained at a police station, an impression of his footwear may be taken without the appropriate consent if—

(a) he is detained in consequence of his arrest for a recordable offence, or has been charged with a recordable offence, or informed that he will be reported for a recordable offence; and

(b) he has not had an impression taken of his footwear in the course of the investigation of the offence by the police.

(4) Where a person mentioned in paragraph (a) of subsection (3) above has already had an impression taken of his footwear in the course of the investigation of the offence by the police, that fact shall be disregarded for the purposes of that subsection if the impression of his footwear taken previously is—

(a) incomplete; or

(b) is not of sufficient quality to allow satisfactory analysis, comparison or matching (whether in the case in question or generally).

(5) If an impression of a person's footwear is taken at a police station, whether with or without the appropriate consent—

(a) before it is taken, an officer shall inform him that it may be the subject of a speculative search; and

(b) the fact that the person has been informed of this possibility shall be recorded as soon as is practicable after the impression has been taken, and if he is detained at a police station, the record shall be made on his custody record.

(6) In a case where, by virtue of subsection (3) above, an impression of a person's footwear is taken without the appropriate consent—

(a) he shall be told the reason before it is taken; and

(b) the reason shall be recorded on his custody record as soon as is practicable after the impression is taken.

(7) The power to take an impression of the footwear of a person detained at a police station without the appropriate consent shall be exercisable by any constable.

(8) Nothing in this section applies to any person—

(a) arrested or detained under the terrorism provisions;

(b) arrested under an extradition arrest power.]

Amendments (Textual)

F74. S. 61. A inserted (1.1.2006) by Serious Organised Crime and Police Act 2005 (c. 15), ss. 118. (2), 178; S.I. 2005/3495, art. 2. (1)(p)

Modifications etc. (not altering text)

C52. S. 61. A extended (1.1.2006) by Police Reform Act 2002 (c. 30), s. 38, Sch. 4 para. 33. A (as inserted by Serious Organied Crime and Police Act 2005 (c. 15), ss. 122, 178, Sch. 8 para. 16); S.I. 2005/3495, art. 2. (q)(r)

C53. S. 61. A applied (with modifications) (31.12.2006) by The Police and Criminal Evidence Act 1984 (Application to the Armed Forces) Order 2006 (S.I. 2006/2015), arts. 2, 3, Schs. 1-3

62 Intimate samples.

(1) [F75. Subject to section 63. B below] An intimate sample may be taken from a person in police detention only—

(a) if a police officer of at least the rank of [F76inspector] authorises it to be taken; and

(b) if the appropriate consent is given.

[F77. (1. A)An intimate sample may be taken from a person who is not in police detention but from whom, in the course of the investigation of an offence, two or more non-intimate samples suitable for the same means of analysis have been taken which have proved insufficient—

(a) if a police officer of at least the rank of [F76inspector] authorises it to be taken; and

(b) if the appropriate consent is given.]

(2) An officer may only give an authorisation [F78under subsection (1) or (1. A) above] if he has

reasonable grounds—

(a) for suspecting the involvement of the person from whom the sample is to be taken in a [F79recordable offence]; and

(b) for believing that the sample will tend to confirm or disprove his involvement.

[F80. (2. A)An intimate sample may be taken from a person where—

(a) two or more non-intimate samples suitable for the same means of analysis have been taken from the person under section 63. (3. E) below (persons convicted of offences outside England and Wales etc) but have proved insufficient;

(b) a police officer of at least the rank of inspector authorises it to be taken; and

(c) the appropriate consent is given.

(2. B)An officer may only give an authorisation under subsection (2. A) above if the officer is satisfied that taking the sample is necessary to assist in the prevention or detection of crime.]

(3) An officer may give an authorisation under subsection (1) [F81or (1. A)] [F82or (2. A)] above orally or in writing but, if he gives it orally, he shall confirm it in writing as soon as is practicable.

(4) The appropriate consent must be given in writing.

[F83. (5)Before an intimate sample is taken from a person, an officer shall inform him of the following—

(a) the reason for taking the sample;

(b) the fact that authorisation has been given and the provision of this section under which it has been given; and

(c) if the sample was taken at a police station, the fact that the sample may be the subject of a speculative search.

(6) The reason referred to in subsection (5)(a) above must include, except in a case where the sample is taken under subsection (2. A) above, a statement of the nature of the offence in which it is suspected that the person has been involved.

(7) After an intimate sample has been taken from a person, the following shall be recorded as soon as practicable—

(a) the matters referred to in subsection (5)(a) and (b) above;

(b) if the sample was taken at a police station, the fact that the person has been informed as specified in subsection (5)(c) above; and

(c) the fact that the appropriate consent was given.]

(8) If an intimate sample is taken from a person detained at a police station, the matters required to be recorded by subsection (7) F84... above shall be recorded in his custody record.

[F85. (9)In the case of an intimate sample which is a dental impression, the sample may be taken from a person only by a registered dentist.

(9. A)In the case of any other form of intimate sample, except in the case of a sample of urine, the sample may be taken from a person only by—

(a) a registered medical practitioner; or

(b) a registered health care professional.]

(10) Where the appropriate consent to the taking of an intimate sample from person was refused without good cause, in any proceedings against that person for an offence—

(a) the court, in determining—

F86. (i). . . . .

(ii) whether there is a case to answer; and

F87 [F88. (aa)a judge, in deciding whether to grant an application made by the accused under[F89 paragraph 2 of Schedule 3 to the Crime and Disorder Act 1998 (applications for dismissal); and]]

(b) the court or jury, in determining whether that person is guilty of the offence charged, F90may draw such inferences from the refusal as appear proper . . ..

(11) Nothing in this section [F91applies to the taking of a specimen for the purposes of any of the provisions of][F92sections 4 to 11 of the Road Traffic Act 1988][F93or of sections 26 to 38 of the Transport and Works Act 1992] .

[F94. (12)Nothing in this section applies to a person arrested or detained under the terrorism provisions; and subsection (1. A) shall not apply where the non-intimate samples mentioned in that subsection were taken under paragraph 10 of Schedule 8 to the Terrorism Act 2000.]

Amendments (Textual)

F75. Words in s. 62 inserted (20.6.2001 for specified purposes and otherwise 2.7.2001) by 2000 c. 43, s. 74, Sch. 7 para. 78; S.I. 2001/2232, art. 2. (k)(m)(i)

F76. Word in s. 62. (1)(a)(1. A)(a) substituted (1.4.2003) by 2001 c. 16, ss. 80. (1), 138. (2); S.I. 2003/708, art. 2. (h)

F77. S. 62. (1. A) inserted (10.4.1995) by 1994 c. 33, s. 54. (2); S.I. 1995/721, art. 2, Sch.

F78. Words in s. 62. (2) inserted (10.4.1995) by 1994 c. 33, s. 54. (3)(a); S.I. 1995/721, art. 2, Sch.

F79. Words in s. 62. (2)(a) substituted (10.4.1995) by 1994 c. 33, s. 54. (3)(b); S.I. 1995/721, art. 2, Sch.

F80. S. 62. (2. A)(2. B) inserted (7.3.2011) by Crime and Security Act 2010 (c. 17), ss. 3. (2), 59. (1); S.I. 2011/414, art. 2. (b)

F81. Words in s. 62. (3) inserted (10.4.1995) by 1994 c. 33, s. 54. (4); S.I. 1995/721, art. 2, Sch.

F82. Words in s. 62. (3) inserted (7.3.2011) by Crime and Security Act 2010 (c. 17), ss. 3. (3), 59. (1); S.I. 2011/414, art. 2. (b)

F83. S. 62. (5)-(7) substituted for s. 62. (5)-(7. A) (7.3.2011) by Crime and Security Act 2010 (c. 17), ss. 4. (4), 59. (1); S.I. 2011/414, art. 2. (b)

F84. Words in s. 62. (8) repealed (7.3.2011) by Crime and Security Act 2010 (c. 17), ss. 4. (5), 59. (1); S.I. 2011/414, art. 2. (b)

F85. S. 62. (9)(9. A) substituted (1.4.2003) for s. 62. (9) by Police Reform Act 2002 (c. 30), ss. 54. (1), 108. (2)-(5); S.I. 2003/808, art. 2. (e)

F86. S. 62. (10)(a)(i) repealed (18.6.2012 for specified purposes, 5.11.2012 for specified purposes, 28.5.2013 for specified purposes) by Criminal Justice Act 2003 (c. 44), s. 336. (3)(4), Sch. 3 para. 56. (2)(a), Sch. 37 Pt. 4; S.I. 2012/1320, art. 4. (1)(c)(d)(2)(3) (with art. 5) (see S.I. 2012/2574, art. 4. (2) and S.I. 2013/1103, art. 4); S.I. 2012/2574, art. 2. (2)(3)(c)(d), Sch. (with arts. 3 4) (as amended (4.11.2012) by S.I. 2012/2761, art. 2) (with S.I. 2013/1103, art. 4); S.I. 2013/1103, art. 2. (1)(c)(d)(2)(3) (with arts. 3 4)

F87. Words in s. 62. (10)(aa) substituted for s. 62. (10)(aa)(i)(ii) (9.5.2005 for specified purposes, 18.6.2012 for specified purposes, 5.11.2012 for specified purposes, 28.5.2013 for specified purposes) by Criminal Justice Act 2003 (c. 44), s. 336. (3)(4), Sch. 3 para. 56. (2)(b); S.I. 2005/1267, art. 2. (1)(2)(a), Sch. Pt. 1; S.I. 2012/1320, art. 4. (1)(c)(2)(3) (with art. 5) (see S.I. 2012/2574, art. 4. (2) and S.I. 2013/1103, art. 4); S.I. 2012/2574, art. 2. (2)(3)(c), Sch. (with arts. 3 4) (as amended (4.11.2012) by S.I. 2012/2761, art. 2) (with S.I. 2013/1103, art. 4); S.I. 2013/1103, art. 2. (1)(c)(2)(3) (with arts. 3 4)

F88. S. 62. (10)(aa) inserted (3.2.1995) by 1994 c. 33, s. 168. (3), Sch. 9 para. 24; S.I. 1995/127, art. 2. (1), Sch. Appendix A

F89. S. 62. (10)(aa): words substituted (9.5.2005 for certain purposes and otherwise prosp.) for s. 62. (10)(aa)(i)(ii) by Criminal Justice Act 2003 (c. 44), ss. 41, 336, Sch. 3 Pt. 2 para. 56. (2)(b); S.I. 2005/1267, art. 2. (1)(2)(a), Sch. Pt. 1 para. 1. (1)(l)

F90. Words in s. 62. (10) repealed (10.4.1995) by 1994 c. 33, s. 168. (3), Sch. 11; S.I. 1995/721, art. 2, Sch. Appendix B

F91. Words in s. 62. (11) substituted (1.4.2003) by Police Reform Act 2002 (c. 30), ss. 53. (2)(a), 108. (2)-(5); S.I. 2003/808, art. 2. (d)

F92. Words substituted by Road Traffic (Consequential Provisions) Act 1988 (c. 54, SIF 107:1), s. 4, Sch. 3 para. 27. (4)

F93. Words in s. 62. (11) inserted (1.4.2003) by Police Reform Act 2002 (c. 30), ss. 53. (2)(b), 108. (2)-(5); S.I. 2003/808, art. 2. (d)

F94. S. 62. (12) substituted (19.2.2001) by 2000 c. 11, s. 125, Sch. 15 para. 8 (with s. 129. (1)); S.I. 2001/421, art. 2

Modifications etc. (not altering text)

C54. S. 62 applied with modifications by S.I. 1985/1800, arts. 3–11, Schs. 1, 2 and 1985/1882, art. 7

S. 62. (1)-(11) applied (with modifications) (10.4.1995) by 1989 c. 4, Sch. 5 para. 7. (6. A)-(6. D) (as inserted by 1994 c. 33, s. 168. (2), Sch. 10 para. 62. (3)); S.I. 1995/721, art. 2, Sch. Appendix A

S. 62. (1)-(11) applied (with modifications) (10.4.1995) by 1989 c. 4, s. 15. (11)-(14) (as inserted by 1994 c. 33, s. 168. (2), Sch. 10 para. 62. (2); S.I. 1995/721, art. 2, Sch. Appendix A)

S. 62. (1)-(3)(5)-(7)(7. A)(9)(10) applied (with modifications) (1.2.1997) by S.I. 1997/15, art. 2. (1), Sch.

S. 62. (4)(6) applied (1.2.1997) by S.I. 1997/15, art. 2. (1), Sch.

C55. S. 62 modified (2.8.1993) by S.I. 1993/1813, art. 6, Sch. 3 para. 3. (2)(3); s. 62 modified by the said S.I. 1993/1813, art. 6, Sch. 3 para. 3 as incorporated (with modifications) (1.12.1997) by S.I. 1994/1405, art. 6, Sch. 3 para. 4

C56. S. 62 applied (with modifications) (31.12.2006) by The Police and Criminal Evidence Act 1984 (Application to the Armed Forces) Order 2006 (S.I. 2006/2015), arts. 2, 3, Schs. 1-3

C57. S. 62 applied (with modifications) (4.11.2015) by The Police and Criminal Evidence Act 1984 (Application to Revenue and Customs) Order 2015 (S.I. 2015/1783), arts. 1, 3. (1), Sch. 1 (with art. 3. (2), (3), 4-19, Sch. 2)

C58. S. 62. (1)(2) applied (with modifications) (25.6.2013) by The Police and Criminal Evidence Act 1984 (Application to immigration officers and designated customs officials in England and Wales) Order 2013 (S.I. 2013/1542), arts. 1, 12. (2)-(4), Sch. 2 (with arts. 13-31)

C59. S. 62. (3)-(12) applied (with modifications) (25.6.2013) by The Police and Criminal Evidence Act 1984 (Application to immigration officers and designated customs officials in England and Wales) Order 2013 (S.I. 2013/1542), arts. 1, 12. (2)-(4), Sch. 2 (with arts. 13-31)

63. Other samples.

(1) Except as provided by this section, a non-intimate sample may not be taken from a person without the appropriate consent.

(2) Consent to the taking of a non-intimate sample must be given in writing.

[F95. (2. A)A non-intimate sample may be taken from a person without the appropriate consent if two conditions are satisfied.

(2. B)The first is that the person is in police detention in consequence of his arrest for a recordable offence.

(2. C)The second is that—

(a) he has not had a non-intimate sample of the same type and from the same part of the body taken in the course of the investigation of the offence by the police, or

(b) he has had such a sample taken but it proved insufficient.]

(3) A non-intimate sample may be taken from a person without the appropriate consent if—

(a) he F96. . . is being held in custody by the police on the authority of a court; and

(b) an officer of at least the rank of [F97inspector] authorises it to be taken without the appropriate consent.

[F98. (3. ZA)A non-intimate sample may be taken from a person without the appropriate consent if (before or after the coming into force of this subsection) he has been arrested for a recordable offence and released and—

(a) F99... he has not had a non-intimate sample of the same type and from the same part of the body taken from him in the course of the investigation of the offence by the police; or

(b) F100... he has had a non-intimate sample taken from him in the course of that investigation but—

(i) it was not suitable for the same means of analysis, or

(ii) it proved insufficient.], or

[F101. (iii)subsection (3. AA) below applies.]

[F102. (3. A)A non-intimate sample may be taken from a person (whether or not he is in police detention or held in custody by the police on the authority of a court) without the appropriate

121

consent if he has been charged with a recordable offence or informed that he will be reported for such an offence and—

(a) he has not had a non-intimate sample taken from him in the course of the investigation of the offence by the police; or

(b) he has had a non-intimate sample taken from him in the course of that investigation but—

(i) it was not suitable for the same means of analysis, or

(ii) it proved [F103insufficient, or

(iii) subsection (3. AA) below applies; or]

(c) he has had a non-intimate sample taken from him in the course of that investigation and—

(i) the sample has been destroyed pursuant to section [F104 63. R] below or any other enactment, and

(ii) it is disputed, in relation to any proceedings relating to the offence, whether a DNA profile relevant to the proceedings is derived from the sample.]

[F105. (3. AA)This subsection applies where the investigation was discontinued but subsequently resumed, and before the resumption of the investigation—

(a) any DNA profile derived from the sample was destroyed pursuant to section 63. D(3) below, and

(b) the sample itself was destroyed pursuant to section 63. R(4), (5) or (12) below.]

[F106. (3. B)Subject to this section, a non-intimate sample may be taken from a person without the appropriate consent if (before or after the coming into force of this subsection)—

(a) he has been convicted of a recordable offence, [F107 or]

(b) he has been given a caution in respect of a recordable offence which, at the time of the caution, he has admitted, [F108 and]

F109. (c). . . . .

either of the conditions mentioned in subsection (3. BA) below is met.

(3. BA)The conditions referred to in subsection (3. B) above are—

(a) a non-intimate sample has not been taken from the person since he was convicted [F110 or cautioned];

(b) such a sample has been taken from him since then but—

(i) it was not suitable for the same means of analysis, or

(ii) it proved insufficient.

(3. BB)A non-intimate sample may only be taken as specified in subsection (3. B) above with the authorisation of an officer of at least the rank of inspector.

(3. BC)An officer may only give an authorisation under subsection (3. BB) above if the officer is satisfied that taking the sample is necessary to assist in the prevention or detection of crime.]

[F111. (3. C)A non-intimate sample may also be taken from a person without the appropriate consent if he is a person to whom section 2 of the Criminal Evidence (Amendment) Act 1997 applies (persons detained following acquittal on grounds of insanity or finding of unfitness to plead).]

[F112. (3. E)Subject to this section, a non-intimate sample may be taken without the appropriate consent from a person if—

(a) under the law in force in a country or territory outside England and Wales the person has been convicted of an offence under that law (whether before or after the coming into force of this subsection and whether or not he has been punished for it);

(b) the act constituting the offence would constitute a qualifying offence if done in England and Wales (whether or not it constituted such an offence when the person was convicted); and

(c) either of the conditions mentioned in subsection (3. F) below is met.

(3. F)The conditions referred to in subsection (3. E)(c) above are—

(a) the person has not had a non-intimate sample taken from him on a previous occasion under subsection (3. E) above;

(b) he has had such a sample taken from him on a previous occasion under that subsection but—

(i) the sample was not suitable for the same means of analysis, or

(ii) it proved insufficient.

(3. G)A non-intimate sample may only be taken as specified in subsection (3. E) above with the authorisation of an officer of at least the rank of inspector.

(3. H)An officer may only give an authorisation under subsection (3. G) above if the officer is satisfied that taking the sample is necessary to assist in the prevention or detection of crime.]

(4) An officer may only give an authorisation under subsection (3) above if he has reasonable grounds—

(a) for suspecting the involvement of the person from whom the sample is to be taken in a [F113recordable offence]; and

(b) for believing that the sample will tend to confirm or disprove his involvement.

(5) An officer may give an authorisation under subsection (3) above orally or in writing but, if he gives it orally, he shall confirm it in writing as soon as is practicable.

[F114. (5. A)An officer shall not give an authorisation under subsection (3) above for the taking from any person of a non-intimate sample consisting of a skin impression if—

(a) a skin impression of the same part of the body has already been taken from that person in the course of the investigation of the offence; and

(b) the impression previously taken is not one that has proved insufficient.]

[F115. (6)Where a non-intimate sample is taken from a person without the appropriate consent by virtue of any power conferred by this section—

(a) before the sample is taken, an officer shall inform him of—

(i) the reason for taking the sample;

(ii) the power by virtue of which it is taken; and

(iii) in a case where the authorisation of an officer is required for the exercise of the power, the fact that the authorisation has been given; and

(b) those matters shall be recorded as soon as practicable after the sample is taken.

(7) The reason referred to in subsection (6)(a)(i) above must include, except in a case where the non-intimate sample is taken under subsection (3. B) or (3. E) above, a statement of the nature of the offence in which it is suspected that the person has been involved.]

[F116. (8. B)If a non-intimate sample is taken from a person at a police station, whether with or without the appropriate consent—

(a) before the sample is taken, an officer shall inform him that it may be the subject of a speculative search; and

(b) the fact that the person has been informed of this possibility shall be recorded as soon as practicable after the sample has been taken.]

(9) If a non-intimate sample is taken from a person detained at a police station, the matters required to be recorded by [F117subsection (6) or (8. B)] above shall be recorded in his custody record.

[F118. (9. ZA)The power to take a non-intimate sample from a person without the appropriate consent shall be exercisable by any constable.]

[F119. (9. A)Subsection (3. B) above shall not apply to

[F120. (a)] any person convicted before 10th April 1995 unless he is a person to whom section 1 of the Criminal Evidence (Amendment) Act 1997 applies (persons imprisoned or detained by virtue of pre-existing conviction for sexual offence etc.).] [F121; or

(b) a person given a caution before 10th April 1995.]

[F122. (10)Nothing in this section applies to a person arrested or detained under the terrorism provisions.]

[F123. (11)Nothing in this section applies to a person arrested under an extradition arrest power.]

Amendments (Textual)

F95. S. 63. (2. A)-(2. C) inserted (5.4.2004) by Criminal Justice Act 2003 (c. 44), ss. 10. (2), 336; S.I. 2004/829, art. 2. (1)(2)(a) (subject to art. 2. (3)-(6))

F96. Words in s. 63. (3)(a) repealed (5.4.2004) by Criminal Justice Act 2003 (c. 44), ss. 10. (3), 332, 336, Sch. 37 Pt. 1; S.I. 2004/829, art. 2. (1)(2)(a)(l)(i) (subject to art. 2. (3)-(6))

F97. Word in s. 63. (3)(b) substituted (1.4.2003) by 2001 c. 16, ss. 80. (1), 138. (2); S.I. 2003/708, art. 2. (h)

F98. S. 63. (3. ZA) inserted (7.3.2011) by Crime and Security Act 2010 (c. 17), ss. 2. (5), 59. (1); S.I. 2011/414, art. 2. (b)

F99. Words in s. 63. (3. ZA)(a) omitted (31.1.2017 for specified purposes, 3.4.2017 in so far as not already in force) by virtue of Policing and Crime Act 2017 (c. 3), ss. 59. (3)(a), 183. (1), (5)(e); S.I. 2017/399, reg. 2, Sch. para. 12

F100. Words in s. 63. (3. ZA)(b) omitted (31.1.2017 for specified purposes, 3.4.2017 in so far as not already in force) by virtue of Policing and Crime Act 2017 (c. 3), ss. 59. (3)(b), 183. (1), (5)(e); S.I. 2017/399, reg. 2, Sch. para. 12. Text here

F101. S. 63. (3. ZA)(b)(iii) and word inserted (13.5.2014) by Anti-social Behaviour, Crime and Policing Act 2014 (c. 12), ss. 144. (2)(a), 185. (1) (with ss. 21, 33, 42, 58, 75, 93); S.I. 2014/949, art. 3, Sch. para. 13

F102. S. 63. (3. A) substituted (7.3.2011) by Crime and Security Act 2010 (c. 17), ss. 2. (6), 59. (1); S.I. 2011/414, art. 2. (b)

F103. Words in s. 63. (3. A)(b) substituted (13.5.2014) by Anti-social Behaviour, Crime and Policing Act 2014 (c. 12), ss. 144. (2)(b), 185. (1) (with ss. 21, 33, 42, 58, 75, 93); S.I. 2014/949, art. 3, Sch. para. 13

F104. Word in s. 63. (3. A)(c)(i) substituted (31.10.2013) by Protection of Freedoms Act 2012 (c. 9), s. 120, Sch. 9 para. 3. (2) (with s. 97); S.I. 2013/2104, art. 3. (c)

F105. S. 63. (3. AA) inserted (13.5.2014) by Anti-social Behaviour, Crime and Policing Act 2014 (c. 12), ss. 144. (2)(c), 185. (1) (with ss. 21, 33, 42, 58, 75, 93); S.I. 2014/949, art. 3, Sch. para. 13

F106. S. 63. (3. B)-(3. BC) substituted for s. 63. (3. B) (7.3.2011) by Crime and Security Act 2010 (c. 17), ss. 2. (7), 59. (1); S.I. 2011/414, art. 2. (b)

F107. Word in s. 63. (3. B)(a) inserted (8.4.2013) by Legal Aid, Sentencing and Punishment of Offenders Act 2012 (c. 10), s. 151. (1), Sch. 24 para. 8. (2)(a) (with s. 135. (4)); S.I. 2013/453, art. 4. (f)

F108. Word in s. 63. (3. B)(b) substituted (8.4.2013) by Legal Aid, Sentencing and Punishment of Offenders Act 2012 (c. 10), s. 151. (1), Sch. 24 para. 8. (2)(b) (with s. 135. (4)); S.I. 2013/453, art. 4. (f)

F109. S. 63. (3. B)(c) omitted (8.4.2013) by virtue of Legal Aid, Sentencing and Punishment of Offenders Act 2012 (c. 10), s. 151. (1), Sch. 24 para. 8. (2)(c) (with s. 135. (4)); S.I. 2013/453, art. 4. (f)

F110. Words in s. 63. (3. BA)(a) substituted (8.4.2013) by Legal Aid, Sentencing and Punishment of Offenders Act 2012 (c. 10), s. 151. (1), Sch. 24 para. 8. (3) (with s. 135. (4)); S.I. 2013/453, art. 4. (f)

F111. S. 63. (3. C) inserted (19.3.1997) by 1997 c. 17, s. 2. (1)(2)(a)(3)-(7)

F112. S. 63. (3. E)-(3. H) inserted (7.3.2011) by Crime and Security Act 2010 (c. 17), ss. 3. (4), 59. (1); S.I. 2011/414, art. 2. (b)

F113. Words in s. 63. (4)(a) substituted (10.4.1995) by 1994 c. 33, s. 55. (3); S.I. 1995/721, art. 2, Sch.

F114. S. 63. (5. A) inserted (1.1.2003) by 2001 c. 16, s. 80. (3); S.I. 2002/3032, art. 2. (b)

F115. S. 63. (6)(7) substituted for s. 63. (6)-(8. A) (7.3.2011) by Crime and Security Act 2010 (c. 17), ss. 4. (7), 59. (1); S.I. 2011/414, art. 2. (b)

F116. S. 63. (8. B) inserted (10.4.1995) by 1994 c. 33, s. 168. (2), Sch. 10 para. 58. (a); S.I. 1995/721, art. 2, Sch. Appendix A

F117. Words in s. 63. (9) substituted (7.3.2011) by Crime and Security Act 2010 (c. 17), ss. 4. (8), 59. (1); S.I. 2011/414, art. 2. (b)

F118. S. 63. (9. ZA) inserted (2.12.2002) by Police Reform Act 2002 (c. 30), s. 107, Sch. 7 para. 9. (4); S.I. 2002/2750, art. 2. (b)(ii)

F119. S. 63. (9. A) substituted for the subsection (10) inserted in s. 63 by 1994 c. 33, s. 55. (6) (19.3.1997) by 1997 c. 17, s. 1. (1)(a)(2)(3)(6)

F120. Words in s. 63. (9. A) renumbered as s. 63. (9. A)(a) (7.3.2011) by Crime and Security Act 2010 (c. 17), ss. 2. (8)(a), 59. (1); S.I. 2011/414, art. 2. (b)

F121. S. 63. (9. A)(b) and word inserted (7.3.2011) by Crime and Security Act 2010 (c. 17), ss. 2.

(8)(b), 59. (1); S.I. 2011/414, art. 2. (b)

F122. S. 63. (10) substituted (19.2.2001) by 2000 c. 11, s. 125, Sch. 15 para. 5. (9) (with s. 129. (1));S.I. 2001/421, art. 2

F123. S. 63. (11) inserted (1.1.2004) by Extradition Act 2003 (c. 41), ss. 169. (4), 221; S.I. 2003/3103, art. 2 (subject to savings in Order (as amended by S.I. 2003/3312, art. 2. (2) and S.I. 2003/3258, art. 2. (2)))

Modifications etc. (not altering text)

C60. S. 63 applied with modifications by S.I. 1985/1800, arts. 3–11, Schs. 1, 2 and 1985/1882, art. 8

S. 63. (1)-(9) applied (with modifications) (10.4.1995) by 1989 c. 4, s. 15. (11)-(14) (as inserted by 1994 c. 33, s. 168. (2), Sch. 10 para. 62. (2); S.I. 1995/721, art. 2, Sch. Appendix A)

S. 63. (1)-(9) applied (with modifications) (10.4.1995) by 1989 c. 4, Sch. 5 para. 7. (6. A)-(6. D) (as inserted by 1994 c. 33, s. 168. (2), Sch. 10 para. 62. (3); S.I. 1995/721, art. 2, Sch. Appendix A)

S. 63. (1)(2)(7) applied (1.2.1997) by S.I. 1997/15, art. 2. (1), Sch.

S. 63. (3)-(6)(8)-(8. B) applied (with modifications) (1.2.1997) by S.I. 1997/15, art. 2. (1), Sch.

C61. S. 63 modified (2.8.1993) by S.I. 1993/1813, art. 6, Sch. 3 para. 3. (2)(3); s. 63 modified by the said S.I. 1993/1813, art. 6, Sch. 3 para. 3 as incorporated (with modifications) (1.12.1997) by S.I. 1994/1405, art. 6, Sch. 3 para. 4

C62. S. 63 extended (2.12.2002) Police Reform Act 2002 (c. 30), s. 38, Sch. 4 Pt. 3 para. 31. (a); S.I. 2002/2750, art. 2. (a)(ii)(d)

C63. S. 63 applied (with modifications) (31.12.2006) by The Police and Criminal Evidence Act 1984 (Application to the Armed Forces) Order 2006 (S.I. 2006/2015), arts. 2, 3, Schs. 1-3

C64. S. 63 applied (with modifications) (4.11.2015) by The Police and Criminal Evidence Act 1984 (Application to Revenue and Customs) Order 2015 (S.I. 2015/1783), arts. 1, 3. (1), Sch. 1 (with art. 3. (2), (3), 4-19, Sch. 2)

C65. S. 63. (8. B)(a) modified (2.12.2002) by Police Reform Act 2002 (c. 30), s. 38, Sch. 4 Pt. 3 para. 31. (c); S.I. 2002/2750, art. 2. (a)(ii)(d)

[F124 63. A Fingerprints and samples: supplementary provisions.

[F125. (1)Where a person has been arrested on suspicion of being involved in a recordable offence or has been charged with such an offence or has been informed that he will be reported for such an offence, fingerprints [F126, impressions of footwear] or samples or the information derived from samples taken under any power conferred by this Part of this Act from the person may be checked against—

(a) other fingerprints [F126, impressions of footwear] or samples to which the person seeking to check has access and which are held by or on behalf of [F127any one or more relevant law-enforcement authorities or which] are held in connection with or as a result of an investigation of an offence;

(b) information derived from other samples if the information is contained in records to which the person seeking to check has access and which are held as mentioned in paragraph (a) above.

[F128. (1. ZA)Fingerprints taken by virtue of section 61. (6. A) above may be checked against other fingerprints to which the person seeking to check has access and which are held by or on behalf of any one or more relevant law-enforcement authorities or which are held in connection with or as a result of an investigation of an offence.]

[F129. (1. A) In subsection (1) [F130 and (1. ZA)] above " relevant law-enforcement authority " means—

(a) a police force;

[F131. (b)the [F132 National Crime Agency] ;]

(d) a public authority (not falling within paragraphs (a) to (c)) with functions in any part of the

British Islands which consist of or include the investigation of crimes or the charging of offenders;

(e) any person with functions in any country or territory outside the United Kingdom which—

(i) correspond to those of a police force; or

(ii) otherwise consist of or include the investigation of conduct contrary to the law of that country or territory, or the apprehension of persons guilty of such conduct;

(f) any person with functions under any international agreement which consist of or include the investigation of conduct which is—

(i) unlawful under the law of one or more places,

(ii) prohibited by such an agreement, or

(iii) contrary to international law,

or the apprehension of persons guilty of such conduct.

F129. (1. B)The reference in subsection (1. A) above to a police force is a reference to any of the following—

(a) any police force maintained under section 2 of the Police Act 1996 (c. 16) (police forces in England and Wales outside London);

(b) the metropolitan police force;

(c) the City of London police force;

[F133. (d)the Police Service of Scotland;]

(e) the Police Service of Northern Ireland;

(f) the Police Service of Northern Ireland Reserve;

(g) the Ministry of Defence Police;

(h) the [F134. Royal Navy Police];

(i) the Royal Military Police;

(j) the Royal Air Force Police;

F135. (k) . . . .

(l) the British Transport Police;

(m) the States of Jersey Police Force;

(n) the salaried police force of the Island of Guernsey;

(o) the Isle of Man Constabulary.

F129. (1. C)Where—

(a) fingerprints [F136, impressions of footwear] or samples have been taken from any person in connection with the investigation of an offence but otherwise than in circumstances to which subsection (1) above applies, and

(b) that person has given his consent in writing to the use in a speculative search of the fingerprints [F137, of the impressions of footwear] or of the samples and of information derived from them,

the fingerprints [F138or impressions of footwear] or, as the case may be, those samples and that information may be checked against any of the fingerprints [F139, impressions of footwear], samples or information mentioned in paragraph (a) or (b) of that subsection.

F129. (1. D)A consent given for the purposes of subsection (1. C) above shall not be capable of being withdrawn.]]

[F140. (1. E) Where fingerprints or samples have been taken from any person under section 61. (6) or 63. (3. B) above (persons convicted etc), the fingerprints or samples, or information derived from the samples, may be checked against any of the fingerprints, samples or information mentioned in subsection (1)(a) or (b) above.

(1. F) Where fingerprints or samples have been taken from any person under section 61. (6. D), 62. (2. A) or 63. (3. E) above (offences outside England and Wales etc), the fingerprints or samples, or information derived from the samples, may be checked against any of the fingerprints, samples or information mentioned in subsection (1)(a) or (b) above.]

(2) Where a sample of hair other than pubic hair is to be taken the sample may be taken either by cutting hairs or by plucking hairs with their roots so long as no more are plucked than the person taking the sample reasonably considers to be necessary for a sufficient sample.

(3) Where any power to take a sample is exercisable in relation to a person the sample may be

taken in a prison or other institution to which the M6 Prison Act 1952 applies.

[F141. (3. A)Where—

(a) the power to take a non-intimate sample under section 63. (3. B) above is exercisable in relation to any person who is detained under Part III of the M7 Mental Health Act 1983 in pursuance of—

(i) a hospital order or interim hospital order made following his conviction for the recordable offence in question, or

(ii) a transfer direction given at a time when he was detained in pursuance of any sentence or order imposed following that conviction, or

(b) the power to take a non-intimate sample under section 63. (3. C) above is exercisable in relation to any person,

the sample may be taken in the hospital in which he is detained under that Part of that Act.

Expressions used in this subsection and in the M8 Mental Health Act 1983 have the same meaning as in that Act.

(3. B)Where the power to take a non-intimate sample under section 63. (3. B) above is exercisable in relation to a person detained in pursuance of directions of the Secretary of State under [F142section 92 of the Powers of Criminal Courts (Sentencing) Act 2000] the sample may be taken at the place where he is so detained.]

[F143. (4)Schedule 2. A (fingerprinting and samples: power to require attendance at police station) shall have effect.]]

Amendments (Textual)

F124. S. 63. A inserted (10.4.1995) by 1994 c. 33, s. 56; S.I. 1995/721, art. 2, Sch.

F125. S. 63. A(1)(1. A) substituted for s. 63. A(1) (5.7.1996) by 1996 c. 25, s. 64 (with s. 78. (1))

F126. Words in s. 63. A(1) inserted (1.1.2006) by Serious Organised Crime and Police Act 2005 (c. 15), ss. 118. (3)(a), 178; S.I. 2005/3495, art. 2. (1)(p)

F127. Words in s. 63. A(1)(a) substituted (11.5.2001) by 2001 c. 16, s. 81. (1)

F128. S. 63. A(1. ZA) inserted (7.3.2011) by Serious Organised Crime and Police Act 2005 (c. 15), ss. 117. (5)(a), 178. (8); S.I. 2011/410, art. 2. (c)

F129. S. 63. A(1. A)-(1. D) substituted (11.5.2001) for s. 63. A(1. A) by 2001 c. 16, s. 81. (2)

F130. Words in s. 63. A(1. A) inserted (7.3.2011) by Serious Organised Crime and Police Act 2005 (c. 15), ss. 117. (5)(b), 178. (8); S.I. 2011/410, art. 2. (c)

F131. S. 63. A(1. A)(b) substituted (1.4.2006) for s. 63. A(1. A)(b)(c) by Serious Organised Crime and Police Act 2005 (c. 15), ss. 59, 178, Sch. 4 para. 46; S.I. 2006/378, art. 4. (1), Sch. para. 10 (subject to art. 4. (2)-(7))

F132. Words in s. 63. A(1. A)(b) substituted (7.10.2013) by Crime and Courts Act 2013 (c. 22), s. 61. (2), Sch. 8 para. 186; S.I. 2013/1682, art. 3. (v)

F133. S. 63. A(1. B)(d) substituted (1.4.2013) by The Police and Fire Reform (Scotland) Act 2012 (Consequential Provisions and Modifications) Order 2013 (S.I. 2013/602), art. 1. (2), Sch. 2 para. 19

F134. Words in s. 63. A(1. B)(h) substituted (4.6.2007) by Armed Forces Act 2006 (c. 52), ss. 378, 383, Sch. 16 para. 100. (a); S.I. 2007/1442, art. 2. (1)

F135. S. 63. A(1. B)(k) omitted (1.1.2008) by virtue of and repealed (28.3.2009 for certain purposes and otherwise 31.10.2009) Armed Forces Act 2006 (c. 52), ss. 378, 383, Sch. 16 para. 100. (b), Sch. 17; S.I. 2007/2913, art. 3; S.I. 2009/812, art. 3 (with transitional provisions in S.I. 2009/1059); S.I. 2009/1167, art. 4

F136. Words in s. 63. A(1. C)(a) inserted (1.1.2006) by Serious Organised Crime and Police Act 2005 (c. 15), ss. 118. (3)(b)(i), 178; S.I. 2005/3495, art. 2. (1)(p)

F137. Words in s. 63. A(1. C)(b) inserted (1.1.2006) by Serious Organised Crime and Police Act 2005 (c. 15), ss. 118. (3)(b)(ii), 178; S.I. 2005/3495, art. 2. (1)(p)

F138. Words in s. 63. A(1. C) inserted (1.1.2006) by Serious Organised Crime and Police Act 2005 (c. 15), ss. 118. (3)(b)(iii), 178; S.I. 2005/3495, art. 2. (1)(p)

F139. Words in s. 63. A(1. C) inserted (1.1.2006) by Serious Organised Crime and Police Act 2005 (c. 15), ss. 118. (3)(b)(iv), 178; S.I. 2005/3495, art. 2. (1)(p)

F140. S. 63. A(1. E)(1. F) inserted (7.3.2011) by Crime and Security Act 2010 (c. 17), ss. 5. (1), 59. (1); S.I. 2011/414, art. 2. (b)

F141. S. 63. A(3. A)(3. B) inserted (19.3.1997) by 1997 c. 17, s. 3

F142. Words in s. 63. A(3. B) substituted (25.8.2000) by 2000 c. 6, ss. 165. (1), 168. (1), Sch. 9 para. 97

F143. S. 63. A(4) substituted for s. 63. (4)-(8) (7.3.2011) by Crime and Security Act 2010 (c. 17), ss. 6. (1), 59. (1); S.I. 2011/414, art. 2. (c)

Modifications etc. (not altering text)

C66. S. 63. A(1) restricted (1.9.2001) by 2001 c. 17, s. 34. (1), Sch. 4 para. 7. (3); S.I. 2001/2161, art. 2 (subject to art. 3)

C67. S. 63. A applied (with modifications) (31.12.2006) by The Police and Criminal Evidence Act 1984 (Application to the Armed Forces) Order 2006 (S.I. 2006/2015), arts. 2, 3, Schs. 1-3

C68. S. 63. A amended (1.7.2004) by Railways and Transport Safety Act 2003 (c. 20), ss. 73, 120, Sch. 5 para. 4. (1)(a)(2) (with s. 72); S.I. 2004/1572, art. 3. (ddd)(jjj)

C69. S. 63. A(1) applied (with modifications) (1.2.1997) by S.I. 1997/15, art. 2. (1), Sch.
S. 63. A(2) applied (1.2.1997) by S.I. 1997/15, art. 2. (1), Sch.

C70. S. 63. A(4) extended (2.12.2002) by Police Reform Act 2002 (c. 30), s. 38, Sch. 4 Pt. 3 para. 32; S.I. 2002/2750, art. 2. (a)(ii)(d)

Marginal Citations

M61952 c. 52.

M71983 c. 20.

M81983 c. 20.

[F14463. AAInclusion of DNA profiles on National DNA Database

(1) This section applies to a DNA profile which is derived from a DNA sample and which is retained under any power conferred by any of sections 63. E to 63. L (including those sections as applied by section 63. P).

(2) A DNA profile to which this section applies must be recorded on the National DNA Database.]

Amendments (Textual)

F144. S. 63. AA inserted (31.10.2013) by Protection of Freedoms Act 2012 (c. 9), ss. 23, 120 (with s. 97); S.I. 2013/1814, art. 2. (g)

[F14563. ABNational DNA Database Strategy Board

(1) The Secretary of State must make arrangements for a National DNA Database Strategy Board to oversee the operation of the National DNA Database.

(2) The National DNA Database Strategy Board must issue guidance about the destruction of DNA profiles which are, or may be, retained under this Part of this Act.

(3) A chief officer of a police force in England and Wales must act in accordance with guidance issued under subsection (2).

(4) The National DNA Database Strategy Board may issue guidance about the circumstances in which applications may be made to the Commissioner for the Retention and Use of Biometric Material under section 63. G.

(5) Before issuing any such guidance, the National DNA Database Strategy Board must consult the Commissioner for the Retention and Use of Biometric Material.

(6) The Secretary of State must publish the governance rules of the National DNA Database Strategy Board and lay a copy of the rules before Parliament.

(7) The National DNA Database Strategy Board must make an annual report to the Secretary of State about the exercise of its functions.

(8) The Secretary of State must publish the report and lay a copy of the published report before Parliament.

(9) The Secretary of State may exclude from publication any part of the report if, in the opinion of the Secretary of State, the publication of that part would be contrary to the public interest or prejudicial to national security.]

Amendments (Textual)

F145. S. 63. AB inserted (31.10.2013) by Protection of Freedoms Act 2012 (c. 9), ss. 24, 120 (with s. 97); S.I. 2013/1814, art. 2. (g)

[F14663. B Testing for presence of Class A drugs.

(1) A sample of urine or a non-intimate sample may be taken from a person in police detention for the purpose of ascertaining whether he has any specified Class A drug in his body if

[F147. (a)either the arrest condition or the charge condition is met;

(b) both the age condition and the request condition are met; and

(c) the notification condition is met in relation to the arrest condition, the charge condition or the age condition (as the case may be).]

[F148. (1. A)The arrest condition is that the person concerned has been arrested for an offence but has not been charged with that offence and either—

(a) the offence is a trigger offence; or

(b) a police officer of at least the rank of inspector has reasonable grounds for suspecting that the misuse by that person of a specified Class A drug caused or contributed to the offence and has authorised the sample to be taken.]

(2) [F149. The charge condition is either]—

(a) that the person concerned has been charged with a trigger offence; or

(b) that the person concerned has been charged with an offence and a police officer of at least the rank of inspector, who has reasonable grounds for suspecting that the misuse by that person of any specified Class A drug caused or contributed to the offence, has authorised the sample to be taken.

[F150. (3)The age condition is—

(a) if the arrest condition is met, that the person concerned has attained the age of 18;

(b) if the charge condition is met, that he has attained the age of 14.]

(4) The [F151request] condition is that a police officer has requested the person concerned to give the sample.

[F152. (4. A)The notification condition is that—

(a) the relevant chief officer has been notified by the Secretary of State that appropriate arrangements have been made for the police area as a whole, or for the particular police station, in which the person is in police detention, and

(b) the notice has not been withdrawn.

(4. B)For the purposes of subsection (4. A) above, appropriate arrangements are arrangements for the taking of samples under this section from whichever of the following is specified in the notification—

(a) persons in respect of whom the arrest condition is met;

(b) persons in respect of whom the charge condition is met;

(c) persons who have not attained the age of 18.]

(5) Before requesting the person concerned to give a sample, an officer must—

(a) warn him that if, when so requested, he fails without good cause to do so he may be liable to prosecution, and

(b) in a case within subsection [F153. (1. A)(b) or] (2)(b) above, inform him of the giving of the authorisation and of the grounds in question.

[F154. (5. A)In the case of a person who [F155has not attained the age of 18]—

(a) the making of the request under subsection (4) above;

(b) the giving of the warning and (where applicable) the information under subsection (5) above; and

129

(c) the taking of the sample,

may not take place except in the presence of an appropriate adult.]

[F156. (5. B)If a sample is taken under this section from a person in respect of whom the arrest condition is met no other sample may be taken from him under this section during the same continuous period of detention but—

(a) if the charge condition is also met in respect of him at any time during that period, the sample must be treated as a sample taken by virtue of the fact that the charge condition is met;

(b) the fact that the sample is to be so treated must be recorded in the person's custody record.

(5. C)Despite subsection (1)(a) above, a sample may be taken from a person under this section if—

(a) he was arrested for an offence (the first offence),

(b) the arrest condition is met but the charge condition is not met,

(c) before a sample is taken by virtue of subsection (1) above he would (but for his arrest as mentioned in paragraph (d) below) be required to be released from police detention,

(d) he continues to be in police detention by virtue of his having been arrested for an offence not falling within subsection (1. A) above, and

(e) the sample is taken before the end of the period of 24 hours starting with the time when his detention by virtue of his arrest for the first offence began.

(5. D)A sample must not be taken from a person under this section if he is detained in a police station unless he has been brought before the custody officer.]

(6) A sample may be taken under this section only by a person prescribed by regulations made by the Secretary of State by statutory instrument.

No regulations shall be made under this subsection unless a draft has been laid before, and approved by resolution of, each House of Parliament.

[F157[F158. (6. A)The Secretary of State may by order made by statutory instrument amend—

(a) paragraph (a) of subsection (3) above, by substituting for the age for the time being specified a different age specified in the order, or different ages so specified for different police areas so specified;

(b) paragraph (b) of that subsection, by substituting for the age for the time being specified a different age specified in the order.]

(6. B)A statutory instrument containing an order under subsection (6. A) above shall not be made unless a draft of the instrument has been laid before, and approved by a resolution of, each House of Parliament.]

(7) Information obtained from a sample taken under this section may be disclosed—

(a) for the purpose of informing any decision about granting bail in criminal proceedings (within the meaning of the M9. Bail Act 1976) to the person concerned;

[F159. (aa)for the purpose of informing any decision about the giving of a conditional caution under Part 3 of the Criminal Justice Act 2003 [F160or a youth conditional caution under Chapter 1 of Part 4 of the Crime and Disorder Act 1998] to the person concerned;]

(b) where the person concerned is in police detention or is remanded in or committed to custody by an order of a court or has been granted such bail, for the purpose of informing any decision about his supervision;

(c) where the person concerned is convicted of an offence, for the purpose of informing any decision about the appropriate sentence to be passed by a court and any decision about his supervision or release;

[F161. (ca)for the purpose of an assessment which the person concerned is required to attend by virtue of section 9. (2) or 10. (2) of the Drugs Act 2005;

(cb) for the purpose of proceedings against the person concerned for an offence under section 12. (3) or 14. (3) of that Act;]

(d) for the purpose of ensuring that appropriate advice and treatment is made available to the person concerned.

(8) A person who fails without good cause to give any sample which may be taken from him under this section shall be guilty of an offence.

[F162. (9)F163. . . . .

(10) In this section—

"appropriate adult", in relation to a person who[F164has not attained the age of 18], means—

- his parent or guardian or, if he is in the care of a local authority or voluntary organisation, a person representing that authority or organisation; or

- F165a social worker of a local authority . . . ; or

- if no person falling within paragraph (a) or (b) is available, any responsible person aged 18 or over who is not a police officer or[F166a person employed for, or engaged on, police purposes; and "police purposes" has the meaning given by section 101. (2) of the Police Act 1996];

"relevant chief officer" means—

- in relation to a police area, the chief officer of police of the police force for that police area; or

- in relation to a police station, the chief officer of police of the police force for the police area in which the police station is situated.]]

Amendments (Textual)

F146. S. 63. B inserted (for certain purposes on 20.6.2001, 2.7.2001, 20.5.2002, 2.9.2002, 1.4.2003, 1.4.2004 and otherwise prosp.) by 2000 c. 43, ss. 57. (2), 80. (1); S.I. 2001/2232, art. 2. (f); S.I. 2002/1149, art. 2; S.I. 2002/1862, art. 2; S.I. 2003/709, art. 2; S.I. 2004/780, art. 2

F147. S. 63. B(1)(a)-(c) substituted (1.12.2005) for words in s. 63. B(1) by Drugs Act 2005 (c. 17), ss. 7. (2), 24 (with s. 7. (13)(14)); S.I. 2005/3053, art. 2. (1)(a)

F148. S. 63. B(1. A) inserted (1.12.2005) by Drugs Act 2005 (c. 17), ss. 7. (3), 24 (with s. 7. (13)(14)); S.I. 2005/3053, art. 2. (1)(a)

F149. Words in s. 63. B(2) substituted (1.12.2005) by Drugs Act 2005 (c. 17), ss. 7. (4), 24 (with s. 7. (13)(14)); S.I. 2005/3053, art. 2. (1)(a)

F150. S. 63. B(3) substituted (1.12.2005) by Drugs Act 2005 (c. 17), ss. 7. (5), 24 (with s. 7. (13)(14)); S.I. 2005/3053, art. 2. (1)(a)

F151. Word in s. 63. B(4) substituted (1.12.2005) by Drugs Act 2005 (c. 17), ss. 7. (6), 24 (with s. 7. (13)(14)); S.I. 2005/3053, art. 2. (1)(a)

F152. S. 63. B(4. A)(4. B) inserted (1.12.2005) by Drugs Act 2005 (c. 17), ss. 7. (7), 24; (with s. 7. (13)(14)); S.I. 2005/3053, art. 2. (1)(a)

F153. Words in s. 63. B(5)(b) inserted (1.12.2005) by Drugs Act 2005 (c. 17), ss. 7. (8), 24 (with s. 7. (13)(14)); S.I. 2005/3053, art. 2. (1)(a)

F154. S. 63. B(5. A) inserted (1.8.2004 for certain purposes and otherwise 1.12.2005) by Criminal Justice Act 2003 (c. 44), ss. 5. (3)(b), 336; S.I. 2004/1867, art. 2; S.I. 2005/3055, art. 2

F155. Words in s. 63. B(5. A) substituted (31.1.2017 for specified purposes, 3.4.2017 in so far as not already in force) by Policing and Crime Act 2017 (c. 3), ss. 73. (3)(a), 183. (1), (5)(e); S.I. 2017/399, reg. 2, Sch. para. 22

F156. S. 63. B(5. B)-(5. D) inserted (1.12.2005) by Drugs Act 2005 (c. 17), ss. 7. (9), 24 (with s. 7. (13)(14)); S.I. 2005/3053, art. 2. (1)(a)

F157. S. 63. B(6. A)(6. B) inserted (1.8.2004 for certain purposes and otherwise 1.12.2005) by Criminal Justice Act 2003 (c. 44), ss. 5. (3)(c), 336; S.I. 2004/1867, art. 2; S.I. 2005/3055, art. 2

F158. S. 63. B(6. A) substituted (1.12.2005) by Drugs Act 2005 (c. 17), ss. 7. (10), 24 (with s. 7. (13)(14)); S.I. 2005/3053, art. 2. (1)(a)

F159. S. 63. B(7)(aa) inserted (1.12.2005) by Drugs Act 2005 (c. 17), ss. 7. (11), 24 (with s. 7. (13)(14)); S.I. 2005/3053, art. 2. (1)(a)

F160. Words in s. 63. B(7)(aa) substituted (16.11.2009 in relation to the areas specified in art. 2. (2) of the commencing S.I.) by Criminal Justice and Immigration Act 2008 (c. 4), ss. 148, 153, Sch. 26 para. 20. (2); S.I. 2009/2780, art. 2

F161. S. 63. B(7)(ca)(cb) inserted (1.12.2005) by Drugs Act 2005 (c. 17), ss. 23, 24, Sch. 1 para. 4; S.I. 2005/3053, art. 2. (1)(f)

F162. S. 63. B(9)(10) inserted (1.8.2004 for certain purposes and otherwise 1.12.2005) by Criminal Justice Act 2003 (c. 44), ss. 5. (3)(d), 336; S.I. 2004/1867, art. 2; S.I. 2005/3055, art. 2

F163. S. 63. B(9) repealed (1.12.2005) by Drugs Act 2005 (c. 17), ss. 7. (9), 23, 24 (with s. 7. (13)(14)); S.I. 2005/3053, art. 2. (1)(a)(f)

F164. Words in s. 63. B(10) substituted (31.1.2017 for specified purposes, 3.4.2017 in so far as not already in force) by Policing and Crime Act 2017 (c. 3), ss. 73. (3)(b), 183. (1), (5)(e); S.I. 2017/399, reg. 2, Sch. para. 22

F165. S. 63. B(10): words in definition of "appropriate adult" repealed (1.4.2005 for E. and 1.4.2006 for W.) by Children Act 2004 (c. 31), ss. 64, 67, Sch. 5 Pt. 4; S.I. 2005/394, art. 2. (2)(g); S.I. 2006/885, art. 2. (2)(h)

F166. Words in s. 63. B(10)(c) substituted (31.1.2017 for specified purposes, 3.4.2017 in so far as not already in force) by Policing and Crime Act 2017 (c. 3), ss. 79. (1), 183. (1), (5)(e); S.I. 2017/399, reg. 2, Sch. para. 27

Modifications etc. (not altering text)

C71. S. 63. B(2): power to amend conferred (for certain purposes on 20.6.2001, 2.7.2001, 20.5.2002, 2.9.2002, 1.4.2003, 1.4.2004, 1.4.2005 and 1.12.2005) by 2000 c. 43, ss. 57. (4), 80. (1); S.I. 2001/2232, art. 2. (f); S.I. 2002/1149, art. 2; S.I. 2002/1862, art. 2; S.I. 2003/709, art. 2; S.I. 2004/780, art. 2; S.I. 2005/596, art. 2; S.I. 2005/3054, art. 2

Marginal Citations

M91976 c. 63.

F16763. C Testing for presence of Class A drugs: supplementary.

(1) A person guilty of an offence under section 63. B above shall be liable on summary conviction to imprisonment for a term not exceeding three months, or to a fine not exceeding level 4 on the standard scale, or to both.

(2) A police officer may give an authorisation under section 63. B above orally or in writing but, if he gives it orally, he shall confirm it in writing as soon as is practicable.

(3) If a sample is taken under section 63. B above by virtue of an authorisation, the authorisation and the grounds for the suspicion shall be recorded as soon as is practicable after the sample is taken.

(4) If the sample is taken from a person detained at a police station, the matters required to be recorded by subsection (3) above shall be recorded in his custody record.

(5) Subsections (11) and (12) of section 62 above apply for the purposes of section 63. B above as they do for the purposes of that section; and section 63. B above does not prejudice the generality of sections 62 and 63 above.

(6) In section 63. B above—

"Class A drug" and "misuse" have the same meanings as in the M10. Misuse of Drugs Act 1971; "specified" (in relation to a Class A drug) and "trigger offence" have the same meanings as in Part III of the Criminal Justice and Court Services Act 2000.

Amendments (Textual)

F167. S. 63. C inserted (for certain purposes on 20.6.2001, 2.7.2001, 20.5.2002, 2.9.2002, 1.4.2003, 1.4.2004, 1.4.2005 and otherwise 1.12.2005) by 2000 c. 43, ss. 57. (3)(a), 80. (1); S.I. 2001/2232, art. 2. (f); S.I. 2002/1149, art. 2; S.I. 2002/1862, art. 2; S.I. 2003/709, art. 2; S.I. 2004/780, art. 2; S.I. 2005/596, art. 2; S.I. 2005/3054, art. 2

Marginal Citations

M101971 c. 38.

[F16863. DDestruction of fingerprints and DNA profiles

(1) This section applies to—

(a) fingerprints—

(i) taken from a person under any power conferred by this Part of this Act, or

(ii) taken by the police, with the consent of the person from whom they were taken, in connection with the investigation of an offence by the police, and

(b) a DNA profile derived from a DNA sample taken as mentioned in paragraph (a)(i) or (ii).

(2) Fingerprints and DNA profiles to which this section applies ("section 63. D material") must be

destroyed if it appears to the responsible chief officer of police that—

(a) the taking of the fingerprint or, in the case of a DNA profile, the taking of the sample from which the DNA profile was derived, was unlawful, or

(b) the fingerprint was taken, or, in the case of a DNA profile, was derived from a sample taken, from a person in connection with that person's arrest and the arrest was unlawful or based on mistaken identity.

(3) In any other case, section 63. D material must be destroyed unless it is retained under any power conferred by sections 63. E to 63. O (including those sections as applied by section 63. P).

(4) Section 63. D material which ceases to be retained under a power mentioned in subsection (3) may continue to be retained under any other such power which applies to it.

(5) Nothing in this section prevents a speculative search, in relation to section 63. D material, from being carried out within such time as may reasonably be required for the search if the responsible chief officer of police considers the search to be desirable.]

Amendments (Textual)

F168. S. 63. D inserted (31.10.2013) by Protection of Freedoms Act 2012 (c. 9), ss. 1, 120 (with s. 97); S.I. 2013/1814, art. 2. (a)

Modifications etc. (not altering text)

C72. S. 63. D applied (with modifications) (4.11.2015) by The Police and Criminal Evidence Act 1984 (Application to Revenue and Customs) Order 2015 (S.I. 2015/1783), arts. 1, 3. (1), Sch. 1 (with art. 3. (2), (3), 4-19, Sch. 2)

[F16963. ERetention of section 63. D material pending investigation or proceedings

(1) This section applies to section 63. D material taken (or, in the case of a DNA profile, derived from a sample taken) in connection with the investigation of an offence in which it is suspected that the person to whom the material relates has been involved.

(2) The material may be retained until the conclusion of the investigation of the offence or, where the investigation gives rise to proceedings against the person for the offence, until the conclusion of those proceedings.]

Amendments (Textual)

F169. S. 63. E inserted (31.10.2013) by Protection of Freedoms Act 2012 (c. 9), ss. 2, 120 (with s. 97); S.I. 2013/1814, art. 2. (a)

Modifications etc. (not altering text)

C73. S. 63. E applied (with modifications) (4.11.2015) by The Police and Criminal Evidence Act 1984 (Application to Revenue and Customs) Order 2015 (S.I. 2015/1783), arts. 1, 3. (1), Sch. 1 (with art. 3. (2), (3), 4-19, Sch. 2)

[F17063. FRetention of section 63. D material: persons arrested for or charged with a qualifying offence

(1) This section applies to section 63. D material which—

(a) relates to a person who is arrested for, or charged with, a qualifying offence but is not convicted of that offence, and

(b) was taken (or, in the case of a DNA profile, derived from a sample taken) in connection with the investigation of the offence.

(2) If the person has previously been convicted of a recordable offence which is not an excluded offence, or is so convicted before the material is required to be destroyed by virtue of this section, the material may be retained indefinitely.

[F171. (2. A)In subsection (2), references to a recordable offence include an offence under the law of a country or territory outside England and Wales where the act constituting the offence would constitute a recordable offence if done in England and Wales (and, in the application of subsection (2) where a person has previously been convicted, this applies whether or not the act constituted such an offence when the person was convicted).]

(3) Otherwise, material falling within subsection (4) or (5) may be retained until the end of the retention period specified in subsection (6).

(4) Material falls within this subsection if it—

(a) relates to a person who is charged with a qualifying offence but is not convicted of that offence, and

(b) was taken (or, in the case of a DNA profile, derived from a sample taken) in connection with the investigation of the offence.

(5) Material falls within this subsection if—

(a) it relates to a person who is arrested for a qualifying offence but is not charged with that offence,

(b) it was taken (or, in the case of a DNA profile, derived from a sample taken) in connection with the investigation of the offence, and

(c) the Commissioner for the Retention and Use of Biometric Material has consented under section 63. G to the retention of the material.

(6) The retention period is—

(a) in the case of fingerprints, the period of 3 years beginning with the date on which the fingerprints were taken, and

(b) in the case of a DNA profile, the period of 3 years beginning with the date on which the DNA sample from which the profile was derived was taken (or, if the profile was derived from more than one DNA sample, the date on which the first of those samples was taken).

(7) The responsible chief officer of police or a specified chief officer of police may apply to a District Judge (Magistrates' Courts) for an order extending the retention period.

(8) An application for an order under subsection (7) must be made within the period of 3 months ending on the last day of the retention period.

(9) An order under subsection (7) may extend the retention period by a period which—

(a) begins with the end of the retention period, and

(b) ends with the end of the period of 2 years beginning with the end of the retention period.

(10) The following persons may appeal to the Crown Court against an order under subsection (7), or a refusal to make such an order—

(a) the responsible chief officer of police;

(b) a specified chief officer of police;

(c) the person from whom the material was taken.

(11) In this section—

"excluded offence", in relation to a person, means a recordable offence—

- which—

is not a qualifying offence,

is the only recordable offence of which the person has been convicted, and

was committed when the person was aged under 18, and

- for which the person was not given a relevant custodial sentence of 5 years or more,

"relevant custodial sentence" has the meaning given by section 63. K(6),

"a specified chief officer of police" means—

- the chief officer of the police force of the area in which the person from whom the material was taken resides, or

- a chief officer of police who believes that the person is in, or is intending to come to, the chief officer's police area.]

[F172. (12)For the purposes of the definition of "excluded offence" in subsection (11)—

(a) references to a recordable offence or a qualifying offence include an offence under the law of a country or territory outside England and Wales where the act constituting the offence would constitute a recordable offence or (as the case may be) a qualifying offence if done in England and Wales (whether or not it constituted such an offence when the person was convicted), and

(b) in the application of paragraph (b) of that definition in relation to an offence under the law of a country or territory outside England and Wales, the reference to a relevant custodial sentence of 5 years or more is to be read as a reference to a sentence of imprisonment or other form of detention of 5 years or more.]

Amendments (Textual)

F170. S. 63. F inserted (31.10.2013) by Protection of Freedoms Act 2012 (c. 9), ss. 3, 120 (with s. 97); S.I. 2013/1814, art. 2. (a)

F171. S. 63. F(2. A) inserted (31.1.2017 for specified purposes, 3.4.2017 in so far as not already in force) by Policing and Crime Act 2017 (c. 3), ss. 70. (2), 183. (1), (5)(e); S.I. 2017/399, reg. 2, Sch. para. 20 (with reg. 6)

F172. S. 63. F(12) inserted (31.1.2017 for specified purposes, 3.4.2017 in so far as not already in force) by Policing and Crime Act 2017 (c. 3), ss. 70. (3), 183. (1), (5)(e); S.I. 2017/399, reg. 2, Sch. para. 20 (with reg. 6)

[F17363. GRetention of section 63. D material by virtue of section 63. F(5): consent of Commissioner

(1) The responsible chief officer of police may apply under subsection (2) or (3) to the Commissioner for the Retention and Use of Biometric Material for consent to the retention of section 63. D material which falls within section 63. F(5)(a) and (b).

(2) The responsible chief officer of police may make an application under this subsection if the responsible chief officer of police considers that the material was taken (or, in the case of a DNA profile, derived from a sample taken) in connection with the investigation of an offence where any alleged victim of the offence was, at the time of the offence—

(a) under the age of 18,

(b) a vulnerable adult, or

(c) associated with the person to whom the material relates.

(3) The responsible chief officer of police may make an application under this subsection if the responsible chief officer of police considers that—

(a) the material is not material to which subsection (2) relates, but

(b) the retention of the material is necessary to assist in the prevention or detection of crime.

(4) The Commissioner may, on an application under this section, consent to the retention of material to which the application relates if the Commissioner considers that it is appropriate to retain the material.

(5) But where notice is given under subsection (6) in relation to the application, the Commissioner must, before deciding whether or not to give consent, consider any representations by the person to whom the material relates which are made within the period of 28 days beginning with the day on which the notice is given.

(6) The responsible chief officer of police must give to the person to whom the material relates notice of—

(a) an application under this section, and

(b) the right to make representations.

(7) A notice under subsection (6) may, in particular, be given to a person by—

(a) leaving it at the person's usual or last known address (whether residential or otherwise),

(b) sending it to the person by post at that address, or

(c) sending it to the person by email or other electronic means.

(8) The requirement in subsection (6) does not apply if the whereabouts of the person to whom the material relates is not known and cannot, after reasonable inquiry, be ascertained by the responsible chief officer of police.

(9) An application or notice under this section must be in writing.

(10) In this section—

"victim" includes intended victim,

"vulnerable adult" means a person aged 18 or over whose ability to protect himself or herself from violence, abuse or neglect is significantly impaired through physical or mental disability or illness, through old age or otherwise,

and the reference in subsection (2)(c) to a person being associated with another person is to be read in accordance with section 62. (3) to (7) of the Family Law Act 1996.]

Amendments (Textual)

F173. S. 63. G inserted (31.10.2013) by Protection of Freedoms Act 2012 (c. 9), ss. 3, 120 (with s. 97); S.I. 2013/1814, art. 2. (a)

Modifications etc. (not altering text)

C74. S. 63. G applied (with modifications) (4.11.2015) by The Police and Criminal Evidence Act 1984 (Application to Revenue and Customs) Order 2015 (S.I. 2015/1783), arts. 1, 3. (1), Sch. 1 (with art. 3. (2), (3), 4-19, Sch. 2)

[F17463. HRetention of section 63. D material: persons arrested for or charged with a minor offence

(1) This section applies to section 63. D material which—
    (a) relates to a person who—
(i) is arrested for or charged with a recordable offence other than a qualifying offence,
(ii) if arrested for or charged with more than one offence arising out of a single course of action, is not also arrested for or charged with a qualifying offence, and
(iii) is not convicted of the offence or offences in respect of which the person is arrested or charged, and
    (b) was taken (or, in the case of a DNA profile, derived from a sample taken) in connection with the investigation of the offence or offences in respect of which the person is arrested or charged.
(2) If the person has previously been convicted of a recordable offence which is not an excluded offence, the material may be retained indefinitely.
[F175. (2. A)In subsection (2), the reference to a recordable offence includes an offence under the law of a country or territory outside England and Wales where the act constituting the offence would constitute a recordable offence if done in England and Wales (whether or not it constituted such an offence when the person was convicted).]
(3) In this section "excluded offence" has the meaning given by section 63. F(11) [F176. (read with section 63. F(12))].]

Amendments (Textual)

F174. S. 63. H inserted (31.10.2013) by Protection of Freedoms Act 2012 (c. 9), ss. 4, 120 (with s. 97); S.I. 2013/1814, art. 2. (a)

F175. S. 63. H(2. A) inserted (31.1.2017 for specified purposes, 3.4.2017 in so far as not already in force) by Policing and Crime Act 2017 (c. 3), ss. 70. (4), 183. (1), (5)(e); S.I. 2017/399, reg. 2, Sch. para. 20 (with reg. 6)

F176. Words in s. 63. H(3) inserted (31.1.2017 for specified purposes, 3.4.2017 in so far as not already in force) by Policing and Crime Act 2017 (c. 3), ss. 70. (5), 183. (1), (5)(e); S.I. 2017/399, reg. 2, Sch. para. 20 (with reg. 6)

Modifications etc. (not altering text)

C75. S. 63. H applied (with modifications) (4.11.2015) by The Police and Criminal Evidence Act 1984 (Application to Revenue and Customs) Order 2015 (S.I. 2015/1783), arts. 1, 3. (1), Sch. 1 (with art. 3. (2), (3), 4-19, Sch. 2)

[F17763. IRetention of material: persons convicted of a recordable offence

(1) This section applies, subject to subsection (3), to—

(a) section 63. D material which—

(i) relates to a person who is convicted of a recordable offence, and

(ii) was taken (or, in the case of a DNA profile, derived from a sample taken) in connection with the investigation of the offence, or

(b) material taken under section 61. (6) or 63. (3. B) which relates to a person who is convicted of a recordable offence.

(2) The material may be retained indefinitely.

(3) This section does not apply to section 63. D material to which section 63. K applies.]

Amendments (Textual)

F177. S. 63. I inserted (31.10.2013) by Protection of Freedoms Act 2012 (c. 9), ss. 5, 120 (with s. 97); S.I. 2013/1814, art. 2. (a)

Modifications etc. (not altering text)

C76. S. 63. I applied (with modifications) (4.11.2015) by The Police and Criminal Evidence Act 1984 (Application to Revenue and Customs) Order 2015 (S.I. 2015/1783), arts. 1, 3. (1), Sch. 1 (with art. 3. (2), (3), 4-19, Sch. 2)

[F17863. IARetention of material: persons convicted of an offence outside England and Wales after taking of section 63. D material

(1) This section applies where—

(a) section 63. D material is taken (or, in the case of a DNA profile, derived from a sample taken) in connection with the investigation of an offence,

(b) at any time before the material is required to be destroyed by virtue of this Part of this Act, the person is convicted of an offence under the law of a country or territory outside England and Wales, and

(c) the act constituting the offence mentioned in paragraph (b) would constitute a recordable offence if done in England and Wales.

(2) The material may be retained indefinitely.

(3) This section does not apply where section 63. KA applies.]

Amendments (Textual)

F178. S. 63. IA inserted (31.1.2017 for specified purposes, 3.4.2017 in so far as not already in force) by Policing and Crime Act 2017 (c. 3), ss. 70. (6), 183. (1), (5)(e); S.I. 2017/399, reg. 2, Sch. para. 20 (with reg. 6)

[F17963. JRetention of material: persons convicted of an offence outside England and Wales[F180: other cases]

(1) This section applies to material falling within subsection (2) relating to a person who is convicted of an offence under the law of any country or territory outside England and Wales.

(2) Material falls within this subsection if it is—

(a) fingerprints taken from the person under section 61. (6. D) (power to take fingerprints without consent in relation to offences outside England and Wales), or

(b) a DNA profile derived from a DNA sample taken from the person under section 62. (2. A) or 63. (3. E) (powers to take intimate and non-intimate samples in relation to offences outside England and Wales).

(3) The material may be retained indefinitely.]

Amendments (Textual)

F179. S. 63. J inserted (31.10.2013) by Protection of Freedoms Act 2012 (c. 9), ss. 6, 120 (with s. 97); S.I. 2013/1814, art. 2. (a)

F180. Words in s. 63. J inserted (31.1.2017 for specified purposes, 3.4.2017 in so far as not already in force) by Policing and Crime Act 2017 (c. 3), ss. 70. (7), 183. (1), (5)(e); S.I. 2017/399,

reg. 2, Sch. para. 20 (with reg. 6)
Modifications etc. (not altering text)
C77. S. 63. J applied (with modifications) (4.11.2015) by The Police and Criminal Evidence Act 1984 (Application to Revenue and Customs) Order 2015 (S.I. 2015/1783), arts. 1, 3. (1), Sch. 1 (with art. 3. (2), (3), 4-19, Sch. 2)

[F18163. KRetention of section 63. D material: exception for persons under 18 convicted of first minor offence

(1) This section applies to section 63. D material which—
    (a) relates to a person who—
(i) is convicted of a recordable offence other than a qualifying offence,
(ii) has not previously been convicted of a recordable offence, and
(iii) is aged under 18 at the time of the offence, and
    (b) was taken (or, in the case of a DNA profile, derived from a sample taken) in connection with the investigation of the offence.
[F182. (1. A)In subsection (1)(a)(ii), the reference to a recordable offence includes an offence under the law of a country or territory outside England and Wales where the act constituting the offence would constitute a recordable offence if done in England and Wales (whether or not it constituted such an offence when the person was convicted).]
(2) Where the person is given a relevant custodial sentence of less than 5 years in respect of the offence, the material may be retained until the end of the period consisting of the term of the sentence plus 5 years.
(3) Where the person is given a relevant custodial sentence of 5 years or more in respect of the offence, the material may be retained indefinitely.
(4) Where the person is given a sentence other than a relevant custodial sentence in respect of the offence, the material may be retained until—
    (a) in the case of fingerprints, the end of the period of 5 years beginning with the date on which the fingerprints were taken, and
    (b) in the case of a DNA profile, the end of the period of 5 years beginning with—
(i) the date on which the DNA sample from which the profile was derived was taken, or
(ii) if the profile was derived from more than one DNA sample, the date on which the first of those samples was taken.
(5) But if, before the end of the period within which material may be retained by virtue of this section, the person is again convicted of a recordable offence, the material may be retained indefinitely.
[F183. (5. A)In subsection (5), the reference to a recordable offence includes an offence under the law of a country or territory outside England and Wales where the act constituting the offence would constitute a recordable offence if done in England and Wales.]
(6) In this section, "relevant custodial sentence" means any of the following—
    (a) a custodial sentence within the meaning of section 76 of the Powers of Criminal Courts (Sentencing) Act 2000;
    (b) a sentence of a period of detention and training (excluding any period of supervision) which a person is liable to serve under an order under section 211 of the Armed Forces Act 2006 or a secure training order.]
Amendments (Textual)
F181. S. 63. K inserted (31.10.2013) by Protection of Freedoms Act 2012 (c. 9), ss. 7, 120 (with s. 97); S.I. 2013/1814, art. 2. (a)
F182. S. 63. K(1. A) inserted (31.1.2017 for specified purposes, 3.4.2017 in so far as not already in force) by Policing and Crime Act 2017 (c. 3), ss. 70. (8), 183. (1), (5)(e); S.I. 2017/399, reg. 2, Sch. para. 20 (with reg. 6)
F183. S. 63. K(5. A) inserted (31.1.2017 for specified purposes, 3.4.2017 in so far as not already

in force) by Policing and Crime Act 2017 (c. 3), ss. 70. (9), 183. (1), (5)(e); S.I. 2017/399, reg. 2, Sch. para. 20 (with reg. 6)

Modifications etc. (not altering text)

C78. S. 63. K applied (with modifications) (4.11.2015) by The Police and Criminal Evidence Act 1984 (Application to Revenue and Customs) Order 2015 (S.I. 2015/1783), arts. 1, 3. (1), Sch. 1 (with art. 3. (2), (3), 4-19, Sch. 2)

[F18463. KARetention of section 63. D material under section 63. IA: exception for persons under 18 convicted of first minor offence outside England and Wales

(1) This section applies where—

(a) section 63. D material is taken (or, in the case of a DNA profile, derived from a sample taken) in connection with the investigation of an offence,

(b) at any time before the material is required to be destroyed by virtue of this Part of this Act, the person is convicted of an offence under the law of a country or territory outside England and Wales,

(c) the act constituting the offence mentioned in paragraph (b) would constitute a recordable offence if done in England and Wales but would not constitute a qualifying offence,

(d) the person is aged under 18 at the time of the offence mentioned in paragraph (b), and

(e) the person has not previously been convicted of a recordable offence.

(2) In subsection (1)(e), the reference to a recordable offence includes an offence under the law of a country or territory outside England and Wales where the act constituting the offence would constitute a recordable offence if done in England and Wales (whether or not it constituted such an offence when the person was convicted).

(3) Where the person is sentenced to imprisonment or another form of detention for less than 5 years in respect of the offence mentioned in subsection (1)(b), the section 63. D material may be retained until the end of the period consisting of the term of the sentence plus 5 years.

(4) Where the person is sentenced to imprisonment or another form of detention for 5 years or more in respect of the offence mentioned in subsection (1)(b), the material may be retained indefinitely.

(5) Where the person is given a sentence other than a sentence of imprisonment or other form of detention in respect of the offence mentioned in subsection (1)(b), the material may be retained until the end of the period of 5 years beginning with the date on which the person was arrested for the offence (or, if the person was not arrested for the offence, the date on which the person was charged with it).

(6) But if, before the end of the period within which material may be retained by virtue of this section, the person is again convicted of a recordable offence, the material may be retained indefinitely.

(7) In subsection (6), the reference to a recordable offence includes an offence under the law of a country or territory outside England and Wales where the act constituting the offence would constitute a recordable offence if done in England and Wales.]

Amendments (Textual)

F184. S. 63. KA inserted (31.1.2017 for specified purposes, 3.4.2017 in so far as not already in force) by Policing and Crime Act 2017 (c. 3), ss. 70. (10), 183. (1), (5)(e); S.I. 2017/399, reg. 2, Sch. para. 20 (with reg. 6)

[F18563. LRetention of section 63. D material: persons given a penalty notice

(1) This section applies to section 63. D material which—

(a) relates to a person who is given a penalty notice under section 2 of the Criminal Justice and Police Act 2001 and in respect of whom no proceedings are brought for the offence to which the notice relates, and

(b) was taken (or, in the case of a DNA profile, derived from a sample taken) from the person in connection with the investigation of the offence to which the notice relates.

(2) The material may be retained—

(a) in the case of fingerprints, for a period of 2 years beginning with the date on which the fingerprints were taken,

(b) in the case of a DNA profile, for a period of 2 years beginning with—

(i) the date on which the DNA sample from which the profile was derived was taken, or

(ii) if the profile was derived from more than one DNA sample, the date on which the first of those samples was taken.]

Amendments (Textual)

F185. S. 63. L inserted (31.10.2013) by Protection of Freedoms Act 2012 (c. 9), ss. 8, 120 (with s. 97); S.I. 2013/1814, art. 2. (a)

Modifications etc. (not altering text)

C79. S. 63. L applied (with modifications) (4.11.2015) by The Police and Criminal Evidence Act 1984 (Application to Revenue and Customs) Order 2015 (S.I. 2015/1783), arts. 1, 3. (1), Sch. 1 (with art. 3. (2), (3), 4-19, Sch. 2)

[F18663. MRetention of section 63. D material for purposes of national security

(1) Section 63. D material may be retained for as long as a national security determination made by the responsible chief officer of police has effect in relation to it.

(2) A national security determination is made if the responsible chief officer of police determines that it is necessary for any section 63. D material to be retained for the purposes of national security.

(3) A national security determination—

(a) must be made in writing,

(b) has effect for a maximum of 2 years beginning with the date on which it is made, and

(c) may be renewed.]

Amendments (Textual)

F186. S. 63. M inserted (31.10.2013) by Protection of Freedoms Act 2012 (c. 9), ss. 9, 120 (with s. 97); S.I. 2013/1814, art. 2. (a)

Modifications etc. (not altering text)

C80. S. 63. M applied (with modifications) (4.11.2015) by The Police and Criminal Evidence Act 1984 (Application to Revenue and Customs) Order 2015 (S.I. 2015/1783), arts. 1, 3. (1), Sch. 1 (with art. 3. (2), (3), 4-19, Sch. 2)

[F18763. NRetention of section 63. D material given voluntarily

(1) This section applies to the following section 63. D material—

(a) fingerprints taken with the consent of the person from whom they were taken, and

(b) a DNA profile derived from a DNA sample taken with the consent of the person from whom the sample was taken.

(2) Material to which this section applies may be retained until it has fulfilled the purpose for which it was taken or derived.

(3) Material to which this section applies which relates to—

(a) a person who is convicted of a recordable offence, or

(b) a person who has previously been convicted of a recordable offence (other than a person who has only one exempt conviction),

may be retained indefinitely.

(4) For the purposes of subsection (3)(b), a conviction is exempt if it is in respect of a recordable offence, other than a qualifying offence, committed when the person is aged under 18.

[F188. (5)The reference to a recordable offence in subsection (3)(a) includes an offence under the law of a country or territory outside England and Wales where the act constituting the offence would constitute a recordable offence if done in England and Wales.

(6) The reference to a recordable offence in subsections (3)(b) and (4), and the reference to a qualifying offence in subsection (4), includes an offence under the law of a country or territory outside England and Wales where the act constituting the offence would constitute a recordable offence or (as the case may be) a qualifying offence if done in England and Wales (whether or not it constituted such an offence when the person was convicted).]]

Amendments (Textual)

F187. S. 63. N inserted (31.10.2013) by Protection of Freedoms Act 2012 (c. 9), ss. 10, 120 (with s. 97); S.I. 2013/1814, art. 2. (a)

F188. S. 63. N(5)(6) inserted (31.1.2017 for specified purposes, 3.4.2017 in so far as not already in force) by Policing and Crime Act 2017 (c. 3), ss. 70. (11), 183. (1), (5)(e); S.I. 2017/399, reg. 2, Sch. para. 20 (with reg. 6)

Modifications etc. (not altering text)

C81. S. 63. N applied (with modifications) (4.11.2015) by The Police and Criminal Evidence Act 1984 (Application to Revenue and Customs) Order 2015 (S.I. 2015/1783), arts. 1, 3. (1), Sch. 1 (with art. 3. (2), (3), 4-19, Sch. 2)

[F18963. ORetention of section 63. D material with consent

(1) This section applies to the following material—

(a) fingerprints (other than fingerprints taken under section 61. (6. A)) to which section 63. D applies, and

(b) a DNA profile to which section 63. D applies.

(2) If the person to whom the material relates consents to material to which this section applies being retained, the material may be retained for as long as that person consents to it being retained.

(3) Consent given under this section—

(a) must be in writing, and

(b) can be withdrawn at any time.]

Amendments (Textual)

F189. S. 63. O inserted (31.10.2013) by Protection of Freedoms Act 2012 (c. 9), ss. 11, 120 (with s. 97); S.I. 2013/1814, art. 2. (a)

Modifications etc. (not altering text)

C82. S. 63. O applied (with modifications) (4.11.2015) by The Police and Criminal Evidence Act 1984 (Application to Revenue and Customs) Order 2015 (S.I. 2015/1783), arts. 1, 3. (1), Sch. 1 (with art. 3. (2), (3), 4-19, Sch. 2)

[F190[F19163. PRetention of 63. D material in connection with different offence

(1) Subsection (2) applies if—

(a) section 63. D material is taken (or, in the case of a DNA profile, derived from a sample taken) from a person in connection with the investigation of an offence, and

(b) the person is subsequently arrested for or charged with a different offence, or convicted of or given a penalty notice for a different offence.

(2) Sections 63. E to 63. O and sections 63. Q and 63. T have effect in relation to the material as if

the material were also taken (or, in the case of a DNA profile, derived from a sample taken)—

(a) in connection with the investigation of the offence mentioned in subsection (1)(b),

(b) on the date on which the person was arrested for that offence (or charged with it or given a penalty notice for it, if the person was not arrested).]]

Amendments (Textual)

F190. S. 63. P inserted (31.10.2013) by Protection of Freedoms Act 2012 (c. 9), ss. 12, 120 (with s. 97); S.I. 2013/1814, art. 2. (a)

F191. S. 63. P substituted (13.5.2014) by Anti-social Behaviour, Crime and Policing Act 2014 (c. 12), ss. 145. (1), 185. (1) (with ss. 21, 33, 42, 58, 75, 93, 145. (2)); S.I. 2014/949, art. 3, Sch. para. 13

Modifications etc. (not altering text)

C83. S. 63. P applied (with modifications) (4.11.2015) by The Police and Criminal Evidence Act 1984 (Application to Revenue and Customs) Order 2015 (S.I. 2015/1783), arts. 1, 3. (1), Sch. 1 (with art. 3. (2), (3), 4-19, Sch. 2)

[F19263. QDestruction of copies of section 63. D material

(1) If fingerprints are required by section 63. D to be destroyed, any copies of the fingerprints held by the police must also be destroyed.

(2) If a DNA profile is required by that section to be destroyed, no copy may be retained by the police except in a form which does not include information which identifies the person to whom the DNA profile relates.]

Amendments (Textual)

F192. S. 63. Q inserted (31.10.2013 for specified purposes, 31.1.2014 in so far as not already in force) by Protection of Freedoms Act 2012 (c. 9), ss. 13, 120 (with s. 97); S.I. 2013/1814, arts. 2. (b), 3. (a)

Modifications etc. (not altering text)

C84. S. 63. Q applied (with modifications) (4.11.2015) by The Police and Criminal Evidence Act 1984 (Application to Revenue and Customs) Order 2015 (S.I. 2015/1783), arts. 1, 3. (1), Sch. 1 (with art. 3. (2), (3), 4-19, Sch. 2)

[F19363. RDestruction of samples

(1) This section applies to samples—

(a) taken from a person under any power conferred by this Part of this Act, or

(b) taken by the police, with the consent of the person from whom they were taken, in connection with the investigation of an offence by the police.

(2) Samples to which this section applies must be destroyed if it appears to the responsible chief officer of police that—

(a) the taking of the samples was unlawful, or

(b) the samples were taken from a person in connection with that person's arrest and the arrest was unlawful or based on mistaken identity.

(3) Subject to this, the rule in subsection (4) or (as the case may be) (5) applies.

(4) A DNA sample to which this section applies must be destroyed—

(a) as soon as a DNA profile has been derived from the sample, or

(b) if sooner, before the end of the period of 6 months beginning with the date on which the sample was taken.

(5) Any other sample to which this section applies must be destroyed before the end of the period of 6 months beginning with the date on which it was taken.

(6) The responsible chief officer of police may apply to a District Judge (Magistrates' Courts) for an order to retain a sample to which this section applies beyond the date on which the sample would otherwise be required to be destroyed by virtue of subsection (4) or (5) if—

(a) the sample was taken from a person in connection with the investigation of a qualifying offence, and

(b) the responsible chief officer of police considers that the condition in subsection (7) is met.

(7) The condition is that, having regard to the nature and complexity of other material that is evidence in relation to the offence, the sample is likely to be needed in any proceedings for the offence for the purposes of—

(a) disclosure to, or use by, a defendant, or

(b) responding to any challenge by a defendant in respect of the admissibility of material that is evidence on which the prosecution proposes to rely.

(8) An application under subsection (6) must be made before the date on which the sample would otherwise be required to be destroyed by virtue of subsection (4) or (5).

(9) If, on an application made by the responsible chief officer of police under subsection (6), the District Judge (Magistrates' Courts) is satisfied that the condition in subsection (7) is met, the District Judge may make an order under this subsection which—

(a) allows the sample to be retained for a period of 12 months beginning with the date on which the sample would otherwise be required to be destroyed by virtue of subsection (4) or (5), and

(b) may be renewed (on one or more occasions) for a further period of not more than 12 months from the end of the period when the order would otherwise cease to have effect.

(10) An application for an order under subsection (9) (other than an application for renewal)—

(a) may be made without notice of the application having been given to the person from whom the sample was taken, and

(b) may be heard and determined in private in the absence of that person.

(11) A sample retained by virtue of an order under subsection (9) must not be used other than for the purposes of any proceedings for the offence in connection with which the sample was taken.

(12) A sample that ceases to be retained by virtue of an order under subsection (9) must be destroyed.

(13) Nothing in this section prevents a speculative search, in relation to samples to which this section applies, from being carried out within such time as may reasonably be required for the search if the responsible chief officer of police considers the search to be desirable.]

Amendments (Textual)

F193. S. 63. R inserted (31.10.2013 for specified purposes) by Protection of Freedoms Act 2012 (c. 9), ss. 14, 120 (with s. 97); S.I. 2013/1814, art. 2. (c)

Modifications etc. (not altering text)

C85. S. 63. R applied (with modifications) (4.11.2015) by The Police and Criminal Evidence Act 1984 (Application to Revenue and Customs) Order 2015 (S.I. 2015/1783), arts. 1, 3. (1), Sch. 1 (with art. 3. (2), (3), 4-19, Sch. 2)

[F19463. SDestruction of impressions of footwear

(1) This section applies to impressions of footwear—

(a) taken from a person under any power conferred by this Part of this Act, or

(b) taken by the police, with the consent of the person from whom they were taken, in connection with the investigation of an offence by the police.

(2) Impressions of footwear to which this section applies must be destroyed unless they are retained under subsection (3).

(3) Impressions of footwear may be retained for as long as is necessary for purposes related to the prevention or detection of crime, the investigation of an offence or the conduct of a prosecution.]

Amendments (Textual)

F194. S. 63. S inserted (31.10.2013) by Protection of Freedoms Act 2012 (c. 9), ss. 15, 120 (with s. 97); S.I. 2013/1814, art. 2. (d)

Modifications etc. (not altering text)

C86. S. 63. S applied (with modifications) (4.11.2015) by The Police and Criminal Evidence Act

1984 (Application to Revenue and Customs) Order 2015 (S.I. 2015/1783), arts. 1, 3. (1), Sch. 1 (with art. 3. (2), (3), 4-19, Sch. 2)

[F19563. TUse of retained material

(1) Any material to which section 63. D, 63. R or 63. S applies must not be used other than—
    (a) in the interests of national security,
    (b) for the purposes of a terrorist investigation,
    (c) for purposes related to the prevention or detection of crime, the investigation of an offence or the conduct of a prosecution, or
    (d) for purposes related to the identification of a deceased person or of the person to whom the material relates.
(2) Material which is required by section 63. D, 63. R or 63. S to be destroyed must not at any time after it is required to be destroyed be used—
    (a) in evidence against the person to whom the material relates, or
    (b) for the purposes of the investigation of any offence.
(3) In this section—
    (a) the reference to using material includes a reference to allowing any check to be made against it and to disclosing it to any person,
    (b) the reference to crime includes a reference to any conduct which—
(i) constitutes one or more criminal offences (whether under the law of England and Wales or of any country or territory outside England and Wales), or
(ii) is, or corresponds to, any conduct which, if it all took place in England and Wales, would constitute one or more criminal offences, and
    (c) the references to an investigation and to a prosecution include references, respectively, to any investigation outside England and Wales of any crime or suspected crime and to a prosecution brought in respect of any crime in a country or territory outside England and Wales.]
Amendments (Textual)
F195. S. 63. T inserted (31.10.2013) by Protection of Freedoms Act 2012 (c. 9), ss. 16, 120 (with s. 97); S.I. 2013/1814, art. 2. (d)
Modifications etc. (not altering text)
C87. S. 63. T applied (with modifications) (4.11.2015) by The Police and Criminal Evidence Act 1984 (Application to Revenue and Customs) Order 2015 (S.I. 2015/1783), arts. 1, 3. (1), Sch. 1 (with art. 3. (2), (3), 4-19, Sch. 2)

[F19663. UExclusions for certain regimes

(1) Sections 63. D to 63. T do not apply to material to which paragraphs 20. A to 20. J of Schedule 8 to the Terrorism Act 2000 (destruction, retention and use of material taken from terrorist suspects) apply.
(2) Any reference in those sections to a person being arrested for, or charged with, an offence does not include a reference to a person—
    (a) being arrested under section 41 of the Terrorism Act 2000, or
    (b) being charged with an offence following an arrest under that section.
(3) Sections 63. D to 63. T do not apply to material to which paragraph 8 of Schedule 4 to the International Criminal Court Act 2001 (requirement to destroy material) applies.
(4) Sections 63. D to 63. T do not apply to material to which paragraph 6 of Schedule 6 to the Terrorism Prevention and Investigation Measures Act 2011 (requirement to destroy material) applies.
(5) [F197 Sections 63. D to 63. T] do not apply to material which is, or may become, disclosable under—
    (a) the Criminal Procedure and Investigations Act 1996, or

(b) a code of practice prepared under section 23 of that Act and in operation by virtue of an order under section 25 of that Act.

[F198. (5. A)A sample that—

(a) falls within subsection (5), and

(b) but for that subsection would be required to be destroyed under section 63. R,

must not be used other than for the purposes of any proceedings for the offence in connection with which the sample was taken.

(5. B)A sample that once fell within subsection (5) but no longer does, and so becomes a sample to which section 63. R applies, must be destroyed immediately if the time specified for its destruction under that section has already passed.]

(6) Sections 63. D to 63. T do not apply to material which—

(a) is taken from a person, but

(b) relates to another person.

(7) Nothing in sections 63. D to 63. T affects any power conferred by—

(a) paragraph 18. (2) of Schedule 2 to the Immigration Act 1971 (power to take reasonable steps to identify a person detained), or

(b) section 20 of the Immigration and Asylum Act 1999 (disclosure of police information to the Secretary of State for use for immigration purposes).]

Amendments (Textual)

F196. S. 63. U inserted (31.10.2013) by Protection of Freedoms Act 2012 (c. 9), ss. 17, 120 (with s. 97); S.I. 2013/1814, art. 2. (d)

F197. Words in s. 63. U(5) substituted (13.5.2014) by Anti-social Behaviour, Crime and Policing Act 2014 (c. 12), ss. 146. (1)(a), 185. (1) (with ss. 21, 33, 42, 58, 75, 93); S.I. 2014/949, art. 3, Sch. para. 13

F198. S. 63. U(5. A)(5. B) inserted (13.5.2014) by Anti-social Behaviour, Crime and Policing Act 2014 (c. 12), ss. 146. (1)(b), 185. (1) (with ss. 21, 33, 42, 58, 75, 93); S.I. 2014/949, art. 3, Sch. para. 13

Modifications etc. (not altering text)

C88. S. 63. U applied (with modifications) (4.11.2015) by The Police and Criminal Evidence Act 1984 (Application to Revenue and Customs) Order 2015 (S.I. 2015/1783), arts. 1, 3. (1), Sch. 1 (with art. 3. (2), (3), 4-19, Sch. 2)

F19964 Destruction of fingerprints and samples.

. . . .

Amendments (Textual)

F199. S. 64 repealed (31.10.2013) by Protection of Freedoms Act 2012 (c. 9), s. 120, Sch. 9 para. 3. (3), Sch. 10 Pt. 1 (with s. 97); S.I. 2013/2104, art. 3. (c)

Modifications etc. (not altering text)

C89. S. 64 applied (with modifications) by S.I. 1985/1882, art. 9

C90. S. 64 applied (1.9.2001) by 2001 c. 17, s. 34. (1), Sch. 4 para. 8; S.I. 2001/2161, art. 2 (subject to art. 3)

C91. S. 64 applied (with modifications) (31.12.2006) by The Police and Criminal Evidence Act 1984 (Application to the Armed Forces) Order 2006 (S.I. 2006/2015), arts. 2, 3, Schs. 1-3

Prospective

[F20064. ZADestruction of samples

(1) A DNA sample to which section 64 applies must be destroyed—

(a) as soon as a DNA profile has been derived from the sample, or

(b) if sooner, before the end of the period of 6 months beginning with the date on which the sample was taken.

(2) Any other sample to which section 64 applies must be destroyed before the end of the period of 6 months beginning with the date on which it was taken.

Amendments (Textual)
F200. Ss. 64. ZA-64. ZN inserted (prosp.) by Crime and Security Act 2010 (c. 17), ss. 14. (2), 59
Prospective

64. ZBDestruction of data given voluntarily

(1) This section applies to—

(a) fingerprints or impressions of footwear taken in connection with the investigation of an offence with the consent of the person from whom they were taken, and

(b) a DNA profile derived from a DNA sample taken in connection with the investigation of an offence with the consent of the person from whom the sample was taken.

(2) Material to which this section applies must be destroyed as soon as it has fulfilled the purpose for which it was taken or derived, unless it is—

(a) material relating to a person who is convicted of the offence,

(b) material relating to a person who has previously been convicted of a recordable offence, other than a person who has only one exempt conviction,

(c) material in relation to which any of sections 64. ZC to 64. ZH applies, or

(d) material which is not required to be destroyed by virtue of consent given under section 64. ZL.

(3) If material to which this section applies leads to the person to whom the material relates being arrested for or charged with an offence other than the offence under investigation—

(a) the material is not required to be destroyed by virtue of this section, and

(b) sections 64. ZD to 64. ZH have effect in relation to the material as if the material was taken (or, in the case of a DNA profile, was derived from material taken) in connection with the investigation of the offence in respect of which the person is arrested or charged.

Amendments (Textual)
F200. Ss. 64. ZA-64. ZN inserted (prosp.) by Crime and Security Act 2010 (c. 17), ss. 14. (2), 59
Prospective

64. ZCDestruction of data relating to a person subject to a control order

(1) This section applies to material falling within subsection (2) relating to a person who—

(a) has no previous convictions or only one exempt conviction, and

(b) is subject to a control order.

(2) Material falls within this subsection if it is—

(a) fingerprints taken from the person, or

(b) a DNA profile derived from a DNA sample taken from the person.

(3) The material must be destroyed before the end of the period of 2 years beginning with the date on which the person ceases to be subject to a control order.

(4) This section ceases to have effect in relation to the material if the person is convicted—

(a) in England and Wales or Northern Ireland of a recordable offence, or

(b) in Scotland of an offence which is punishable by imprisonment,

before the material is required to be destroyed by virtue of this section.

(5) For the purposes of subsection (1)—

(a) a person has no previous convictions if the person has not previously been convicted—

(i) in England and Wales or Northern Ireland of a recordable offence, or

(ii) in Scotland of an offence which is punishable by imprisonment, and

(b) if the person has been previously convicted of a recordable offence in England and Wales or

Northern Ireland, the conviction is exempt if it is in respect of a recordable offence other than a qualifying offence, committed when the person is aged under 18.

(6) For the purposes of that subsection—

(a) a person is to be treated as having been convicted of an offence if—

(i) he has been given a caution in England and Wales or Northern Ireland in respect of the offence which, at the time of the caution, he has admitted, [F201 and]

F202. (ii). . . . .

(b) if a person is convicted of more than one offence arising out of a single course of action, those convictions are to be treated as a single conviction.

(7) In this section—

(a) "recordable offence" has, in relation to a conviction in Northern Ireland, the meaning given by Article 2. (2) of the Police and Criminal Evidence (Northern Ireland) Order 1989, and

(b) "qualifying offence" has, in relation to a conviction in respect of a recordable offence committed in Northern Ireland, the meaning given by Article 53. A of that Order.

Amendments (Textual)

F200. Ss. 64. ZA-64. ZN inserted (prosp.) by Crime and Security Act 2010 (c. 17), ss. 14. (2), 59

F201. Word in s. 64. ZC(6)(a)(i) substituted (8.4.2013) by Legal Aid, Sentencing and Punishment of Offenders Act 2012 (c. 10), s. 151. (1), Sch. 24 para. 9. (a) (with s. 135. (4)); S.I. 2013/453, art. 4. (f)

F202. S. 64. ZC(6)(a)(ii) omitted (8.4.2013) by virtue of Legal Aid, Sentencing and Punishment of Offenders Act 2012 (c. 10), s. 151. (1), Sch. 24 para. 9. (b) (with s. 135. (4)); S.I. 2013/453, art. 4. (f)

Prospective

64. ZDDestruction of data relating to persons not convicted

(1) This section applies to material falling within subsection (2) relating to a person who—

(a) has no previous convictions or only one exempt conviction,

(b) is arrested for or charged with a recordable offence, and

(c) is aged 18 or over at the time of the alleged offence.

(2) Material falls within this subsection if it is—

(a) fingerprints or impressions of footwear taken from the person in connection with the investigation of the offence, or

(b) a DNA profile derived from a DNA sample so taken.

(3) The material must be destroyed—

(a) in the case of fingerprints or impressions of footwear, before the end of the period of 6 years beginning with the date on which the fingerprints or impressions were taken,

(b) in the case of a DNA profile, before the end of the period of 6 years beginning with the date on which the DNA sample from which the profile was derived was taken (or, if the profile was derived from more than one DNA sample, the date on which the first of those samples was taken).

(4) But if, before the material is required to be destroyed by virtue of this section, the person is arrested for or charged with a recordable offence the material may be further retained until the end of the period of 6 years beginning with the date of the arrest or charge.

(5) This section ceases to have effect in relation to the material if the person is convicted of a recordable offence before the material is required to be destroyed by virtue of this section.

Amendments (Textual)

F200. Ss. 64. ZA-64. ZN inserted (prosp.) by Crime and Security Act 2010 (c. 17), ss. 14. (2), 59

Prospective

64. ZEDestruction of data relating to persons under 18 not convicted: recordable offences other than qualifying offences

(1) This section applies to material falling within subsection (2) relating to a person who—

(a) has no previous convictions or only one exempt conviction,

(b) is arrested for or charged with a recordable offence other than a qualifying offence, and

(c) is aged under 18 at the time of the alleged offence.

(2) Material falls within this subsection if it is—

(a) fingerprints or impressions of footwear taken from the person in connection with the investigation of the offence, or

(b) a DNA profile derived from a DNA sample so taken.

(3) The material must be destroyed—

(a) in the case of fingerprints or impressions of footwear, before the end of the period of 3 years beginning with the date on which the fingerprints or impressions were taken,

(b) in the case of a DNA profile, before the end of the period of 3 years beginning with the date on which the DNA sample from which the profile was derived was taken (or, if the profile was derived from more than one DNA sample, the date on which the first of those samples was taken).

(4) But if, before the material is required to be destroyed by virtue of this section, the person is arrested for or charged with a recordable offence—

(a) where the person is aged 18 or over at the time of the alleged offence, the material may be further retained until the end of the period of 6 years beginning with the date of the arrest or charge,

(b) where—

(i) the alleged offence is not a qualifying offence, and

(ii) the person is aged under 18 at the time of the alleged offence,

the material may be further retained until the end of the period of 3 years beginning with the date of the arrest or charge,

(c) where—

(i) the alleged offence is a qualifying offence, and

(ii) the person is aged under 16 at the time of the alleged offence,

the material may be further retained until the end of the period of 3 years beginning with the date of the arrest or charge,

(d) where—

(i) the alleged offence is a qualifying offence, and

(ii) the person is aged 16 or 17 at the time of the alleged offence,

the material may be further retained until the end of the period of 6 years beginning with the date of the arrest or charge,

(e) where—

(i) the person is convicted of the offence,

(ii) the offence is not a qualifying offence,

(iii) the person is aged under 18 at the time of the offence, and

(iv) the person has no previous convictions,

the material may be further retained until the end of the period of 5 years beginning with the date of the arrest or charge.

(5) This section ceases to have effect in relation to the material if, before the material is required to be destroyed by virtue of this section, the person—

(a) is convicted of a recordable offence and is aged 18 or over at the time of the offence,

(b) is convicted of a qualifying offence, or

(c) having a previous exempt conviction, is convicted of a recordable offence.

Amendments (Textual)

F200. Ss. 64. ZA-64. ZN inserted (prosp.) by Crime and Security Act 2010 (c. 17), ss. 14. (2), 59 Prospective

64. ZFDestruction of data relating to persons under 16 not

convicted: qualifying offences

(1) This section applies to material falling within subsection (2) relating to a person who—
    (a) has no previous convictions or only one exempt conviction,
    (b) is arrested for or charged with a qualifying offence, and
    (c) is aged under 16 at the time of the alleged offence.
(2) Material falls within this subsection if it is—
    (a) fingerprints or impressions of footwear taken from the person in connection with the investigation of the offence, or
    (b) a DNA profile derived from a DNA sample so taken.
(3) The material must be destroyed—
    (a) in the case of fingerprints or impressions of footwear, before the end of the period of 3 years beginning with the date on which the fingerprints or impressions were taken,
    (b) in the case of a DNA profile, before the end of the period of 3 years beginning with the date on which the DNA sample from which the profile was derived was taken (or, if the profile was derived from more than one DNA sample, the date on which the first of those samples was taken).
(4) But if, before the material is required to be destroyed by virtue of this section, the person is arrested for or charged with a recordable offence—
    (a) where the person is aged 18 or over at the time of the alleged offence, the material may be further retained until the end of the period of 6 years beginning with the date of the arrest or charge,
    (b) where—
(i) the alleged offence is not a qualifying offence, and
(ii) the person is aged under 18 at the time of the alleged offence,
the material may be further retained until the end of the period of 3 years beginning with the date of the arrest or charge,
    (c) where—
(i) the alleged offence is a qualifying offence, and
(ii) the person is aged under 16 at the time of the alleged offence,
the material may be further retained until the end of the period of 3 years beginning with the date of the arrest or charge,
    (d) where—
(i) the alleged offence is a qualifying offence, and
(ii) the person is aged 16 or 17 at the time of the alleged offence,
the material may be further retained until the end of the period of 6 years beginning with the date of the arrest or charge,
    (e) where—
(i) the person is convicted of the offence,
(ii) the offence is not a qualifying offence,
(iii) the person is aged under 18 at the time of the offence, and
(iv) the person has no previous convictions,
the material may be further retained until the end of the period of 5 years beginning with the date of the arrest or charge.
(5) This section ceases to have effect in relation to the material if, before the material is required to be destroyed by virtue of this section, the person—
    (a) is convicted of a recordable offence and is aged 18 or over at the time of the offence,
    (b) is convicted of a qualifying offence, or
    (c) having a previous exempt conviction, is convicted of a recordable offence.
Amendments (Textual)
F200. Ss. 64. ZA-64. ZN inserted (prosp.) by Crime and Security Act 2010 (c. 17), ss. 14. (2), 59
Prospective

64. ZGDestruction of data relating to persons aged 16 or 17 not convicted: qualifying offences

(1) This section applies to material falling within subsection (2) relating to a person who—

    (a) has no previous convictions or only one exempt conviction,

    (b) is arrested for or charged with a qualifying offence, and

    (c) is aged 16 or 17 at the time of the alleged offence.

(2) Material falls within this subsection if it is—

    (a) fingerprints or impressions of footwear taken from the person in connection with the investigation of the offence, or

    (b) a DNA profile derived from a DNA sample so taken.

(3) The material must be destroyed—

    (a) in the case of fingerprints or impressions of footwear, before the end of the period of 6 years beginning with the date on which the fingerprints or impressions were taken,

    (b) in the case of a DNA profile, before the end of the period of 6 years beginning with the date on which the DNA sample from which the profile was derived was taken (or, if the profile was derived from more than one DNA sample, the date on which the first of those samples was taken).

(4) But if, before the material is required to be destroyed by virtue of this section, the person is arrested for or charged with a recordable offence—

    (a) where the person is aged 18 or over at the time of the alleged offence, the material may be further retained until the end of the period of 6 years beginning with the date of the arrest or charge,

    (b) where—

(i) the alleged offence is not a qualifying offence, and

(ii) the person is aged under 18 at the time of the alleged offence,

the material may be further retained until the end of the period of 3 years beginning with the date of the arrest or charge,

    (c) where—

(i) the alleged offence is a qualifying offence, and

(ii) the person is aged 16 or 17 at the time of the alleged offence,

the material may be further retained until the end of the period of 6 years beginning with the date of the arrest or charge,

    (d) where—

(i) the person is convicted of the offence,

(ii) the offence is not a qualifying offence,

(iii) the person is aged under 18 at the time of the offence, and

(iv) the person has no previous convictions,

the material may be further retained until the end of the period of 5 years beginning with the date of the arrest or charge.

(5) This section ceases to have effect in relation to the material if, before the material is required to be destroyed by virtue of this section, the person—

    (a) is convicted of a recordable offence and is aged 18 or over at the time of the offence,

    (b) is convicted of a qualifying offence, or

    (c) having a previous exempt conviction, is convicted of a recordable offence.

Amendments (Textual)

F200. Ss. 64. ZA-64. ZN inserted (prosp.) by Crime and Security Act 2010 (c. 17), ss. 14. (2), 59

Prospective

64. ZHDestruction of data relating to persons under 18 convicted of a recordable offence other than a qualifying offence

(1) This section applies to material falling within subsection (2) relating to a person who—

(a) has no previous convictions,

(b) is convicted of a recordable offence other than a qualifying offence, and

(c) is aged under 18 at the time of the offence.

(2) Material falls within this subsection if it is—

(a) fingerprints or impressions of footwear taken from the person in connection with the investigation of the offence, or

(b) a DNA profile derived from a DNA sample so taken.

(3) The material must be destroyed—

(a) in the case of fingerprints or impressions of footwear, before the end of the period of 5 years beginning with the date on which the fingerprints or impressions were taken,

(b) in the case of a DNA profile, before the end of the period of 5 years beginning with the date on which the DNA sample from which the profile was derived was taken (or, if the profile was derived from more than one DNA sample, the date on which the first of those samples was taken).

(4) But if, before the material is required to be destroyed by virtue of this section, the person is arrested for or charged with a recordable offence—

(a) where the person is aged 18 or over at the time of the alleged offence, the material may be further retained until the end of the period of 6 years beginning with the date of the arrest or charge,

(b) where—

(i) the alleged offence is not a qualifying offence, and

(ii) the person is aged under 18 at the time of the alleged offence,

the material may be further retained until the end of the period of 3 years beginning with the date of the arrest or charge,

(c) where—

(i) the alleged offence is a qualifying offence, and

(ii) the person is aged under 16 at the time of the alleged offence,

the material may be further retained until the end of the period of 3 years beginning with the date of the arrest or charge,

(d) where—

(i) the alleged offence is a qualifying offence, and

(ii) the person is aged 16 or 17 at the time of the alleged offence,

the material may be further retained until the end of the period of 6 years beginning with the date of the arrest or charge.

(5) This section ceases to have effect in relation to the material if the person is convicted of a further recordable offence before the material is required to be destroyed by virtue of this section.

Amendments (Textual)

F200. Ss. 64. ZA-64. ZN inserted (prosp.) by Crime and Security Act 2010 (c. 17), ss. 14. (2), 59 Prospective

64. ZISections 64. ZB to 64. ZH: supplementary provision

(1) Any reference in section 64. ZB or sections 64. ZD to 64. ZH to a person being charged with an offence includes a reference to a person being informed that he will be reported for an offence.

(2) For the purposes of those sections—

(a) a person has no previous convictions if the person has not previously been convicted of a recordable offence, and

(b) if the person has been previously convicted of a recordable offence, the conviction is exempt if it is in respect of a recordable offence other than a qualifying offence, committed when the person is aged under 18.

(3) For the purposes of those sections, a person is to be treated as having been convicted of an offence if—

(a) he has been given a caution in respect of the offence which, at the time of the caution, he has admitted, or

F203. (b). . . . .

(4) If a person is convicted of more than one offence arising out of a single course of action, those convictions are to be treated as a single conviction for the purpose of any provision of those sections relating to an exempt, first or subsequent conviction.

(5) Subject to the completion of any speculative search that the responsible chief officer of police considers necessary or desirable, material falling within any of sections 64. ZD to 64. ZH must be destroyed immediately if it appears to the chief officer that—

(a) the arrest was unlawful,

(b) the taking of the fingerprints, impressions of footwear or DNA sample concerned was unlawful,

(c) the arrest was based on mistaken identity, or

(d) other circumstances relating to the arrest or the alleged offence mean that it is appropriate to destroy the material.

(6) "Responsible chief officer of police" means the chief officer of police for the police area—

(a) in which the samples, fingerprints or impressions of footwear were taken, or

(b) in the case of a DNA profile, in which the sample from which the DNA profile was derived was taken.

Amendments (Textual)

F200. Ss. 64. ZA-64. ZN inserted (prosp.) by Crime and Security Act 2010 (c. 17), ss. 14. (2), 59

F203. S. 64. ZI(3)(b) omitted (8.4.2013) by virtue of Legal Aid, Sentencing and Punishment of Offenders Act 2012 (c. 10), s. 151. (1), Sch. 24 para. 10 (with s. 135. (4)); S.I. 2013/453, art. 4. (f)

Prospective

64. ZJDestruction of fingerprints taken under section 61(6. A)

Fingerprints taken from a person by virtue of section 61. (6. A) (taking fingerprints for the purposes of identification) must be destroyed as soon as they have fulfilled the purpose for which they were taken.

Amendments (Textual)

F200. Ss. 64. ZA-64. ZN inserted (prosp.) by Crime and Security Act 2010 (c. 17), ss. 14. (2), 59

Prospective

64. ZKRetention for purposes of national security

(1) Subsection (2) applies if the responsible chief officer of police determines that it is necessary for—

(a) a DNA profile to which section 64 applies, or

(b) fingerprints to which section 64 applies, other than fingerprints taken under section 61. (6. A),

to be retained for the purposes of national security.

(2) Where this subsection applies—

(a) the material is not required to be destroyed in accordance with sections 64. ZB to 64. ZH, and

(b) section 64. ZN(2) does not apply to the material,

for as long as the determination has effect.

(3) A determination under subsection (1) has effect for a maximum of 2 years beginning with the date on which the material would otherwise be required to be destroyed, but a determination may be renewed.

(4) "Responsible chief officer of police" means the chief officer of police for the police area—

(a) in which the fingerprints were taken, or

(b) in the case of a DNA profile, in which the sample from which the DNA profile was derived was taken.

Amendments (Textual)
F200. Ss. 64. ZA-64. ZN inserted (prosp.) by Crime and Security Act 2010 (c. 17), ss. 14. (2), 59
Prospective

64. ZLRetention with consent

(1) If a person consents in writing to the retention of fingerprints, impressions of footwear or a DNA profile to which section 64 applies, other than fingerprints taken under section 61. (6. A)—

(a) the material is not required to be destroyed in accordance with sections 64. ZB to 64. ZH, and

(b) section 64. ZN(2) does not apply to the material.

(2) It is immaterial for the purposes of subsection (1) whether the consent is given at, before or after the time when the entitlement to the destruction of the material arises.

(3) Consent given under this section can be withdrawn at any time.

Amendments (Textual)
F200. Ss. 64. ZA-64. ZN inserted (prosp.) by Crime and Security Act 2010 (c. 17), ss. 14. (2), 59
Prospective

64. ZMDestruction of copies, and notification of destruction

(1) If fingerprints or impressions of footwear are required to be destroyed by virtue of any of sections 64. ZB to 64. ZJ, any copies of the fingerprints or impressions of footwear must also be destroyed.

(2) If a DNA profile is required to be destroyed by virtue of any of those sections, no copy may be kept except in a form which does not include information which identifies the person to whom the DNA profile relates.

(3) If a person makes a request to the responsible chief officer of police to be notified when anything relating to the person is destroyed under any of sections 64. ZA to 64. ZJ, the responsible chief officer of police or a person authorised by the chief officer or on the chief officer's behalf must within three months of the request issue the person with a certificate recording the destruction.

(4) "Responsible chief officer of police" means the chief officer of police for the police area—

(a) in which the samples, fingerprints or impressions of footwear which have been destroyed were taken, or

(b) in the case of a DNA profile which has been destroyed, in which the samples from which the DNA profile was derived were taken.

Amendments (Textual)
F200. Ss. 64. ZA-64. ZN inserted (prosp.) by Crime and Security Act 2010 (c. 17), ss. 14. (2), 59
Prospective

64. ZNUse of retained material

(1) Any material to which section 64 applies which is retained after it has fulfilled the purpose for which it was taken or derived must not be used other than—

(a) in the interests of national security,

(b) for the purposes of a terrorist investigation,

(c) for purposes related to the prevention or detection of crime, the investigation of an offence or the conduct of a prosecution, or

(d) for purposes related to the identification of a deceased person or of the person to whom the material relates.

(2) Material which is required to be destroyed by virtue of any of sections 64. ZA to 64. ZJ, or of section 64. ZM, must not at any time after it is required to be destroyed be used—

(a) in evidence against the person to whom the material relates, or

(b) for the purposes of the investigation of any offence.

(3) In this section—

(a) the reference to using material includes a reference to allowing any check to be made against it and to disclosing it to any person,

(b) the reference to crime includes a reference to any conduct which—

(i) constitutes one or more criminal offences (whether under the law of a part of the United Kingdom or of a country or territory outside the United Kingdom), or

(ii) is, or corresponds to, any conduct which, if it all took place in any one part of the United Kingdom, would constitute one or more criminal offences, and

(c) the references to an investigation and to a prosecution include references, respectively, to any investigation outside the United Kingdom of any crime or suspected crime and to a prosecution brought in respect of any crime in a country or territory outside the United Kingdom.]

Amendments (Textual)

F200. Ss. 64. ZA-64. ZN inserted (prosp.) by Crime and Security Act 2010 (c. 17), ss. 14. (2), 59

[F20464. A Photographing of suspects etc.

(1) A person who is detained at a police station may be photographed—

(a) with the appropriate consent; or

(b) if the appropriate consent is withheld or it is not practicable to obtain it, without it.

[F205. (1. A)A person falling within subsection (1. B) below may, on the occasion of the relevant event referred to in subsection (1. B), be photographed elsewhere than at a police station—

(a) with the appropriate consent; or

(b) if the appropriate consent is withheld or it is not practicable to obtain it, without it.

(1. B)A person falls within this subsection if he has been—

(a) arrested by a constable for an offence;

(b) taken into custody by a constable after being arrested for an offence by a person other than a constable;

(c) made subject to a requirement to wait [F206with a community support officer or a community support volunteer under paragraph 7 of Schedule 3. B] to the Police Reform Act 2002 ("the 2002 Act");]

[F207. (ca)given a direction by a constable under section 35 of the Anti-social Behaviour, Crime and Policing Act 2014;]

(d) given a penalty notice by a constable F208... under Chapter 1 of Part 1 of the Criminal Justice and Police Act 2001, a penalty notice by a constable under section 444. A of the Education Act 1996, or a fixed penalty notice by a constable in uniform under section 54 of the Road Traffic Offenders Act 1988;

[F209. (e)given a fixed penalty notice by a community support officer or community support volunteer who is authorised to give the notice by virtue of his or her designation under section 38 of the Police Reform Act 2002;]

(f) given a notice in relation to a relevant fixed penalty offence (within the meaning of paragraph 1 of Schedule 5 to the 2002 Act) by an accredited person by virtue of accreditation specifying that that paragraph applies to him.[F210; or

(g) given a notice in relation to a relevant fixed penalty offence (within the meaning of Schedule 5. A to the 2002 Act) by an accredited inspector by virtue of accreditation specifying that paragraph 1 of Schedule 5. A to the 2002 Act applies to him.]

(2) A person proposing to take a photograph of any person under this section—

(a) may, for the purpose of doing so, require the removal of any item or substance worn on or over the whole or any part of the head or face of the person to be photographed; and

(b) if the requirement is not complied with, may remove the item or substance himself.

(3) Where a photograph may be taken under this section, the only persons entitled to take the photograph are [F211constables].

(4) A photograph taken under this section—

(a) may be used by, or disclosed to, any person for any purpose related to the prevention or detection of crime, the investigation of an offence or the conduct of a prosecution [F212or to the enforcement of a sentence]; and

(b) after being so used or disclosed, may be retained but may not be used or disclosed except for a purpose so related.

(5) In subsection (4)—

(a) the reference to crime includes a reference to any conduct which—

(i) constitutes one or more criminal offences (whether under the law of a part of the United Kingdom or of a country or territory outside the United Kingdom); or

(ii) is, or corresponds to, any conduct which, if it all took place in any one part of the United Kingdom, would constitute one or more criminal offences;

and

(b) the references to an investigation and to a prosecution include references, respectively, to any investigation outside the United Kingdom of any crime or suspected crime and to a prosecution brought in respect of any crime in a country or territory outside the United Kingdom.[F213; and

(c) "sentence" includes any order made by a court in England and Wales when dealing with an offender in respect of his offence.]

(6) References in this section to taking a photograph include references to using any process by means of which a visual image may be produced; and references to photographing a person shall be construed accordingly.

[F214. (6. A)In this section, a "photograph" includes a moving image, and corresponding expressions shall be construed accordingly.]

[F215. (7)Nothing in this section applies to a person arrested under an extradition arrest power.]]

Amendments (Textual)

F204 S. 64. A inserted (14.12.2001) by 2001 c. 24, s. 92

F205. S. 64. A(1. A)(1. B) inserted (1.1.2006) by Serious Organised Crime and Police Act 2005 (c. 15), ss. 116. (2), 178; S.I. 2005/3495, art. 2. (1)(o)

F206. Words in s. 64. A(1. B)(c) substituted (31.1.2017 for specified purposes, 15.12.2017 in so far as not already in force) by Policing and Crime Act 2017 (c. 3), s. 183. (1)(5)(e), Sch. 12 para. 7. (3)(a); S.I. 2017/1139, reg. 2. (k) (as amended by S.I. 2017/1162, reg. 2)

F207. S. 64. A(1. B)(ca) substituted (20.10.2014) by Anti-social Behaviour, Crime and Policing Act 2014 (c. 12), s. 185. (1), Sch. 11 para. 4 (with ss. 21, 33, 42, 58, 75, 93); S.I. 2014/2590, art. 3. (g)(i)

F208. Words in s. 64. A(1. B)(d) omitted (8.4.2013) by virtue of Legal Aid, Sentencing and Punishment of Offenders Act 2012 (c. 10), s. 151. (1), Sch. 23 para. 13; S.I. 2013/453, art. 4. (e)

F209. S. 64. A(1. B)(e) substituted (31.1.2017 for specified purposes, 15.12.2017 in so far as not already in force) by Policing and Crime Act 2017 (c. 3), s. 183. (1)(5)(e), Sch. 12 para. 7. (3)(b); S.I. 2017/1139, reg. 2. (k) (as amended by S.I. 2017/1162, reg. 2)

F210. S. 64. A(1. B)(g) and preceding word inserted (1.4.2007) by Police and Justice Act 2006 (c. 48), ss. 52, 53, Sch. 14 para. 11; S.I. 2007/709, art. 3. (o)(p) (subject to arts. 6, 7)

F211. Words in s. 64. A(3) substituted (2.12.2002) by Police Reform Act 2002 (c. 30), s. 107, Sch. 7 para. 9. (5); S.I. 2002/2750, art. 2. (b)(ii)

F212. Words in s. 64. A(4)(a) inserted (1.8.2005) by Serious Organised Crime and Police Act 2005 (c. 15), ss. 116. (3), 178; S.I. 2005/2026, art. 2. (c)

F213. S. 64. A(5)(c) and preceding word inserted (1.8.2005) by Serious Organised Crime and Police Act 2005 (c. 15), ss. 116. (4), 178; S.I. 2005/2026, art. 2. (c)

F214. S. 64. A(6. A) inserted (1.8.2005) by Serious Organised Crime and Police Act 2005 (c. 15), ss. 116. (5), 178; S.I. 2005/2026, art. 2. (c)

F215. S. 64. A(7) inserted (1.1.2004) by Extradition Act 2003 (c. 41), ss. 169. (5), 221; S.I. 2003/3103, art. 2 (subject to savings in Order (as amended by S.I. 2003/3312, art. 2. (2) and S.I. 2003/3258, art. 2. (2)))

Modifications etc. (not altering text)

C92. S. 64. A extended (2.12.2002) by Police Reform Act 2002 (c. 30), s. 38, Sch. 4 para. 33; S.I. 2002/2750, art. 2. (a)(ii)(d)

C93. S. 64. A applied (with modifications) (31.12.2006) by The Police and Criminal Evidence Act 1984 (Application to the Armed Forces) Order 2006 (S.I. 2006/2015), arts. 2, 3, Schs. 1-3

C94. S. 64. A(1. A) extended (1.1.2006) by Police Reform Act 2002 (c. 30), ss. 38, 108. (2)-(5), Sch. 4 Pt. 1 para. 15. ZA (as inserted by Serious Organised Crime and Police Act 2005 (c. 15), ss. 122, 178, Sch. 8 Pt. 1 para. 12; S.I. 2005/3495, art. 2. (1)(q)(r))

S. 64. A(1. A) extended (1.1.2006) by Police Reform Act 2002 (c. 30), ss. 41, 108. (2)-(5), Sch. 5 para. 9. ZA (as inserted by Serious Organised Crime and Police Act 2005 (c. 15), ss. 122, 178, Sch. 8 Pt. 2 para. 21; S.I. 2005/3495, art. 2. (1)(q)(r))

C95. S. 64. A(1. B)(f) modified (27.1.2010) by Police Reform Act 2002 (c. 30), Sch. 5 para. 1. (3. A) (as inserted by Local Government and Public Involvement in Health Act 2007 (c. 28), s. 133. (3)(a); S.I. 2010/112, art. 2. (e)

65 Part V—supplementary.

In this Part of this Act—

[F216 "analysis", in relation to a skin impression, includes comparison and matching;]

"appropriate consent" means—

- in relation to a person who [F217has attained the age of 18 years], the consent of that person;
- in relation to a person who has not attained that age but has attained the age of 14 years, the consent of that person and his parent or guardian; and
- in relation to a person who has not attained the age of 14 years, the consent of his parent or guardian;

[F218"DNA profile" means any information derived from a DNA sample;

"DNA sample" means any material that has come from a human body and consists of or includes human cells;]

[F219 "extradition arrest power" means any of the following—

- a Part 1 warrant (within the meaning given by the Extradition Act 2003) in respect of which a certificate under section 2 of that Act has been issued;
- section 5 of that Act;
- a warrant issued under section 71 of that Act;
- a provisional warrant (within the meaning given by that Act).]

F220 . . . .

[F221 "fingerprints", in relation to any person, means a record (in any form and produced by any method) of the skin pattern and other physical characteristics or features of—

- any of that person's fingers; or
- either of his palms;]

[F222"intimate sample" means—

- a sample of blood, semen or any other tissue fluid, urine or pubic hair;
- a dental impression;
- [F223a swab taken from any part of a person's genitals (including pubic hair) or from a person's body orifice other than the mouth;]]

[F224"intimate search" means a search which consists of the physical examination of a person's body orifices other than the mouth;]

[F225"non-intimate sample" means—

- a sample of hair other than pubic hair;

- a sample taken from a nail or from under a nail;
- [F226a swab taken from any part of a person's body other than a part from which a swab taken would be an intimate sample;]
- saliva;
- [F227a skin impression;]]

[F228"offence", in relation to any country or territory outside England and Wales, includes an act punishable under the law of that country or territory, however it is described;]

[F229"registered dentist" has the same meaning as in the M11 Dentists Act 1984;

[F230"registered health care professional" means a person (other than a medical practitioner) who is—
- a registered nurse; or
- a registered member of a health care profession which is designated for the purposes of this paragraph by an order made by the Secretary of State;]

[F231"the responsible chief officer of police", in relation to material to which section 63. D or 63. R applies, means the chief officer of police for the police area—
- in which the material concerned was taken, or
- in the case of a DNA profile, in which the sample from which the DNA profile was derived was taken;

"section 63. D material" means fingerprints or DNA profiles to which section 63. D applies;]

[F232"skin impression", in relation to any person, means any record (other than a fingerprint) which is a record " in any form and produced by any method) of the skin pattern and other physical characteristics or features of the whole or any part of his foot or of any other part of his body;]

"speculative search", in relation to a person's fingerprints or samples, means such a check against other fingerprints or samples or against information derived from other samples as is referred to in section 63. A(1) above;

"sufficient" and "insufficient", in relation to a sample, means [F233 (subject to subsection (2) below)] sufficient or insufficient (in point of quantity or quality) for the purpose of enabling information to be produced by the means of analysis used or to be used in relation to the sample.]

[F234"the terrorism provisions" means section 41 of the Terrorism Act 2000, and any provision of Schedule 7 to that Act conferring a power of detention; and

"terrorism" has the meaning given in section 1 of that Act.]

[F235"terrorist investigation" has the meaning given by section 32 of that Act;]

F236. . . F237. . .

[F238. (1. A)A health care profession is any profession mentioned in section 60. (2) of the Health Act 1999 (c. 8) other than the profession of practising medicine and the profession of nursing.

(1. B)An order under subsection (1) shall be made by statutory instrument and shall be subject to annulment in pursuance of a resolution of either House of Parliament.]

[F239. (2)References in this Part of this Act to a sample's proving insufficient include references to where, as a consequence of—
   (a) the loss, destruction or contamination of the whole or any part of the sample,
   (b) any damage to the whole or a part of the sample, or
   (c) the use of the whole or a part of the sample for an analysis which produced no results or which produced results some or all of which must be regarded, in the circumstances, as unreliable, the sample has become unavailable or insufficient for the purpose of enabling information, or information of a particular description, to be obtained by means of analysis of the sample.]

[F240. (2. A)In subsection (2), the reference to the destruction of a sample does not include a reference to the destruction of a sample under section 63. R (requirement to destroy samples).

(2. B)Any reference in sections 63. F, 63. H, 63. P or 63. U to a person being charged with an offence includes a reference to a person being informed that the person will be reported for an offence.]

[F241. (3)For the purposes of this Part, a person has in particular been convicted of an offence under the law of a country or territory outside England and Wales if—

(a) a court exercising jurisdiction under the law of that country or territory has made in respect of such an offence a finding equivalent to a finding that the person is not guilty by reason of insanity; or

(b) such a court has made in respect of such an offence a finding equivalent to a finding that the person is under a disability and did the act charged against him in respect of the offence.]

Amendments (Textual)

F216. Words in s. 65. (1) inserted (1.1.2003) by 2001 c. 16, s. 80. (5)(a); S.I. 2002/3032, art. 2. (b)

F217. Words in s. 65. (1) substituted (31.1.2017 for specified purposes, 3.4.2017 in so far as not already in force) by Policing and Crime Act 2017 (c. 3), ss. 73. (4), 183. (1), (5)(e); S.I. 2017/399, reg. 2, Sch. para. 22

F218. Words in s. 65. (1) inserted (31.10.2013) by Protection of Freedoms Act 2012 (c. 9), ss. 18. (2)(a), 120 (with s. 97); S.I. 2013/1814, art. 2. (d)

F219. S. 65: definition of "extradition arrest power" inserted (1.1.2004) by Extradition Act 2003 (c. 41), ss. 169. (6), 221; S.I. 2003/3103, art. 2 (subject to savings in Order (as amended by S.I. 2003/3312, art. 2. (2) and S.I. 2003/3258, art. 2. (2)))

F220. S. 65. (1): definitions of "drug trafficking" and "drug trafficking offence" repealed (24.3.2003) by Proceeds of Crime Act 2002 (c. 29), ss. 457, 458. (1)(3), Sch. 12; S.I. 2003/333, art. 2. (1), Sch. (as amended by S.I. 2003/531, arts. 3, 4)

F221. S. 65. (1): definition of "fingerprints" substituted (1.1.2003) by 2001 c. 16, s. 78. (8): S.I. 2002/3032, art. 2. (a)

F222. Definition of "intimate sample" in s. 65 substituted (10.4.1995) by 1994 c. 33, s. 58. (2); S.I. 1995/721, art. 2, Sch.

F223. S. 65. (1): words in the definition of "intimate sample" substituted (1.7.2005) by Serious Organised Crime and Police Act 2005 (c. 15), ss. 119. (2), 178; S.I. 2005/1521, art. 3. (1)(g)

F224. Definition of "intimate search" in s. 65 inserted (10.4.1995) by 1994 c. 33, s. 59. (1); S.I. 1995/721, art. 2, Sch.

F225. Definition of "non-intimate sample" substituted (10.4.1995) by 1994 c. 33, s. 58. (3); S.I. 1995/721, art. 2, Sch.

F226. S. 65. (1): words in the definition of "non-intimate sample" substituted (1.7.2005) by Serious Organised Crime and Police Act 2005 (c. 15), ss. 119. (3), 178; S.I. 2005/1521, art. 3. (1)(g)

F227. S. 65. (1): words in the definition of "non-intimate sample" substituted (1.1.2003) by 2001 c. 16, s. 80. (5)(b); S.I. 2002/3032, art. 2. (b)

F228. Words in s. 65. (1) inserted (7.3.2011) by Crime and Security Act 2010 (c. 17), ss. 3. (5), 59. (1); S.I. 2011/414, art. 2. (b)

F229. Definitions of "registered dentist", "speculative search" and "sufficient" and "insufficient" in s. 65 inserted (10.4.1995) by 1994 c. 33, s. 58. (4); S.I. 1995/721, art. 2, Sch.

F230. Definition of "registered health care professional" in s. 65 inserted (1.10.2002 for specified purposes otherwise 1.4.2003.) by Police Reform Act 2002 (c. 30), ss. {54. (2)}, 108. (2)-(5); S.I. 2002/2306, art. 4. (d); S.I. 2003/808, art. 2. (e)

F231. Words in s. 65. (1) inserted (31.10.2013) by Protection of Freedoms Act 2012 (c. 9), ss. 18. (2)(b), 120 (with s. 97); S.I. 2013/1814, art. 2. (d)

F232. S. 65. (1): definition of "skin impression" inserted (1.1.2003) by 2001 c. 16, s. 80. (5)(c); S.I. 2002/3032, art. 2. (b)

F233. S. 65. (1): words in definition of "sufficient" and "insufficient" inserted (1.1.2003) by 2001 c. 16, s. 80. (5)(d); S.I. 2002/3032, art. 2. (b)

F234. Definitions of " the terrorism provisions" and " terrorism" in s. 65 substituted (19.2.2001) by 2000 c. 11, s. 125, Sch. 15 para. 5. (10) (with s 129. (1)); S.I. 2001/421, art. 2

F235. Words in s. 65. (1) inserted (31.10.2013) by Protection of Freedoms Act 2012 (c. 9), ss. 18. (2)(c), 120 (with s. 97); S.I. 2013/1814, art. 2. (d)

F236. Word repealed by Criminal Justice Act 1988 (c. 33, SIF 39:1), s. 170. (2), Sch. 16

F237. Words in s. 65. (1) repealed (24.3.2003) by Proceeds of Crime Act 2002 (c. 29), ss. 457, 458. (1)(3), Sch. 12; S.I. 2003/333, art. 2. (1), Sch. (as amended by S.I. 2003/531, arts. 3, 4)

F238. S. 65. (1. A)(1. B) inserted (1.10.2002 for specified purposes otherwise 1.4.2003) by Police Reform Act 2002 (c. 30), ss. 54. (3), 108. (2)-(5); S.I. 2002/2306, art. 4. (d); S.I. 2003/808, art. 2. (e)

F239. S. 65. (2) inserted (1.1.2003) by 2001 c. 16, s. 80. (6); S.I. 2002/3032, art. 2. (b)

F240. S. 65. (2. A)(2. B) inserted (31.10.2013) by Protection of Freedoms Act 2012 (c. 9), ss. 18. (3), 120 (with s. 97); S.I. 2013/1814, art. 2. (d)

F241. S. 65. (3) inserted (7.3.2011) by Crime and Security Act 2010 (c. 17), ss. 3. (6), 59. (1); S.I. 2011/414, art. 2. (b)

Modifications etc. (not altering text)

C96. S. 65 applied with modifications: by S.I. 1985/1882, art. 10; (1.2.1997) by S.I. 1997/15, art. 2. (1), Sch.

S. 65 applied (with modifications) (31.12.2006) by The Police and Criminal Evidence Act 1984 (Application to the Armed Forces) Order 2006 (S.I. 2006/2015), arts. 2, 3, Schs. 1-3

C97. S. 65 applied (with modifications) (25.6.2013) by The Police and Criminal Evidence Act 1984 (Application to immigration officers and designated customs officials in England and Wales) Order 2013 (S.I. 2013/1542), arts. 1, 12. (2)-(4), Sch. 2 (with arts. 13-31)

Marginal Citations

M11 1984 c. 24.

[F242 65. A "Qualifying offence"

(1) In this Part, "qualifying offence" means—
   (a) an offence specified in subsection (2) below, or
   (b) an ancillary offence relating to such an offence.
(2) The offences referred to in subsection (1)(a) above are—
   (a) murder;
   (b) manslaughter;
   (c) false imprisonment;
   (d) kidnapping;
   [F243. (da)an offence of indecent exposure;
   (db) an offence under section 4 of the Vagrancy Act 1824, committed by a person by wilfully, openly, lewdly, and obscenely exposing his person with intent to insult any female;
   (dc) an offence under section 28 of the Town Police Clauses Act 1847, committed by a person by wilfully and indecently exposing his person;]
   (e) an offence under section 4, 16, 18, 20 to 24 or 47 of the Offences Against the Person Act 1861;
   (f) an offence under section 2 or 3 of the Explosive Substances Act 1883;
   [F244. (fa)an offence under section 1 of the Infant Life (Preservation) Act 1929;]
   (g) an offence under section 1 of the Children and Young Persons Act 1933;
   [F245. (ga)an offence under section 1 of the Infanticide Act 1938;
   (gb) an offence under section 12 or 13 of the Sexual Offences Act 1956, other than an offence committed by a person where the other person involved in the conduct constituting the offence consented to it and was aged 16 or over;
   (gc) an offence under any other section of that Act, other than sections 18 and 32;
   (gd) an offence under section 128 of the Mental Health Act 1959;
   (ge) an offence under section 1 of the Indecency with Children Act 1960;]
   (h) an offence under section 4. (1) of the Criminal Law Act 1967 committed in relation to murder;
   [F246. (ha)an offence under section 5 of the Sexual Offences Act 1967;]
   (i) an offence under sections 16 to 18 of the Firearms Act 1968;
   (j) an offence under [F247 section 8, 9] or 10 of the Theft Act 1968 or an offence under section 12. A of that Act involving an accident which caused a person's death;

[F248. (ja)an offence under section 1. (1) of the Genocide Act 1969;]

(k) an offence under section 1 of the Criminal Damage Act 1971 required to be charged as arson;

[F249. (ka)an offence under section 54 of the Criminal Law Act 1977;]

(l) an offence under section 1 of the Protection of Children Act 1978;

(m) an offence under section 1 of the Aviation Security Act 1982;

(n) an offence under section 2 of the Child Abduction Act 1984;

[F250. (na)an offence under section 1 of the Prohibition of Female Circumcision Act 1985;

(nb) an offence under section 1 of the Public Order Act 1986;]

(o) an offence under section 9 of the Aviation and Maritime Security Act 1990;

[F251. (oa)an offence under section 3 of the Sexual Offences (Amendment) Act 2000;

(ob) an offence under section 51 of the International Criminal Court Act 2001;

(oc) an offence under section 1, 2 or 3 of the Female Genital Mutilation Act 2003;]

(p) an offence under any of sections 1 to 19, 25, 26, 30 to 41, 47 to 50, 52, 53, 57 to [F252 59. A] , 61 to 67, 69 and 70 of the Sexual Offences Act 2003;

(q) an offence under section 5 of the Domestic Violence, Crime and Victims Act 2004;

(r) an offence for the time being listed in section 41. (1) of the Counter-Terrorism Act 2008.

[F253. (s)an offence under section 2 of the Modern Slavery Act 2015 (human trafficking).]]

(3) The Secretary of State may by order made by statutory instrument amend subsection (2) above.

(4) A statutory instrument containing an order under subsection (3) above shall not be made unless a draft of the instrument has been laid before, and approved by resolution of, each House of Parliament.

(5) In subsection (1)(b) above "ancillary offence", in relation to an offence, means—

(a) aiding, abetting, counselling or procuring the commission of the offence;

(b) an offence under Part 2 of the Serious Crime Act 2007 (encouraging or assisting crime) in relation to the offence (including, in relation to times before the commencement of that Part, an offence of incitement);

(c) attempting or conspiring to commit the offence.]

Amendments (Textual)

F242. S. 65. A inserted (7.3.2011) by Crime and Security Act 2010 (c. 17), ss. 7, 59. (1); S.I. 2011/414, art. 2. (f)

F243. Ss. 65. A(2)(da)-(dc) inserted (11.11.2013) by The Police and Criminal Evidence Act 1984 (Amendment: Qualifying Offences) Order 2013 (S.I. 2013/2774), arts. 1, 2. (2)

F244. S. 65. A(2)(fa) inserted (11.11.2013) by The Police and Criminal Evidence Act 1984 (Amendment: Qualifying Offences) Order 2013 (S.I. 2013/2774), arts. 1, 2. (3)

F245. Ss. 65. A(2)(ga)-(ge) inserted (11.11.2013) by The Police and Criminal Evidence Act 1984 (Amendment: Qualifying Offences) Order 2013 (S.I. 2013/2774), arts. 1, 2. (4)

F246. S. 65. A(2)(ha) inserted (11.11.2013) by The Police and Criminal Evidence Act 1984 (Amendment: Qualifying Offences) Order 2013 (S.I. 2013/2774), arts. 1, 2. (5)

F247. Words in s. 65. A(2)(j) substituted (31.10.2013) by Protection of Freedoms Act 2012 (c. 9), ss. 18. (4), 120 (with s. 97); S.I. 2013/1814, art. 2. (d)

F248. S. 65. A(2)(ja) inserted (11.11.2013) by The Police and Criminal Evidence Act 1984 (Amendment: Qualifying Offences) Order 2013 (S.I. 2013/2774), arts. 1, 2. (6)

F249. S. 65. A(2)(ka) inserted (11.11.2013) by The Police and Criminal Evidence Act 1984 (Amendment: Qualifying Offences) Order 2013 (S.I. 2013/2774), arts. 1, 2. (7)

F250. S. 65. A(2)(na)(nb) inserted (11.11.2013) by The Police and Criminal Evidence Act 1984 (Amendment: Qualifying Offences) Order 2013 (S.I. 2013/2774), arts. 1, 2. (8)

F251. Ss. 65. A(2)(oa)-(oc) inserted (11.11.2013) by The Police and Criminal Evidence Act 1984 (Amendment: Qualifying Offences) Order 2013 (S.I. 2013/2774), arts. 1, 2. (9)

F252. Word in s. 65. A(2)(p) substituted (6.4.2013) by Protection of Freedoms Act 2012 (c. 9), s. 120, Sch. 9 para. 137 (with s. 97); S.I. 2013/470, art. 2. (d) (with arts. 5-8)

F253. S. 65. A(2)(s) inserted (31.7.2015) by Modern Slavery Act 2015 (c. 30), s. 61. (1), Sch. 5 para. 3; S.I. 2015/1476, reg. 2. (j)

[F25465. BPersons convicted of an offence"

(1) For the purposes of this Part, any reference to a person who is convicted of an offence includes a reference to—

(a) a person who has been given a caution in respect of the offence which, at the time of the caution, the person has admitted,

(b) a person who has been warned or reprimanded under section 65 of the Crime and Disorder Act 1998 for the offence,

(c) a person who has been found not guilty of the offence by reason of insanity, or

(d) a person who has been found to be under a disability and to have done the act charged in respect of the offence.

(2) This Part, so far as it relates to persons convicted of an offence, has effect despite anything in the Rehabilitation of Offenders Act 1974.

(3) But a person is not to be treated as having been convicted of an offence if that conviction is a disregarded conviction or caution by virtue of section 92 of the Protection of Freedoms Act 2012.

(4) If a person is convicted of more than one offence arising out of a single course of action, those convictions are to be treated as a single conviction for the purposes of calculating under sections 63. F, 63. H and 63. N whether the person has been convicted of only one offence.

(5) See also section 65. (3) (which deals with findings equivalent to those mentioned in subsection (1)(c) or (d) by courts which exercise jurisdiction under the laws of countries or territories outside England and Wales).]

Amendments (Textual)

F254. S. 65. B inserted (31.10.2013) by Protection of Freedoms Act 2012 (c. 9), ss. 18. (5), 120 (with s. 97); S.I. 2013/1814, art. 2. (d)

Part V—supplementary.

65 Part V—supplementary.

In this Part of this Act—

[F1 "analysis", in relation to a skin impression, includes comparison and matching;]

"appropriate consent" means—

- in relation to a person who [F2has attained the age of 18 years], the consent of that person;

- in relation to a person who has not attained that age but has attained the age of 14 years, the consent of that person and his parent or guardian; and

- in relation to a person who has not attained the age of 14 years, the consent of his parent or guardian;

[F3"DNA profile" means any information derived from a DNA sample;

"DNA sample" means any material that has come from a human body and consists of or includes human cells;]

[F4 "extradition arrest power" means any of the following—

- a Part 1 warrant (within the meaning given by the Extradition Act 2003) in respect of which a certificate under section 2 of that Act has been issued;

- section 5 of that Act;

- a warrant issued under section 71 of that Act;

- a provisional warrant (within the meaning given by that Act).]

F5 . . . .

[F6 "fingerprints", in relation to any person, means a record (in any form and produced by any method) of the skin pattern and other physical characteristics or features of—

161

- any of that person's fingers; or
- either of his palms;]
[F7"intimate sample" means—
- a sample of blood, semen or any other tissue fluid, urine or pubic hair;
- a dental impression;
- [F8a swab taken from any part of a person's genitals (including pubic hair) or from a person's body orifice other than the mouth;]]
[F9"intimate search" means a search which consists of the physical examination of a person's body orifices other than the mouth;]
[F10"non-intimate sample" means—
- a sample of hair other than pubic hair;
- a sample taken from a nail or from under a nail;
- [F11a swab taken from any part of a person's body other than a part from which a swab taken would be an intimate sample;]
- saliva;
- [F12a skin impression;]]
[F13"offence", in relation to any country or territory outside England and Wales, includes an act punishable under the law of that country or territory, however it is described;]
[F14"registered dentist" has the same meaning as in the M1 Dentists Act 1984;
[F15"registered health care professional" means a person (other than a medical practitioner) who is—
- a registered nurse; or
- a registered member of a health care profession which is designated for the purposes of this paragraph by an order made by the Secretary of State;]
[F16"the responsible chief officer of police", in relation to material to which section 63. D or 63. R applies, means the chief officer of police for the police area—
- in which the material concerned was taken, or
- in the case of a DNA profile, in which the sample from which the DNA profile was derived was taken;
"section 63. D material" means fingerprints or DNA profiles to which section 63. D applies;]
[F17"skin impression", in relation to any person, means any record (other than a fingerprint) which is a record " in any form and produced by any method) of the skin pattern and other physical characteristics or features of the whole or any part of his foot or of any other part of his body;]
"speculative search", in relation to a person's fingerprints or samples, means such a check against other fingerprints or samples or against information derived from other samples as is referred to in section 63. A(1) above;
"sufficient" and "insufficient", in relation to a sample, means [F18 (subject to subsection (2) below)] sufficient or insufficient (in point of quantity or quality) for the purpose of enabling information to be produced by the means of analysis used or to be used in relation to the sample.]
[F19"the terrorism provisions" means section 41 of the Terrorism Act 2000, and any provision of Schedule 7 to that Act conferring a power of detention; and
"terrorism" has the meaning given in section 1 of that Act.]
[F20"terrorist investigation" has the meaning given by section 32 of that Act;]
F21. . . F22. . .
[F23. (1. A)A health care profession is any profession mentioned in section 60. (2) of the Health Act 1999 (c. 8) other than the profession of practising medicine and the profession of nursing.
(1. B)An order under subsection (1) shall be made by statutory instrument and shall be subject to annulment in pursuance of a resolution of either House of Parliament.]
[F24. (2)References in this Part of this Act to a sample's proving insufficient include references to where, as a consequence of—
    (a) the loss, destruction or contamination of the whole or any part of the sample,
    (b) any damage to the whole or a part of the sample, or

162

(c) the use of the whole or a part of the sample for an analysis which produced no results or which produced results some or all of which must be regarded, in the circumstances, as unreliable, the sample has become unavailable or insufficient for the purpose of enabling information, or information of a particular description, to be obtained by means of analysis of the sample.]

[F25. (2. A)In subsection (2), the reference to the destruction of a sample does not include a reference to the destruction of a sample under section 63. R (requirement to destroy samples). (2. B)Any reference in sections 63. F, 63. H, 63. P or 63. U to a person being charged with an offence includes a reference to a person being informed that the person will be reported for an offence.]

[F26. (3)For the purposes of this Part, a person has in particular been convicted of an offence under the law of a country or territory outside England and Wales if—

(a) a court exercising jurisdiction under the law of that country or territory has made in respect of such an offence a finding equivalent to a finding that the person is not guilty by reason of insanity; or

(b) such a court has made in respect of such an offence a finding equivalent to a finding that the person is under a disability and did the act charged against him in respect of the offence.]

Amendments (Textual)

F1. Words in s. 65. (1) inserted (1.1.2003) by 2001 c. 16, s. 80. (5)(a); S.I. 2002/3032, art. 2. (b)

F2. Words in s. 65. (1) substituted (31.1.2017 for specified purposes, 3.4.2017 in so far as not already in force) by Policing and Crime Act 2017 (c. 3), ss. 73. (4), 183. (1), (5)(e); S.I. 2017/399, reg. 2, Sch. para. 22

F3. Words in s. 65. (1) inserted (31.10.2013) by Protection of Freedoms Act 2012 (c. 9), ss. 18. (2)(a), 120 (with s. 97); S.I. 2013/1814, art. 2. (d)

F4. S. 65: definition of "extradition arrest power" inserted (1.1.2004) by Extradition Act 2003 (c. 41), ss. 169. (6), 221; S.I. 2003/3103, art. 2 (subject to savings in Order (as amended by S.I. 2003/3312, art. 2. (2) and S.I. 2003/3258, art. 2. (2)))

F5. S. 65. (1): definitions of "drug trafficking" and "drug trafficking offence" repealed (24.3.2003) by Proceeds of Crime Act 2002 (c. 29), ss. 457, 458. (1)(3), Sch. 12; S.I. 2003/333, art. 2. (1), Sch. (as amended by S.I. 2003/531, arts. 3, 4)

F6. S. 65. (1): definition of "fingerprints" substituted (1.1.2003) by 2001 c. 16, s. 78. (8): S.I. 2002/3032, art. 2. (a)

F7. Definition of "intimate sample" in s. 65 substituted (10.4.1995) by 1994 c. 33, s. 58. (2); S.I. 1995/721, art. 2, Sch.

F8. S. 65. (1): words in the definition of "intimate sample" substituted (1.7.2005) by Serious Organised Crime and Police Act 2005 (c. 15), ss. 119. (2), 178; S.I. 2005/1521, art. 3. (1)(g)

F9. Definition of "intimate search" in s. 65 inserted (10.4.1995) by 1994 c. 33, s. 59. (1); S.I. 1995/721, art. 2, Sch.

F10. Definition of "non-intimate sample" substituted (10.4.1995) by 1994 c. 33, s. 58. (3); S.I. 1995/721, art. 2, Sch.

F11. S. 65. (1): words in the definition of "non-intimate sample" substituted (1.7.2005) by Serious Organised Crime and Police Act 2005 (c. 15), ss. 119. (3), 178; S.I. 2005/1521, art. 3. (1)(g)

F12. S. 65. (1): words in the definition of "non-intimate sample" substituted (1.1.2003) by 2001 c. 16, s. 80. (5)(b); S.I. 2002/3032, art. 2. (b)

F13. Words in s. 65. (1) inserted (7.3.2011) by Crime and Security Act 2010 (c. 17), ss. 3. (5), 59. (1); S.I. 2011/414, art. 2. (b)

F14. Definitions of "registered dentist", "speculative search" and "sufficient" and "insufficient" in s. 65 inserted (10.4.1995) by 1994 c. 33, s. 58. (4); S.I. 1995/721, art. 2, Sch.

F15. Definition of "registered health care professional" in s. 65 inserted (1.10.2002 for specified purposes otherwise 1.4.2003.) by Police Reform Act 2002 (c. 30), ss. {54. (2)}, 108. (2)-(5); S.I. 2002/2306, art. 4. (d); S.I. 2003/808, art. 2. (e)

F16. Words in s. 65. (1) inserted (31.10.2013) by Protection of Freedoms Act 2012 (c. 9), ss. 18. (2)(b), 120 (with s. 97); S.I. 2013/1814, art. 2. (d)

F17. S. 65. (1): definition of "skin impression" inserted (1.1.2003) by 2001 c. 16, s. 80. (5)(c); S.I.

2002/3032, art. 2. (b)

F18. S. 65. (1): words in definition of "sufficient" and "insufficient" inserted (1.1.2003) by 2001 c. 16, s. 80. (5)(d); S.I. 2002/3032, art. 2. (b)

F19. Definitions of " the terrorism provisions" and " terrorism" in s. 65 substituted (19.2.2001) by 2000 c. 11, s. 125, Sch. 15 para. 5. (10) (with s 129. (1)); S.I. 2001/421, art. 2

F20. Words in s. 65. (1) inserted (31.10.2013) by Protection of Freedoms Act 2012 (c. 9), ss. 18. (2)(c), 120 (with s. 97); S.I. 2013/1814, art. 2. (d)

F21. Word repealed by Criminal Justice Act 1988 (c. 33, SIF 39:1), s. 170. (2), Sch. 16

F22. Words in s. 65. (1) repealed (24.3.2003) by Proceeds of Crime Act 2002 (c. 29), ss. 457, 458. (1)(3), Sch. 12; S.I. 2003/333, art. 2. (1), Sch. (as amended by S.I. 2003/531, arts. 3, 4)

F23. S. 65. (1. A)(1. B) inserted (1.10.2002 for specified purposes otherwise 1.4.2003) by Police Reform Act 2002 (c. 30), ss. 54. (3), 108. (2)-(5); S.I. 2002/2306, art. 4. (d); S.I. 2003/808, art. 2. (e)

F24. S. 65. (2) inserted (1.1.2003) by 2001 c. 16, s. 80. (6); S.I. 2002/3032, art. 2. (b)

F25. S. 65. (2. A)(2. B) inserted (31.10.2013) by Protection of Freedoms Act 2012 (c. 9), ss. 18. (3), 120 (with s. 97); S.I. 2013/1814, art. 2. (d)

F26. S. 65. (3) inserted (7.3.2011) by Crime and Security Act 2010 (c. 17), ss. 3. (6), 59. (1); S.I. 2011/414, art. 2. (b)

Modifications etc. (not altering text)

C1. S. 65 applied with modifications: by S.I. 1985/1882, art. 10; (1.2.1997) by S.I. 1997/15, art. 2. (1), Sch.

S. 65 applied (with modifications) (31.12.2006) by The Police and Criminal Evidence Act 1984 (Application to the Armed Forces) Order 2006 (S.I. 2006/2015), arts. 2, 3, Schs. 1-3

C2. S. 65 applied (with modifications) (25.6.2013) by The Police and Criminal Evidence Act 1984 (Application to immigration officers and designated customs officials in England and Wales) Order 2013 (S.I. 2013/1542), arts. 1, 12. (2)-(4), Sch. 2 (with arts. 13-31)

Marginal Citations

M11984 c. 24.

Part VI Codes of Practice—General

Part VI Codes of Practice—General

66 Codes of practice.

The Secretary of State shall issue codes of practice in connection with—

(a) the exercise by police officers of statutory powers—

(i) to search a person without first arresting him; F1. . .

(ii) to search a vehicle without making an arrest;[F2 or

(iii) to arrest a person;]

(b) the detention, treatment, questioning and identification of persons by police officers;

(c) searches of premises by police officers; and

(d) the seizure of property found by police officers on persons or premises.

[F3. (2)Codes shall (in particular) include provision in connection with the exercise by police officers of powers under section 63. B above.]

[F4. (3)Nothing in this section requires the Secretary of State to issue a code of practice in relation to any matter falling within the code of practice issued under section 47. AB(2) of the Terrorism Act 2000 (as that code is altered or replaced from time to time) (code of practice in relation to terrorism powers to search persons and vehicles and to stop and search in specified locations).]

Amendments (Textual)

F1. S. 66: "in subsection (1)(a)" word at the end of sub-paragraph (i) repealed (1.1.2006) by virtue of Serious Organised Crime and Police Act 2005 (c. 15), ss. 110. (3)(a), 178, Sch. 17 Pt. 2; S.I. 2005/3495, art. 2. (1)(m)(t)(u)(xxiv)

F2. S. 66: "in subsection (1)(a)" sub-paragraph (ii) and word inserted (1.1.2006) by virtue of Serious Organised Crime and Police Act 2005 (c. 15), ss. 110. (3)(b), 178; S.I. 2005/3495, art. 2. (1)(m)

F3. S. 66. (2) inserted "at the end of s. 66" (for certain purposes on 20.6.2001, 2.7.2001, 20.5.2002, 2.9.2002, 1.4.2003, 1.4.2004, 1.4.2005 and otherwise 1.12.2005) by virtue of 2000 c. 43, ss. 57. (3)(a), 80. (1); S.I. 2001/2232, art. 2. (f); S.I. 2002/1149, art. 2; S.I. 2002/1862, art. 2; S.I. 2003/709, art. 2; S.I. 2004/780, art. 2; S.I. 2005/596, art. 2; S.I. 2005/3054, art. 2

F4. S. 66. (3) inserted (10.7.2012) by Protection of Freedoms Act 2012 (c. 9), s. 120, Sch. 9 para. 21 (with s. 97); S.I. 2012/1205, art. 4. (k)

Modifications etc. (not altering text)

C1. S. 66 modified (18.3.2011) by Terrorism Act 2000 (Remedial) Order 2011 (S.I. 2011/631), art. 1, Sch. 2 paras. 1, 2 (with art. 6)

C2. S. 66 applied (with modifications) (4.11.2015) by The Police and Criminal Evidence Act 1984 (Application to Revenue and Customs) Order 2015 (S.I. 2015/1783), arts. 1, 3. (1), Sch. 1 (with art. 3. (2), (3), 4-19, Sch. 2)

67 Codes of practice—supplementary.

[F5. (1) In this section, " code " means a code of practice under section 60, 60. A or 66.

(2) The Secretary of State may at any time revise the whole or any part of a code.

(3) A code may be made, or revised, so as to—

　(a) apply only in relation to one or more specified areas,

　(b) have effect only for a specified period,

　(c) apply only in relation to specified offences or descriptions of offender.

(4) Before issuing a code, or any revision of a code, the Secretary of State must consult—

　(a) [F6such persons as appear to the Secretary of State to represent the views of police and crime commissioners,

　(aa) the Mayor's Office for Policing and Crime,

　(ab) the Common Council of the City of London,]

　(b) [F7the National Police Chiefs' Council],

　(c) the General Council of the Bar,

　(d) the Law Society of England and Wales,

　(e) the Institute of Legal Executives, and

　(f) such other persons as he thinks fit.

[F8. (4. A)The duty to consult under subsection (4) does not apply to a revision of a code where the Secretary of State considers that—

　(a) the revision is necessary in consequence of legislation, and

　(b) the Secretary of State has no discretion as to the nature of the revision.

(4. B)Where, in consequence of subsection (4. A), a revision of a code is issued without prior consultation with the persons mentioned in subsection (4), the Secretary of State must (at the same time as issuing the revision) publish a statement that, in his or her opinion, paragraphs (a) and (b) of subsection (4. A) apply to the revision.

(4. C)In subsection (4. A), "legislation" means any provision of—

　(a) an Act,

　(b) subordinate legislation within the meaning of the Interpretation Act 1978.]

(5) A code, or a revision of a code, does not come into operation until the Secretary of State by order so provides.

(6) The power conferred by subsection (5) is exercisable by statutory instrument.

(7) An order bringing a code into operation may not be made unless a draft of the order has been laid before Parliament and approved by a resolution of each House.

(7. A)An order bringing a revision of a code into operation must be laid before Parliament if the order has been made without a draft having been so laid and approved by a resolution of each House.

(7. B)When an order or draft of an order is laid, the code or revision of a code to which it relates must also be laid.

(7. C)No order or draft of an order may be laid until the consultation required by subsection (4) has taken place.

(7. D)An order bringing a code, or a revision of a code, into operation may include transitional or saving provisions.]

F9. (8). . . . .

(9) Persons other than police officers who are charged with the duty of investigating offences or charging offenders shall in the discharge of that duty have regard to any relevant provision of F10. . . a code.

[F11. (9. A)Persons on whom powers are conferred by—

(a) any designation under section 38 or 39 of the Police Reform Act 2002 (c. 30) (police powers for [F12civilian staff] [F13and volunteers]), or

(b) any accreditation under section 41 of that Act (accreditation under community safety accreditation schemes),

F14shall have regard to any relevant provision of a code . . . in the exercise or performance of the powers and duties conferred or imposed on them by that designation or accreditation.]

(10) A failure on the part—

(a) of a police officer to comply with any provision of F15. . . a code; F16. . .

(b) of any person other than a police officer who is charged with the duty of investigating offences or charging offenders to have regard to any relevant provision of F17. . . a code in the discharge of that duty, [F18, or

(c) of a person designated under section 38 or 39 or accredited under section 41 of the Police Reform Act 2002 (c. 30) to have regard to any relevant provision of F19. . . a code in the exercise or performance of the powers and duties conferred or imposed on him by that designation or accreditation,]

shall not of itself render him liable to any criminal or civil proceedings.

(11) In all criminal and civil proceedings any F20. . . code shall be admissible in evidence; and if any provision of F20. . . a code appears to the court or tribunal conducting the proceedings to be relevant to any question arising in the proceedings it shall be taken into account in determining that question.

[F21. (12) In subsection (11) " criminal proceedings " includes service proceedings.

(13) In this section " service proceedings " means proceedings before a court (other than a civilian court) in respect of a service offence; and "service offence" and "civilian court" here have the same meanings as in the Armed Forces Act 2006.]

Amendments (Textual)

F5. S. 67. (1)-(7. D) substituted (20.1.2004) for s. 67. (1)-(7. C) by Criminal Justice Act 2003 (c. 44), ss. 11. (1), 336; S.I. 2004/81, art. 2. (1)(2)(a)

F6. S. 67. (4)(a)-(ab) substituted for s. 67. (4)(a) (16.1.2012) by Police Reform and Social Responsibility Act 2011 (c. 13), s. 157. (1), Sch. 16 para. 163. (2); S.I. 2011/3019, art. 3, Sch. 1 (with Sch. 2 para. 47)

F7. Words in s. 67. (4)(b) substituted (31.1.2017 for specified purposes, 3.4.2017 in so far as not already in force) by Policing and Crime Act 2017 (c. 3), s. 183. (1)(5)(e), Sch. 14 paras. 4, 5. (a); S.I. 2017/399, reg. 2, Sch. para. 41

F8. S. 67. (4. A)-(4. C) inserted (31.1.2017 for specified purposes, 3.4.2017 in so far as not already in force) by Policing and Crime Act 2017 (c. 3), ss. 78, 183. (1), (5)(e); S.I. 2017/399, reg. 2, Sch. para. 26

F9. S. 67. (8) repealed (1.4.1999) by 1996 c. 16, s. 103. (3), Sch. 9 Pt. II; S.I. 1999/533, art. 2. (a)

F10. Word in s. 67. (9) repealed (20.1.2004) by Criminal Justice Act 2003 (c. 44), ss. 332, 336, Sch. 37 Pt. 1; S.I. 2004/81, art. 2. (1)(2)(g)(i)

F11. S. 67. (9. A) inserted (2.12.2002) by Police Reform Act 2002 (c. 30), s. 107, Sch. 7 para. 9. (7); S.I. 2002/2750, art. 2. (b)(ii)

F12. Words in s. 67. (9. A)(a) substituted (16.1.2012) by Police Reform and Social Responsibility Act 2011 (c. 13), s. 157. (1), Sch. 16 para. 163. (3); S.I. 2011/3019, art. 3, Sch. 1

F13. Words in s. 67. (9. A)(a) inserted (31.1.2017 for specified purposes, 15.12.2017 in so far as not already in force) by Policing and Crime Act 2017 (c. 3), s. 183. (1)(5)(e), Sch. 12 para. 7. (4); S.I. 2017/1139, reg. 2. (k) (as amended by S.I. 2017/1162, reg. 2)

F14. Words in s. 67. (9. A) repealed (20.1.2004) by Criminal Justice Act 2003 (c. 44), ss. 332, 336, Sch. 37 Pt. 1; S.I. 2004/81, art. 2. (1)(2)(g)(i)

F15. Word in s. 67. (10)(a) repealed (20.1.2004) by Criminal Justice Act 2003 (c. 44), ss. 332, 336, Sch. 37 Pt. 1; S.I. 2004/81, art. 2. (1)(2)(g)(i)

F16. S. 67. (10): the word "or" after paragraph (a) repealed (2.12.2002) by Police Reform Act 2002 (c. 30), s. 107, Sch. 8; S.I. 2002/2750, art. 2. (b)(iii)(b)

F17. Word in s. 67. (10)(b) repealed (20.1.2004) by Criminal Justice Act 2003 (c. 44), ss. 332, 336, Sch. 37 Pt. 1; S.I. 2004/81, art. 2. (1)(2)(g)(i)

F18. S. 67. (10)(c) and preceding word "or" inserted (2.12.2002) by Police Reform Act 2002 (c. 30), s. 107, Sch. 7 para. 9. (8); S.I. 2002/2750, art. 2. (b)(ii)

F19. Word in s. 67. (10)(c) repealed (20.1.2004) by Criminal Justice Act 2003 (c. 44), ss. 332, 336, Sch. 37 Pt. 1; S.I. 2004/81, art. 2. (1)(2)(g)(i)

F20. Word in s. 67. (11) repealed (20.1.2004) by Criminal Justice Act 2003 (c. 44), ss. 332, 336, Sch. 37 Pt. 1; S.I. 2004/81, art. 2. (1)(2)(g)(i)

F21. S. 67. (12)(13) substituted (28.3.2009 for certain purposes and otherwise 31.10.2009) for s. 67. (12) by Armed Forces Act 2006 (c. 52), ss. 378, 383, Sch. 16 para. 101; S.I. 2009/812, art. 3 (with transitional provisions in S.I. 2009/1059); S.I. 2009/1167, art. 4

Modifications etc. (not altering text)

C3. S. 67 applied (with modifications) (4.11.2015) by The Police and Criminal Evidence Act 1984 (Application to Revenue and Customs) Order 2015 (S.I. 2015/1783), arts. 1, 3. (1), Sch. 1 (with art. 3. (2), (3), 4-19, Sch. 2)

C4. S. 67. (9) excluded (12.4.2010) by 2002 c. 29 s. 377. ZB (as inserted by The Northern Ireland Act 1998 (Devolution of Policing and Justice Functions) Order 2010) (S.I. 2010/976), arts. 1. (2), 12, {Sch. 14 para. 68}; S.I. 2010/977, art. 1. (2)

C5. S. 67. (9) excluded (24.2.2003) by Proceeds of Crime Act 2002 (c. 29), ss. 377. (9)(a), 458; S.I. 2003/120, art. 2, Sch. (subject to transitional provisions and savings in arts. 3-7 (as amended by S.I. 2003/333, art. 14 which in turn is amended by S.I. 2003/531, arts. 3 and 4))

Part VII Documentary Evidence in Criminal Proceedings

Part VII Documentary Evidence in Criminal Proceedings

Modifications etc. (not altering text)

C1. Pt. VII modified (2.10.2000) by S.I. 2000/2370, rule 27. (2), Sch. 3 Pt. III para. 18. (a)

Pt. VII modified (2.10.2000) by S.I. 2000/2371, rule 27. (2), Sch. 3 Pt. III para. 18. (a)

Pt. VII modified (2.10.2000) by S.I. 2000/2372, rule 27. (2), Sch. 3 Pt. III para. 18. (a)

68. . . . . F1.

F269. . . . .

F370. . . . .

71 Microfilm copies.

In any proceedings the contents of a document may (whether or not the document is still in existence) be proved by the production of an enlargement of a microfilm copy of that document or of the material part of it, authenticated in such manner as the court may approve.
[F4. F5... concerned are proceedings before a magistrates' court inquiring into an offence as examining justices this section shall have effect with the omission of the words "authenticated in such manner as the court may approve."]

Extent Information
E1. S. 71 extends to England and Wales only with exceptions as regards courts martial, see s. 120. (1)(6)-(8)

72 Part VII—supplementary.

(1) In this Part of this Act—
[F6"copy", in relation to a document, means anything onto which information recorded in the document has been copied, by whatever means and whether directly or indirectly, and "statement" means any representation of fact, however made; and]
"proceedings" means criminal proceedings, including[F7 service proceedings.]
[F8. (1. A)In subsection (1) "service proceedings" means proceedings before a court (other than a civilian court) in respect of a service offence; and "service offence" and "civilian court" here have the same meanings as in the Armed Forces Act 2006.]
(2) Nothing in this Part of this Act shall prejudice any power of a court to exclude evidence (whether by preventing questions from being put or otherwise) at its discretion.

Extent Information
E2. S. 72 extends to England and Wales only with exceptions as regards courts martial, see s. 120. (1)(6)-(8)

Amendments (Textual)

F6. Definitions of "copy" and "statement" in s. 72. (1) substituted (31.1.1997) by 1995 c. 38, s. 15. (1), Sch. 1 para. 9. (2) (with ss. 1. (3), 6. (4)(5), 14); S.I. 1996/3217, art. 2

F7. S. 72. (1): words in definition of "proceedings" substituted (28.3.2009 for certain purposes and otherwise 31.10.2009) for paras. (a)-(c) by Armed Forces Act 2006 (c. 52), ss. 378. (1), 383, Sch. 16 para. 102. (2); S.I. 2009/812, art. 3 (with transitional provisions in S.I. 2009/1059); S.I. 2009/1167, art. 4

F8. S. 72. (1. A) inserted (28.3.2009 for certain purposes and otherwise 31.10.2009) by Armed Forces Act 2006 (c. 52), ss. 378. (1), 383, Sch. 16 para. 102. (3); S.I. 2009/812, art. 3 (with transitional provisions in S.I. 2009/1059); S.I. 2009/1167, art. 4

Part VII—supplementary.

72 Part VII—supplementary.

(1) In this Part of this Act—

[F1"copy", in relation to a document, means anything onto which information recorded in the document has been copied, by whatever means and whether directly or indirectly, and "statement" means any representation of fact, however made; and]

"proceedings" means criminal proceedings, including[F2 service proceedings.]

[F3. (1. A)In subsection (1) "service proceedings" means proceedings before a court (other than a civilian court) in respect of a service offence; and "service offence" and "civilian court" here have the same meanings as in the Armed Forces Act 2006.]

(2) Nothing in this Part of this Act shall prejudice any power of a court to exclude evidence (whether by preventing questions from being put or otherwise) at its discretion.

Extent Information

E1. S. 72 extends to England and Wales only with exceptions as regards courts martial, see s. 120. (1)(6)-(8)

Amendments (Textual)

F1. Definitions of "copy" and "statement" in s. 72. (1) substituted (31.1.1997) by 1995 c. 38, s. 15. (1), Sch. 1 para. 9. (2) (with ss. 1. (3), 6. (4)(5), 14); S.I. 1996/3217, art. 2

F2. S. 72. (1): words in definition of "proceedings" substituted (28.3.2009 for certain purposes and otherwise 31.10.2009) for paras. (a)-(c) by Armed Forces Act 2006 (c. 52), ss. 378. (1), 383, Sch. 16 para. 102. (2); S.I. 2009/812, art. 3 (with transitional provisions in S.I. 2009/1059); S.I. 2009/1167, art. 4

F3. S. 72. (1. A) inserted (28.3.2009 for certain purposes and otherwise 31.10.2009) by Armed Forces Act 2006 (c. 52), ss. 378. (1), 383, Sch. 16 para. 102. (3); S.I. 2009/812, art. 3 (with transitional provisions in S.I. 2009/1059); S.I. 2009/1167, art. 4

Part VIII Evidence in Criminal Proceedings— General

Part VIII Evidence in Criminal Proceedings—General

Modifications etc. (not altering text)

C1. Pt. VIII modified (2.10.2000) by S.I. 2000/2370, rule 27. (2), Sch. 3 Pt. III para. 18. (a)

Pt. VIII modified (2.10.2000) by S.I. 2000/2371, rule 27. (2), Sch. 3 Pt. III para. 18. (a)

Pt. VIII modified (2.10.2000) by S.I. 2000/2372, rule 27. (2), Sch. 3 Pt. III para. 18. (a)

73 Proof of convictions and acquittals.

(1) Where in any proceedings the fact that a person has in the United Kingdom [F1or any other member State] been convicted or acquitted of an offence otherwise than by a Service court is admissible in evidence, it may be proved by producing a certificate of conviction or, as the case may be, of acquittal relating to that offence, and proving that the person named in the certificate as having been convicted or acquitted of the offence is the person whose conviction or acquittal of the offence is to be proved.

(2) For the purposes of this section a certificate of conviction or of acquittal—

(a) shall, as regards a conviction or acquittal on indictment, consist of a certificate, signed by the [F2proper officer] of the court where the conviction or acquittal took place, giving the substance and effect (omitting the formal parts) of the indictment and of the conviction or acquittal; and

(b) shall, as regards a conviction or acquittal on a summary trial, consist of a copy of the conviction or of the dismissal of the information, signed by the [F2proper officer] of the court where the conviction or acquittal took place or by the [F2proper officer] of the court, if any, to which a memorandum of the conviction or acquittal was sent[F3; and

(c) shall, as regards a conviction or acquittal by a court in a member State (other than the United Kingdom), consist of a certificate, signed by the proper officer of the court where the conviction or acquittal took place, giving details of the offence, of the conviction or acquittal, and of any sentence;]

and a document purporting to be a duly signed certificate of conviction or acquittal under this section shall be taken to be such a certificate unless the contrary is proved.

[F4. (3)In subsection (2) above "proper officer" means—

(a) in relation to a magistrates' court in England and Wales, the [F5designated officer] for the court; and

(b) in relation to any other court [F6in the United Kingdom], the clerk of the court, his deputy or any other person having custody of the court record [F7, and

(c) in relation to any court in another member State ("the EU court"), a person who would be the proper officer of the EU court if that court were in the United Kingdom.]]

(4) The method of proving a conviction or acquittal authorised by this section shall be in addition to and not to the exclusion of any other authorised manner of proving a conviction or acquittal.

Extent Information

E1. S. 73 extends to England and Wales only with exceptions as regards courts martial, see s. 120. (1)(6)-(8)

Amendments (Textual)

F1. Words in s. 73. (1) inserted (15.8.2010) by Coroners and Justice Act 2009 (c. 25), ss. 144, 182, Sch. 17 para. 13. (2) (with s. 180, Sch. 22); S.I. 2010/1858, art. 3. (a)(d)(vii)

F2. Words in s. 73. (2)(a)(b) substituted (1.4.2001) by 1999 c. 22, s. 90, Sch. 13 para. 128. (1)(2) (with Sch. 14 para. 7. (2)); S.I. 2001/916, art. 2

F3. S. 73. (2)(c) and preceding word inserted (15.8.2010) by Coroners and Justice Act 2009 (c. 25), ss. 144, 182, Sch. 17 para. 13. (3) (with s. 180, Sch. 22); S.I. 2010/1858, art. 3. (a)(d)(vii)

F4. S. 73. (3) substituted (1.4.2001) by 1999 c. 22, ss. 90, Sch. 13 para. 128. (1)(3) (with Sch. 14 para. 7. (2)); S.I. 2001/916, art. 2

F5. Words in s. 73. (3)(a) substituted (1.4.2005) by Courts Act 2003 (c. 39), ss. 109. (1), 110, Sch. 8 para. 285; S.I. 2005/910, art. 3. (y)

F6. Words in s. 73. (3)(b) inserted (15.8.2010) by Coroners and Justice Act 2009 (c. 25), ss. 144, 182, Sch. 17 para. 13. (4)(a) (with s. 180, Sch. 22); S.I. 2010/1858, art. 3. (a)(d)(vii)

F7. S. 73. (3)(c) and preceding word added (15.8.2010) by Coroners and Justice Act 2009 (c. 25), ss. 144, 182, Sch. 17 para. 13. (4)(b) (with s. 180, Sch. 22); S.I. 2010/1858, art. 3. (a)(d)(vii)

74 Conviction as evidence of commission of offence.

(1) In any proceedings the fact that a person other than the accused has been convicted of an offence by or before any court in the United Kingdom [F8or any other member State] or by a Service court outside the United Kingdom shall be admissible in evidence for the purpose of proving, [F9that that person committed that offence, where evidence of his having done so is admissible] , whether or not any other evidence of his having committed that offence is given.
(2) In any proceedings in which by virtue of this section a person other than the accused is proved to have been convicted of an offence by or before any court in the United Kingdom [F10or any other member State] or by a Service court outside the United Kingdom, he shall be taken to have committed that offence unless the contrary is proved.
(3) In any proceedings where evidence is admissible of the fact that the accused has committed an offence, F11. . . , if the accused is proved to have been convicted of the offence—
   (a) by or before any court in the United Kingdom [F12or any other member State]; or
   (b) by a Service court outside the United Kingdom,
he shall be taken to have committed that offence unless the contrary is proved.
(4) Nothing in this section shall prejudice—
   (a) the admissibility in evidence of any conviction which would be admissible apart from this section; or
   (b) the operation of any enactment whereby a conviction or a finding of fact in any proceedings is for the purposes of any other proceedings made conclusive evidence of any fact.
Amendments (Textual)
F8. Words in s. 74. (1) inserted (15.8.2010) by Coroners and Justice Act 2009 (c. 25), ss. 144, 182, Sch. 17 para. 14. (2) (with s. 180, Sch. 22); S.I. 2010/1858, art. 3. (a)(d)(vii)
F9. Words in s. 74. (1) substituted (15.12.2004) by Criminal Justice Act 2003 (c. 44), 331, 336, {Sch. 36 para. 85. (2)}; S.I. 2004/3033, art. 3. (1)(2)(d)
F10. Words in s. 74. (2) inserted (15.8.2010) by Coroners and Justice Act 2009 (c. 25), ss. 144, 182, Sch. 17 para. 14. (3) (with s. 180, Sch. 22); S.I. 2010/1858, art. 3. (a)(d)(vii)
F11. Words in s. 74. (3) repealed (15.12.2004) by Criminal Justice Act 2003 (c. 44), ss. 331, 332, 336, Sch. 36 para. 85. (3), Sch. 37 Pt. 5; S.I. 2004/3033, art. 3. (1)(2)(d)(e)(i)
F12. Words in s. 74. (3)(a) inserted (15.8.2010) by Coroners and Justice Act 2009 (c. 25), ss. 144, 182, Sch. 17 para. 14. (4) (with s. 180, Sch. 22); S.I. 2010/1858, art. 3. (a)(d)(vii)
Modifications etc. (not altering text)
C2. S. 74 modified (2.10.2000) by S.I. 2000/2370, rule 27. (2), Sch. 3 Pt. III para. 18. (b)
S. 74 modified (2.10.2000) by S.I. 2000/2371, rule 27. (2), Sch. 3 Pt. III para. 18. (b)
S. 74 modified (2.10.2000) by S.I. 2000/2372, rule 27. (2), Sch. 3 Pt. III para. 18. (b)

75 Provisions supplementary to section 74.

(1) Where evidence that a person has been convicted of an offence is admissible by virtue of section 74 above, then without prejudice to the reception of any other admissible evidence for the purpose of identifying the facts on which the conviction was based—
   (a) the contents of any document which is admissible as evidence of the conviction; and
   [F13. (b)the contents of—
(i) the information, complaint, indictment or charge-sheet on which the person in question was convicted, or
(ii) in the case of a conviction of an offence by a court in a member State (other than the United Kingdom), any document produced in relation to the proceedings for that offence which fulfils a purpose similar to any document or documents specified in sub-paragraph (i),]
shall be admissible in evidence for that purpose.
(2) Where in any proceedings the contents of any document are admissible in evidence by virtue of subsection (1) above, a copy of that document, or of the material part of it, purporting to be

certified or otherwise authenticated by or on behalf of the court or authority having custody of that document shall be admissible in evidence and shall be taken to be a true copy of that document or part unless the contrary is shown.

(3) Nothing in any of the following—

(a) [F14. Section 14 of the Powers of Criminal Courts (Sentencing) Act 2000](under which a conviction leading to probation or discharge is to be disregarded except as mentioned in that section);

[F15. (aa)section 187 of the Armed Forces Act 2006 (which makes similar provision in respect of service convictions);]

(b) [F16section 247 of the Criminal Procedure (Scotland) Act 1995] (which makes similar provision in respect of convictions on indictment in Scotland); and

(c) section 8 of the Probation Act (Northern Ireland) 1950 (which corresponds to section 13 of the Powers of Criminal Courts Act 1973) or any legislation which is in force in Northern Ireland for the time being and corresponds to that section,

shall affect the operation of section 74 above; and for the purposes of that section any order made by a court of summary jurisdiction in Scotland under section 182 or section 183 of the said Act of 1975 shall be treated as a conviction.

(4) Nothing in section 74 above shall be construed as rendering admissible in any proceedings evidence of any conviction other than a subsisting one.

Extent Information

E2. S. 75 extends to England and Wales only with exceptions as regards courts martial, see s. 120. (1)(6)-(8)

Amendments (Textual)

F13. S. 75. (1)(b) substituted (15.8.2010) by Coroners and Justice Act 2009 (c. 25), ss. 144, 182, Sch. 17 para. 15 (with s. 180, Sch. 22); S.I. 2010/1858, art. 3. (a)(d)(vii)

F14. Words in s. 75. (3)(a) substituted (25.8.2000) by 2000 c. 6, ss. 165, 168. (1), Sch. 9 para. 98

F15. S. 75. (3)(aa) inserted (28.3.2009 for certain purposes and otherwise 31.10.2009) by Armed Forces Act 2006 (c. 52), ss. 378, 383, Sch. 16 para. 103; S.I. 2009/812, art. 3 (with transitional provisions in S.I. 2009/1059); S.I. 2009/1167, art. 4

F16. Words in s. 75. (3)(b) substituted (1.4.1996) by 1995 c. 40, ss. 5, 7. (2), Sch. 4 para. 55. (a)

Confessions

76 Confessions.

(1) In any proceedings a confession made by an accused person may be given in evidence against him in so far as it is relevant to any matter in issue in the proceedings and is not excluded by the court in pursuance of this section.

(2) If, in any proceedings where the prosecution proposes to give in evidence a confession made by an accused person, it is represented to the court that the confession was or may have been obtained—

(a) by oppression of the person who made it; or

(b) in consequence of anything said or done which was likely, in the circumstances existing at the time, to render unreliable any confession which might be made by him in consequence thereof, the court shall not allow the confession to be given in evidence against him except in so far as the prosecution proves to the court beyond reasonable doubt that the confession (notwithstanding that it may be true) was not obtained as aforesaid.

(3) In any proceedings where the prosecution proposes to give in evidence a confession made by an accused person, the court may of its own motion require the prosecution, as a condition of allowing it to do so, to prove that the confession was not obtained as mentioned in subsection (2) above.

(4) The fact that a confession is wholly or partly excluded in pursuance of this section shall not affect the admissibility in evidence—

(a) of any facts discovered as a result of the confession; or

(b) where the confession is relevant as showing that the accused speaks, writes or expresses himself in a particular way, of so much of the confession as is necessary to show that he does so.

(5) Evidence that a fact to which this subsection applies was discovered as a result of a statement made by an accused person shall not be admissible unless evidence of how it was discovered is given by him or on his behalf.

(6) Subsection (5) above applies—

(a) to any fact discovered as a result of a confession which is wholly excluded in pursuance of this section; and

(b) to any fact discovered as a result of a confession which is partly so excluded, if the fact is discovered as a result of the excluded part of the confession.

(7) Nothing in Part VII of this Act shall prejudice the admissibility of a confession made by an accused person.

(8) In this section "oppression" includes torture, inhuman or degrading treatment, and the use or threat of violence (whether or not amounting to torture).

F17. (9). . . . .

Extent Information

E3. S. 76 extends to England and Wales only with exceptions as regards courts martial, see s. 120. (1)(6)-(8)

Amendments (Textual)

F17. S. 76. (9) repealed (18.6.2012 for specified purposes, 5.11.2012 for specified purposes, 28.5.2013 for specified purposes) by Criminal Justice Act 2003 (c. 44), s. 336. (3)(4), Sch. 3 para. 56. (4), Sch. 37 Pt. 4; S.I. 2012/1320, art. 4. (1)(c)(d)(2)(3) (with art. 5) (see S.I. 2012/2574, art. 4. (2) and S.I. 2013/1103, art. 4); S.I. 2012/2574, art. 2. (2)(3)(c)(d), Sch. (with arts. 3 4) (as amended (4.11.2012) by S.I. 2012/2761, art. 2) (with S.I. 2013/1103, art. 4); S.I. 2013/1103, art. 2. (1)(c)(d)(2)(3) (with arts. 3 4)

Modifications etc. (not altering text)

C3. S. 76 modified (2.10.2000) by S.I. 2000/2370, rule 27. (2), Sch. 3 Pt. III para. 18. (c)

S. 76 modified (2.10.2000) by S.I. 2000/2371, rule 27. (2), Sch. 3 Pt. III para. 18. (c)

S. 76 modified (2.10.2000) by S.I. 2000/2370, rule 27. (2), Sch. 3 Pt. III para. 18. (c)

[F1876. AConfessions may be given in evidence for co-accused

(1) In any proceedings a confession made by an accused person may be given in evidence for another person charged in the same proceedings (a co-accused) in so far as it is relevant to any matter in issue in the proceedings and is not excluded by the court in pursuance of this section.

(2) If, in any proceedings where a co-accused proposes to give in evidence a confession made by an accused person, it is represented to the court that the confession was or may have been obtained—

(a) by oppression of the person who made it; or

(b) in consequence of anything said or done which was likely, in the circumstances existing at the time, to render unreliable any confession which might be made by him in consequence thereof, the court shall not allow the confession to be given in evidence for the co-accused except in so far as it is proved to the court on the balance of probabilities that the confession (notwithstanding that it may be true) was not so obtained.

(3) Before allowing a confession made by an accused person to be given in evidence for a co-accused in any proceedings, the court may of its own motion require the fact that the confession was not obtained as mentioned in subsection (2) above to be proved in the proceedings on the balance of probabilities.

(4) The fact that a confession is wholly or partly excluded in pursuance of this section shall not

affect the admissibility in evidence—

(a) of any facts discovered as a result of the confession; or

(b) where the confession is relevant as showing that the accused speaks, writes or expresses himself in a particular way, of so much of the confession as is necessary to show that he does so.

(5) Evidence that a fact to which this subsection applies was discovered as a result of a statement made by an accused person shall not be admissible unless evidence of how it was discovered is given by him or on his behalf.

(6) Subsection (5) above applies—

(a) to any fact discovered as a result of a confession which is wholly excluded in pursuance of this section; and

(b) to any fact discovered as a result of a confession which is partly so excluded, if the fact is discovered as a result of the excluded part of the confession.

(7) In this section "oppression" includes torture, inhuman or degrading treatment, and the use or threat of violence (whether or not amounting to torture).]

Amendments (Textual)

F18. S. 76. A inserted (4.4.2005) by Criminal Justice Act 2003 (c. 44), ss. 128. (1), 336; S.I. 2005/950, art. 2. (1), Sch. 1 para. 6 (subject to art. 2. (2), Sch. 2) (as amended by S.I. 2005/2122, art. 2)

77 Confessions by mentally handicapped persons.

(1) Without prejudice to the general duty of the court at a trial on indictment [F19with a jury] to direct the jury on any matter on which it appears to the court appropriate to do so, where at such a trial—

(a) the case against the accused depends wholly or substantially on a confession by him; and

(b) the court is satisfied—

(i) that he is mentally handicapped; and

(ii) that the confession was not made in the presence of an independent person,

the court shall warn the jury that there is special need for caution before convicting the accused in reliance on the confession, and shall explain that the need arises because of the circumstances mentioned in paragraphs (a) and (b) above.

(2) In any case where at the summary trial of a person for an offence it appears to the court that a warning under subsection (1) above would be required if the trial were on indictment [F20with a jury] , the court shall treat the case as one in which there is a special need for caution before convicting the accused on his confession.

[F21. (2. A)In any case where at the trial on indictment without a jury of a person for an offence it appears to the court that a warning under subsection (1) above would be required if the trial were with a jury, the court shall treat the case as one in which there is a special need for caution before convicting the accused on his confession.]

(3) In this section—

"independent person" does not include a police officer or a person employed for, or engaged on, police purposes;

"mentally handicapped", in relation to a person, means that he is in a state of arrested or incomplete development of mind which includes significant impairment of intelligence and social functioning; and

"police purposes" has the meaning assigned to it by [F22section 101. (2) of the M1. Police Act 1996].

Extent Information

E4. S. 77 extends to England and Wales only with exceptions as regards courts martial, see s. 120. (1)(6)-(8)

Amendments (Textual)

F19. Words in s. 77. (1) inserted (24.7.2006 for E.W. and 8.1.2007 for N.I.) by Criminal Justice

Act 2003 (c. 44), ss. 331, 336, Sch. 36 Pt. 4 para. 48. (2); S.I. 2006/1835, art. 2. (g)(h) (subject to art. 3); S.I. 2006/3422, art. 2. (c)(i)

F20. Words in s. 77. (2) inserted (24.7.2006 for E.W. and 8.1.2007 for N.I.) by Criminal Justice Act 2003 (c. 44), ss. 331, 336, Sch. 36 Pt. 4 para. 48. (3); S.I. 2006/1835, art. 2. (g)(h) (subject to art. 3); S.I. 2006/3422, art. 2. (c)(i)

F21. S. 77. (2. A) inserted (24.7.2006 for E.W. and 8.1.2007 for N.I.) by Criminal Justice Act 2003 (c. 44), ss. 331, 336, Sch. 36 Pt. 4 para. 48. (4); S.I. 2006/1835, art. 2. (g)(h) (subject to art. 3); S.I. 2006/3422, art. 2. (c)(i)

F22. Words in the definition of "police purposes" in s. 77. (3) substituted (22.8.1996) by 1996 c. 16, ss. 103. (1), 104. (2), Sch. 7 Pt. II para.38

Modifications etc. (not altering text)

C4. S. 77 excluded (2.10.2000) by S.I. 2000/2370, rule 27. (2), Sch. 3 Pt. III para. 18. (d)

S. 77 excluded (2.10.2000) by S.I. 2000/2371, rule 27. (2), Sch. 3 Pt. III para. 18. (d)

S. 77 excluded (2.10.2000) by S.I. 2000/2372, rule 27. (2), Sch. 3 Pt. III para. 18. (d)

C5. S. 77 applied (with modifications) (4.11.2015) by The Police and Criminal Evidence Act 1984 (Application to Revenue and Customs) Order 2015 (S.I. 2015/1783), arts. 1, 3. (1), Sch. 1 (with art. 3. (2), (3), 4-19, Sch. 2)

C6. S. 77 applied (with modifications) (30.4.2017) by The Police and Criminal Evidence Act 1984 (Application to Labour Abuse Prevention Officers) Regulations 2017 (S.I. 2017/520), regs. 1, 2, 3. (u), Sch.

Marginal Citations

M11996 c. 16

Miscellaneous

78 Exclusion of unfair evidence.

(1) In any proceedings the court may refuse to allow evidence on which the prosecution proposes to rely to be given if it appears to the court that, having regard to all the circumstances, including the circumstances in which the evidence was obtained, the admission of the evidence would have such an adverse effect on the fairness of the proceedings that the court ought not to admit it.

(2) Nothing in this section shall prejudice any rule of law requiring a court to exclude evidence.

F23. (3). . . . .

Extent Information

E5. S. 78 extends to England and Wales only with exceptions as regards courts martial, see s. 120. (1)(6)-(8)

Amendments (Textual)

F23. S. 78. (3) repealed (18.6.2012 for specified purposes, 5.11.2012 for specified purposes, 28.5.2013 for specified purposes) by Criminal Justice Act 2003 (c. 44), s. 336. (3)(4), Sch. 3 para. 56. (5), Sch. 37 Pt. 4; S.I. 2012/1320, art. 4. (1)(c)(d)(2)(3) (with art. 5) (see S.I. 2012/2574, art. 4. (2) and S.I. 2013/1103, art. 4); S.I. 2012/2574, art. 2. (2)(3)(c)(d), Sch. (with arts. 3 4) (as amended (4.11.2012) by S.I. 2012/2761, art. 2) (with S.I. 2013/1103, art. 4); S.I. 2013/1103, art. 2. (1)(c)(d)(2)(3) (with arts. 3 4)

Modifications etc. (not altering text)

C7. S. 78. (1) modified (2.10.2000) by S.I. 2000/2370, rule 27. (2), Sch. 3 Pt. III para. 18. (c)

S. 78. (1) modified (2.10.2000) by S.I. 2000/2371, rule 27. (2), Sch. 3 Pt. III para. 18. (c)

S. 78. (1) modified (2.10.2000) by S.I. 2000/2372, rule 27. (2), Sch. 3 Pt. III para. 18. (c)

79 Time for taking accused's evidence.

If at the trial of any person for an offence—
    (a) the defence intends to call two or more witnesses to the facts of the case; and
    (b) those witnesses include the accused,
the accused shall be called before the other witness or witnesses unless the court in its discretion otherwise directs.
Modifications etc. (not altering text)
C8. S. 79 modified (2.10.2000) by S.I. 2000/2370, rule 27. (2), Sch. 3 Pt. III para. 18. (e)
S. 79 modified (2.10.2000) by S.I. 2000/2371, rule 27. (2), Sch. 3 Pt. III para. 18. (e)
S. 79 modified (2.10.2000) by S.I. 2000/2372, rule 27. (2), Sch. 3 Pt. III para. 18. (e)

80[F24. Competence and] compellability of accused's spouse [F25or civil partner].

F26[(1)In any proceedings the wife or husband of the accused shall be competent to give evidence—
    (a) subject to subsection (4) below, for the prosecution; and
    (b) on behalf of the accused or any person jointly charged with the accused.]
[F27. (2)In any proceedings the [F28spouse or civil partner] of a person charged in the proceedings shall, subject to subsection (4) below, be compellable to give evidence on behalf of that person.
(2. A)In any proceedings the [F28spouse or civil partner] of a person charged in the proceedings shall, subject to subsection (4) below, be compellable—
    (a) to give evidence on behalf of any other person charged in the proceedings but only in respect of any specified offence with which that other person is charged; or
    (b) to give evidence for the prosecution but only in respect of any specified offence with which any person is charged in the proceedings.
(3) In relation to the [F28spouse or civil partner] of a person charged in any proceedings, an offence is a specified offence for the purposes of subsection (2. A) above if—
    (a) it involves an assault on, or injury or a threat of injury to, the [F28spouse or civil partner] or a person who was at the material time under the age of 16;
    (b) it is a sexual offence alleged to have been committed in respect of a person who was at the material time under that age; or
    (c) it consists of attempting or conspiring to commit, or of aiding, abetting, counselling, procuring or inciting the commission of, an offence falling within paragraph (a) or (b) above.
(4) No person who is charged in any proceedings shall be compellable by virtue of subsection (2) or (2. A) above to give evidence in the proceedings.
(4. A)References in this section to a person charged in any proceedings do not include a person who is not, or is no longer, liable to be convicted of any offence in the proceedings (whether as a result of pleading guilty or for any other reason).]
(5) In any proceedings a person who has been but is no longer married to the accused shall be [F29competent and] compellable to give evidence as if that person and the accused had never been married.
[F30. (5. A)In any proceedings a person who has been but is no longer the civil partner of the accused shall be compellable to give evidence as if that person and the accused had never been civil partners.]
(6) Where in any proceedings the age of any person at any time is material for the purposes of subsection (3) above, his age at the material time shall for the purposes of that provision be deemed to be or to have been that which appears to the court to be or to have been his age at that time.
(7) In subsection (3)(b) above "sexual offence" means an offence under [F31the Sexual Offences Act 1956, the M2. Indecency with Children Act M31960, the Sexual Offences Act 1967, section 54 of the M4. Criminal Law Act M51977 or] the M6. Protection of Children Act 1978 [F32or Part

1 of the Sexual Offences Act 2003] [F33, or an offence under section 2 of the Modern Slavery Act 2015 (human trafficking) committed with a view to exploitation that consists of or includes behaviour within section 3. (3) of that Act (sexual exploitation).] .

[F26. (8)The failure of the wife or husband of the accused to give evidence shall not be made the subject of any comment by the prosecution.]

(9) Section 1. (d) of the Criminal Evidence Act 1898 (communications between husband and wife) and section 43. (1) of the M7. Matrimonial Causes Act M81965 (evidence as to marital intercourse) shall cease to have effect.

Extent Information

E6. S. 80 extends to England and Wales only with exceptions as regards courts martial, see s. 120. (1)(6)-(8)

Amendments (Textual)

F24. S. 80: words in side-note omitted (24.7.2002 for E.W.) by virtue of 1999 c. 23, ss. 67. (1), 68. (3), Sch. 4 para. 13. (4) (with Sch. 7 paras. 3. (3), 5. (2)); S.I. 2002/1739, art. 2. (f)

F25. S. 80: words in heading inserted (5.12.2005) by Civil Partnership Act 2004 (c. 33), ss. 261. (1), 263, Sch. 27 para. 97. (4); S.I. 2005/3175, art. 2. (2)

F26. S. 80. (1)(8) repealed (24.7.2002 for E.W.) by 1999 c. 23, ss. 67. (1)(3), 68. (3), Sch. 4 para. 13. (2), Sch. 6 (with Sch. 7 paras. 3. (3), 5. (2)); S.I. 2002/1739. {art. 2. (f)(g)(ii)}

F27. S. 80. (2)-(4. A) substituted for s. 80. (2)-(4) (24.7.2002 for E.W.) by 1999 c. 23, ss. 67. (1), 68. (3), Sch. 4 para. 13. (3) (with Sch. 7 paras. 3. (3), 5. (2)); S.I. 2002/1739, art. 2. (f)

F28. Words in s. 80. (2)(2. A)(3) substituted (5.12.2005) by Civil Partnership Act 2004 (c. 33), ss. 261. (1), 263, Sch. 27 para. 97. (2); S.I. 2005/3175, art. 2. (2)

F29. Words in s. 80. (5) repealed (24.7.2002 for E.W.) by 1999 c. 23, ss. 67. (1)(3), 68. (3), Sch. 4 para. 13. (4), Sch. 6 (with Sch. 7 paras. 3. (3), 5. (2)); S.I. 2002/1739, art. 2. (f)(g)(ii)

F30. S. 80. (5. A) inserted (5.12.2005) by Civil Partnership Act 2004 (c. 33), ss. 261. (1), 263 {Sch. 27 para. 97. (3)}; S.I. 2005/3175, art. 2. (2)

F31. Words in s. 80. (7) repealed (E.W.) (1.5.2004) by Sexual Offences Act 2003 (c. 42), ss. 140, 141, Sch. 7; S.I. 2004/874, art. 2

F32. Words in s. 80. (7) inserted (E.W.) (1.5.2004) by Sexual Offences Act 2003 (c. 42), ss. 139, 141, Sch. 6 para. 28. (2); S.I. 2004/874, art. 2

F33. Words in s. 80. (7) inserted (17.3.2016) by The Modern Slavery Act 2015 (Consequential Amendments) Regulations 2016 (S.I. 2016/244), regs. 1. (1), 5

Modifications etc. (not altering text)

C9. S. 80 modified (2.10.2000) by S.I. 2000/2370, rule 27. (2), Sch. 3 Pt. III para. 18. (f)

S. 80 modified (2.10.2000) by S.I. 2000/2371, rule 27. (2), Sch. 3 Pt. III para. 18. (f)

S. 80 modified (2.10.2000) by S.I. 2000/2372, rule 27. (2), Sch. 3 Pt. III para. 18. (f)

C10. S. 80. (3)(c) modified (1.10.2008) by Serious Crime Act 2007 (c. 27), ss. 63. (1), 91. (1), 94, Sch. 6 para. 9 (with Sch. 13 para. 5); S.I. 2008/2504, art. 2. (a)

Marginal Citations

M21960 c. 33.

M31967 c. 60.

M41977 c. 45.

M51978 c. 37.

M61978 c. 37.

M71965 c. 72.

M81965 c. 72.

[80. AF34. Rule where accused's spouse [F35or civil partner] not compellable.

The failure of the [F36spouse or civil partner] of a person charged in any proceedings to give evidence in the proceedings shall not be made the subject of any comment by the prosecution.]

E7. S. 80. A extends to England and Wales only with exceptions as regards courts martial, see s. 120. (1)(6)-(8)

Amendments (Textual)

F34. S. 80. A inserted (24.7.2002 for E.W.) by 1999 c. 23, s. 67. (1), Sch. 4 para. 14 (with Sch. 7 paras. 3. (3), 5. (2)); S.I. 2002/1739, art. 2. (f)

F35. S. 80. A: words in heading inserted (5.12.2005) by Civil Partnership Act 2004 (c. 33), ss. 261. (1), 263, Sch. 27 para. 98. (b); S.I. 2005/3175, art. 2. (2)

F36. Words in s. 80. A substituted (5.12.2005) by Civil Partnership Act 2004 (c. 33), ss. 261. (1), 263, Sch. 27 para. 98. (a); S.I. 2005/3175, art. 2. (2)

81 Advance notice of expert evidence in Crown Court.

(1) [F37. Criminal Procedure Rules] may make provision for—

(a) requiring any party to proceedings before the court to disclose to the other party or parties any expert evidence which he proposes to adduce in the proceedings; and

(b) prohibiting a party who fails to comply in respect of any evidence with any requirement imposed by virtue of paragraph (a) above from adducing that evidence without the leave of the court.

(2) [F37. Criminal Procedure Rules] made by virtue of this section may specify the kinds of expert evidence to which they apply and may exempt facts or matters of any description specified in the rules.

Amendments (Textual)

F37. Words in s. 81. (1)(2) substituted (1.9.2004) by Courts Act 2003 (c. 39), ss. 109. (1), 110, Sch. 8 para. 286; S.I. 2004/2066, art. 2. (c)(xii) (subject to art. 3)

Modifications etc. (not altering text)

C11. S. 81 excluded (2.10.2000) by S.I. 2000/2370, rule 27. (2), Sch. 3 Pt. III para. 18. (g)

S. 81 excluded (2.10.2000) by S.I. 2000/2371, rule, 27. (2), Sch. 3 Pt. III para. 18. (g)

S. 81 excluded (2.10.2000) by S.I. 2000/2372 rule, 27. (2), Sch. 3 Pt. III para. 18. (g)

Part VIII—supplementary

Modifications etc. (not altering text)

C12. Pt. VIII modified (2.10.2000) by S.I. 2000/2370, rule 27. (2), Sch. 3 Pt. III para. 18. (a)

Pt. VIII modified (2.10.2000) by S.I. 2000/2371 rule, 27. (2), Sch. 3 Pt. III para. 18. (a)

82 Part VIII— interpretation.

(1) In this Part of this Act—

"confession", includes any statement wholly or partly adverse to the person who made it, whether made to a person in authority or not and whether made in words or otherwise;

F38. . . . .

"proceedings" means criminal proceedings, including [F39service proceedings;]

"Service court" means [F40the Court Martial or the Service Civilian Court].

[F41. (1. A)In subsection (1) "service proceedings" means proceedings before a court (other than a civilian court) in respect of a service offence; and "service offence" and "civilian court" here have the same meanings as in the Armed Forces Act 2006.]

(2) F42. . . . .

(3) Nothing in this Part of this Act shall prejudice any power of a court to exclude evidence (whether by preventing questions from being put or otherwise) at its discretion.

Extent Information

E8. S. 82 extends to England and Wales only with exceptions as regards courts martial, see s. 120. (1)(6)-(8)

Amendments (Textual)

F38. S. 82. (1): definition of "court-martial" repealed (28.3.2009 for certain purposes and otherwise prosp.) by Armed Forces Act 2006 (c. 52), ss. 378, 383, Sch. 16 para. 104. (2)(a), Sch. 17; S.I. 2009/812, art. 3 (with transitional provisions in S.I. 2009/1059)

F39. S. 82. (1): words in definition of "Proceedings" substituted (28.3.2009 for certain purposes and otherwise 31.10.2009) for "paragraphs (a) to (c)" by virtue of Armed Forces Act 2006 (c. 52), ss. 378, 383 {Sch. 16 para. 104. (2)(b)}; S.I. 2009/812, art. 3 (with transitional provisions in S.I. 2009/1059); S.I. 2009/1167, art. 4

F40. S. 82. (1): words in definition of "Service Court" substituted (28.3.2009 for certain purposes and otherwise 31.10.2009) by Armed Forces Act 2006 (c. 52), ss. 378, 383 {Sch. 16 para. 104. (2)(c)}; S.I. 2009/812, art. 3 (with transitional provisions in S.I. 2009/1059); S.I. 2009/1167, art. 4

F41. S. 82. (1. A) inserted (28.3.2009 for certain purposes and otherwise 31.10.2009) by Armed Forces Act 2006 (c. 52), ss. 378, 383, Sch. 16 para. 104. (3); S.I. 2009/812, art. 3 (with transitional provisions in S.I. 2009/1059); S.I. 2009/1167, art. 4

F42. S. 82. (2) repealed (28.3.2009 for certain purposes and otherwise prosp.) by Armed Forces Act 2006 (c. 52), ss. 378, 383, Sch. 16 para. 104. (4), Sch. 17; S.I. 2009/812, art. 3 (with transitional provisions in S.I. 2009/1059)

Modifications etc. (not altering text)

C13. S. 82 applied (with modifications) (30.4.2017) by The Police and Criminal Evidence Act 1984 (Application to Labour Abuse Prevention Officers) Regulations 2017 (S.I. 2017/520), regs. 1, 2, 3. (v), Sch.

C14. S. 82. (1) modified (24.4.2009 for certain purposes and 31.10.2009 otherwise) by The Armed Forces Act 2006 (Transitional Provisions etc) Order 2009 (S.I. 2009/1059), arts. 1. (3), 205, Sch. 1 para. 28. (1)

Part VIII—supplementary

Modifications etc. (not altering text)

C1. Pt. VIII modified (2.10.2000) by S.I. 2000/2370, rule 27. (2), Sch. 3 Pt. III para. 18. (a)
Pt. VIII modified (2.10.2000) by S.I. 2000/2371 rule, 27. (2), Sch. 3 Pt. III para. 18. (a)

82 Part VIII— interpretation.

(1) In this Part of this Act—

"confession", includes any statement wholly or partly adverse to the person who made it, whether made to a person in authority or not and whether made in words or otherwise;

F1. . . . .

"proceedings" means criminal proceedings, including [F2service proceedings;]

"Service court" means [F3the Court Martial or the Service Civilian Court].

[F4. (1. A)In subsection (1) "service proceedings" means proceedings before a court (other than a civilian court) in respect of a service offence; and "service offence" and "civilian court" here have the same meanings as in the Armed Forces Act 2006.]

(2) F5. . . . .

(3) Nothing in this Part of this Act shall prejudice any power of a court to exclude evidence (whether by preventing questions from being put or otherwise) at its discretion.

Extent Information

E1. S. 82 extends to England and Wales only with exceptions as regards courts martial, see s. 120. (1)(6)-(8)

Amendments (Textual)

Part VIII— interpretation.

82 Part VIII— interpretation.

(1) In this Part of this Act—

"confession", includes any statement wholly or partly adverse to the person who made it, whether made to a person in authority or not and whether made in words or otherwise;

F1. . . . .

"proceedings" means criminal proceedings, including [F2service proceedings;]

"Service court" means [F3the Court Martial or the Service Civilian Court].

[F4. (1. A)In subsection (1) "service proceedings" means proceedings before a court (other than a civilian court) in respect of a service offence; and "service offence" and "civilian court" here have the same meanings as in the Armed Forces Act 2006.]

(2) F5. . . . .

(3) Nothing in this Part of this Act shall prejudice any power of a court to exclude evidence (whether by preventing questions from being put or otherwise) at its discretion.

Extent Information

E1. S. 82 extends to England and Wales only with exceptions as regards courts martial, see s. 120. (1)(6)-(8)

2009/1059); S.I. 2009/1167, art. 4

F3. S. 82. (1): words in definition of "Service Court" substituted (28.3.2009 for certain purposes and otherwise 31.10.2009) by Armed Forces Act 2006 (c. 52), ss. 378, 383 {Sch. 16 para. 104. (2)(c)}; S.I. 2009/812, art. 3 (with transitional provisions in S.I. 2009/1059); S.I. 2009/1167, art. 4

F4. S. 82. (1. A) inserted (28.3.2009 for certain purposes and otherwise 31.10.2009) by Armed Forces Act 2006 (c. 52), ss. 378, 383, Sch. 16 para. 104. (3); S.I. 2009/812, art. 3 (with transitional provisions in S.I. 2009/1059); S.I. 2009/1167, art. 4

F5. S. 82. (2) repealed (28.3.2009 for certain purposes and otherwise prosp.) by Armed Forces Act 2006 (c. 52), ss. 378, 383, Sch. 16 para. 104. (4), Sch. 17; S.I. 2009/812, art. 3 (with transitional provisions in S.I. 2009/1059)

Modifications etc. (not altering text)

C1. S. 82 applied (with modifications) (30.4.2017) by The Police and Criminal Evidence Act 1984 (Application to Labour Abuse Prevention Officers) Regulations 2017 (S.I. 2017/520), regs. 1, 2, 3. (v), Sch.

C2. S. 82. (1) modified (24.4.2009 for certain purposes and 31.10.2009 otherwise) by The Armed Forces Act 2006 (Transitional Provisions etc) Order 2009 (S.I. 2009/1059), arts. 1. (3), 205, Sch. 1 para. 28. (1)

Part IX Police Complaints and Discipline

Part IX Police Complaints and Discipline

Modifications etc. (not altering text)
C1. Pt. IX (ss. 83–105) restricted by S.I. 1985/520, reg. 11

F183. . . . .

Amendments (Textual)
F1. S. 83 repealed (1.4.1999) by 1996 c. 16, s. 103. (3), Sch. 9 Pt. II; S.I. 1999/533, art. 2. (a)

Handling of complaints etc.

F284. . . . .

Amendments (Textual)
F2. S. 84 repealed (1.4.1999) by 1996 c. 16, s. 103. (3), Sch. 9 Pt. II; S.I. 1999/533, art. 2. (a)

F385. . . . .

Amendments (Textual)
F3. S. 85 repealed (1.4.1999) by 1996 c. 16, s. 103. (3), Sch. 9 Pt. II; S.I. 1999/533, art. 2. (a)

F486. . . . .

Amendments (Textual)
F4. S. 86 repealed (1.4.1999) by 1996 c. 16, s. 103. (3), Sch. 9 Pt. II; S.I. 1999/533, art. 2. (a)

F587. . . . .

Amendments (Textual)
F5. S. 87 repealed (1.4.1999) by 1996 c. 16, s. 103. (3), Sch. 9 Pt. II; S.I. 1999/533, art. 2. (a)

F688. . . . .

Amendments (Textual)
F6. S. 88 repealed (1.4.1999) by 1996 c. 16, s. 103. (3), Sch. 9 Pt. II; S.I. 1999/533, art. 2. (a)

F789. . . . .

Amendments (Textual)
F7. S. 89 repealed (1.4.1999) by 1996 c. 16, s. 103. (3), Sch. 9 Pt. II; S.I. 1999/533, art. 2. (a)

F890. . . . .

Amendments (Textual)
F8. S. 90 repealed (1.4.1999) by 1996 c. 16, s. 103. (3), Sch. 9 Pt. II; S.I. 1999/533, art. 2. (a)

F991. . . . .

Amendments (Textual)
F9. S. 91 repealed (1.4.1999) by 1996 c. 16, s. 103. (3), Sch. 9 Pt. II; S.I. 1999/533, art. 2. (a)

F1092. . . . .

Amendments (Textual)
F10. S. 92 repealed (1.4.1999) by 1996 c. 16, s. 103. (3), Sch. 9 Pt. II; S.I. 1999/533, art. 2. (a)

F1193. . . . .

Amendments (Textual)
F11. S. 93 repealed (1.4.1999) by 1996 c. 16, s. 103. (3), Sch. 9 Pt. II; S.I. 1999/533, art. 2. (a)

F1294. . . . .

Amendments (Textual)
F12. S. 94 repealed (1.4.1999) by 1996 c. 16, s. 103. (3), Sch. 9 Pt. II; S.I. 1999/533, art. 2. (a)

F1395. . . . .

Amendments (Textual)
F13. S. 95 repealed (1.4.1999) by 1996 c. 16, s. 103. (3), Sch. 9 Pt. II; S.I. 1999/533, art. 2. (a)

F1496. . . . .

Amendments (Textual)
F14. S. 96 repealed (1.4.1999) by 1996 c. 16, s. 103. (3), Sch. 9 Pt. II; S.I. 1999/533, art. 2. (a)

F1597. . . . .

Amendments (Textual)
F15. S. 97 repealed (1.4.1999) by 1996 c. 16, s. 103. (3), Sch. 9 Pt. II; S.I. 1999/533, art. 2. (a)

F1698. . . . .

Amendments (Textual)
F16. S. 98 repealed (1.4.1999) by 1996 c. 16, s. 103. (3), Sch. 9 Pt. II; S.I. 1999/533, art. 2. (a)

F1799. . . . .

Amendments (Textual)
F17. S. 99 repealed (1.4.1999) by 1996 c. 16, s. 103. (3), Sch. 9 Pt. II; S.I. 1999/533, art. 2. (a)

F18100. . . . .

Amendments (Textual)
F18. S. 100 repealed (1.4.1999) by 1996 c. 16, s. 103. (3), Sch. 9 Pt. II; S.I. 1999/533, art. 2. (a)

Amendments of discipline provisions

F19101. . . . .

Amendments (Textual)
F19. S. 101 repealed (1.4.1999) by 1996 c. 16, s. 103. (3), Sch. 9 Pt. II; S.I. 1999/533, art. 2. (a)

F20102. . . . .

Amendments (Textual)
F20. S. 102 repealed (1.4.1999) by 1996 c. 16, s. 103. (3), Sch. 9 Pt. II; S.I. 1999/533, art. 2. (a)

F21103. . . . .

Amendments (Textual)
F21. S. 103 repealed (1.4.1999) by 1996 c. 16, s. 103. (3), Sch. 9 Pt. II; S.I. 1999/533, art. 2. (a)

General

F22104. . . . .

Amendments (Textual)
F22. S. 104 repealed (1.4.1999) by 1996 c. 16, s. 103. (3), Sch. 9 Pt. II; S.I. 1999/533, art. 2. (a)

F23105. . . . .

Amendments (Textual)
F23. S. 105 repealed (1.4.1999) by 1996 c. 16, s. 103. (3), Sch. 9 Pt. II; S.I. 1999/533, art. 2. (a)

Part X Police—General

Part X Police—General

F1106. . . . .

Amendments (Textual)
F1. S. 106 repealed (22.8.1996) by 1996 c. 16, ss. 103. (3), 104. (1), Sch. 9 Pt.I

107 Police officers performing duties of higher rank.

(1) For the purpose of any provision of this Act or any other Act under which a power in respect of the investigation of offences or the treatment of persons in police custody is exercisable only by or with the authority of a police officer of at least the rank of superintendent, an officer of the rank of chief inspector shall be treated as holding the rank of superintendent if

[F2. (a)he has been authorised by an officer holding a rank above the rank of superintendent to exercise the power or, as the case may be, to give his authority for its exercise, or

(b) he is acting during the absence of an officer holding the rank of superintendent who has authorised him, for the duration of that absence, to exercise the power or, as the case may be, to give his authority for its exercise.]

(2) For the purpose of any provision of this Act or any other Act under which such a power is exercisable only by or with the authority of an officer of at least the rank of inspector, an officer of the rank of sergeant shall be treated as holding the rank of inspector if he has been authorised by an officer of at least the rank of [F3superintendent] to exercise the power or, as the case may be, to give his authority for its exercise.

Amendments (Textual)
F2. Words in s. 107. (1) substituted (1.4.1995) by 1994 c. 29, s. 44, Sch. 5 Pt. II para. 35. (2); S.I. 1994/3262, art. 4,Sch.
F3. Word in s. 107. (2) substituted (1.4.1995) by 1994 c. 29, s. 44, Sch. 5 Pt. II para. 35. (3); S.I. 1994/3262, art. 4,Sch.
Modifications etc. (not altering text)
C1. S. 107 applied with modifications by S.I. 1985/1800, arts. 3–11, Schs. 1, 2 (as amended by S.I. 1987/439, art. 3)
C2. S. 107 applied (with modifications) (4.11.2015) by The Police and Criminal Evidence Act 1984 (Application to Revenue and Customs) Order 2015 (S.I. 2015/1783), arts. 1, 3. (1), Sch. 1 (with art. 3. (2), (3), 4-19, Sch. 2)
C3. S. 107. (2) applied (with modifications) (25.6.2013) by The Police and Criminal Evidence Act 1984 (Application to immigration officers and designated customs officials in England and Wales) Order 2013 (S.I. 2013/1542), arts. 1, 12. (2)-(4), Sch. 2 (with arts. 13-31)
C4. S. 107. (2) applied (with modifications) (25.6.2013) by The Police and Criminal Evidence Act 1984 (Application to immigration officers and designated customs officials in England and Wales) Order 2013 (S.I. 2013/1542), arts. 1, 3. (2)-(4), Sch. 1 (with arts. 4-11)

108 Deputy chief constables.

F4. . . . .

Amendments (Textual)

F4. S. 108 repealed (21.7.2008) by Statute Law (Repeals) Act 2008 (c. 12), s. 1. (1), Sch. 1 Pt. 6

F5109. . . . .

Amendments (Textual)

F5. S. 109 repealed (22.8.1996) by 1996 c. 16, ss. 103. (3), 104. (1), Sch. 9 Pt.I

110 Functions of special constables in Scotland.S

F6. . . . .

Amendments (Textual)

F6. S. 110 repealed (21.7.2008) by Statute Law (Repeals) Act 2008 (c. 12), s. 1. (1), Sch. 1 Pt. 6

111 Regulations for Police Forces and Police Cadets—Scotland.S

(1) In section 26 to the M1. Police (Scotland) Act 1967 (regulations as to government and administration of police forces)—

    (a) after subsection (1) there shall be inserted the following subsection—

"(1. A)Regulations under this section may authorise the Secretary of State, the police authority or the chief constable to make provision for any purpose specified in the regulations."; and

    (b) at the end there shall be inserted the following subsection—

"(10)Any statutory instrument made under this section shall be subject to annulment in pursuance of a resolution of either House of Parliament.".

(2) In section 27 of the said Act of 1967 (regulations for police cadets) in subsection (3) for the word "(9)" there shall be substituted the words "(1. A), (9) and (10)".

Marginal Citations

M11967 c. 77.

F7112. . . . . .S+N.I.

Amendments (Textual)

F7. S. 112 repealed (22.8.1996) by 1996 c. 16, ss. 103. (3), 104. (1), Sch. 9 Pt.I

Part XI Miscellaneous and Supplementary

Part XI Miscellaneous and Supplementary

Modifications etc. (not altering text)

C1. Pt. XI incorporated (E.W.S.) (16.5.2008) by The London Gateway Port Harbour Empowerment Order 2008 (S.I. 2008/1261), art. 52

113. Application of Act to Armed Forces.

[F1. (1)The Secretary of State may by order make provision in relation to—

    (a) investigations of service offences,

(b) persons arrested under a power conferred by or under the Armed Forces Act 2006,

(c) persons charged under that Act with service offences,

(d) persons in service custody, or

(e) persons convicted of service offences,

which is equivalent to that made by any provision of Part 5 of this Act (or this Part of this Act so far as relating to that Part), subject to such modifications as the Secretary of State considers appropriate.]

(2) Section 67. (9) above shall not have effect in relation to investigations of [F2service offences].

(3) The Secretary of State shall issue a code of practice, or a number of such codes, for persons other than police officers who are [F3 concerned with—

(a) the exercise of powers conferred by or under Part 3 of the Armed Forces Act 2006; or

(b) investigations of service offences.]

[F4. (3. A)In subsections (4) to (10), "code" means a code of practice under subsection (3).]

(4) F5. Without prejudice to the generality of subsection (3) above, a code . . . may contain provisions, in connection with [F6the powers mentioned in subsection (3)(a) above or the [F7investigations] mentioned in subsection (3)(b) above], as to the following matters—

(a) the [F8audio recording] of interviews;

(b) searches of persons and premises; and

(c) the seizure of things found on searches.

[F9. (5)The Secretary of State may at any time revise the whole or any part of a code.

(6) A code may be made, or revised, so as to—

(a) apply only in relation to one or more specified areas,

(b) have effect only for a specified period,

(c) apply only in relation to specified offences or descriptions of offender.

(7) The Secretary of State must lay a code, or any revision of a code, before Parliament.]

(8) A failure on the part of any person to comply with any provision of a code F10. . . shall not of itself render him liable to any criminal or civil proceedings except those to which this subsection applies.

[F11. (9)Subsection (8) above applies to proceedings in respect of an offence under a provision of Part 1 of the Armed Forces Act 2006 other than section 42 (criminal conduct).]

(10) In all criminal and civil proceedings any F12. . . code shall be admissible in evidence and if any provision of F12. . . a code appears to the court or tribunal conducting the proceedings to be relevant to any question arising in the proceedings it shall be taken into account in determining that question.

(11) F13. . . . .

(12) Parts VII and VIII of this Act have effect for the purposes of [F14 service proceedings] subject to any modifications which the Secretary of State may by order specify.

[F15. (12. A)In this section—

"service offence" has the meaning given by section 50 of the Armed Forces Act 2006;

"criminal proceedings" includes service proceedings;

"service proceedings" means proceedings before a court (other than a civilian court) in respect of a service offence; and

"civilian court" has the meaning given by section 374 of the Armed Forces Act 2006;

and section 376. (1) and (2) of that Act (meaning of "convicted" in relation to summary hearings and the SAC) apply for the purposes of subsection (1)(e) above as they apply for the purposes of that Act.]

(13) An order under this section shall be made by statutory instrument and shall be subject to annulment in pursuance of a resolution of either House of Parliament.

[F16. (14)Section 373. (5) and (6) of the Armed Forces Act 2006 (supplementary provisions) apply in relation to an order under this section as they apply in relation to an order under that Act.]

Amendments (Textual)

F1. S. 113. (1) substituted (28.3.2009 for certain purposes and otherwise 31.10.2009) by Armed Forces Act 2006 (c. 52), ss. 378. (1), 383, Sch. 16 para. 105. (2); S.I. 2009/812, art. 3 (with transitional provisions in S.I. 2009/1059); S.I. 2009/1167, art. 4

F2. Words in s. 113. (2) substituted (28.3.2009 for certain purposes and otherwise 31.10.2009) by Armed Forces Act 2006 (c. 52), ss. 378. (1), 383, Sch. 16 para. 105. (3); S.I. 2009/812, art. 3 (with transitional provisions in S.I. 2009/1059); S.I. 2009/1167, art. 4

F3. Words in s. 113. (3) substituted (28.3.2009 for certain purposes and otherwise 31.10.2009) by Armed Forces Act 2006 (c. 52), ss. 378. (1), 383, Sch. 16 para. 105. (4); S.I. 2009/812, art. 3 (with transitional provisions in S.I. 2009/1059); S.I. 2009/1167, art. 4

F4. S. 113. (3. A) inserted (20.1.2004) by Criminal Justice Act 2003 (c. 44), ss. 11. (3), 336; S.I. 2004/81, art. 2. (1)(2)(a)

F5. Words in s. 113. (4) repealed (20.1.2004) by Criminal Justice Act 2003 (c. 44), ss. 332, 336, Sch. 37 Pt. 1; S.I. 2004/81, art. 2. (1)(2)(g)(i)

F6. Words in s. 113. (4) substituted (30.9.2003) by 2001 c. 19, ss. 13. (1)(4), 39. (2) (with s. 16. (7)); S.I. 2003/2268, art. 2

F7. Word in s. 113. (4) substituted (28.3.2009 for certain purposes and otherwise 31.10.2009) by Armed Forces Act 2006 (c. 52), ss. 378. (1), 383, Sch. 16 para. 105. (5); S.I. 2009/812, art. 3 (with transitional provisions in S.I. 2009/1059); S.I. 2009/1167, art. 4

F8. Words in s. 113. (4)(a) substituted (31.1.2017 for specified purposes, 31.3.2017 in so far as not already in force) by Policing and Crime Act 2017 (c. 3), ss. 76. (3), 183. (5)(e)(6)(a)

F9. S. 113. (5)-(7) substituted (20.1.2004) by Criminal Justice Act 2003 (c. 44), ss. 11. (4), 336; S.I. 2004/81, art. 2. (1)(2)(a)

F10. Words in s. 113. (8) repealed (20.1.2004) by Criminal Justice Act 2003 (c. 44), ss. 332, 336, Sch. 37 Pt. 1; S.I. 2004/81, art. 2. (1)(2)(g)(i)

F11. S. 113. (9) substituted (28.3.2009 for certain purposes and otherwise 31.10.2009) by Armed Forces Act 2006 (c. 52), ss. 378. (1), 383, Sch. 16 para. 105. (6); S.I. 2009/812, art. 3 (with transitional provisions in S.I. 2009/1059); S.I. 2009/1167, art. 4

F12. Word in s. 113. (10) repealed (20.1.2004) by Criminal Justice Act 2003 (c. 44), ss. 332, 336, Sch. 37 Pt. 1; S.I. 2004/81, art. 2. (1)(2)(g)(i)

F13. S. 113. (11) repealed (28.3.2009 for certain purposes and otherwise prosp.) by Armed Forces Act 2006 (c. 52), ss. 378, 383, Sch. 16 para. 105. (7), Sch. 17; S.I. 2009/812, art. 3 (with transitional provisions in S.I. 2009/1059)

F14. Words in s. 113. (12) substituted (28.3.2009 for certain purposes and otherwise 31.10.2009) by Armed Forces Act 2006 (c. 52), ss. 378. (1), 383, Sch. 16 para. 105. (8); S.I. 2009/812, art. 3 (with transitional provisions in S.I. 2009/1059); S.I. 2009/1167, art. 4

F15. S. 113. (12. A) inserted (28.3.2009 for certain purposes and otherwise 31.10.2009) by Armed Forces Act 2006 (c. 52), ss. 378. (1), 383, Sch. 16 para. 105. (9); S.I. 2009/812, art. 3 (with transitional provisions in S.I. 2009/1059); S.I. 2009/1167, art. 4

F16. S. 113. (14) added (28.3.2009 for certain purposes and otherwise 31.10.2009) by Armed Forces Act 2006 (c. 52), ss. 378. (1), 383, Sch. 16 para. 105. (10); S.I. 2009/812, art. 3 (with transitional provisions in S.I. 2009/1059); S.I. 2009/1167, art. 4

Modifications etc. (not altering text)

C2. S. 113. (1) modified (24.4.2009 for certain purposes and 31.10.2009 otherwise) by The Armed Forces Act 2006 (Transitional Provisions etc) Order 2009 (S.I. 2009/1059), arts. 1. (3), 205, Sch. 1 para. 28. (2)

C3. S. 113. (2)(3)(b) modified (24.4.2009 for certain purposes and 31.10.2009 otherwise) by The Armed Forces Act 2006 (Transitional Provisions etc) Order 2009 (S.I. 2009/1059), arts. 1. (3), 205, Sch. 1 para. 28. (3)

C4. S. 113. (12) applied (with modifications) (2.10.2000) by S.I. 2000/2370, rule 27. (1)(e)(2)

S. 113. (12) applied (with modifications) (2.10.2000) by S.I. 2000/2371, rule 27. (1)(d)(2)

S. 113. (12) applied (with modifications) (2.10.2000) by S.I. 2000/2372, rule 27. (1)(d)(2)

114[F17. Application of Act to Revenue and Customs]

(1) "Arrested", "arresting", "arrest" and "to arrest" shall respectively be substituted for "detained", "detaining", "detention" and "to detain" wherever in the customs and excise Acts, as defined in section 1. (1) of the M1. Customs and Excise Management Act 1979, those words are used in relation to persons.

(2) The Treasury may by order direct—

(a) that any provision of this Act which relates to investigations of offences conducted by police officers or to persons detained by the police shall apply, subject to such modifications as the order may specify, to [F18investigations conducted by officers of Revenue and Customs] or to [F19persons detained by officers of Revenue and Customs;] and

(b) that, in relation to [F20investigations of offences conducted by officers of Revenue and Customs]—

(i) this Act shall have effect as if the following [F21sections] were inserted after section 14—

"14. A Exception for [F22. Revenue and Customs].

Material in the possession of a person who acquired or created it in the course of any trade, business, profession or other occupation or for the purpose of any paid or unpaid office [F23and which relates to a matter in relation to which Her Majesty's Revenue and Customs have functions,] is neither excluded material nor special procedure material for the purposes of any enactment such as is mentioned in section 9. (2) above.

[F2414. BRevenue and Customs: restriction on other powers to apply for production of documents

(1) An officer of Revenue and Customs may make an application for the delivery of, or access to, documents under a provision specified in subsection (3) only if the condition in subsection (2) is satisfied.

(2) The condition is that the officer thinks that an application under Schedule 1 would not succeed because the material required does not consist of or include special procedure material.

(3) The provisions are—

(a) section 20. BA of, and Schedule 1. AA to, the Taxes Management Act 1970 (serious tax fraud);

(b) paragraph 11 of Schedule 11 to the Value Added Tax Act 1994 (VAT);

(c) paragraph 4. A of Schedule 7 to the Finance Act 1994 (insurance premium tax);

(d) paragraph 7 of Schedule 5 to the Finance Act 1996 (landfill tax);

(e) paragraph 131 of Schedule 6 to the Finance Act 2000 (climate change levy);

(f) paragraph 8 of Schedule 7 to the Finance Act 2001 (aggregates levy);

(g) Part 6 of Schedule 13 to the Finance Act 2003 (stamp duty land tax)."; and

(ii) section 55 above shall have effect as if it related only to things such as are mentioned in subsection (1)(a) of that section.

[F25. (d)that where an officer of Revenue and Customs searches premises in reliance on a warrant under section 8 of, or paragraph 12 of Schedule 1 to, this Act (as applied by an order under this subsection) the officer shall have the power to search persons found on the premises—

(i) in such cases and circumstances as are specified in the order, and

(ii) subject to any conditions specified in the order; and

(e) that powers and functions conferred by a provision of this Act (as applied by an order under this subsection) may be exercised only by officers of Revenue and Customs acting with the authority (which may be general or specific) of the Commissioners for Her Majesty's Revenue and Customs.]

[F26. (2. A)A certificate of the Commissioners that an officer of Revenue and Customs had authority under subsection (2)(e) to exercise a power or function conferred by a provision of this

Act shall be conclusive evidence of that fact.]

[F27. (3)An order under subsection (2)—

(a) may make provision that applies generally or only in specified cases or circumstances,

(b) may make different provision for different cases or circumstances,

(c) may, in modifying a provision, in particular impose conditions on the exercise of a function, and

(d) shall not be taken to limit a power under section 164 of the Customs and Excise Management Act 1979.]

(4) F28. . . . .

(5) An order under this section shall be made by statutory instrument and shall be subject to annulment in pursuance of a resolution of either House of Parliament.]

Amendments (Textual)

F17. S. 114 heading substituted (8.11.2007) by virtue of Finance Act 2007 (c. 11), ss. 82. (11), 84. (5); S.I. 2007/3166, art. 2

F18. Words in s. 114. (2)(a) substituted (8.11.2007) by Finance Act 2007 (c. 11), ss. 82. (2)(a), 84. (5); S.I. 2007/3166, art. 2

F19. Words in s. 114. (2)(a) substituted (8.11.2007) by Finance Act 2007 (c. 11), ss. 82. (2)(b), 84. (5); S.I. 2007/3166, art. 2

F20. Words in s. 114. (2)(b) substituted (8.11.2007) by Finance Act 2007 (c. 11), ss. 82. (3), 84. (5); S.I. 2007/3166, art. 2

F21. Words in s. 114. (2)(b)(i) substituted (8.11.2007) by Finance Act 2007 (c. 11), ss. 82. (4), 84. (5); S.I. 2007/3166, art. 2

F22. Words in s. 114. (2)(b)(i) substituted (8.11.2007) by Finance Act 2007 (c. 11), ss. 82. (5)(b), 84. (5); S.I. 2007/3166, art. 2

F23. Words in s. 114. (2)(b)(i) substituted (8.11.2007) by Finance Act 2007 (c. 11),), {ss. 82. (5)(a)}, 84. (5); S.I. 2007/3166, art. 2

F24. Words in s. 114. (2)(b)(i) inserted (8.11.2007) by Finance Act 2007 (c. 11), ss. 82. (6), 84. (5); S.I. 2007/3166, art. 2

F25. S. 114. (2)(d)(e) inserted (8.11.2007) by Finance Act 2007 (c. 11), ss. 82. (8), 84. (5); S.I. 2007/3166, art. 2

F26. S. 114. (2. A) inserted (8.11.2007) by Finance Act 2007 (c. 11), ss. 82. (9), 84. (5); S.I. 2007/3166, art. 2

F27. S. 114. (3) substituted (8.11.2007) by Finance Act 2007 (c. 11), ss. 82. (10), 84. (5); S.I. 2007/3166, art. 2

F28. S. 114. (4) repealed (18.4.2005) by Commissioners for Revenue and Customs Act 2005 (c. 11), ss. 50, 52, 53. (1), Sch. 4 para. 31, Sch. 5; S.I. 2005/1126, art. 2. (2)(h)(i)

Modifications etc. (not altering text)

C5. S. 114 excluded (18.4.2005) by Commissioners for Revenue and Customs Act 2005 (c. 11), ss. 16, 53. (1), Sch. 2 Pt. 1 para. 7; S.I. 2005/1126, art. 2. (2)(d)

C6. S. 114. (2) extended (1.4.2003) by 2001 c. 16, ss. 67, 138. (2); S.I. 2003/708, art. 2. (c)

Marginal Citations

M11979 c. 2.

[F29114. ZAApplication of Act to Welsh Revenue Authority

(1) The Welsh Ministers may by regulations—

(a) direct that any provision of this Act which relates to investigations of offences conducted by police officers or to the detention of persons by the police is to apply, subject to such modifications as the regulations may specify, to investigations of offences conducted by the Welsh Revenue Authority ("WRA") or to the detention of persons by WRA in connection with such investigations;

(b) make provision permitting a person exercising a function conferred on WRA by the regulations to use reasonable force in the exercise of such a function;

(c) specify that where premises are searched by WRA in reliance on a warrant under section 8 of, or paragraph 12 of Schedule 1 to, this Act (as applied by regulations under paragraph (a)) persons found on the premises may be searched—

(i) in such cases and circumstances as are specified in the regulations, and

(ii) subject to any conditions specified in the regulations.

(2) Regulations under subsection (1) may—

(a) make provision that applies generally or only in specified cases,

(b) make different provision for different cases or circumstances, and

(c) may, in modifying a provision, in particular impose conditions on the exercise of a function.

(3) The power to make regulations under subsection (1) is exercisable by statutory instrument.

(4) A statutory instrument containing regulations under subsection (1) may not be made unless a draft of the instrument has been laid before, and approved by a resolution of, the National Assembly for Wales.]

Amendments (Textual)

F29. S. 114. ZA inserted (25.1.2018) by Tax Collection and Management (Wales) Act 2016 (anaw 6), ss. 185. (1), 194. (2); S.I. 2018/33, art. 2. (j)

[F30114. A Power to apply Act to officers of the Secretary of State etc.

(1) The Secretary of State may by order direct that—

(a) the provisions of Schedule 1 to this Act so far as they relate to special procedure material, and

(b) the other provisions of this Act so far as they relate to the provisions falling within paragraph (a) above,

shall apply, with such modifications as may be specified in the order, for the purposes of investigations falling within subsection (2) as they apply for the purposes of investigations of offences conducted by police officers.

(2) An investigation falls within this subsection if—

(a) it is conducted by an officer of the department of [F31the Secretary of State for Business, Energy and Industrial Strategy] or by another person acting on that Secretary of State's behalf;

(b) it is conducted by that officer or other person in the discharge of a duty to investigate offences; and

(c) the investigation relates to [F32an indictable offence] or to anything which there are reasonable grounds for suspecting has involved the commission of [F32an indictable offence] .

(3) The investigations for the purposes of which provisions of this Act may be applied with modifications by an order under this section include investigations of offences committed, or suspected of having been committed, before the coming into force of the order or of this section.

(4) An order under this section shall be made by statutory instrument and shall be subject to annulment in pursuance of a resolution of either House of Parliament.]

Amendments (Textual)

F30. S. 114. A inserted (11.7.2001) by 2001 c 16, ss. 85, 138. (4)

F31. Words in s. 114. A(2)(a) substituted (9.11.2016) by The Secretaries of State for Business, Energy and Industrial Strategy, for International Trade and for Exiting the European Union and the Transfer of Functions (Education and Skills) Order 2016 (S.I. 2016/992), art. 1. (2), Sch. para. 4 (with art. 13)

F32. Words in s. 114. A(2)(c) substituted (1.1.2006) by Serious Organised Crime and Police Act 2005 (c. 15), ss. 111, 178, Sch. 7 Pt. 3 para. 43. (11); S.I. 2005/3495, art. 2. (1)(m)

[F33114. BApplication of Act to labour abuse prevention officers

(1) The Secretary of State may by regulations apply any provision of this Act which relates to investigations of offences conducted by police officers to investigations of labour market offences conducted by labour abuse prevention officers.

(2) The regulations may apply provisions of this Act with any modifications specified in the regulations.

(3) In this section "labour abuse prevention officer" means an officer of the Gangmasters and Labour Abuse Authority who—

(a) falls within subsection (4), and

(b) is authorised (whether generally or specifically) by the Secretary of State for the purposes of this section.

(4) An officer of the Gangmasters and Labour Abuse Authority falls within this subsection if he or she is—

(a) acting for the purposes of the Employment Agencies Act 1973 (see section 8. A of that Act),

(b) acting for the purposes of the National Minimum Wage Act 1998 (see section 13 of that Act),

(c) acting for the purposes of the Gangmasters (Licensing) Act 2004 as an enforcement officer within the meaning of section 15 of that Act,

(d) acting for the purposes of Part 1 or 2 of the Modern Slavery Act 2015 (see sections 11. A and 30. A of that Act), or

(e) acting for any other purpose prescribed in regulations made by the Secretary of State.

(5) The investigations for the purposes of which provisions of this Act may be applied by regulations under this section include investigations of offences committed, or suspected of having been committed, before the coming into force of the regulations or of this section.

(6) Regulations under this section are to be made by statutory instrument.

(7) Regulations under this section may make—

(a) different provision for different purposes;

(b) provision which applies generally or for particular purposes;

(c) incidental, supplementary, consequential, transitional or transitory provision or savings.

(8) Regulations under subsection (4)(e) may, in particular, make such provision amending, repealing or revoking any enactment as the Secretary of State considers appropriate in consequence of any provision made by the regulations.

(9) A statutory instrument containing regulations under subsection (4)(e) may not be made unless a draft of the instrument has been laid before, and approved by a resolution of, each House of Parliament.

(10) Any other statutory instrument containing regulations under this section is subject to annulment in pursuance of a resolution of either House of Parliament.

(11) In this section—

"enactment" includes an enactment contained in subordinate legislation within the meaning of the Interpretation Act 1978;

"labour market offence" has the meaning given in section 3 of the Immigration Act 2016.]

Amendments (Textual)

F33. S. 114. B inserted (12.7.2016) by Immigration Act 2016 (c. 19), ss. 12. (1), 94. (1); S.I. 2016/603, reg. 3. (b)

115 Expenses.

Any expenses of a Minister of the Crown incurred in consequence of the provisions of this Act, including any increase attributable to those provisions in sums payable under any other Act, shall be defrayed out of money provided by Parliament.

116 Meaning of "serious arrestable offence".

F34. . . . .

Amendments (Textual)
F34. S. 116 repealed (1.1.2006) by Serious Organised Crime and Police Act 2005 (c. 15), ss. 111, 174, 178, Sch. 7 Pt. 3 para. 43. (12), Sch. 17 Pt. 2; S.I. 2005/3495, art. 2. (1)(m)(t)(u)(xxiv)
Modifications etc. (not altering text)
C7. S. 116 applied (1.11.1999) by 1999 c. 8, s. 24. (10)(a); S.I. 1999/2793, art. 2. (1)(b), Sch. 2

117 Power of constable to use reasonable force.

Where any provision of this Act—
    (a) confers a power on a constable; and
    (b) does not provide that the power may only be exercised with the consent of some person, other than a police officer,
the officer may use reasonable force, if necessary, in the exercise of the power.

Modifications etc. (not altering text)
C8. S. 117 applied (with modifications) (1.1.1986) by S.I. 1985/1882, art. 11;
S. 117 applied (with modifications) (1.2.1997) by S.I. 1997/15, art. 2. (1), Sch.
S. 117 applied (with modifications) (31.12.2006) by The Police and Criminal Evidence Act 1984 (Application to the Armed Forces) Order 2006 (S.I. 2006/2015), arts. 2, 3, Schs. 1-3
C9. S. 117 applied (with modifications) (30.4.2017) by The Police and Criminal Evidence Act 1984 (Application to Labour Abuse Prevention Officers) Regulations 2017 (S.I. 2017/520), regs. 1, 2, 3. (v), Sch.

118 General interpretation.

(1) In this Act—
F35. . . . .
[F36[F37"British Transport Police Force" means the constables appointed under section 53 of the British Transport Commission Act 1949 (c. xxix);]
"designated police station" has the meaning assigned to it by section 35 above;
"document" [F38means anything in which information of any description is recorded.];
F39. . . . .
"item subject to legal privilege" has the meaning assigned to it by section 10 above;
"parent or guardian" means—
    - in the case of a child or young person in the care of a local authority, that authority; F40 . . .
    - F40. . . . .
"premises" has the meaning assigned to it by section 23 above;
"recordable offence" means any offence to which regulations under section 27 above apply;
"vessel" includes any ship, boat, raft or other apparatus constructed or adapted for floating on water.
(2) [F41. Subject to subsection (2. A)] a person is in police detention for the purposes of this Act if—
    [F42. (a)he has been taken to a police station after being arrested for an offence or after being arrested under section 41 of the Terrorism Act 2000, or]
    (b) he is arrested at a police station after attending voluntarily at the station or accompanying a constable to it,
and is detained there or is detained elsewhere in the charge of a constable, except that a person who is at a court after being charged is not in police detention for those purposes.
[F43. (2. A)Where a person is in another's lawful custody by virtue of paragraph F44... 34. (1) or 35. (3) of Schedule 4 to the Police Reform Act 2002, he shall be treated as in police detention.]]
Extent Information

E1. For the extent of this Act see s. 120. (11)

Amendments (Textual)

F35. S. 118. (1): definition of "arrestable offence" repealed (1.1.2006) by Serious Organised Crime and Police Act 2005 (c. 15), ss. 111, 174. (2), 178, Sch. 7 Pt. 1 para. 24. (2), Sch. 17 Pt. 2; S.I. 2005/3495, art. 2. (1)(m)(t)(u)(xxiv)

F36. S. 118. (1): definition of "British Transport Police Force" ceased to have effect (1.7.2004) by virtue of Railways and Transport Safety Act 2003 (c. 20), ss. 73, 120, Sch. 5 para. 4. (1)(b)(2) (with s. 72); S.I. 2004/1572, art. 3. (ddd)(jjj)

F37. Words in s. 118. (1) inserted (14.12.2001) by 2001 c 24, s. 101, Sch. 7 para. 14

F38. Words in definition of "document" in s. 118. (1) substituted (31.1.1997) by 1995 c. 38, s. 15. (1), Sch. 1 para. 9. (3) (with ss. 1. (3), 6. (4)(5), 14); S.I. 1996/3217, art. 2

F39. Definition of "intimate search" in s. 118. (1) repealed (10.4.1995) by 1994 c. 33, s. 168. (3), Sch. 11; S.I. 1995/721, art. 2, Sch. Appendix B

F40. In s. 118, paragraph (b) of definition and the word immediately preceding it repealed (E.W.)(14.10.1991) by Children Act 1989 (c. 41, SIF 20), s. 108. (7), Sch. 15 (with Sch. 14 paras. 1. (1), 27. (4)); S.I. 1991/828, art. 3. (2)

F41. Words in s. 118. (2) inserted (2.12.2002) by Police Reform Act 2002 (c. 30), s. 107, Sch. 7 para. 9. (9); S.I. 2002/2750, art. 2. (b)(ii)

F42. S. 118. (2)(a) substituted (19.2.2001) by 2000 c. 11, s. 125. (1), Sch. 15 para. 5. (12); S.I. 2001/421, art. 2

F43. S. 118. (2. A) inserted (2.12.2002) by Police Reform Act 2002 (c. 30), s. 107, Sch. 7 para. 9. (9); S.I. 2002/2750, art. 2. (b)(ii)

F44. Word in s. 118. (2. A) omitted (22.2.2018) by virtue of The Policing and Crime Act 2017 (Consequential Amendments) Regulations 2018 (S.I. 2018/226), regs. 1, 5. (2)

Modifications etc. (not altering text)

C10. S. 118 applied with modifications by S.I. 1985/1882, arts. 3, 10

C11. S. 118 amended (1.7.2004) by Railways and Transport Safety Act 2003 (c. 20), ss. 73, 120, Sch. 5 para. 4. (1)(a)(2) (with s. 72); S.I. 2004/1572, art. 3. (ddd)(jjj)

C12. S. 118 applied (with modifications) (30.4.2017) by The Police and Criminal Evidence Act 1984 (Application to Labour Abuse Prevention Officers) Regulations 2017 (S.I. 2017/520), regs. 1, 2, 3. (w), Sch.

119 Amendments and repeals.

(1) The enactments mentioned in Schedule 6 to this Act shall have effect with the amendments there specified.

(2) The enactments mentioned in Schedule 7 to this Act (which include enactments already obsolete or unnecessary) are repealed to the extent specified in the third column of that Schedule.

(3) The repeals in Parts II and IV of Schedule 7 to this Act have effect only in relation to criminal proceedings.

120 Extent.

(1) Subject to the following provisions of this section, this Act extends to England and Wales only.

(2) The following extend to Scotland only—

F45. . .

F45. . .

section 111;

section 112. (1); and

section 119. (2), so far as it relates to the provisions of the M2. Pedlars Act 1871 repealed by Part VI of Schedule 7.

(3) The following extend to Northern Ireland only—

section 6. (4); and

section 112. (2).

(4) The following extend to England and Wales and Scotland—

section 6. (1) and (2);

section 7;

F46. . .

F46. . .

F46. . .

section 119. (2), so far as it relates to section 19 of the M3. Pedlars Act 1871.

(5) The following extend to England and Wales, Scotland and Northern Ireland—

section 6. (3);

[F47section 9. (2. A);]

F48. . .

section 114. (1).

[F49. (6)Nothing in subsection (1) affects—

(a) the extent of section 113. (1) to (7) and (12) to (14);

(b) the extent of the relevant provisions so far as they relate to service proceedings.]

(8) In this section "the relevant provisions" means—

[F50. (a)section 67. (11) to (13);]

(c) Parts VII and VIII of this Act, except paragraph 10 of Schedule 3;

[F51. (d)section 113. (8) to (10).]

[F52. (8. A)In this section "service proceedings" means proceedings before a court (other than a civilian court) in respect of a service offence; and "service offence" and "civilian court" here have the same meanings as in the Armed Forces Act 2006."

(8. B)Section 384 of the Armed Forces Act 2006 (Channel Islands, Isle of Man and British overseas territories) applies in relation to the provisions mentioned in subsection (6)(a) and (b) above as it applies in relation to that Act.]

F53. (9. A)Section 119. (1), so far as it relates to any provision amended by Part II of Schedule 6, extends to any place to which that provision extends.

(10) Section 119. (2), so far as it relates—

(a) to any provision contained in—

the M4. Army Act 1955;

the M5. Air Force Act 1955;

the M6. Armed Forces Act 1981; or

the M7. Value Added Tax Act 1983;

(b) to any provision mentioned in Part VI of Schedule 7, other than section 18 of the M8. Pedlars Act 1871,

extends to any place to which that provision extends.

(11) So far as any of the following—

section 115;

in section 118, the definition of "document";

this section;

section 121; and

section 122,

has effect in relation to any other provision of this Act, it extends to any place to which that provision extends.

Amendments (Textual)

F45. Words in s. 120. (2) repealed (21.7.2008) by Statute Law (Repeals) Act 2008 (c. 12), s. 1. (1), Sch. 1 Pt. 6

F46. Words in s. 120. (4) repealed (21.7.2008) by Statute Law (Repeals) Act 2008 (c. 12), s. 1. (1), Sch. 1 Pt. 6

F47. Words in s. 120. (5) inserted (1.8.2001) by 2001 c. 16, s. 86. (2); S.I. 2001/2223, art. 3. (e)

F48. Words in s. 120. (5) repealed (21.7.2008) by Statute Law (Repeals) Act 2008 (c. 12), s. 1. (1), Sch. 1 Pt. 6

F49. S. 120. (6) substituted (28.3.2009 for certain purposes and otherwise 31.10.2009) for s. 120. (6)(7) by Armed Forces Act 2006 (c. 52), ss. 378, 383, Sch. 16 para. 106. (2); S.I. 2009/812, art. 3 (with transitional provisions in S.I. 2009/1059); S.I. 2009/1167, art. 4

F50. S. 120. (8)(a) substituted (28.3.2009 for certain purposes and otherwise 31.10.2009) for s. 120. (8)(a)(b) by Armed Forces Act 2006 (c. 52), ss. 378, 383, Sch. 16 para. 106. (3)(a); S.I. 2009/812, art. 3 (with transitional provisions in S.I. 2009/1059); S.I. 2009/1167, art. 4

F51. S. 120. (8)(d) substituted (28.3.2009 for certain purposes and otherwise 31.10.2009) for s. 120. (8)(d)(e) by Armed Forces Act 2006 (c. 52), ss. 378, 383, Sch. 16 para. 106. (3)(b); S.I. 2009/812, art. 3 (with transitional provisions in S.I. 2009/1059); S.I. 2009/1167, art. 4

F52. S. 120. (8. A)(8. B) substituted (28.3.2009 for certain purposes and otherwise 31.10.2009) for s. 120. (9) by Armed Forces Act 2006 (c. 52), ss. 378, 383, Sch. 16 para. 106. (4); S.I. 2009/812, art. 3 (with transitional provisions in S.I. 2009/1059); S.I. 2009/1167, art. 4

F53. S. 120. (9. A) re-numbered from subsection (9) by Criminal Justice Act 1988 (c. 33, SIF 39:1), s. 170. (1), Sch. 15 para. 101

Marginal Citations

M21871 c. 96.

M31871 c. 96.

M41955 c. 18.

M51955 c. 19.

M61981 c. 55.

M71983 c. 55.

M81871 c. 96.

121 Commencement.

(1) This Act, except section 120 above, this section and section 122 below, shall come into operation on such day as the Secretary of State may by order made by statutory instrument appoint, and different days may be so appointed for different provisions and for different purposes.

(2) Different days may be appointed under this section for the coming into force of section 60 above in different areas.

(3) When an order under this section provides by virtue of subsection (2) above that section 60 above shall come into force in an area specified in the order, the duty imposed on the Secretary of State by that section shall be construed as a duty to make an order under it in relation to interviews in that area.

(4) An order under this section may make such transitional provision as appears to the Secretary of State to be necessary or expedient in connection with the provisions thereby brought into operation.

Subordinate Legislation Made

P1. S. 121 power partly exercised by S.I.1991/2686

S. 121 power partly exercised (8.11.1992); 9.11.1992 appointed for specified provision by S.I. 1992/2802, art.2.

S. 121 power of appointment conferred by s. 121. (1) previously exercised: S.I. 1984/2002, 1985/623, 1934

122 Short title.

This Act may be cited as the Police and Criminal Evidence Act 1984.

Schedules

Schedule 1. Special Procedure

Section 9.

Modifications etc. (not altering text)

C1. Ss. 8, 9, 15, 16, 17. (1)(b)(2) (4), 18-20, 21, 22. (1)-(4), 28, 29, 30. (1)-(4)(a)(5)-(11), 31, 32. (1)-(9), 34. (1)-(5), 35, 36, 37, 39, 40-44, 50, 51. (d), 52, 54, 55, 64. (1)-(4)(5)(6), Sch. 1 applied with modifications by S.I. 1985/1800, arts. 3-11, Schs. 1, 2

C2. Sch. 1 extended (10.6.1991) by Criminal Justice (International Co-operation) Act 1990 (c. 5, SIF 39:1), s. 7. (1); S.I. 1991/1072, art. 2, Sch. Pt. I

Sch. 1 extended (17.5.1996) by S.I. 1996/1296, art. 16. (1).

Sch. 1: power to apply conferred (30.9.2003) by 2001 c. 19, ss. 6. (2), 39. (2) (with s. 16. (7)); S.I. 2003/2268, art. 2

C3. Sch. 1 applied (with modifications) (2.12.2002) by Police Reform Act 2002 (c. 30), s. 38, Sch. 4 para. 17. (a)(b); S.I. 2002/2750, art. 2. (a)(ii)(d)

Sch. 1 applied (with modifications) (14.10.2002) by The Police and Criminal Evidence Act 1984 . (Department of Trade and Industry Investigations) Order 2002 (S.I. 2002/2326), arts. 3, 4

C4. Sch. 1 incorporated (16.5.2008) by The London Gateway Port Harbour Empowerment Order 2008 (S.I. 2008/1261), art. 52

C5. Sch. 1 applied (with modifications) (25.6.2013) by The Police and Criminal Evidence Act 1984 (Application to immigration officers and designated customs officials in England and Wales) Order 2013 (S.I. 2013/1542), arts. 1, 3. (2)-(4), Sch. 1 (with arts. 4-11)

C6. Sch. 1 applied (with modifications) (25.6.2013) by The Police and Criminal Evidence Act 1984 (Application to immigration officers and designated customs officials in England and Wales) Order 2013 (S.I. 2013/1542), arts. 1, 12. (2)-(4), Sch. 2 (with arts. 13-31)

C7. Sch. 1 applied (with modifications) (30.4.2017) by The Police and Criminal Evidence Act 1984 (Application to Labour Abuse Prevention Officers) Regulations 2017 (S.I. 2017/520), regs. 1, 2, 3. (e), Sch.

Making of orders by [F1judge]

Amendments (Textual)

F1. Sch. 1: words in cross-heading substituted (1.4.2005) by Courts Act 2003 (c. 39), ss. 65, 110, Sch. 4 para. 6. (1); S.I. 2005/910, art. 3. (u)

1. If on an application made by a constable a [F2judge] is satisfied that one or other of the sets of access conditions is fulfilled, he may make an order under paragraph 4 below.

Amendments (Textual)

F2. Words in Sch. 1 para. 1 substituted (1.4.2005) by Courts Act 2003 (c. 39), ss. 65, 110, Sch. 4 para. 6. (1); S.I. 2005/910, art. 3. (u)

2. The first set of access conditions is fulfilled if—

(a) there are reasonable grounds for believing—

(i) that [F3an indictable offence] has been committed;

(ii) that there is material which consists of special procedure material or includes special procedure material and does not also include excluded material on premises specified in the application [F4, or on premises occupied or controlled by a person specified in the application (including all such premises on which there are reasonable grounds for believing that there is such material as it is reasonably practicable so to specify);]

(iii) that the material is likely to be of substantial value (whether by itself or together with other material) to the investigation in connection with which the application is made; and

(iv) that the material is likely to be relevant evidence;

(b) other methods of obtaining the material—

(i) have been tried without success; or

(ii) have not been tried because it appeared that they were bound to fail; and

(c) it is in the public interest, having regard—

(i) to the benefit likely to accrue to the investigation if the material is obtained; and

(ii) to the circumstances under which the person in possession of the material holds it,

that the material should be produced or that access to it should be given.

Amendments (Textual)

F3. Words in Sch. 1 para. 2. (a)(i) substituted (1.1.2006) by Serious Organised Crime and Police Act 2005 (c. 15), ss. 111, 178, Sch. 7 Pt. 3 para. 43. (13); S.I. 2005/3495, art. 2. (1)(m)

F4. Words in Sch. 1 para. 2. (a)(ii) added (1.1.2006) by Serious Organised Crime and Police Act 2005 (c. 15), ss. 113. (11), 178; S.I. 2005/3495, art. 2. (1)(n)

3. The second set of access conditions is fulfilled if—

(a) there are reasonable grounds for believing that there is material which consists of or includes excluded material or special procedure material on premises specified in the application [F5, or on premises occupied or controlled by a person specified in the application (including all such premises on which there are reasonable grounds for believing that there is such material as it is reasonably practicable so to specify);]

(b) but for section 9. (2) above a search of [F6such premises] for that material could have been authorised by the issue of a warrant to a constable under an enactment other than this Schedule; and

(c) the issue of such a warrant would have been appropriate.

Amendments (Textual)

F5. Words in Sch. 1 para. 3. (a) added (1.1.2006) by Serious Organised Crime and Police Act 2005 (c. 15), ss. 113. (11), 178; S.I. 2005/3495, art. 2. (1)(n)

F6. Words in Sch. 1 para. 3. (b) substituted (1.1.2006) by Serious Organised Crime and Police Act 2005 (c. 15), ss. 113. (12), 178; S.I. 2005/3495, art. 2. (1)(n)

4. An order under this paragraph is an order that the person who appears to the [F7judge] to be in possession of the material to which the application relates shall—

(a) produce it to a constable for him to take away; or

(b) give a constable access to it,

not later than the end of the period of seven days from the date of the order or the end of such longer period as the order may specify.

Amendments (Textual)

F7. Words in Sch. 1 para. 4 substituted (1.4.2005) by Courts Act 2003 (c. 39), ss. 65, 110, Sch. 4 para. 6. (1); S.I. 2005/910, art. 3. (u)

5. Where the material consists of information [F8stored in any electronic form]—

(a) an order under paragraph 4. (a) above shall have effect as an order to produce the material in a form in which it can be taken away and in which it is visible and legible [F9or from which it can readily be produced in a visible and legible form]; and

(b) an order under paragraph 4. (b) above shall have effect as an order to give a constable access to the material in a form in which it is visible and legible.

Amendments (Textual)

F8. Words in Sch. 1 para. 5 substituted (1.4.2003) by 2001 c. 16, ss. 70, 138. (2), Sch. 2 Pt. 2 para. 14. (a); S.I. 2003/708, art. 2. (k)

F9. Words in Sch. 1 para. 5. (a) inserted (1.4.2003) by 2001 c. 16, ss. 70, 138. (2), Sch. 2 Pt. 2 para. 14. (b); S.I. 2003/708, art. 2. (k)

6. For the purposes of sections 21 and 22 above material produced in pursuance of an order under paragraph 4. (a) above shall be treated as if it were material seized by a constable.

Notices of applications for orders

7. An application for an order under paragraph 4 above [F10 that relates to material that consists of or includes journalistic material] shall be made inter partes.

Amendments (Textual)
F10. Words in Sch. 1 para. 7 inserted (26.5.2015) by Deregulation Act 2015 (c. 20), ss. 82. (3)(a), 115. (7); S.I. 2015/994, art. 6. (o)

8. Notice of an application for [F11 an order under paragraph 4 above that relates to material that consists of or includes journalistic material] may be served on a person either by delivering it to him or by leaving it at his proper address or by sending it by post to him in a registered letter or by the recorded delivery service.

Amendments (Textual)
F11. Words in Sch. 1 para. 8 substituted (26.5.2015) by Deregulation Act 2015 (c. 20), ss. 82. (3)(b), 115. (7); S.I. 2015/994, art. 6. (o)

9[F12 Notice of an application for an order under paragraph 4 above that relates to material that consists of or includes journalistic material] may be served—

(a) on a body corporate, by serving it on the body's secretary or clerk or other similar officer; and

(b) on a partnership, by serving in on one of the partners.

Amendments (Textual)
F12. Words in Sch. 1 para. 9 substituted (26.5.2015) by Deregulation Act 2015 (c. 20), ss. 82. (3)(c), 115. (7); S.I. 2015/994, art. 6. (o)

10. For the purposes of [F13 paragraph 8] , and of section 7 of the M1. Interpretation Act 1978 in its application to [F13 paragraph 8] , the proper address of a person, in the case of secretary or clerk or other similar officer of a body corporate, shall be that of the registered or principal office of that body, in the case of a partner of a firm shall be that of the principal office of the firm, and in any other case shall be the last known address of the person to be served.

Amendments (Textual)
F13. Words in Sch. 1 para. 10 substituted (26.5.2015) by Deregulation Act 2015 (c. 20), ss. 82. (3)(d), 115. (7); S.I. 2015/994, art. 6. (o)
Marginal Citations
M11978 c. 30.

11. Where notice of an application for an order under paragraph 4 above has been served on a person, he shall not conceal, destroy, alter or dispose of the material to which the application relates except—

(a) with the leave of a judge; or

(b) with the written permission of a constable,

until—

(i) the application is dismissed or abandoned; or

(ii) he has complied with an order under paragraph 4 above made on the application.

Issue of warrants by [F14judge]

Amendments (Textual)
F14. Sch.1: words in cross-heading substituted (1.4.2005) by Courts Act 2003 (c. 39), ss. 65, 110, Sch. 4 para. 6. (1); S.I. 2005/910, art. 3. (u)

12. If on an application made by a constable a [F15judge]—

(a) is satisfied—

(i) that either set of access conditions is fulfilled; and

(ii) that any of the further conditions set out in paragraph 14 below is also fulfilled [F16in relation to each set of premises specified in the application] ; or

(b) is satisfied—

(i) that the second set of access conditions is fulfilled; and

(ii) that an order under paragraph 4 above relating to the material has not been complied with, he may issue a warrant authorising a constable to enter and search the premises [F17 or (as the case may be) all premises occupied or controlled by the person referred to in paragraph 2. (a)(ii) or 3. (a), including such sets of premises as are specified in the application (an "all premises warrant")] .

Amendments (Textual)
F15. Words in Sch. 1 para. 12 substituted (1.4.2005) by Courts Act 2003 (c. 39), ss. 65, 110, Sch. 4 para. 6. (1); S.I. 2005/910, art. 3. (u)
F16. Words in Sch. 1 para. 12. (a)(ii) inserted (1.1.2006) by Serious Organised Crime and Police Act 2005 (c. 15), ss. 113. (13)(a), 178; S.I. 2005/3495, art. 2. (1)(n)
F17. Words in Sch. 1 para. 12 inserted (1.1.2006) by Serious Organised Crime and Police Act 2005 (c. 15), ss. 113. (13)(b), 178; S.I. 2005/3495, art. 2. (1)(n)

[F1812. AThe judge may not issue an all premises warrant unless he is satisfied—
(a) that there are reasonable grounds for believing that it is necessary to search premises occupied or controlled by the person in question which are not specified in the application, as well as those which are, in order to find the material in question; and
(b) that it is not reasonably practicable to specify all the premises which he occupies or controls which might need to be searched.]

Amendments (Textual)
F18. Sch. 1 para. 12. A inserted (1.1.2006) by Serious Organised Crime and Police Act 2005 (c. 15), ss. 113. (14), 178; S.I. 2005/3495, art. 2. (1)(n)

13. A constable may seize and retain anything for which a search has been authorised under paragraph 12 above.
14. The further conditions mentioned in paragraph 12 (a)(ii) above are—
(a) that it is not practicable to communicate with any person entitled to grant entry to the premises F19. . . ;
(b) that it is practicable to communicate with a person entitled to grant entry to the premises but it is not practicable to communicate with any person entitled to grant access to the material;
(c) that the material contains information which—
(i) is subject to a restriction or obligation such as is mentioned in section 11. (2)(b) above; and
(ii) is likely to be disclosed in breach of it if a warrant is not issued;
(d) that service of notice of an application for an order under paragraph 4 above may seriously prejudice the investigation.

Amendments (Textual)
F19. Words in Sch. 1 para. 14. (a) repealed (1.1.2006) by Serious Organised Crime and Police Act 2005 (c. 15), ss. 113. (15), 178, Sch. 17 Pt. 2; S.I. 2005/3495, art. 2. (1)(n)(t)(u)(xxiv)

15. (1)If a person fails to comply with an order under paragraph 4 above, a [F20judge] may deal with him as if he had committed a contempt of the Crown Court.
(2) Any enactment relating to contempt of the Crown Court shall have effect in relation to such a failure as if it were such a contempt.

Amendments (Textual)
F20. Words in Sch. 1 para. 15 substituted (1.4.2005) by Courts Act 2003 (c. 39), ss. 65, 110, Sch. 4 para. 6. (1); S.I. 2005/910, art. 3. (u)

[F21. Procedural rules

Amendments (Textual)
F21. Sch. 1 para. 15. A and cross-heading inserted (26.5.2015) by Deregulation Act 2015 (c. 20), ss. 82. (3)(e), 115. (7); S.I. 2015/994, art. 6. (o)

15. ACriminal Procedure Rules may make provision about proceedings under this Schedule, other than proceedings for an order under paragraph 4 above that relates to material that consists of or includes journalistic material.]

Costs

16. The costs of any application under this Schedule and of anything done or to be done in pursuance of an order made under it shall be in the discretion of the judge.

[F22. Interpretation

Amendments (Textual)
F22. Sch. 1 para. 17 inserted (1.4.2005) by Courts Act 2003 (c. 39), ss. 65, 110, Sch. 4 para. 6. (2); S.I. 2005/910, art. 3. (u)
17. In this Schedule "judge" means a Circuit judge [F23, a qualifying judge advocate (within the meaning of the Senior Courts Act 1981)] or a District Judge (Magistrates' Courts).]
Amendments (Textual)
F23. Words in Sch. 1 para. 17 inserted (2.4.2012) by Armed Forces Act 2011 (c. 18), s. 32. (3), Sch. 2 para. 11. (2); S.I. 2012/669, art. 4. (c)

Schedule 2. Specific offences which are arrestable offences

Amendments (Textual)
F1. Sch. 1. A repealed (1.1.2006) by Serious Organised Crime and Police Act 2005 (c. 15), ss. 111, 174, 178, Sch. 7 Pt. 1 para. 24. (3), Sch. 17 Pt. 2; S.I. 2005/3495, art. 2. (1)(m)(t)(u)(xxiv)
F2. Sch. 1. A inserted (1.10.2002) by Police Reform Act 2002 (c. 30), s. 48, Sch. 6; S.I. 2002/2306, art. 2. (d)(iv)

Wildlife and Countryside Act 1981.

9. An offence under section 1. (1) or (2) or 6 of the Wildlife and Countryside Act 1981 (c. 69) (taking, possessing, selling etc. of wild birds) in respect of a bird included in Schedule 1 to that Act or any part of, or anything derived from, such a bird.

11. AAn offence of contravening a provision of an Order in Council under section 60 of that Act (air navigation order) where the offence relates to—
(a) a provision which prohibits specified behaviour by a person in an aircraft towards or in relation to a member of the crew, or
(b) a provision which prohibits a person from being drunk in an aircraft, in so far as it applies to passengers.

Schedule 3. Fingerprinting and samples: power to require attendance at police station

Section 63. A(4)
Amendments (Textual)
F1. Sch. 2. A inserted (E.W.) (7.3.2011 except for the insertion of Sch. 2. A paras. 4, 12) by Crime

and Security Act 2010 (c. 17), ss. 6. (2), 59. (1); S.I. 2011/414, art. 2. (d)

Part 1. Fingerprinting

Persons arrested and released

1. (1)A constable may require a person to attend a police station for the purpose of taking his fingerprints under section 61. (5. A).

(2) The power under sub-paragraph (1) above may not be exercised in a case falling within [F2 section 61. (5. A)(b)(i)] (fingerprints taken on previous occasion insufficient etc) after the end of the period of six months beginning with the day on which the appropriate officer was informed that section 61. (3. A)(a) or (b) applied.

(3) In sub-paragraph (2) above " appropriate officer " means the officer investigating the offence for which the person was arrested.

[F3. (4)The power under sub-paragraph (1) above may not be exercised in a case falling within section 61. (5. A)(b)(ii) (fingerprints destroyed where investigation interrupted) after the end of the period of six months beginning with the day on which the investigation was resumed.]

Amendments (Textual)

F2. Words in Sch. 2. A para. 1. (2) substituted (13.5.2014) by Anti-social Behaviour, Crime and Policing Act 2014 (c. 12), s. 185. (1), Sch. 11 para. 86. (2)(a) (with ss. 21, 33, 42, 58, 75, 93); S.I. 2014/949, art. 3, Sch. para. 23. (e)

F3. Sch. 2. A para. 1. (4) inserted (13.5.2014) by Anti-social Behaviour, Crime and Policing Act 2014 (c. 12), s. 185. (1), Sch. 11 para. 86. (2)(b) (with ss. 21, 33, 42, 58, 75, 93); S.I. 2014/949, art. 3, Sch. para. 23. (e)

Persons charged etc

2. (1)A constable may require a person to attend a police station for the purpose of taking his fingerprints under section 61. (5. B).

(2) The power under sub-paragraph (1) above may not be exercised after the end of the period of six months beginning with—

(a) in a case falling within section 61. (5. B)(a) (fingerprints not taken previously), the day on which the person was charged or informed that he would be reported, or

(b) in a case falling within [F4 section 61. (5. B)(b)(i)] (fingerprints taken on previous occasion insufficient etc), the day on which the appropriate officer was informed that section 61. (3. A)(a) or (b) applied. [F5, or

(c) in a case falling within section 61. (5. B)(b)(ii) (fingerprints destroyed where investigation interrupted), the day on which the investigation was resumed.]

(3) In sub-paragraph (2)(b) above " appropriate officer " means the officer investigating the offence for which the person was charged or informed that he would be reported.

Amendments (Textual)

F4. Words in Sch. 2. A para. 2. (2)(b) substituted (13.5.2014) by Anti-social Behaviour, Crime and Policing Act 2014 (c. 12), s. 185. (1), Sch. 11 para. 86. (3)(a) (with ss. 21, 33, 42, 58, 75, 93); S.I. 2014/949, art. 3, Sch. para. 23. (e)

F5. Sch. 2. A para. 2. (2)(c) and word inserted (13.5.2014) by Anti-social Behaviour, Crime and Policing Act 2014 (c. 12), s. 185. (1), Sch. 11 para. 86. (3)(b) (with ss. 21, 33, 42, 58, 75, 93); S.I. 2014/949, art. 3, Sch. para. 23. (e)

Persons convicted etc of an offence in England and Wales

3. (1)A constable may require a person to attend a police station for the purpose of taking his fingerprints under section 61. (6).

(2) Where the condition in section 61. (6. ZA)(a) is satisfied (fingerprints not taken previously), the power under sub-paragraph (1) above may not be exercised after the end of the period of two years beginning with—

(a) the day on which the person was convicted [F6 or cautioned] , or

(b) if later, the day on which this Schedule comes into force.

(3) Where the condition in section 61. (6. ZA)(b) is satisfied (fingerprints taken on previous occasion insufficient etc), the power under sub-paragraph (1) above may not be exercised after the end of the period of two years beginning with—

(a) the day on which an appropriate officer was informed that section 61. (3. A)(a) or (b) applied, or

(b) if later, the day on which this Schedule comes into force.

(4) In sub-paragraph (3)(a) above " appropriate officer " means an officer of the police force which investigated the offence in question.

(5) Sub-paragraphs (2) and (3) above do not apply where the offence is a qualifying offence (whether or not it was such an offence at the time of the conviction [F7 or caution]).

Amendments (Textual)

F6. Words in Sch. 2. A para. 3. (2)(a) substituted (8.4.2013) by Legal Aid, Sentencing and Punishment of Offenders Act 2012 (c. 10), s. 151. (1), Sch. 24 para. 11. (2)(a) (with s. 135. (4)); S.I. 2013/453, art. 4. (f)

F7. Words in Sch. 2. A para. 3. (5) substituted (8.4.2013) by Legal Aid, Sentencing and Punishment of Offenders Act 2012 (c. 10), s. 151. (1), Sch. 24 para. 11. (2)(b) (with s. 135. (4)); S.I. 2013/453, art. 4. (f)

Persons subject to a control order

F84. . . . .

Amendments (Textual)

F8. Sch. 2. A para. 4 omitted (15.12.2011) by virtue of Terrorism Prevention and Investigation Measures Act 2011 (c. 23), s. 31. (2), Sch. 7 para. 2 (with Sch. 8)

Persons convicted etc of an offence outside England and Wales

5. A constable may require a person to attend a police station for the purpose of taking his fingerprints under section 61. (6. D).

Multiple attendance

6. (1)Where a person's fingerprints have been taken under section 61 on two occasions in relation to any offence, he may not under this Schedule be required to attend a police station to have his fingerprints taken under that section in relation to that offence on a subsequent occasion without the authorisation of an officer of at least the rank of inspector.

(2) Where an authorisation is given under sub-paragraph (1) above—

(a) the fact of the authorisation, and

(b) the reasons for giving it,

shall be recorded as soon as practicable after it has been given.

Part 2. Intimate samples

Persons suspected to be involved in an offence

7. A constable may require a person to attend a police station for the purpose of taking an intimate sample from him under section 62. (1. A) if, in the course of the investigation of an offence, two or more non-intimate samples suitable for the same means of analysis have been taken from him but have proved insufficient.

Persons convicted etc of an offence outside England and Wales

8. A constable may require a person to attend a police station for the purpose of taking a sample from him under section 62. (2. A) if two or more non-intimate samples suitable for the same means of analysis have been taken from him under section 63. (3. E) but have proved insufficient.

Part 3. Non-intimate samples

Persons arrested and released

9. (1)A constable may require a person to attend a police station for the purpose of taking a non-intimate sample from him under section 63. (3. ZA).
(2) The power under sub-paragraph (1) above may not be exercised in a case falling [F9 within section 63. (3. ZA)(b)(i) or (ii)] (sample taken on a previous occasion not suitable etc) after the end of the period of six months beginning with the day on which the appropriate officer was informed of the matters specified in section 63. (3. ZA)(b)(i) or (ii).
(3) In sub-paragraph (2) above, " appropriate officer " means the officer investigating the offence for which the person was arrested.
[F10. (4)The power under sub-paragraph (1) above may not be exercised in a case falling within section 63. (3. ZA)(b)(iii) (sample, and any DNA profile, destroyed where investigation interrupted) after the end of the period of six months beginning with the day on which the investigation was resumed.]
Amendments (Textual)
F9. Words in Sch. 2. A para. 9. (2) substituted (13.5.2014) by Anti-social Behaviour, Crime and Policing Act 2014 (c. 12), s. 185. (1), Sch. 11 para. 86. (4)(a) (with ss. 21, 33, 42, 58, 75, 93); S.I. 2014/949, art. 3, Sch. para. 23. (e)
F10. Sch. 2. A para. 9. (4) inserted (13.5.2014) by Anti-social Behaviour, Crime and Policing Act 2014 (c. 12), s. 185. (1), Sch. 11 para. 86. (4)(b) (with ss. 21, 33, 42, 58, 75, 93); S.I. 2014/949, art. 3, Sch. para. 23. (e)

Persons charged etc

10. (1)A constable may require a person to attend a police station for the purpose of taking a non-intimate sample from him under section 63. (3. A).
(2) The power under sub-paragraph (1) above may not be exercised in a case falling within section 63. (3. A)(a) (sample not taken previously) after the end of the period of six months beginning with the day on which he was charged or informed that he would be reported.
(3) The power under sub-paragraph (1) above may not be exercised in a case falling [F11 within section 63. (3. A)(b)(i) or (ii)] (sample taken on a previous occasion not suitable etc) after the end of the period of six months beginning with the day on which the appropriate officer was informed of the matters specified in section 63. (3. A)(b)(i) or (ii).
(4) In sub-paragraph (3) above " appropriate officer " means the officer investigating the offence for which the person was charged or informed that he would be reported.

[F12. (5)The power under sub-paragraph (1) above may not be exercised in a case falling within section 63. (3. A)(b)(iii) (sample, and any DNA profile, destroyed where investigation interrupted) after the end of the period of six months beginning with the day on which the investigation was resumed.]

Amendments (Textual)

F11. Words in Sch. 2. A para. 10. (3) substituted (13.5.2014) by Anti-social Behaviour, Crime and Policing Act 2014 (c. 12), s. 185. (1), Sch. 11 para. 86. (5)(a) (with ss. 21, 33, 42, 58, 75, 93); S.I. 2014/949, art. 3, Sch. para. 23. (e)

F12. Sch. 2. A para. 10. (5) inserted (13.5.2014) by Anti-social Behaviour, Crime and Policing Act 2014 (c. 12), s. 185. (1), Sch. 11 para. 86. (5)(b) (with ss. 21, 33, 42, 58, 75, 93); S.I. 2014/949, art. 3, Sch. para. 23. (e)

Persons convicted etc of an offence in England and Wales

11. (1)A constable may require a person to attend a police station for the purpose of taking a non-intimate sample from him under section 63. (3. B).

(2) Where the condition in section 63. (3. BA)(a) is satisfied (sample not taken previously), the power under sub-paragraph (1) above may not be exercised after the end of the period of two years beginning with—

(a) the day on which the person was convicted [F13 or cautioned] , or

(b) if later, the day on which this Schedule comes into force.

(3) Where the condition in section 63. (3. BA)(b) is satisfied (sample taken on a previous occasion not suitable etc), the power under sub-paragraph (1) above may not be exercised after the end of the period of two years beginning with—

(a) the day on which an appropriate officer was informed of the matters specified in section 63. (3. BA)(b)(i) or (ii), or

(b) if later, the day on which this Schedule comes into force.

(4) In sub-paragraph (3)(a) above " appropriate officer " means an officer of the police force which investigated the offence in question.

(5) Sub-paragraphs (2) and (3) above do not apply where—

(a) the offence is a qualifying offence (whether or not it was such an offence at the time of the conviction [F14 or caution]), or

(b) he was convicted before 10th April 1995 and is a person to whom section 1 of the Criminal Evidence (Amendment) Act 1997 applies.

Amendments (Textual)

F13. Words in Sch. 2. A para. 11. (2)(a) substituted (8.4.2013) by Legal Aid, Sentencing and Punishment of Offenders Act 2012 (c. 10), s. 151. (1), Sch. 24 para. 11. (3)(a) (with s. 135. (4)); S.I. 2013/453, art. 4. (f)

F14. Words in Sch. 2. A para. 11. (5)(a) substituted (8.4.2013) by Legal Aid, Sentencing and Punishment of Offenders Act 2012 (c. 10), s. 151. (1), Sch. 24 para. 11. (3)(b) (with s. 135. (4)); S.I. 2013/453, art. 4. (f)

Persons subject to a control order

F1512. . . . .

Amendments (Textual)

F15. Sch. 2. A para. 12 omitted (15.12.2011) by virtue of Terrorism Prevention and Investigation Measures Act 2011 (c. 23), s. 31. (2), Sch. 7 para. 2 (with Sch. 8)

Persons convicted etc of an offence outside England and Wales

13. A constable may require a person to attend a police station for the purpose of taking a non-intimate sample from him under section 63. (3. E).

Multiple exercise of power

14. (1)Where a non-intimate sample has been taken from a person under section 63 on two occasions in relation to any offence, he may not under this Schedule be required to attend a police station to have another such sample taken from him under that section in relation to that offence on a subsequent occasion without the authorisation of an officer of at least the rank of inspector.
(2) Where an authorisation is given under sub-paragraph (1) above—
(a) the fact of the authorisation, and
(b) the reasons for giving it,
shall be recorded as soon as practicable after it has been given.

Part 4. General and supplementary

Requirement to have power to take fingerprints or sample

15. A power conferred by this Schedule to require a person to attend a police station for the purposes of taking fingerprints or a sample under any provision of this Act may be exercised only in a case where the fingerprints or sample may be taken from the person under that provision (and, in particular, if any necessary authorisation for taking the fingerprints or sample under that provision has been obtained).

Date and time of attendance

16. (1)A requirement under this Schedule—
(a) shall give the person a period of at least seven days within which he must attend the police station; and
(b) may direct him so to attend at a specified time of day or between specified times of day.
(2) In specifying a period or time or times of day for the purposes of sub-paragraph (1) above, the constable shall consider whether the fingerprints or sample could reasonably be taken at a time when the person is for any other reason required to attend the police station.
(3) A requirement under this Schedule may specify a period shorter than seven days if—
(a) there is an urgent need for the fingerprints or sample for the purposes of the investigation of an offence; and
(b) the shorter period is authorised by an officer of at least the rank of inspector.
(4) Where an authorisation is given under sub-paragraph (3)(b) above—
(a) the fact of the authorisation, and
(b) the reasons for giving it,
shall be recorded as soon as practicable after it has been given.
(5) If the constable giving a requirement under this Schedule and the person to whom it is given so agree, it may be varied so as to specify any period within which, or date or time at which, the person must attend; but a variation shall not have effect unless confirmed by the constable in writing.

Enforcement

17. A constable may arrest without warrant a person who has failed to comply with a requirement under this Schedule.]

Schedule 4. Minor and Consequential Amendments

Section 119.
Modifications etc. (not altering text)
C1. Sch. 6 incorporated (16.5.2008) by The London Gateway Port Harbour Empowerment Order 2008 (S.I. 2008/1261), art. 52

Part I England and Wales

Game Act 1831 (c. 32)

1. The following section shall be inserted after section 31 of the Game Act 1831—
"31. A Powers of constables in relation to trespassers.
The powers conferred by section 31 above to require a person found on land as mentioned in that section to quit the land and to tell his christian name, surname, and place of abode shall also be exercisable by a police constable.".

Metropolitan Police Act 1839 (c. 47)

2. In section 39 of the Metropolitan Police Act 1839 (fairs within the metropolitan police district) after the word "amusement" there shall be inserted the words "shall be guilty of an offence".

Railway Regulation Act 1840 (c. 97)

3. In section 16 of the Railway Regulation Act 1840 (persons obstructing officers of railway company or trespassing upon railway) for the words from "and" in the third place where it occurs to "justice," in the third place where it occurs there shall be substituted the words ", upon conviction by a magistrates' court, at the discretion of the court,".

London Hackney Carriages Act 1843 (c. 86)

4. In section 27 of the London Hackney Carriages Act 1843 (no person to act as driver of carriage without consent of proprietor) for the words after "constable" there shall be substituted the words "if necessary, to take charge of the carriage and every horse in charge of any person unlawfully acting as a driver and to deposit the same in some place of safe custody until the same can be applied for by the proprietor.".

Town Gardens Protection Act 1863 (c. 13)

5. In section 5 of the Town Gardens Protection Act 1863 (penalty for injuring garden) for the words from the beginning to "district" there shall be substituted the words "Any person who throws any rubbish into any such garden, or trespasses therein, or gets over the railings or fence, or steals or damages the flowers or plants, or commits any nuisance therein, shall be guilty of an offence and".

Parks Regulation Act 1872 (c. 15)

6. The following section shall be substituted for section 5 of the Parks Regulation Act 1872 (apprehension of offender whose name or residence is not known)—
"5. Any person who—

(a) within the view of a park constable acts in contravention of any of the said regulations in the park where the park constable has jurisdiction; and

(b) when required by any park constable or by any police constable to give his name and address gives a false name or false address,

shall be liable on summary conviction to a penalty of an amount not exceeding level 1 on the standard scale, as defined in section 75 of the Criminal Justice Act 1982.".

Dogs (Protection of Livestock) Act 1953 (c. 28)

7. In the Dogs (Protection of Livestock) Act 1953 the following section shall be inserted after section 2—
"2. A Power of justice of the peace to authorise entry and search.
If on an application made by a constable a justice of the peace is satisfied that there are reasonable grounds for believing—

(a) that an offence under this Act has been committed; and

(b) that the dog in respect of which the offence has been committed is on premises specified in the application,

he may issue a warrant authorising a constable to enter and search the premises in order to identify the dog.".

Army Act 1955 (c. 18)Air Force Act 1955 (c. 19)

8. F1. . . . .
Amendments (Textual)
F1. Sch. 6 para. 8 repealed (28.3.2009 for certain purposes and otherwise prosp.) by Armed Forces Act 2006 (c. 52), ss. 378, 383, Sch. 17; S.I. 2009/812, art. 3 (with transitional provisions in S.I. 2009/1059)

Sexual Offences Act 1956 (c. 69)

9. F2. . . . .
Amendments (Textual)
F2. Sch. 6 Pt. 1 para. 9 repealed (1.5.2004) by Sexual Offences Act 2003 (c. 42), ss. 140, 141, Sch. 7; S.I. 2004/874, art. 2

Game Laws (Amendment) Act 1960 (c. 36)

10. In subsection (1) of section 2 of the Game Laws (Amendment) Act 1960 (power of police to enter on land) for the words "purpose of exercising any power conferred on him by the foregoing section" there shall be substituted the words "purpose—

(a) of exercising in relation to him the powers under section 31 of the Game Act 1831 which section 31. A of that Act confers on police constables; or

(b) of arresting him in accordance with section 25 of the Police and Criminal Evidence Act 1984.".

11. In subsection (1) of section 4 of that Act (enforcement powers) for the words from "under", in the first place where it occurs, to "thirty-one" there shall be substituted the words ", in accordance

with section 25 of the Police and Criminal Evidence Act 1984, for an offence under section one or section nine of the M1. Night Poaching Act 1828, or under section thirty".
Marginal Citations
M11828 c. 69.

Betting, Gaming and Lotteries Act 1963 (c. 2)

12. F3. . . . .
Amendments (Textual)
F3. Sch. 6 para. 12 repealed (1.9.2007) by Gambling Act 2005 (c. 19), ss. 356, 358, Sch. 17 (with ss. 352, 354); S.I. 2006/3272, art. 2. (4) (with savings in art. 6, Sch. 4) (as amended by S.I. 2006/3361, art. 2)

Deer Act 1963 (c. 36)

F413. . . . .
Amendments (Textual)
F4. Sch. 6 para. 13 repealed (25.10.1991) by Deer Act 1991 (c. 54, SIF 4:3), ss. 17. (6), 18. (3), Sch4

Police Act 1964 (c. 48)

F514. . . . .
Amendments (Textual)
F5. Sch. 6 paras. 14-15 repealed (1.4.1995) by 1994 c. 29, s. 93, Sch. 9 Pt.1; S.I. 1994/3262, art. 4,Sch..
F615. . . . .
Amendments (Textual)
F6. Sch. 6 paras. 14-15 repealed (1.4.1995) by 1994 c. 29, s. 93, Sch. 9 Pt.1; S.I. 1994/3262, art. 4, Sch..
16. . . . . F7.
Amendments (Textual)
F7. Sch. 6 para. 16 repealed by Police Officers (Central Service) Act 1989 (c. 11, SIF 95), s. 3, Sch.

Criminal Law Act 1967 (c. 58)

17. F8. . . . .
Amendments (Textual)
F8. Sch. 6 para. 17 repealed (1.1.2006) by Serious Organised Crime and Police Act 2005 (c. 15), ss. 174, 178, Sch. 17 Pt. 2; S.I. 2005/3495, art. 2. (1)(m)(t)(u)(xxiv)

Theatres Act 1968 (c. 54)

18. In section 15. (1) of the Theatres Act 1968 (powers of entry and inspection) for the words "fourteen days" there shall be substituted the words "one month".

Children and Young Persons Act 1969 (c. 54)

19. In the Children and Young Persons Act 1969— F9.

(a) . . . .

(b) the following section shall be substituted for section 29—

"29. A child or young person arrested in pursuance of a warrant shall not be released unless he or his parent or guardian (with or without sureties) enters into a recognisance for such amount as the custody officer at the police station where he is detained considers will secure his attendance at the hearing of the charge; and the recognisance entered into in pursuance of this section may, if the custody officer thinks fit, be conditioned for the attendance of the parent or guardian at the hearing in addition to the child or young person.".

Amendments (Textual)

F9. Sch. 6 para. 19. (a) repealed (14.10.1991) by Children Act 1989 (c. 41, SIF 20), s. 108. (7), Sch. 15 (with Sch. 14 paras. 1. (1), 27. (4)); S.I. 1991/828, art. 3. (2)

Immigration Act 1971 (c. 77)

20. In section 25. (3) of the Immigration Act 1971 for the words "A constable or" there shall be substituted the word "An".

Criminal Justice Act 1972 (c. 71)

21. In subsection (1) of section 34 of the Criminal Justice Act 1972 (powers of constable to take drunken offender to treatment centre) for the words from the beginning to "section the" there shall be substituted the words "On arresting an offender for an offence under—

    (a) section 12 of the Licensing Act 1872; or

    (b) section 91. (1) of the Criminal Justice Act 1967,

a ".

F10 . . .

Amendments (Textual)

F10. Sch. 6 para. 22 repealed (14.10.1991) by Children Act 1989 (c. 41, SIF 20), s. 108. (7), Sch.15 (with Sch. 14 paras. 1. (1), 27. (4)); S.I. 1991/828, art. 3. (2)

F1122. . . . .

Amendments (Textual)

F11. Sch. 6 para. 22 repealed (14.10.1991) by Children Act 1989 (c. 41, SIF 20), s. 108. (7), Sch.15 (with Sch. 14 paras. 1. (1), 27. (4)); S.I. 1991/828, art. 3. (2)

Deer Act 1980 (c. 49)

F1223. . . . .

Amendments (Textual)

F12. Sch. 6 para. 23 repealed (25.10.1991) by Deer Act 1991 (c. 54, SIF 4:3), ss. 17. (6), 18. (3), Sch.4

Animal Health Act 1981 (c. 22)

24. In subsection (5) of section 60 of the Animal Health Act 1981 (enforcement powers) for the words "a constable or other officer" there shall be substituted the words "an officer other than a constable".

Wildlife and Countryside Act 1981 (c. 69)

25. In subsection (2) of section 19 of the Wildlife and Countryside Act 1981 (enforcement powers) after the words "subsection (1)" there shall be inserted the words "or arresting a person, in accordance with section 25 of the Police and Criminal Evidence Act 1984, for such an offence".

Mental Health Act 1983 (c. 20)

26. In section 135. (4) of the Mental Health Act 1983 for the words "the constable to whom it is addressed", in both places where they occur, there shall be substituted the words "a constable".

27. . . . . F13.

Amendments (Textual)

F13. Sch. 6 para. 27 repealed by Prevention of Terrorism (Temporary Provisions) Act 1989 (c. 4, SIF 39:2), s. 25. (2), Sch. 9 Pt. I

Part II Other Amendments

Army Act 1955 (c. 18)

28. F14. . . . .

Amendments (Textual)

F14. Sch. 6 para. 28 repealed (28.3.2009 for certain purposes and otherwise prosp.) by Armed Forces Act 2006 (c. 52), ss. 378, 383, Sch. 17; S.I. 2009/812, art. 3 (with transitional provisions in S.I. 2009/1059)

Air Force Act 1955 (c. 19)

29. F15. . . . .

Amendments (Textual)

F15. Sch. 6 para. 29 repealed (28.3.2009 for certain purposes and otherwise prosp.) by Armed Forces Act 2006 (c. 52), ss. 378, 383, Sch. 17; S.I. 2009/812, art. 3 (with transitional provisions in S.I. 2009/1059)

Police (Scotland) Act 1967 (c. 77)

30. In section 6. (2) of the Police (Scotland) Act 1967 (constables below rank of assistant chief constable) for the words "an assistant chief constable or a constable holding the office of deputy chief constable" there shall be substituted the words "a deputy chief constable or an assistant chief constable".

31. In section 7. (1) of that Act (ranks) after the words "chief constable," there shall be inserted the words "deputy chief constable,".

32. In section 26. (7) of that Act (disciplinary authority) immediately before the words "deputy chief constable" there shall be inserted the word "any".

33. In section 31. (2) of that Act (compulsory retirement of chief constable etc.) for the words "the deputy or an assistant chief constable" there shall be substituted the words "a deputy or assistant chief constable".

Courts-Martial (Appeals) Act 1968 (c. 20)

F1634. . . . .

House of Commons Disqualification Act 1975 (c. 24)Northern Ireland Assembly Disqualification Act 1975 (c. 25)

35. In Part II of Schedule 1 to the House of Commons Disqualification Act 1975 and Part II of Schedule 1 to the Northern Ireland Assembly Disqualification Act 1975 (bodies of which all members are disqualified under those Acts) there shall be inserted at the appropriate place in alphabetical order—
"The Police Complaints Authority".

Armed Forces Act 1976 (c. 52)

F1736. . . . .

Customs and Excise Management Act 1979 (c. 2)

37. The following subsection shall be substituted for section 138. (4) of the Customs and Excise Management Act 1979—
"(4)Where any person has been arrested by a person who is not an officer—
   (a) by virtue of this section; or
   (b) by virtue of section 24 of the Police and Criminal Evidence Act 1984 in its application to offences under the customs and excise Acts,
the person arresting him shall give notice of the arrest to an officer at the nearest convenient office of customs and excise.".
38. In section 161 of that Act—
(a) in subsection (3), for the words from "that officer" to the end of the subsection there shall be substituted the words "any officer and any person accompanying an officer to enter and search the building or place named in the warrant within one month from that day"; and
(b) in subsection (4), for the words "person named in a warrant under subsection (3) above" there shall be substituted the words "other person so authorised".

Betting and Gaming Duties Act 1981 (c. 63)

39. In the following provisions of the Betting and Gaming Duties Act 1981, namely—
F18. (a). . . . .
(b) F19. . . . .
(c) F19. . . . .
(d) F19. . . . .
for the words "fourteen days" there shall be substituted the words "one month".

Car Tax Act 1983 (c. 53)

40. F20. . . . .

Amendments (Textual)

F20. Sch. 9 para. 40 repealed (22.7.2004) by Statute Law (Repeals) Act 2004 (c. 14), ss. 1. (1), {Sch. 1 Pt. 9 Group 5}

Value Added Tax Act 1983 (c. 55)

F2141. . . . .

Amendments (Textual)

F21. Sch. 6 para. 41 repealed (1.9.1994) by 1994 c. 23, ss. 100. (2), 101. (1), Sch. 15

Schedule 5. Repeals

Section 119.

Modifications etc. (not altering text)

C1. Sch. 7 incorporated (16.5.2008) by The London Gateway Port Harbour Empowerment Order 2008 (S.I. 2008/1261), art. 52

Part I Enactments Repealed in Consequence of Parts I to V

Chapter | Short title | Extent of repeal |

5 Geo. 4. c. 83. | Vagrancy Act 1824. | Section 8. |

| | Section 13. |

1 & 2 Will. 4. c. 32. | Game Act 1831. | In section 31, the words "or for any police constable". |

2 & 3 Vict. c. 47. | Metropolitan Police Act 1839. | Section 34. |

| | In section 38, the words from "it" to "and" in the sixth place where it occurs. |

| | In section 39, the words "to take into custody". |

| | In section 47, the words "take into custody" and the words ", and every person so found". |

| | In section 54, the words from "And" to the end of the section. |

| | In section 62, the words from "may" in the first place where it occurs to "and" in the second place where it occurs. |

| | Sections 63 to 67. |

3 & 4 Vict. c. 50. | Canals (Offences) Act 1840. | The whole Act. |

5 & 6 Vict. c. 55. | Railway Regulation Act 1842. | In section 17, the words "or for any special constable duly appointed,". |

8 & 9 Vict. c. 20. | Railways Clauses Consolidation Act 1845. | In section 104, the words "and all constables, gaolers, and police officers,". |

10 & 11 Vict. c. 89 | Town Police Clauses Act 1847. | In section 15, the words "may be taken into custody, without a warrant, by any constable, or" and the words from "Provided" to the end of the section. |

| | In section 28, the words from "and" in the first place where it occurs to "offence" in the second place where it occurs. |

14 & 15 Vict. c. 19 | Prevention of Offences Act 1851. | Section 11. |

23 & 24 Vict. c. 32. | Ecclesiastical Courts Jurisdiction Act 1860. | In section 3, the words "constable or" |

24 & 25 Vict. c. 100. | Offences against the Person Act 1861. | In section 65, the words "in the daytime". |

34 & 35 Vict. c. 96. | Pedlars Act 1871. | Sections 18 and 19. |

35 & 36 Vict. c. 93. | Pawnbrokers Act 1872. | In section 36, the words ", within the hours of

business,". |

38 & 39 Vict. c. 17. | Explosives Act 1875. | In section 78, the words "a constable, or". |

52 & 53 Vict. c. 18. | Indecent Advertisements Act 1889. | Section 6. |

52 & 53 Vict. c. 57. | Regulation of Railways Act 1889. | In section 5(2), the words "or any constable". |

8 Edw. 7. c. 66. | Public Meeting Act 1908. | In section 1, in subsection (3) the words from "and" in the sixth place where it occurs to the end of the subsection. |

1 & 2 Geo. 5. c. 28. | Official Secrets Act 1911. | In section 9(1), the words "named therein". |

15 & 16 Geo. 5. c. 71. | Public Health Act 1925. | Section 74(2) and (3). |

23 & 24 Geo. 5. c. 12. | Children and Young Persons Act 1933. | Section 10(2). |

| | Section 13(1) and (2). |

| | In section 40, in subsection (1) the words "named therein" and in subsection (4) the words "addressed to and". |

11 & 12 Geo. 6. c. 58. | Criminal Justice Act 1948. | Section 68. |

1 & 2 Eliz. 2. c. 14. | Prevention of Crime Act 1953. | Section 1(3). |

3 & 4 Eliz. 2. c. 28. | Children and Young Persons (Harmful Publications) Act 1955. | In section 3(1), the words "named therein". |

4 & 5 Eliz. 2. c. 69. | Sexual Offences Act 1956. | Section 40. |

| | In section 43(1), the word "named". |

5 & 6 Eliz. 2. c. 53. | Naval Discipline Act 1957. | In section 106(1), the words from "may" in the first place where it occurs to "and". |

7 & 8 Eliz. 2. c. 66. | Obscene Publications Act 1959. | In section 3(1), the words ", within fourteen days from the date of the warrant,". |

8 & 9 Eliz. 2. c. 36. | Game Laws (Amendment) Act 1960. | Section 1. |

1963 c. 2. | Betting, Gaming and Lotteries Act 1963. | In section 51(1), the words "at any time within fourteen days from the time of the issue of the warrant" and the words "arrest and". |

1963 c. 36. | Deer Act 1963. | Section 5(1)(c). |

1964 c. 26. | Licensing Act 1964. | Section 187(5). |

1967 c. 58. | Criminal Law Act 1967. | Section 2. |

1968 c. 27. | Firearms Act 1968. | In section 46(1), the words "named therein". |

| | Section 50. |

1968 c. 52. | Caravan Sites Act 1968. | Section 11(5). |

1968 c. 60. | Theft Act 1968. | Section 12(3). |

| | Section 26(2). |

1968 c. 65. | Gaming Act 1968. | Section 5(2). |

| | In section 43, in subsection (4), the words "at any time within fourteen days from the time of the issue of the warrant", and in subsection (5)(b), the words "arrest and". |

1970 c. 30. | Conservation of Seals Act 1970. | Section 4(1)(a). |

1971 c. 38. | Misuse of Drugs Act 1971. | Section 24. |

1971 c. 77. | Immigration Act 1971. | In Schedule 2, in paragraph 17(2), the words "acting for the police area in which the premises are situated," and the words "at any time or times within one month from the date of the warrant". |

1972 c. 20. | Road Traffic Act 1972. | Section 19(3). |

| | Section 164(2). |

1972 c. 27. | Road Traffic (Foreign Vehicles) Act 1972. | Section 3(2). |

1972 c. 71. | Criminal Justice Act 1972. | Section 34(3). |

1973 c. 57. | Badgers Act 1973. | Section 10(1)(b). |

1974 c. 6. | Biological Weapons Act 1974. | In section 4(1), the words "named therein". |

1976 c. 32. | Lotteries and Amusements Act 1976. | In section 19, the words "at any time within 14 days from the time of the issue of the warrant". |

1976 c. 58. | International Carriage of Perishable Foodstuffs Act 1976. | Section 11(6). |

1977 c. 45. | Criminal Law Act 1977. | Section 11. |

| | Section 62. |

1979 c. 2. | Customs and Excise Management Act 1979. | In section 138, in subsections (1) and (2), the words "or constable". |

1980 c. 43. | Magistrates' Courts Act 1980. | Section 49. |

1980 c. 49. | Deer Act 1980. | Section 4(1)(c). |

1980 c. 66. | Highways Act 1980. | Section 137(2). |

1980 c. x. | County of Merseyside Act 1980. | Section 33. |

1980 c. xi. | West Midlands County Council Act 1980. | Section 42. |

1981 c. 14. | Public Passenger Vehicles Act 1981. | Section 25(2). |

1981 c. 22. | Animal Health Act 1981. | In section 60, subsection (3), in subsection (4) the words "or apprehending", and in subsection (5) the words "constable or", in the second place where they occur. |

1981 c. 42. | Indecent Displays (Control) Act 1981. | Section 2(1). |

| | In section 2(3), the words "within fourteen days from the date of issue of the warrant". |

1981 c. 47. | Criminal Attempts Act 1981. | Section 9(4). |

1981 c. 69. | Wildlife and Countryside Act 1981. | Section 19(1)(c). |

1982 c. 48. | Criminal Justice Act 1982. | Section 34. |

1983 c. 2. | Representation of the People Act 1983. | In section 97(3), the words from "and" in the fifth place where it occurs to "him" in the third place where it occurs. |

| | . . . F1 |

1983 c. 20. | Mental Health Act 1983. | In Section 135, in subsections (1) and (2), the words "named in the warrant". |

Amendments (Textual)

F1. Words repealed by Representation of the People Act 1985 (c. 50, SIF 42), s. 28, Sch. 5

Part II Enactments Repealed in Relation to Criminal Proceedings in Consequence of Part VII

Chapter | Short title | Extent of repeal |

1971 c. liv. | Cornwall County Council Act 1971. | Section 98(4). |

1972 c. xlvii. | Hampshire County Council Act 1972. | Section 86(2). |

Part III Enactments Repealed Generally in Consequence of Part VII

Chapter | Short title | Extent of repeal |

3 & 4 Eliz. 2. c. 18. | Army Act 1955. | In section 198(1), the words "of this section and of sections 198A and 198B of this Act". |

| | Sections 198A and 198B. |

3 & 4 Eliz. 2. c. 19. | Air Force Act 1955. | In section 198(1), the words "of this section and of sections 198A and 198B of this Act". |

| | Sections 198A and 198B. |

1965 c. 20. | Criminal Evidence Act 1965. | The whole Act. |

1969 c. 48. | Post Office Act 1969. | In section 93(4), the words "the Criminal Evidence Act 1965 and". |

| | In Schedule 4, paragraph 77. |

1981 c. 55. | Armed Forces Act 1981. | Section 9. |

1981 c. xviii. | County of Kent Act 1981. | Section 82. |

1983 c. 55. | Value Added Tax Act 1983. | In Schedule 7, paragraph 7(7) and (8). |

Part IV Enactments Repealed in Relation to Criminal

Proceedings in Consequence of Part VIII

Chapter | Short title | Extent of repeal |
14 & 15 Vict. c. 99. | Evidence Act 1851. | Section 13. |
28 & 29 Vict. c. 18. | Criminal Procedure Act 1865. | In section 6, the words from "and a certificate" onwards. |
34 & 35 Vict. c. 112. | Prevention of Crimes Act 1871. | Section 18 except the words "A previous conviction in any one part of the United Kingdom may be proved against a prisoner in any other part of the United Kingdom.". |

Part V Enactments Repealed Generally in Consequence of Part VIII

Chapter | Short title | Extent of repeal |
16 & 17 Vict. c. 83. | Evidence (Amendment) Act 1853. | Section 3. |
46 & 47 Vict. c. 3. | Explosive Substances Act 1883. | Section 4(2). |
58 & 59 Vict. c. 24. | Law of Distress Amendment Act 1895. | Section 5. |
61 & 62 Vict. c. 36. | Criminal Evidence Act 1898. | In section 1, the words "and the wife or husband, as the case may be, of the person so charged" the words (in paragraph (b)) "or of the wife or husband, as the case may be, of the person so charged" and paragraphs (c) and (d). |
	Section 4.
	In section 6(1), the words from "notwithstanding" to the end.
	The Schedule.
4 & 5 Geo. 5, c. 58.	Criminal Justice Administration Act 1914.	Section 28(3).
19 & 20 Geo. 5. c. 34.	Infant Life (Preservation) Act 1929.	Section 2(5).
23 & 24 Geo. 5. c. 12.	Children and Young Persons Act 1933.	Section 15.
	Section 26(5).
4 & 5 Eliz. 2. c. 69.	Sexual Offences Act 1956.	Section 12(2) and (3).
	Section 15(4) and (5).
	Section 16(2) and (3).
	Section 39.
	In Schedule 3, the entry relating to section 15 of the Children and Young Persons Act 1933.
8 & 9 Eliz. 2. c. 33. | Indecency with Children Act 1960. | In section 1, subsection (2) and in subsection (3) the words "except in section 15 (which relates to the competence as a witness of the wife or husband of the accused)". |
1965 c. 72. | Matrimonial Causes Act 1965. | Section 43(1). |
1968 c. 60. | Theft Act 1968. | Section 30(3). |
1970 c. 55. | Family Income Supplements Act 1970. | Section 12(5). |
1973 c. 38. | Social Security Act 1973. | In Schedule 23, paragraph 4. |
1975 c. 14. | Social Security Act 1975. | Section 147(6). |
1975 c. 16. | Industrial Injuries and Diseases (Old Cases) Act 1975. | Section 10(4). |
1975 c. 61. | Child Benefit Act 1975. | Section 11(8). |
1976 c. 71. | Supplementary Benefits Act 1976. | Section 26(5). |
1977 c. 45. | Criminal Law Act 1977. | In section 54(3), the words "subsection (2) (competence of spouse of accused to give evidence)". |
1978 c. 37. | Protection of Children Act 1978. | Section 2(1). |
1979 c. 18. | Social Security Act 1979. | Section 16. |
1980 c. 43. | Magistrates' Courts Act 1980. | In Schedule 7, paragraph 4. |
1982 c. 24. | Social Security and Housing Benefits Act 1982. | Section 21(6). |

Part VI Miscellaneous Repeals

Chapter | Short title | Extent of repeal |
2 & 3 Vict. c. 47. | Metropolitan Police Act 1839. | Section 7. |
34 & 35 Vict. c. 96. | Pedlars Act 1871. | In section 18, the words from "or" where secondly occurring to "Act," and the words from "and forthwith" to the end of the section. |
1964 c. 48. | Police Act 1964. | Section 49. |
| | Section 50. |
1967 c. 77. | Police (Scotland) Act 1967. | Section 5(3) and section 17(6). |
1972 c. 11. | Superannuation Act 1972. | In Schedule 1, the reference to the Police Complaints Board. |
1975 c. 24. | House of Commons Disqualification Act 1975. | In Part II of Schedule 1, the entry relating to the Police Complaints Board. |
1975 c. 25. | Northern Ireland Assembly Disqualification Act 1975. | In Part II of Schedule 1, the entry relating to the Police Complaints Board. |
1976 c. 46. | Police Act 1976. | section 1(1) to (4). |
	Sections 2 to 13.
	Section 14(2).
	In the Schedule, paragraphs 1 to 3, in paragraph 4, the words "remuneration" and "allowances" and paragraphs 5 to 13.

Open Government Licence v3.0

Printed in Great Britain
by Amazon

49909718R00124